KU-791-205

MEDIEVAL WORLDS

A SOURCEBOOK

Edited by

Roberta Anderson *and*
Dominic Aidan Bellenger

NOTTINGHAM UNIVERSITY LIBRARY

Routledge
Taylor & Francis Group

LONDON AND NEW YORK

First published 2003
by Routledge
11 New Fetter Lane, London EC4P 4EE

Simultaneously published in the USA and Canada
by Routledge
29 West 35th Street, New York, NY 10001

Routledge is an imprint of the Taylor & Francis Group

© 2003 Roberta Anderson and Dominic Aidan Bellenger

Typeset in Baskerville and Univers by
Florence Production Ltd, Stoodleigh, Devon
Printed and bound in Great Britain by
TJ International Ltd, Padstow, Cornwall

All rights reserved. No part of this book may be
reprinted or reproduced or utilised in any form or by any electronic,
mechanical, or other means, now known or hereafter invented, including
photocopying and recording, or in any information storage or retrieval
system, without permission in writing from the publishers.

British Library Cataloguing in Publication Data
A catalogue record for this book is available from the British Library

Library of Congress Cataloging in Publication Data
has been applied for

ISBN 0–415–25308–X (hbk)
ISBN 0–415–25309–8 (pbk)

100462502 3

CONTENTS

DOCUMENTS

The world of the crusades

The world of the feudal kingdom

The English political world

The world of the outsider

The world of women

The world of the mind

The world of the countryside

The world of the town

The medieval world self-observed

WELLS CATHEDRAL: A MEDIEVAL WORLD (PLATES)

꡴

ACKNOWLEDGEMENTS

This book is not only a result of the collaboration of the editors but owes much to previous scholars, translators and publishers; the editors are conscious of being dwarfs on the shoulders of giants.

We are most grateful to Richard Neale for the use of photographs of Wells Cathedral from his private collection. Every effort has been made to obtain permission to reproduce copyright material. If any proper acknowledgement has not been made, we would invite copyright holders to inform us of the oversight.

We acknowledge permission for the use of the following copyright material:

Ö. Thorssen, *The Sagas of Icelanders* by Leifur Eiricksson (Allen Lane, The Penguin Press, 2000) © Leifur Eiricksson Publishing, 2000.

D. Ayerst and A. Fisher, *Records of Christianity. Vol. II: Christendom* (Blackwell, Oxford, 1977).

A. P. D'Entreves (ed.), J. G. Dawson (trans.) *Aquinas: Selected Political Writings* (Blackwell, Oxford, 1965).

R. Barber (trans.) *Bestiary* (Boydell, Woodbridge, 1999).

J. M. Upton-Ward, *The Rule of the Templars* (Boydell, Woodbridge, 1992).

Augustine (trans.) C. T. Wilcox, *Treatises on Marriage and other subjects*, Fathers of the Church Series, Vol. 27 (Catholic University of America Press, Washington, 1955).

L. Eberle (trans.) *The Rule of the Master* (Cistercian Publications, Michigan, 1977).

U. Ó Maidín (trans.) *The Celtic Monk* (Cistercian Publications, Michigan, 1966).

F. Barlow (ed. and trans.) *The Life of King Edward Who Rests at Westminster*, 2nd edn (Clarendon Press, Oxford, 1992).

B. Colgrave and R. A. B. Mynors (eds), *Venerable Bede, Ecclesiastical History of the English People* (Clarendon Press, Oxford, 1979).

A. Gewirth (trans.) *Marsilius of Padua: the Defender of Peace* (Columbia University Press, New York, 1967).

B. Scott James (trans.) *The Letters of St Bernard of Clairvaux*, 2nd edn (Continuum, Stroud, 1998).

J. McCann, *The Rule of St Benedict* (Continuumn, Burns and Oates, 1952).

F. Davey, *Willaim Wey: An English Pilgrim to Compostella in 1456* (CSJ, 2000) CSJ, 27 Blackfriars Road, London SE1 8NY. www.csj.org.uk

P. McNulty (trans.) *St Peter Damien: Selected Writings on the Spiritual Life* (Faber & Faber, 1959).

B. Garton (trans.) *The Metrical Life of Saint Hugh* (Lincoln Cathedral Publications, Lincoln, 1986).

G. A. Loud, T. Wiedemann (trans.) *The History of the Tyrants of Sicily by 'Hugo Falcandus' 1154–69* (Manchester University Press, Manchester, 1998).

H. Bettenson (trans.) *Documents of the Christian Church*, 3rd edn, C. Maunder (ed.) (Oxford University Press, Oxford, 1993).

B. Davies and G. R. Evans (eds) *Anselm of Canterbury, The Major Works* (Oxford University Press, Oxford, 1998).

C. F. J. Martin (trans.) *On the Six Days of Creation: A Translation of the Hexaëmeron* (Oxford University Press, Oxford, 1999) © The British Academy, 1996. Reproduced by permission from *Robert Grosseteste: On the Six Days of Creation*.

L. Thorpe (trans.) *The Life of Charlemagne* (Penguin, 1970) © Professor Lewis Thorpe, 1969.

P. Matarasso (trans., ed.) *The Cistercian World: Monastic Writings of the Twelfth Century* (Penguin, 1993, Harmondsworth) © Pauline Matarasso, 1993.

J. J. O'Meara (trans.) *Gerald of Wales, The History and Topography of Ireland* (Penguin, Harmondsworth, 1982) © John J. O'Meara, 1954, 1982.

W. Granger Ryan, (trans.) *Jacobus de Voragine, The Golden Legend* (Princeton University Press, New Jersey, 1993) © 1993 by Princeton University Press, reprinted by permission of Princeton University Press.

A. R. Meyers (ed.) *English Historical Documents, 1327–1485*, Vol. IV (Routledge, Eyre & Spottiswoode, Oxford, 1969).

D. C. Douglas and G. W. Greenaway *English Historical Documents, 1042–1189*, Vol. II (Routledge, Eyre & Spottiswoode, 1953).

M. Summers, *The Geography of Witchcraft* (Routledge & Kegan Paul, 1978).

Cyril C. Richardson (ed.) (trans.) *Early Christian Fathers*, Library of Christian Classics Vol. I (SCM Press, 1953).

E. Colledge, B. McGinn (trans.) *Meister Eckhart, the Essential Sermons, Commentaries, Treatises and Defence* (SPCK, 1981).

A. Erlande-Brandenburg, *The Cathedral Builders of the Middle Ages* (Thames & Hudson, 1995).

Aelfric: *Those Who Pray, Work, and Fight, Aelfric's Grammar* (W. W. Norton & Co., www.wwnorton.com/nael/nto/middle/estates/aelfricfrm.htm).

D. Herlihy (ed. and trans.) *Medieval Culture and Society* (Walker & Co., 1968).

PREFACE

The moderns and the post-moderns have scant regard for the wisdom of their ancestors and little knowledge of their common tradition. The term 'medieval' is often
used in a pejorative sense when addressing questions of punishment and civilisation,
seemingly forgetting contemporary horrors. This is unfortunate. The period from
the decline of the Western Roman Empire in the fourth century to the Fall of
Constantinople in 1453, which has been called the Middle Ages since the Enlightenment, is a complex of inter-related worlds in which a search for a coherent system
of knowledge and an artistic sublimity, which reached its apogee in the Gothic
cathedral, are as characteristic as the disorder, violence and superstition which cast
their shadow on all societies.

This collection of medieval documents is not an apologia for a return to the Middle
Ages or a black paper on the superiority of a Gothic education. Its translations, drawn
from books old and new, are not scholarly editions but a cross-section of materials
which are intended to act as an introduction to the period which goes far beyond
conventional medieval history. One of the editors, reading medieval history at a
medieval university, managed to spend two years without discussing cultural or
scientific developments in the period. In this collection such omissions are fully
addressed.

The selected sources range from administrative documents to poetry and reflect the
diversity of the period. They are focused on western Europe, Christendom as then
understood, but it is hoped that the balance of materials is Eurocentric rather than
Anglocentric. The book has emerged from a collaborative taught course on the
Middle Ages given by the two editors at Bath Spa University College since 1996.

THE EDITORS

Roberta Anderson was educated in Hampshire and has degrees in History and English (BA) and The English Renaissance, Politics, Patronage and Literature (MA). She received her PhD in 2000 for her work on the foreign diplomatic representatives to the court of James VI and I. In addition to publishing several papers on the early modern period she is a lecturer in medieval and early modern history in the School of Historical and Cultural Studies, Bath Spa University College.

Dominic Aidan Bellenger is Prior of the Benedictine Abbey of Downside in Somerset. He was educated at Finchley Grammar School and Jesus College, Cambridge, where he received his PhD in 1978 for his work on French exiled clergy in Great Britain during the French Revolution. He has published several books, contributed to many others, and has written numerous articles, principally on Anglo-French relations, the history of monastic and religious orders, and the English Catholic community. A former Head Master of Downside School, he is a fellow of the Society of Antiquaries, the Royal Historical Society and the Royal Society of Arts.

GLOSSARY

Abbot	The superior of a monastery (abbey) from the Latin *Abbas* (father).
Absolution	Forgiveness of sins through the ministry of the Church or release from excommunication.
Advowson	Right of appointing clerics to benefices.
Albigensians	Heretic sect of Cathars whose name derives from the Albi region of Southern France.
Anathema	The solemnisation of excommunication.
Anante	A fee paid to the Pope for an ecclesiastical preferment, originally the whole of the first year's income from the office, thus the name from the Latin *annus*, year.
Angevins	The Plantagenet kings of England from Henry II to Richard who were also dukes of Anjou.
Anti-Pope	Rival factions in the Catholic Church from 1378 to 1417 led to the Great Schism or division of the Church. The unauthorised claimants to the papacy are designated Anti-Popes.
Archbishop	A bishop with a diocese of his own who also presided over an ecclesiastical province of several dioceses and over which he had metropolitan jurisdiction. His powers included summoning provincial councils and presiding at elections.
Benefice	An ecclesiastical living or preferment which gave status and financial support to its holder.
Bishop	The principal priest of a diocese who exercised the apostolic authority in his area, ordaining priests and administering his See. The highest order of ministers in the Christian church. The word bishop is an Anglo-Saxon corruption of the Latin *episcopus*.
Borough	A town whose legal liberties and privileges are incorporated in a charter.
Canon	(a) A priest or cleric who is part of a corporation of clergy like a cathedral or a collegiate church. Also applied to a member of a religious order living according to a rule (*regular canons*). Cathedral canons, not usually living a rule of life, are called secular canons. (b) An individual item of legislation.
Canon Law	The law of the Catholic Church which developed in the Middle Ages and was given substance by papal letters (decretals).

Canonisation	The process of making saints in the Catholic Church in which men and women are enrolled in the *canon* or list of saints.
Corpus Christi	*Christ's Body*, a Christian feast instituted in 1264 to celebrate the real presence of Christ in the Eucharist and to celebrate the doctrine of transubstantiation.
Cardinal	From the Latin *cardo* (a hinge), a member of what amounted to the senate of the Roman Church who, during the course of the Middle Ages, emerged as the electors of the Pope. The college of cardinals consisted of cardinal bishops, priests and deacons.
Chamber	A financial department of the Royal Household.
Chancery	Writing office and secretariat of the household government of a king or pope, presided over by a chancellor.
Chantry	An endowed chapel for the celebration of Masses for founders and other purposes.
Close Rolls	Grants from the Crown to individuals sealed and closed for confidentiality.
Commendation	An act of submission to a feudal lord by which a man became the vassal of that lord.
Council	A meeting of ecclesiastics, also known as a synod, which dealt with church disputes and resulted in legislation in the form of canons.
Cenobite	From Greek for 'living in community': a religious in vows living in a community as contrasted to a hermit, living alone.
Conversi	A name used for lay brothers in monasteries, presumably alluding to the 'conversion' in maturity.
Curia	The court or place where the sovereign resided with his chief officials and household. Term frequently applied to the papal court.
Decretals	see Canon Law.
Diocese	Territory ruled by a bishop.
Escheat	Reversion of land to the Crown in case of failure to produce heirs.
Eucharist	The re-enactment of the Last Supper also known as the Mass, one of the central sacraments of the Christian Church.
Exchequer	Financial department originating in the *Curia Regis*.
Excommunication	The ritual exclusion of a person or church by the appropriate authority.
Fealty	An oath of fidelity sworn by a man to his master or lord.
Fee	A feudal term for a payment by a retainer in cash or kind.
Feretory	A shrine in which a saint's relics are venerated.
Feria	In ecclesiastical language a *feria*, despite its literal meaning as a feast, is applied to a day on which no feast falls.
Friars	Religious brotherhood more centralised than the monastic orders and dedicated to poverty and preaching.
Gilds (Guilds)	Associations for religious, social and professional purposes.
Glebe	Land held by the local parish priest.
Hansa or Hanseatic League	A confederation of north German towns which dominated the trade of the Baltic and North Sea.
Holy See	The papal seat of authority, the city of Rome.
Homage	Submission of a tenant to his lord in return for protection.

Hussites	Followers of Jan Hus (d. 1415), the Bohemian reformer, condemned for heresy by the Council of Constance in 1414.
Heresy	A mistaken belief about the central teachings of the Christian faith.
Indulgence	Remission of temporal penalty due to forgiven sin given by the Pope.
Interdict	Church prohibition of ecclesiastical functions imposed on persons or places.
Investiture	Public transfer of property or rights marked by a public ceremony and often involving symbols of office.
Jubilee	Year in which a special 'indulgence' is given, sometimes called a 'holy year'. The first was in 1300.
Justiciar	In the eleventh to thirteenth centuries the effective viceroy of a king during absence abroad.
Legate	An ecclesiastic of high rank, usually a cardinal, representing the Pope on a mission.
Lollards	Followers of John Wyclif (d. 1384), condemned as heretics.
Liturgy	Prescribed order of a church service.
Mendicant	A beggar in a literal sense, often applied as a title to friars who, in theory, owned nothing and depended on charity.
Monk	A religious who lives under a rule of life in the enclosure of a monastery and takes vows of renunciation and stability.
Nominalism	A scholastic theory which suggests that 'universals' (abstract nouns like 'goodness') are not real entities but only 'names'. The alternative theory is 'realism' which maintains the real existence of universals.
Lectio	Literally, reading, from the Latin. Applied to slow meditative reading for monks.
Obedientaries	Officials of monasteries.
Outremer	'Beyond the seas': the name given to the Crusader kingdoms.
Orthodox	Name given to the Eastern Church after the split or schism of Rome and Byzantium in 1054.
Orders	The status of clerk of holy orders was divided into the major orders of bishops, priests and deacons (who had sacramental authority) and minor orders which gave status but not authority. Entry to the clerical state was controlled by the bishops and shown by a tonsure or clerical haircut.
Opus Dei	Latin for work of God. Applied to monastic work of liturgy and the canonical hours.
Pallium	Circular band of white woollen material with two hanging straps and marked with black crosses worn by the Pope and given to archbishops to show metropolitan status.
Papacy	See Pope.
Penance	An act of repentance for a sin or crime.
Pope	The bishop of Rome known as *papa* (father) of the Western Church. Also known as *Pontifex Maximus*, thus pontiff or pontifical, bridge builder (from Latin *pons*, bridge).
Prelate	A holder of high office in the church, from the Latin *prelatus*, meaning 'set over' others.
Province	A group of diocese under the jurisdiction of an archbishop.

Reich	German empire.
Sacrament	Defined by St Augustine (354–430) as 'the visible form of invisible grace' and applied widely in the Middle Ages to sacred actions. Gradually, in the West, restricted to seven: baptism, confirmation, Eucharist, penance, anointing of the sick, holy orders and matrimony.
Schism	see Anti-Pope.
Scholasticism	Method used by medieval thinkers founded on logic and intended to assist in the exposition and reconciliation of the Bible, the writings of the Church Fathers and classical philosophical texts, especially Aristotle, to create a unified system.
Simony	The attempt to purchase spiritual gifts with money, taken from Simon Magus in the *Acts of the Apostles*. It became particularly associated with the buying and selling of church offices.
Subinfeudation	Holders of hereditary fiefs granting land to sub-vassals on terms similar to those by which they held the land.
Synod	see Council
Transubstantiation	The doctrine that the bread and wine of the Eucharist is changed into the real presence of the body and blood of Christ through the action of the priest.
Troubadour	A poet and musician, especially in southern France, who provided court entertainment.
Unction	Anointing with consecrated oil as part of a ceremony of consecration.
Villein	An unfree peasant in England, similar to serf (Latin, *servus*, a slave), bound to land.

৪৶ Abbreviations ৶ঌ

Schroder, *Disciplinary Decrees*	H. J. Schroder (trans.) *Disciplinary Decrees of the General Councils* (1937).
Douglas and Greenaway, *English Historical Documents*	D. C. Douglas and G. W. Greenaway, *English Historical Documents 1042–1189* (1953) Vol. II.
Ayerst and Fisher, *Records*	D. Ayerst and A. Fisher, *Records of Christianity. Vol. II: Christendom* (1977).
Herlihy, *Culture and Society*	D. Herlihy (ed. and trans.) *Medieval Culture and Society* (1968).
Bland *Economic History*	A. E. Bland, P. A. Brown and R. H. Tawney (comp. and ed.) *English Economic History* (1930).
Henderson, *Select Historical Documents*	E. F. Henderson (ed. and trans.) *Select Historical Documents of the Middle Ages* (1925).
Bettenson, *Christian Church*	H. Bettenson (trans.) *Documents of the Christian Church* (Oxford, 1950).
Tierney, *Crisis of Church*	B. Tierney, *The Crisis of Church and State, 1050–1300* (New Jersey, 1964).
EETS	Early English Text Society

INTRODUCTION
TO MEDIEVAL WORLDS

The decline and fall of the Roman Empire in the West was a slow process. The revival of interest in antiquity was also somewhat protracted. It is therefore a broad-brush convenience to label the gap between the Classical civilisation of Greece and Rome and that of the Renaissance, roughly speaking the centuries between the fourth and the fifteenth, as the 'Middle Ages'. To some historians this medieval period is little better than a black hole, a dark age of superstition and regression, of no importance in the great tradition of human progress. To others, much to the delight of writers of fiction, it is an age of faith and romance, full of colour and splendour with a perfectly balanced communal society based on co-operation and benevolence. This book makes neither assumption, but hopes that its documentation will allow the Middle Ages to speak for themselves and their claim to be the bedrock of modern European society.

Periodisation can distort the nuances and contrasts that make historical study vital, and it is with this risk in mind that we dare to divide the medieval millennium into three unequal but nevertheless distinct eras.

The early Middle Ages, from the end of the fourth century to *c.* 1100, saw the unifying forces of Roman imperialism give way to a network of small, self-sufficient communities. These often consisted of peasant farmers, bound to the land and generally also to the local lord who, in return for their labour, provided the peasants with housing, stock, and perhaps, most importantly, protection. The barbarian invasions, the later onslaughts of Magyars and Vikings, and the emergence of Islam were all parts of the external forces that transformed the late antique world into the medieval one. In this world the Christian Church, and especially the monasteries, provided a local focus with a wider vision. The 'Dark Ages', blighted by more than their fair share of natural disasters, were also the 'Benedictine centuries' in which the vestiges of the ancient world were collated and preserved. The unifying imperial ideal itself, shadowed in the institution of the papacy and in the survival of the texts of Roman law, was given a new channel among the Christianised barbarians. The 'conversion of Europe' to Christianity was given its greatest affirmation in 800 AD with the coronation of Charles, king of the Franks, as the first holy Roman emperor, Charlemagne. Consecrated kingship replaced warlords as the norm of government.

The high or central Middle Ages, the twelfth and thirteenth centuries, witnessed marked population growth and outward expansion, both military and mercantile, together with the evolution of more complex forms of government, representative or otherwise, particularly in the prosperous cities. All this was made possible by favourable climatic conditions, in which the cultivation of high protein crops, coupled by technological advances in agriculture, created an agricultural surplus to feed the expanding towns and cities. It was the era of the cathedral and the crusade, the age of the Gothic. The backbone of this urban revitalisation was the new merchant class who, in the course of time, were able to amass great fortunes and become urban leaders and, in city-states, the key figures in government. Education moved from the monastery to the university, new ideas flowed in from the Arab world, and the great tradition of the Classical world was reclaimed. The new orders of monks and friars brought vitality to the institutional Church. It is not without reason that the twelfth century, borrowing the historical language of the early modern period, has been called a unity of both renaissance and reformation.

The third chronological division, from *c.* 1300 to *c.* 1500, was characterised by a defensive contraction of Christendom, again in both military and commercial terms, while a mood of foreboding pervaded the literature of the period. Vernacular writings became more sophisticated and authoritative: Dante's *Divina commedia* was written in Italian, Chaucer's *Canterbury Tales* in English. Although Constantinople fell to the Turks in 1453 and the Balkans fell under Ottoman rule, occasional crusading ventures by the Christian powers were at best half-hearted, the energies of the emerging nation states of Europe being channelled instead into warfare between themselves, undertaken by increasingly professional armies. The background to this lay in famine and failed harvests that ended the long run of population increase and economic expansion. It was nature itself that delivered the most devastating blow of all: the 'Black Death'. Plague and pestilence cut a swathe through the continent, killing many millions. The secure institutions of the high Middle Ages seemed fundamentally compromised. Papal authority was challenged by conciliarism; lay piety and individualistic faith countered monastic spiritual dominance. The Middle Ages died hard but, by the fifteenth century, much of the world explored by this book was a distant memory.

In subsequent chapters the selected texts convey the depth of the medieval achievement: its faith, its structures, its ideas, its magnificence and folly, the lives of its people. The subject matter of the texts is diverse and the style and form of the documents range from the administrative record to the poetic evocation. The texts, mainly translated from Latin originals, are arranged thematically and preceded by historical overviews. Medieval texts, always originally in manuscript before the introduction of printing with movable type in the fifteenth century, have a surprising variety of theme and approach and do not reflect a totally clerical world. They suggest something of the excitement and surprise of medieval life. Reading and writing were much more social activities than in the modern world, with written dialogues reflecting conversations, disputes and exchanges of letters. Medieval texts reflect not only a conscious 'handing on' (*traditio*) but a 'chain' (*concatenatio*) of shared and borrowed words and concepts. Much emphasis was placed on the authority of ancient writers, notably the Bible and the Fathers of the Church, and there was a conscious re-use of words and complete passages; plagiarism was a concept foreign to the minds of medieval writers. This collection of texts does not purport to be a collection of the 'best' of medieval writing, nor does it present texts of a standard length. The main objective has been to provide the reader with a stimulating variety of sources, a *florilegium* in the best medieval sense.

The medieval West was not a monolithic world but more a series of inter-related entities dependent on each other. William Langland, the English poet of the fourteenth century, describes the vision of a plain full of people, of his hero Piers Plowman.

❧ 1.1 William Langland, *The Vision of Piers Plowman* ❧

The Induction

In a summer season when the sun was softest,
Shrouded in a smock, in shepherd's clothing,
In the habit of a hermit of unholy living
I went through this world to witness wonders.
On a May morning on a Malvern hillside
I saw strange sights like scenes of Faerie.
I was weary of wandering and went to rest
By the bank of a brook in a broad meadow.
As I lay and leaned and looked on the water
I slumbered and slept, so sweetly it murmured.   10

Then I met with marvellous visions.
I was in a wilderness; where, I knew not.
I looked up at the East at the high sun,
And saw a tower on a toft artfully fashioned.
A deep dale was beneath with a dungeon in it,
And deep ditches and dark, dreadful to see.
A fair field full of folk I found between them,
With all manner of men, the meanest and the richest,
Working and wandering as the world demanded.
Some put them to the plough and practised hardship   20
In setting and sowing and seldom had leisure;
They won what wasters consumed in gluttony.
Some practised pride and quaint behaviour,
And came disguised in clothes and features.
Prayer and penance prevailed with many.
For the love of our Lord they lived in strictness,
To have bliss hereafter and heavenly riches.
Hermits and anchorites held to their dwellings,
Gave up the course of country roving
And all lusty living that delights the body.   30
Some turned to trade; they tried barter;

And seemed in our sight to succeed better.
Some men were mirthful, learned minstrelsies,
And got gold as gleemen – a guiltless practice.
Yet jesters and janglers, Judas' children,
Feigned idle fancies and wore fools' clothing,
But had wit if they wished to work as others.
What Paul has preached I proffer without glossing:
Qui loquitur turpiloquium, is Lucifer's servant.

Bidders and beggars ride about the country   40
With bread to the brim in their bags and bellies;

They feign that they are famished and fight in the ale-house.
God wot, they go in gluttony to their chambers
And rise with ribaldry, like Robert's children.
Sleep and sloth pursue them always.

Pilgrims and palmers were plighted together
To seek Saint James and saints in Rome.
They went on their way with many wise stories,
And had leave to lie for a lifetime after.
I saw some who said that they sought for relics;   50
In each tale that they told their tongue would always
Speak more than was so, it seemed to my thinking.

A host of hermits with hocked staves
Went to Walsingham with their wenches behind them.
These great lubbers and long, who were loath to labour,
Clothed themselves in copes to be distinguished from others,
And robed themselves as hermits to roam at their leisure.
There I found friars of all the four orders,
Who preached to the people for the profit of their bellies,
And glossed the gospel to their own good pleasure;   60
They coveted their copes, and construed it to their liking.
Many master-brothers may clothe themselves to their fancy,
For their money and their merchandise multiply together.
Since charity has turned chapman to shrive lords and ladies,
Strange sights have been seen in a few short years.
Unless they and Holy Church hold closer together
The worst misery of man will mount up quickly.

There a pardoner preached as priest of the parish,
And brought out a bull with a bishop's signet,
Said that he himself might assoil all men   70
Of all falsehood in fasting and vows that were broken.
Common folk confided in him and liked his preaching,
And crept up on cowed knees and kissed his pardons.
He abused them with brevets and blinded their eyesight;
His devil's devices drew rings and brooches.
They gave their gold to keep gluttons,
And believed in liars and lovers of lechery.
If the bishop were blessed and worth both his ears
His seal would not be sent to deceive the people.
But the power of the bishop is not this preacher's licence,   80
For the parish priest and the pardoner share the profits together
Which the poor of the parish would have if these were honest.

Because parishes were poor since the pestilence season,
Parsons and parish priests petitioned the bishops
For a licence to leave and live in London
And sing there for simony, for silver is sweet.

Bishops and bachelors, both masters and doctors,
Who have cures under Christ and are crowned with the tonsure,
In sign of their service to shrive the parish,
To pray and preach and give the poor nourishment,   90
Lodge in London in Lent and the long year after,
Some are counting coins in the king's chamber,
Or in exchequer and chancery challenging his debts
From wards and wardmotes, waifs and strays.
Some serve as servants to lords and ladies
And sit in the seats of steward and butler.
They hear mass and matins and many of their hours
Are done without devotion. There is danger that at last
Christ in his consistory will curse many.

I pondered on the power which Peter was given   100
To bind and to unbind as the Book tells us.
He left it with love at our Lord's commandment
And in care of four virtues, which are fairest of all virtues,
These are called cardinal, or hinges to the gateway
Where Christ is in his kingdom; they close it to many
And open it to many others and show them heaven's glory.
Yet I dare not deny that the dignity of Peter
Is in cardinals at court who command this title
And presume on its power in the pontiff's election.
The election belongs to love and to learning.   110
I might but I must not speak more of their college.

Then there came a king in the company of knighthood.
The might of the Commune made him a ruler.
Common Wit came after and created advisers,
As a council for the king and for the common safety.
The king and the clergy and the company of knighthood
Decreed that the commons should contrive their welfare.
Common Wit and the Commune made craftsmen and tradesmen,
And put others to the plough for the people's profit,
To till and to toil as true life bade them.   120
The king and the Commune and Common Wit also
Ordained loyalty and law, and each man knew his own.

Then a fool came forth, a long lean fellow,
And knelt to the king and spoke like a cleric:
'Christ keep you, my king, and all your kingdom also,
So live in your land that loyalty may love you,
And righteous rule be rewarded in heaven!'
Then high in the air an angel from heaven
Spoke loudly in Latin, that laymen might never   130
Either judge or justify or object to opinions,
But suffer and serve; and thus spoke the angel:
Sum rex, sum Princeps; neutrum fortasse deinceps;

O qui jura regis Christi specialia Regis,
Hoc quod agas melius, justus es, esto pius!
Nudum jus a te vestiri vult pietate,
Qualia vis metere, talia grana sere.
Si jus nudatur, nudo de jure metatur;
Si seritur pietas, de pietate metas!

Then a glutton of language, a scandalous jester,
Answered the angel, who hovered above them: 140
Dum rex a regere dicatur nomen habere;
Nomen habet sine re, nisi studet jura tenere.

Then the crowd of the commons cried out in Latin
To the king's council for all to construe it:
Praecepta regis sunt nobis vincula legis.

A rabble of rats ran suddenly hither
With a swarm of small mice sporting among them.
They came to a council for the common profit.
A cat of the court would come at his pleasure
Sport and spring and seize whom he fancied.   150
Play with them perilously and push them before him.
'We dread the danger and dare not come forward,
And if we grudge him his game he will grieve us further,
Scratch us or claw us or take us in his clutches,
And make life loathsome before he leave us.
If we had the wit to withstand his pleasure
We might be lords aloft and live at our leisure.'

A rat of renown, a ready speaker,
Sought for the sovereign salve for his people:
'I have seen men,' he said, 'in the city of London   160
Bearing bright chains about their shoulders,
On cunning collars; they go at random
Through warren and waste as their will inclines them.
And at other times elsewhere, as I hear reported.
If they bore bells, I believe, by heaven,
One might hear where they went and run away!
So,' said the speaker, 'reason shows clearly
That we should buy a bell of brass, or bright silver,
Clasp it on a collar, and for the common profit
Hang it on the cat's head, and then we may hear him   170
When he roams or is at rest or runs to frolic.
When his mood is mild we may move at pleasure,
And appear in his presence when he is playfully minded,
And be ware of his wrath and wary of his coming.'
The rabble of rats thought his reasons clever;
But when the bell was brought and bound to the collar,
There was no rat in all the rout, for the realm of Louis,

Who dared bind the bell about the cat's shoulders,
Nor hang it on the cat's head to win all England.
They granted themselves cowards and their counsel feeble, 180
And their labour was lost and all their long sessions.

Then a mouse of importance, and of merit, as I thought him,
Strode forth sternly and stood before the council,
And with the rout of rats reasoned as follows:
'If we killed the cat there would still come another,
To catch us and all our kin, though we crept under benches.
So I counsel the commune to let the cat wander,
And never be bold to bring him the collar.
For my sire said, seven years past,
Where the cat is a kitten the court is in sorrow. 190
So Holywrit witnesses; who will may read it:
Vae terrae ubi puer rex est, etc.
For no one could rest for rats in the night.
While the cat catches rabbits he cares for us little,
But feeds wholly on that venison – never defame him!
A little loss is better than a long sorrow,
And the raids of a robber than ruin forever.
We mice would demolish the malt of many,
And the rout of rats rend men's clothing,
If that cat of the court could not control you. 200
For if you rats had your way you could not rule yourselves.
For my part,' said the mouse, 'I see so much further,
That neither the cat nor the kitten should be grieved at my counsel.
Neither complain I at the collar that cost me nothing.
If it had cost me a crown I should never confess it.
We must suffer our rulers to roam at their pleasure
Uncoupled or coupled, and catch what they will.
And I warn the wise to watch out for themselves.'
What this dream may mean, you men who are clever,
Divine, for I dare not, by dear God in heaven! 210

Hundreds in silk hoods hovered about me,
They seemed to be sergeants who served in the court rooms,
Took pounds for pence, and pled for justice,
Nor for the love of our Lord unlocked their lips ever.
Better measure the mist on Malvern hillsides,
Than hear a mumble from their mouths till money is promised.
I saw in the press, as you shall hear hereafter,
Barons and burgesses and village bondmen,
Bakers and butchers and brewers without number,
Wool-websters and weavers of linen, 220
Tailors and tinkers and tollmen in markets,
Masons and miners and many other craftsmen.
All lived in labour. But others leapt forward,
Dykemen and diggers who do their work badly,

And drive out the long day with *Dieu vous sauve, dame Emme!*
Cooks and their knaves cried, 'Hot pies, hot!
Good geese and bacon! Come dine, Come!'
Taveners too were tossed in the turmoil,
'White wine of Alsace and red wine of Gascony,
Rhine and Rochelle digest the roast!' –   230
I saw all this sleeping, and seven times more.

Source: H. W. Wells (trans.) *William Langland,*
The Vision of Piers Plowman (1935) pp. 3–10

The plain of Piers Plowman is not so strange a landscape to modern men and women but the mentality of the period had some fundamental differences. Many of these stemmed from the dominance of the spiritual ideal of Christianity which presented the world as part of a divine order in which this world, the earthly city, was merely a staging post on the journey towards the heavenly city where life was to be truly fulfilled.

---

৯ 1.2 St Augustine, *The City of God* ৬৩

The grounds of the concord and discord between the cities of heaven and earth.

But they that live not according to faith, angle for all their peace in the sea of temporal profits: whereas the righteous live in full expectation of the glories to come, using the occurrences of this world, but as pilgrims, not to abandon their course towards God for mortal respects, but thereby to assist the infirmity of the corruptible flesh, and make it more able to encounter with toil and trouble. Wherefore the necessaries of this life are common, both to the faithful and the infidel, and to both their families: but the ends of their two usages thereof are far different.

The faithless, 'worldly city' aims at earthly peace, and settles the self therein, only to have an uniformity of the citizens' wills in matters only pertaining to mortality. And the 'Heavenly City', or rather that part thereof, which is as yet a pilgrim on earth and lives by faith, uses this peace also: as it should, it leaves this mortal life, wherein such a peace is requisite, and therefore lives (while it is here on earth) as if it were in captivity, and having received the promise of redemption, and divers spiritual gifts as seals thereof, it willingly obeys such laws of the 'temporal city' as order the things pertaining to the sustenance of this mortal life, to the end that both the cities might observe a peace in such things as are pertinent hereunto. But because that the 'earthly city' has some members whom the Holy Scriptures utterly disallow, and who standing either too well affected to the devils, or being deluded by them, believed that each thing had a peculiar deity over it, and belonged to the charge of a several god: as the body to one, the soul to another, and in the body itself the head to one, the neck to another, and so of every member: as likewise of the soul, one had the wit, another the learning, a third the wrath, a fourth the desire: as also in other necessaries or accidents belonging to man's life, the cattle, the corn, the wine, the oil, the woods, the monies, the navigation, the wars, the marriages, the generations, each being a several charge unto a particular power, whereas the citizens of the 'Heavenly State' acknowledged but one only God, to whom that worship, which is called λατρεία was peculiarly and solely due; hence came it that the 'two hierarchies' could not be combined in one religion, but must needs dissent herein, so that the good part was fain to bear the pride and persecution of the bad, had not their own multitude sometimes, and the providence of God continually stood for their protection.

This 'celestial society' while it is here on earth, increases itself out of all languages, never respecting the temporal laws that are made against so good and religious a practice: yet not breaking, but observing their diversity in divers nations, all which do tend unto the preservation of earthly peace, if they oppose not the adoration of one only God. So that you see, the 'Heavenly City' observes and respects this temporal peace here on earth, and the coherence of men's wills in honest morality, as far as it may with a safe conscience; yea, and so far desires it, making use of it for the attainment of the peace eternal: which is so truly worthy of that name, as that the orderly and uniform combination of men in the fruition of God, and of one another in God, is to be accounted the reasonable creature's only peace, which being once attained, mortality is banished, and life then is the true life indeed, nor is the carnal body any more an encumbrance to the soul, by corruptibility, but is now become spiritual, perfected and entirely subject unto the sovereignty of the will.

This peace is that unto which the pilgrim in faith refers the other which he has here in his pilgrimage, and then lives he according to faith, when all that he does for the obtaining hereof is by himself referred unto God, and his neighbour withal, because being a citizen, he must not be all for himself, but sociable in his life and actions.

> **Source:** J. Healey (trans.) *The City of God* (1931)
> pp. 152–154

Medieval people, at one level, had no abiding city and the pilgrim can be taken as a type of the medieval ideal, institutionalised by the medieval papacy in the *Jubilee Indulgence*.

ॐ 1.3 Boniface VIII proclaims the first Jubilee: ॐ
20 February 1300

Bishop Boniface, servant of the servants of God, in perpetual memory of this matter.

The relation of the ancients is trustworthy, to the effect that, to those going to the famous church of the Prince of the Apostles in the City, great remissions and indulgences, of their sins have been granted.

1   We therefore who, as is the duty of our office, do seek and most willingly procure the salvation of individuals, considering each and all such remissions and indulgences as valid and helpful, do confirm and approve them by apostolic

authority; and do also renew them and furnish them with the sanction of the present writing.

2   In order, therefore, that the most blessed apostles Peter and Paul may be the more honoured the more their churches in the City shall be devoutly frequented by the faithful, and that the faithful themselves, by the bestowal of spiritual gifts, may feel themselves the more regenerated through such frequenting: we, by the mercy of almighty God, and trusting in the merits and authority of those same ones his apostles, by the counsel of our brethren and from the plenitude of the apostolic power, do concede, in this present year and in every hundredth year to come, not only full and free, but the very fullest, pardon of all their sins to all who in this present year 1300, counting from the feast just past of the nativity of our Lord Jesus Christ, and in every hundredth year to come, shall reverently go to those churches, having truly repented and confessed, or being about to truly repent and confess.

3   Decreeing that those who wish to become partakers of such indulgence conceded by us, if they are Romans shall go to those churches on at least thirty days, consecutively or at intervals, and at least once in the day; but if they be pilgrims or foreigners, they shall in like manner go on fifteen days. Each one, however, shall be the more deserving and shall more efficaciously obtain the indulgence, the more often and the more, devoutly he shall frequent those churches. Let no man whatever infringe this page of our decree, or oppose it with rash daring. But if any one shall presume to attempt this he shall know that he is about to incur the indignation of almighty God and of His blessed apostles Peter and Paul.

Given at Rome, in St. Peters, on the 23rd day of February 1300, in the sixth year of our pontificate.

> Source: E. F. Henderson (ed. and trans.) *Select Historical Documents of the Middle Ages* (1925) pp. 349–350

The Divine Order, however, was widely seen as reflected in the human order of things and no more clearly than in the individual's place in society, his role indeed determined more by his station, his *ordo*, than by his personality. The three orders of society were given an eloquent exposition by the Anglo-Saxon monk Aelfric (*c.* 955–1020), whose chief concern seems to be to distinguish the duties of the clergy – monks and priests – from those of the warrior class.

---

۶ 1.4 Aelfric: Those who pray, work and fight ۶

It is well known that in this world
there are three orders, set in unity:
these are *laboratores, oratores, bellatores.*
Laboratores are those who labour for our living;
Oratores are those who plead for our peace with God;

Bellatores are those who battle to protect our towns
and defend our land against an invading army.
Now the farmer works to provide our food,
And the worldly warrior must fight against our foes,
and the servant of God must always pray for us
and fight spiritually against invisible foes.
Therefore greater is the struggle of the monks
against the invisible devils who lay traps around us,
than that of worldly men who contend against carnal foes
and fight in plain sight against men they can see.
Now worldly warriors must not to the worldly battle
force the servants of God away from the spiritual battle,
for it will be better for them that the invisible enemies
be defeated than the visible ones.
And it would do great harm were they to forsake God's service
and turn to the worldly battle, which is none of their business.
Julian the Apostate and the cruel Caesar
wanted to compel priests to worldly warfare,
as well as the holy monks, and ordered them thrown in prison.
Then was Apollonius, abbot of the Egyptians,
locked up in prison with his brothers in faith.
But God's angel came to him in prison by night
with heavenly light and unlocked the prison.
Also the centurion who had locked them in there
came in the morning with a great multitude
and said that his house collapsed suddenly with an earthquake,
and his dearest men lay fallen there dead.
And he bade the saints to go away from there,
and they went back into the wilderness with hymns of praise.
God's servants must preserve their innocence,
just as Christ set the example Himself
when he commanded Peter to put up his sword,
and healed through his might the man's ear,
which Peter had cut off, and demonstrated His goodness.
Now the monk who bows to Saint Benedict's rule
and gives up all things of the world, why will he go back
to worldly weapons and forsake his warfare
against invisible foes so as to offend his Creator?
The servant of God may not fight together with men of the world
if he is to have speed in spiritual warfare.
There was no holy servant of God after His Saviour's suffering
who would ever defile his hands by fighting,
but they bore the tortures of infidel tormentors
and gave up their lives in innocence
for God's faith, and now they live with God,
because they would not even kill a bird.

Source: Cited in http://www.wwnorton.com/nael/
nto/middle/estates/aelfricfrm.htm

The clergy's near monopoly of learning sometimes distorts the study of the medieval period but the interplay between 'the three orders' has also been confused by later attempts to systematise a series of relationships which often owed more to local variation and custom than to a universally accepted law. Into this category comes the ideal of feudalism. The term feudalism is an abstract term coined in the nineteenth century to highlight the features of the state of society in western Europe in the Middle Ages. The word comes from the Latin *feudum* (or *feodum*), but is often taken to refer to property held from a landlord by a tenant in return for a rent in the form of service. Mutuality in the three orders was assisted by related services.

The first of the three orders, the clergy, was a complex of persons, representing both the hierarchical church of the bishop, priest and clerks and the charismatic church of the religious 'orders' who contributed their individual gifts to the Church. All those who were baptised (the critical rite of initiation in the sacramental life of the Church) were members of the Church but the first *ordo* were those particularly set aside for prayer. The search for sanctity, wholeness in the heavenly kingdom, was not reserved for the first *ordo* but the majority of those dead Christians honoured for particular deeds were full-time clergy. Their model was the early martyrs.

---

১৯ 1.5 From Justin Martyr, *Apologia*, I ৯৩

Certainly we do not honour with many sacrifices and floral garlands the objects that men have fashioned, set up in temples, and called gods. We know that they are lifeless and dead and do not represent the form of God – for we do not think of God as having the kind of form which some claim that they imitate to be honoured – but rather exhibit the names and shapes of the evil demons who have manifested themselves [to men]. You know well enough without our mentioning it how the craftsmen prepare their material, scraping and cutting and moulding and beating. And often they make what they call gods out of vessels used for vile purposes, changing and transforming by art merely their appearance. We consider it not only irrational but an insult to God, whose glory and form are ineffable, to give his name to corruptible things which themselves need care. You are well aware that craftsmen in these [things] are impure and – not to go into details – given to all kinds of vice; they even corrupt their own slave girls who work along with them. What an absurdity, that dissolute men should be spoken of as fashioning or remaking gods for public veneration, and that you should appoint such people as guardians of the temples where they are set up – not considering that it is unlawful to think or speak of men as guardians of gods. . . .

When you hear that we look for a kingdom, you rashly suppose that we mean something merely human. But we speak of a Kingdom with God, as is clear from our confessing Christ when you bring us to trial, though we know that death is the penalty for this confession. For if we looked for a human kingdom we would deny it in order to save our lives, and would try to remain in hiding in order to obtain the things we look for. But since we do not place our hopes on the present [order], we are not troubled by being put to death, since we will have to die somehow in any case. . . .

What sound-minded man will not admit that we are not godless, since we worship the Fashioner of the universe, declaring him, as we have been taught, to have no need of blood and libations and incense, but praising him by the word of prayer and thanksgiving for all that he has given us? We have learned that the only honour worthy of him is, not to consume by fire the things he has made for our nourishment, but to devote them to our use and those in need, in thankfulness to him sending up solemn prayers and hymns for our creation and all the means of health, for the variety of creatures and the changes of the seasons, and sending up our petitions that we may live again in incorruption through our faith in him. It is Jesus Christ who has taught us these things, having been born for this purpose and crucified under Pontius Pilate, who was procurator in Judea in the time of Tiberius Caesar. We will show that we honour him in accordance with reason, having learned that he is the Son of the true God himself, and holding him to be in the second place and the prophetic Spirit in the third rank. It is for this that they charge us with madness, saying that we give the second place after the unchanging and ever-existing God and begetter of all things to a crucified man, not knowing the mystery involved in this, to which we ask you to give your attention as we expound it.

> **Source: C. C. Richardson (ed.) (trans.)** *Early Christian Fathers* **(1953) pp. 246–247, 249**

The second order, those who fight, were also idealised from an early period of the Middle Ages, and the chivalric ideal, presenting the soldier as the Christian knight, often hides from view the brutality of medieval battle.

---

৪৯ 1.6 Diaz de Gamez, *The Unconquered Knight* ৩৩

Now is it fitting that I should tell what it is to be a knight: whence comes this name of knight; what manner of a man a knight should be to have a right to be called a knight; and what profit the good knight is to the country wherein he lives. I tell you that men call knight the man who, of custom, rides upon a horse. He who, of custom, rides upon another mount, is no knight; but he who rides upon a horse is not for that reason a knight; he only is rightly called a knight, who makes it his calling. Knights have not been chosen to ride an ass or a mule; they have not been taken from among feeble or timid or cowardly souls, but from among men who are strong and full of energy, bold and without fear; and for this reason there is no other beast that so befits a knight as a good horse.

Thus have horses been found that in the thick of battle have shewn themselves as loyal to their masters as if they had been men. There are horses who are so strong, fiery, swift, and faithful, that a brave man, mounted on a good horse, may do more in an hour of fighting than ten or mayhap a hundred could have done afoot. For this reason do men rightly call him knight.

What is required of a good knight? That he should be noble. What means noble and nobility? That the heart should be governed by the virtues. By what virtues?

By the four that I have already named. These four virtues are sisters and so bound up one with the other, that he who has one, has all, and he who lacks one, lacks the others also. So the virtuous knight should be wary and prudent, just in the doing of justice, continent and temperate, enduring and courageous; and withal he must have great faith in God, hope at His glory, that he may attain the guerdon of the good that he has done, and finally he must have charity and the love of his neighbour.

Of what profit is a good knight? I tell you that through good knights is the king and the kingdom honoured, protected, feared, and defended. I tell you that the king, when he sends forth a good knight with an army and entrusts him with a great emprise, on sea or on land, has in him a pledge of victory. I tell you that without good knights, the king is like a man who has neither feet nor hands.

> Source: J. Evans (trans.) *The Unconquered Knight*
> (1926) p. 5

୫∾୰ଔ

In the *Song of Roland* the pattern of chivalry develops further. This is an account which tells how Charlemagne and his peers, under Roland, take on the might of Muslim Spain under the Emir Marsillion. Marsillion is a treacherous man and throughout the work the autocracy of the Emir is contrasted with the monarchy of Charlemagne. Roland leads his men boldly and fights with heroism. It is an epic of chivalry and revenge. Roland dies at the end of his great stand against Marsillion and the remainder of the poem is concerned with the vengeance which Charlemagne takes for the death of his men.

୫∾ 1.7 *The Song of Roland* ∾ଔ

CLXXI

When Roland saw that life had fled,
And with face to, earth his comrade dead,
He thus bewept him, soft and still:
'Ah, friend, thy prowess wrought thee ill!
So many days and years gone by
We lived together, thou and I:
And thou hast never done me wrong,
Nor I to thee, our lifetime long.
Since thou art dead, to live is pain.'
He swooned on Veillantif again,
Yet may not unto earth be cast,
His golden stirrups held him fast.

CLXXII

When passed away had Roland's swoon,
With sense restored, he saw full soon

What ruin lay beneath his view.
His Franks have perished all save two —
The archbishop and Walter of Hum alone.
From the mountain-side hath Walter flown,
Where he met in battle the bands of Spain,
And the heathen won and his men were slain.
In his own despite to the vale he came;
Called unto Roland, his aid to claim.
'Ah, count! brave gentleman, gallant peer!
Where art thou? With thee I know not fear.
I am Walter, who vanquished Maelgut of yore,
Nephew to Drouin, the old and hoar.
For knightly deeds I was once thy friend.
I fought the Saracen to the end;
My lance is shivered, my shield is cleft,
Of my broken mail are but fragments left.
I bear in my body eight thrusts of spear;
I die, but I sold my life right dear.'
Count Roland heard as he spake the word,
Pricked his steed, and anear him spurred.

CLXXIV

In Roland's sorrow his wrath arose,
Hotly he struck at the heathen foes,
Nor left he one of a score alive;
Walter slew six, the archbishop five.
The heathens cry, 'What a felon thee!
Look to it, lords, that they shall not flee.
Dastard is he who confronts them not;
Craven, who lets them depart this spot.'
Their cries and shoutings begin once more,
And from every side on the Franks they pour.

CLXXX

Count Roland never hath loved the base,
Nor the proud of heart, nor the dastard race, —
Nor knight, but if he were vassal good, —
And he spake to Turpin, as there he stood;
'On foot are you, on horseback I;
For your love I halt, and stand you by.
Together for good and ill we hold;
I will not leave you for man of mould.
We will pay the heathen their onset back,
Nor shall Durindana of blows be slack.'
'Base,' said Turpin, 'who spares to smite:
When the Emperor comes, he will all requite.'

CLXXXI

The heathens said, 'We were born to shame.
This day for our disaster came:
Our lords and leaders in battle lost,
And Karl at hand with his marshalled host;
We hear the trumpets of France ring out,
And the cry *"Montjoie!"* their rallying shout.
Roland's pride is of such a height,
Not to be vanquished by mortal wight;
Hurl we our missiles, and hold aloof.'
And the word they spake, they put in proof; –
They flung, with all their strength and craft,
Javelin, barb, and plumed shaft.
Roland's buckler was torn and frayed,
His cuirass broken and disarrayed,
Yet entrance none to his flesh they made.
From thirty wounds Veillantif bled,
Beneath his rider they cast him, dead;
Then from the field have the heathen flown:
Roland remaineth, on foot, alone.

CLXXXII

The heathens fly in rage and dread;
To the land of Spain have their footsteps sped;
Nor can Count Roland make pursuit –
Slain is his steed, and he rests afoot;
To succour Turpin he turned in haste,
The golden helm from his head unlaced,
Ungirt the corselet from his breast,
In stripes divided his silken vest;
The archbishop's wounds hath he staunched and bound,
His arms about him softly wound;
On the green sward gently his body laid,
And, with tender greeting, thus him prayed:
'For a little space, let me take farewell;
Our dear companions, who round us fell,
I go to seek; if I haply find,
I will place them at thy feet reclined.'
'Go,' said Turpin; 'the field is thine –
To God the glory, 'tis thine and mine.'

CLXXXIX

Roland feeleth his death is near,
His brain is oozing by either ear.
For his peers he prayed – God keep them well;
Invoked the angel Gabriel.
That none reproach him, his horn he clasped;

His other hand Durindana grasped;
Then, far as quarrel from crossbow sent,
Across the march of Spain he went.
Where, on a mound, two trees between,
Four flights of marble steps were seen;
Backward he fell, on the field to lie,
And he swooned anon, for the end was nigh.

CXC

High were the mountains and high the trees,
Bright shone the marble terraces;
On the green grass Roland hath swooned away.
A Saracen spied him where he lay:
Stretched with the rest, he had feigned him dead,
His face and body with blood bespread.
To his feet he sprang, and in haste he hied, –
He was fair and strong and of courage tried,
In pride and wrath he was overbold, –
And on Roland, body and arms, laid hold.
'The nephew of Karl is overthrown!;
'To Araby bear I this sword, mine own.'
He stooped to grasp it, but as he drew,
Roland returned to his sense anew.

CXCI

He saw the Saracen seize his sword;
His eyes he oped, and he spake one word:
'Thou art not one of our band, I trow,'
And he clutched the horn he would ne'er forego;
On the golden crest he smote him full,
Shattering steel and bone and skull,
Forth from his head his eyes he beat,
And cast him lifeless before his feet
'Miscreant, makest thou then so free,
As, right or wrong, to lay hand on me?
Who hears it will deem thee a madman born;
Behold the mouth of mine ivory horn
Broken for thee, and the gems and gold
Around its rim to earth are rolled.'

CXCII

Roland feeleth his eyesight reft,
Yet he stands erect with what strength is left;
From his bloodless cheek is the hue dispelled,
But his Durindana all bare he held.
In front a dark brown rock arose –
He smote upon it ten grievous blows.

Grated the steel as it struck the flint,
Yet it brake not, nor bore its edge one dint.
'Mary, Mother, be thou mine aid!
Ah, Durindana, my ill-starred blade,
I may no longer thy guardian be!
What fields of battle I won with thee!
What realms and regions 'twas ours to gain,
Now the lordship of Carlemaine!
Never shalt thou possessor know
Who would turn from face of mortal foe;
A gallant vassal so long thee bore,
Such as France the free shall know no more.'

CXCV

That death was on him he knew full well;
Down from his head to his heart it fell.
On the grass beneath a pine-tree's shade,
With face to earth, his form he laid,
Beneath him placed he his horn and sword,
And turned his face to the heathen horde.
Thus hath he done the sooth to show,
That Karl and his warriors all may know,
That the gentle count a conqueror died.
Mea Culpa full oft he cried;
And, for all his sins, unto God above,
In sign of penance, he raised his glove.

CXCVI

Roland feeleth his hour at hand;
On a knoll he lies towards the Spanish land.
With one hand beats he upon his breast:
'In thy sight, O God, be my sins confessed.
From my hour of birth, both the great and small,
Down to this day, I repent of all.'
As his glove he raises to God on high,
Angels of heaven descend him nigh.

CXCVII

Beneath a pine was his resting-place,
To the land of Spain hath he turned his face,
On his memory rose full many a thought –
Of the lands he won and the fields he fought;
Of his gentle France, of his kin and line;
Of his nursing father, King Karl benign; –
He may not the tear and sob control,
Nor yet forgets he his parting soul.
To God's compassion he makes his cry:

'O Father true, who canst not lie,
Who didst Lazarus raise unto life agen,
And Daniel shield in the lions' den;
Shield my soul from its peril, due
For the sins I sinned my lifetime through.'
He did his right-hand glove uplift –
Saint Gabriel took from his hand the gift;
Then drooped his head upon his breast,
And with clasped hands he went to rest.
God from on high sent down to him
One of his angel Cherubim –
Saint Michael of Peril of the sea,
Saint Gabriel in company –
From heaven they came for that soul of price,
And they bore it with them to Paradise.

Source: J. O'Hagan (trans.) *The Song of Roland* (1883)
pp. 137–152

Fully developed as a mythological medieval world by the fifteenth century, chivalry and chivalric literature perhaps reached its acme in the Arthurian writings which have such force that many have mistaken them for reality.

ᚠᚱ 1.8 Sir Thomas Malory, *Le Morte D'Arthur* ᚱᚠ

Chapter XIV

How Sir Galahad departed, and how he was commanded to go to the Castle of Maidens to destroy the wicked custom.

Now will I depart, said Galahad, for I have much on hand, for many good knights be full busy about it, and this knight and I were in the same quest of the Sangreal. Sir, said a good man, for his sin he was thus wounded; and I marvel, said the good man, how ye durst take upon you so rich a thing as the high order of knighthood without clean confession, and that was the cause ye were bitterly wounded. For the way on the right hand betokeneth the highway of our Lord Jesu Christ, and the way of a good true good liver. And the other way betokeneth the way of sinners and of misbelievers. And when the devil saw your pride and presumption, for to take you in the quest of the Sangreal, that made you to be overthrown, for it may not be enchieved but by virtuous living. Also, the writing on the cross was a signification of heavenly deeds, and of knightly deeds in God's works, and no knightly deeds in worldly works. And pride is head of all deadly sins, that caused this knight to depart from Galahad. And where thou tookest the crown of gold thou sinnest in covetise and in theft: all this were no knightly deeds. And this Galahad, the holy knight, the which fought with the two knights, the two knights signify the two deadly sins which were wholly in this knight Melias; and they might not withstand you, for ye are without deadly sin.

Now departed Galahad from thence, and betaught them all unto God. Sir Melias said: My lord Galahad, as soon as I may ride I shall seek you. God send you health, said Galahad, and so took his horse and departed, and rode many journeys forward and backward, as adventure would lead him. And at the last it happened him to depart from a place or a castle the which was named Abblasoure; and he had heard no mass, the which he was wont ever to hear or ever he departed out of any castle or place, and kept that for a custom. Then Sir Galahad came unto a mountain where he found an old chapel, and found there nobody, for all, all was desolate; and there he kneeled before the altar, and besought God of wholesome counsel. So as he prayed he heard a voice that said: Go thou now, thou adventurous knight, to the Castle of Maidens, and there do thou away the wicked customs.

Chapter XV

How Sir Galahad fought with the knights of the castle, and destroyed the wicked custom.

When Sir Galahad heard this he thanked God, and took his horse; and he had not ridden but half a mile, he saw in the valley afore him a strong castle with deep ditches, and there ran beside it a fair river that hight Severn; and there he met with a man of great age, and either saluted other, and Galahad asked him the castle's name. Fair sir, said he, it is the Castle of Maidens. That is a cursed castle, said Galahad, and all they that be conversant therein, for all pity is out thereof, and all hardiness and mischief is therein. Therefore, I counsel you, sir knight, to turn again. Sir, said Galahad, wit you well I shall not turn again. Then looked Sir Galahad on his arms that nothing failed him, and then he put his shield afore him; and anon there met him seven fair maidens, the which said unto him: Sir knight, ye ride here in a great folly, for ye have the water to pass over. Why should I not pass the water? said Galahad. So rode he away from them and met with a squire that said: Knight, those knights in the castle defy you, and defenden you ye go no further till that they wit what ye would. Fair sir, said Galahad, I come for to destroy the wicked custom of this castle. Sir, an ye will abide by that ye shall have enough to do. Go you now, said Galahad, and haste my needs.

Then the squire entered into the castle. And anon after there came out of the castle seven knights, and all were brethren. And when they saw Galahad they cried: Knight, keep thee, for we assure thee nothing but death. Why, said Galahad, will ye all have ado with me at once? Yea, said they, thereto mayst thou trust. Then Galahad put forth his spear and smote the foremost to the earth, that near he brake his neck. And therewithal the other smote him on his shield great strokes, so that their spears brake. Then Sir Galahad drew out his sword, and set upon them so hard that it was marvel to see it, and so through great force he made them to forsake the field; and Galahad chased them till they entered into the castle, and so passed through the castle at another gate.

And there met Sir Galahad an old man clothed in religious clothing, and said: Sir, have here the keys of this castle. Then Sir Galahad opened the gates, and saw so much people in the streets that he might not number them, and all said: Sir, ye be welcome, for long have we abiden here our deliverance. Then came to him a gentlewoman and said: These knights be fled, but they will come again this night, and here to begin again their evil custom. What will ye that I shall do? said Galahad. Sir, said the gentlewoman, that ye send after all the knights hither that hold their lands of this castle, and make them to swear for to use the customs that were used heretofore of old time. I will well, said Galahad. And there she brought him an horn of ivory, bounden with gold richly, and said: Sir, blow this horn which will be heard two mile about this castle. When Sir Galahad had blown the horn he set him down upon a bed.

Then came a priest to Galahad, and said: Sir, it is past a seven year agone that these seven brethren came into this castle, and harboured with the lord of this castle that night the Duke Lianour, and he was lord of all this country. And when they espied the duke's daughter, that was a full fair woman, then by their false covin they made debate betwixt themself, and the duke of his goodness would have departed them, and there they slew him and his eldest son. And then they took the maiden and the treasure of the castle. And then by great force they held all the knights of this castle against their will under their obeissance, and in great service and truage, robbing and pilling the poor common people of all that they had. So it happened on a day the duke's daughter said: Ye have done unto me great wrong to slay mine own father, and my brother, and thus to hold our lands: not for then, she said, ye shall not hold this castle for many years, for by one knight ye shall be overcome. Thus she prophesied seven years agone. Well, said the seven knights, sithen ye say so, there shall never lady nor knight pass this castle but they shall abide maugre their heads, or die therefore, till that knight be come by whom we shall lose this castle. And therefore is it called the Maidens' Castle, for they have devoured many maidens. Now, said Galahad, is she here for whom this castle was lost? Nay sir, said the priest, she was dead within these three nights after that she was thus enforced; and sithen have they kept her younger sister, which endureth great pains with no other ladies.

By this were the knights of the country come, and then he made them do homage and fealty to the king's daughter, and set them in great ease of heart. And in the morn there came one to Galahad and told him how that Gawaine, Gareth, and Uwaine, had slain the seven brethren. I suppose well, said Sir Galahad, and took his armour and his horse, and commended them unto God.

Source: Sir Thomas Malory, Le Morte D'Arthur, 2 vols
(1903) Vol. II, pp. 244–248

ꙮ 1.9 M. R. Ridley, *Sir Gawain and The Green Knight* ꙮ

Chapter III: The Three Days

The first day, and the hunting of the deer
Quite early, before the dawn came, the folk in the castle rose, and those that were for the road summoned their grooms, and the grooms made haste to saddle their horses,

got ready all their gear, and packed their bags. Then they dressed in their finest riding clothes, and mounted, and took hold of their reins, and went each his way. And the lord of the castle was up as early as any of them, ready dressed for the hunt with many of his knights. He heard Mass, and then ate a hasty breakfast, and was ready with his horn for the hunting-field. Before there was even a glimmer of dawn over the land he and his men were mounted, and the kennel-men coupled the hounds, and opened the kennel doors, and called the hounds out, blowing clear on the horns the three long notes. The hounds bayed as they heard them, and made a great clamour, as the huntsmen whipped in and turned back those that went straying off on false scents. There were a hundred hunters, the best horsemen in the country. The keepers of the deer-hounds went to their hunting stations, and cast off the couples, and the horns rang loud and clear through the forest.

At the first sound of the hunt all the wild creatures trembled, and the deer huddled together in the valley, half mad for fear, and then hastened to the high ground, but they were turned back by the beaters who shouted aloud at them. They let the harts go their way, and the noble bucks, with their high-held heads and their fine antlers, for the lord had given orders that in the close season there was to be no hunting of the male deer. But the hinds were ringed in with shouts of 'Hay!' and 'Ware!' and the does were driven down with great clamour to the bottoms of the valleys. There you might see, as the bowmen loosed, the curving flight of the arrows. At each turn in the wood there flashed a shaft, that bit into the brown hides with its broad head, and the deer cried out as they fell bleeding in death along the hillsides. The hounds coursed hard after them, and the hunters with their horns followed the hounds, with blasts on the horns that rang as though the cliffs were splitting. Any beasts that escaped the bowmen were pulled down and killed at the resayts, after they had been harassed from the high ground and driven down to the streams in the valleys. The men at the low-lying stations were skilled, and the greyhounds so strong that they gripped the deer and tore them down as soon as they came in sight. The lord was carried away with joy of the hunting, and now he galloped, and now he dismounted to watch the death of a deer, and he drove hard all day till the night fell.

Meantime, while the lord took his delight in hunting along the woods, the good knight Gawain lay in his soft bed, keeping snug till the light of day gleamed on the walls of his room, with the curtains round him and the gay coverlet over him. And as he lay there dozing he heard a little timid noise at his door, and then heard it quickly open. He brought his head up out of the clothes and lifted a corner of the curtain and took a cautious glance to see what this might be. It was the lady, lovely to look on, that closed the door behind her very softly and quietly, and stole towards the bed.

Gawain did not know what to do, so he lay down again quietly and behaved as though he was still asleep. The lady crept noiselessly over the floor to the bed, and lifted the curtain, came inside and sat down on the edge of the bed, and stayed there a long time to watch him when he woke. Gawain lay there a long time wondering what this might mean, for it seemed to him very strange; but then he said to himself, 'Perhaps it would be better to ask straight out what she desires.' So he woke up and stretched himself, turned towards her and opened his eyes, and pretended to be astonished, and crossed himself, to preserve himself from any harm. The lady sat there, with her lovely pink and white cheeks, and her sweet lips, and laughing at him.

'Good morning, Sir Gawain,' said she gaily, 'you are a careless sleeper, that lets a lady slip thus to your bedside without hearing her. Now you are caught, and unless we can make a truce I shall imprison you in your bed, be sure of that.' And she laughed as she made fun of him.

'Good morning, sweet lady,' said Gawain cheerfully, 'everything shall be done to me as you like and I am well content, for I yield myself as your prisoner, and pray you for favour; that, I think, is the best I can do, and there is no way out of it.' So he laughed back at her. 'But,' said he, 'fair lady, will you then grant me a boon and release prisoner for long enough to let him get up and out of his bed and get himself dressed? Then I should be in better case to talk with you.'

'No, no, dear knight,' said the sweet lady, 'you are not to get out of your bed. I have a better idea than that. I shall tuck you up where you are, and then talk with my knight that I have caught. You are Sir Gawain, whom all men hold in honour wherever in the world you ride your ways, and you win great praise among lords and among ladies and among all men that live for your honour and your courtesy. And now here you are, and we are by our two selves. My lord and his men are hunting afar, the knights in the castle are in their beds and so are my maidens, and the door is shut and close latched. And since I have here in this house the knight that is the honoured favourite of all the world, I shall spend my time well while it lasts in talking to him. I am wholly yours, your humble servant, to do with as you please.'

'Faith,' said Gawain, 'that rejoices my heart, even though I am far below what you have said of me. I am unworthy, and I know it, of the honour that you do me. But, if you will, it would be pure joy to me to put myself wholly at your service, to do your pleasure whether in word or deed.'

'Good faith, Sir Gawain,' said the lady; 'if I held light the goodness and the prowess that please all others, that would be poor courtesy. There are ladies enough who would give all the jewels and the gold that they possess to have you, dear knight, in their power, as I have you, to talk to you and hear your courtly answers, and have you comfort them and soothe their cares. I give praise to the Lord who rules the heavens that I have by His grace here under my hand the desire of all the world.'

So the lovely lady spoke sweetly to him, and he made courteous answer.

'Madam,' said Gawain, 'Mary reward you for the noble generosity you have shown me. There are many who just copy other men, and the courtesy they show me is far beyond my deserts; but your kindness comes from your own heart, that does not know how to be less than courteous to any man.'

'Nay,' said the lady, 'it is far otherwise. Were I the fairest and noblest of all women alive, and had I all the wealth of the world in my hands, so that I could choose as I would from all the men on earth a lover to my liking, there is no man I would choose before you, seeing all that I have found in you of beauty and courtesy and gay spirits, all that I had heard of you before, and now find to be true.'

'My noble lady,' said Gawain, 'you could have chosen far better, but none the less I am very proud that you hold me so high. I am your servant, and I hold you my queen; I offer myself as your true knight, and may Christ reward you for accepting my service.'

Thus they spoke of many things till past mid-morning, and the lady behaved as though she loved him dearly. But Gawain met her with his perfect courtesy, yet a little distantly, and she thought 'even if I were the loveliest maiden on earth, he left his love-making behind him when he set out on this journey,' for she remembered the grim task that lay before him, and the stroke that might strike him down, which he could not escape. So she spoke of leaving him, and he did not stop her.

She bade him good day, and glanced at him with a laugh, and as she stood by him she surprised him with make-believe severity. 'I thank you for my entertainment. But I begin to wonder whether you are Gawain at all.'

'Why so?' he asked anxiously, fearing that in some way his words had failed in courtesy.

'Bless you!' she said, 'so good and courteous a knight as Gawain is famed to be, the very pattern of knightly manners, could not have talked so long with a lady without asking her for a kiss, even if only by some trifle of a hint at the end of a speech.'

'Be it as you wish,' said Gawain. 'Surely I will kiss you at your bidding. That is no more than your knight's duty; and besides, I should hate to displease you, so you need not ask twice.'

Then she came to him, and bent sweetly down, and put her arms round him and kissed him. They commended each other to the keeping of Christ, and she quietly opened the door and went out.

Gawain rose and hastened to dress, called his servant, and chose his raiment. When he was arrayed he went gladly to Mass, and then to the meal that was ready for him, and made good cheer all day till the moon rose. There was never a knight had a gayer time, with two such worthy ladies to entertain him, the elder and the younger, and the three of them had much happiness together. Meantime the lord of the castle was off all day at his hunting, chasing the hinds over heath and through woodland. And by the time that the sun drew down to the west they had killed does and hinds almost beyond counting. Then all the hunters flocked together at the end of the day and made a quarry of all the deer, and undid them. Each man had his due portion, and on a hide they laid out parts to feed the hounds. Then they blew the kill, and the hounds bayed, and they took up the carcases, and turned homewards, winding as they rode many clear notes on the horns. And as daylight ended, the whole company was back in the great castle where the knight lived secure. There they found ease, and bright fires kindled. And as the lord came in Gawain met him, and they were glad to greet each other again.

Then the lord commanded all the company to gather in the great hall, and the ladies to come down with their maidens. And then before them all he bade men bring in the venison. And he called laughingly to Gawain and told him the tally of all the swift deer, and showed him what fine condition they had been in.

'How does this please you?' said he. 'Have I done well? Have I deserved your thanks by my skill in the field?'

'Indeed,' said Gawain, 'this is the finest kill in a day's hunting that I have seen in seven years in winter-time.'

'I hand it over to you,' said the knight, 'for by our covenant you can claim it for your own.'

'True,' said Gawain, 'and I say the same to you. What I have with honour won in this house I make it over to you with as good will.' And he threw his arms round his neck and gave him a kiss as near to the sweetness of the lady's as he could manage. 'There are my winnings,' he said, 'they are all that I can show for my day, but I would hand them over as freely if they were worth more.'

'Good,' said the other, 'and I thank you. Maybe it is the richer prize of the two, if only you would tell me where you were clever enough to win it.'

'That was not in the covenant,' said Gawain, 'so ask me no more; you have been given all that is due you, and do not suspect otherwise.' They laughed and made merry, and went to supper, where new delicacies were laid ready for them.

Then they sat by the fireside in the lord's own room and servants brought them goblet after goblet of choice wine. And in their laughing talk they made again the same agreement that they made the day before, that, whatever changes fortune should bring in their winnings, they would exchange their new gains when they met the next night. And they pledged each other to this as before in a special goblet of wine. Then they said good night, and they all went happily to their beds.

Source: M. R. Ridley, *Sir Gawain and the Green Knight* (1968) pp. 60–70

One of the most eloquent expressions of chivalry was the development of heraldry, from the twelfth century onwards, as a way of identifying families in a symbolic language of pictures. It developed from the battlefield marking of shields and the shield remained the conventional frame for designs. Coats of arms became prized possessions, annexed to particular families and ensuring the stability of the knightly class. In England, along with the pictorial language, a descriptive language emerged, in a debased Norman-French vocabulary. In 1484 the College of Arms, under the Garter King of Arms, was formally created.

The third order generally lacks a voice and the condition of medieval peasantry has frequently been depicted bleakly even if the counter-legend of 'Merry England' with a healthy – organically fed – population also persists. Peasant life was not an invariable; soil and climate saw to that, and, given *Piers the Plowman* and Chaucer, the peasant's life (within the disposition of Christ's love for all) could at times be 'idealised'.

᭡ 1.10 Geoffrey Chaucer, *The Canterbury Tales* ᭡

With him there was his brother, a ploughman,
Who'd fetched and carried many a load of dung;
A good and faithful labourer was he,
Living in peace and perfect charity.
God he loved best, and that with all his heart,
At all times, good and bad, no matter what;
And next he loved his neighbour as himself.
He'd thresh, and ditch, and also dig and delve,
And for Christ's love would do as much again
If he could manage it, for all poor men,
And ask no hire. He paid his tithes in full,
On what he earned and on his goods as well.
He wore a smock, and rode upon a mare.

Source: Geoffrey Chaucer, *The Canterbury Tales* (trans.) D. Wright (Oxford, 1986) p. 14

The life of pre-industrial society has often been seen presented as a static one, and in general terms the medieval world had many fixed points. The structures of the Roman Empire continued, after the collapse of the Western Empire, to not only cast its spell but also to provide an administrative and legal model to both secular and ecclesiastical institutions, not least the papacy. The search for a Christian Empire in the West, reflecting Constantine's in the East, was a continuous and sometimes painful one.

1.11 Eusebius: *The Christian Empire* (AD 336)

The Virtues of the Christian Emperor (5.1–4)

1   And in this hope (i.e. of the heavenly kingdom) our divinely-favoured emperor partakes even in this present life, gifted as he is by God with native virtues, and having received into his soul the outflowings of His favour. His reason he derives from the universal Reason (i.e. the Word): he is wise by communion with wisdom; good by participation in good; just by sharing injustice; prudent by fellowship with prudence, and brave by sharing in

2   the heavenly power. And truly may he deserve the imperial tide, who has formed his soul to royal virtues, according to the standard of that celestial kingdom. . . .

3   Let then our emperor, on the testimony of truth itself, be declared alone worthy of the title; who is dear to the Supreme Sovereign himself; who alone is free, nay, who is truly lord: above the thirst of wealth, superior to sexual desire; victorious even over natural pleasures, controlling, not controlled by, anger and passion. He is indeed an emperor, and bears a title corresponding to his deeds; a victor in truth, who has gained the victory over those passions which overmaster the rest of men: whose character is formed after the Divine original of the Supreme Sovereign, and whose mind reflects, as in a mirror, the radiance of His virtues. Hence is our emperor perfect in prudence, in goodness, in justice in courage, in piety, in devotion to God: he truly and only is a philosopher since he knows himself, and is fully aware that supplies of every blessing are showered on him from a source quite external to himself, even from heaven itself. Declaring the august title of supreme authority by the splendour of his vesture, he alone worthily wears that imperial purple which so well becomes him.

Source: **J. Stevenson (ed.) *A New Eusebius: documents illustrative of the history of the Church to AD 337* (1968) pp. 393–394**

The Latin language remained, in a babel of vernaculars, the channel of education and cult. The Roman Church provided a focus for unity for the far-flung Christian community. The barbarian invasions had provided both a valuable source of new blood and a unifying cause for the West to fight for, even later to be superseded by the hatred of the Greek civilisation of New Rome or Byzantium and the developing challenge of Islam.

Alongside these 'unifying' tendencies, all underpinned by an often undercharged economy, was a parallel movement which favoured centrifugalism. Localities were, given the difficulties of transport and a general lack of a money economy, defended doggedly and retained a strong personal identity. As the centuries progressed the idea of 'nations' developed, not 'nation' states in our present sense, but areas designated by a commonality of culture. The Western world expanded gradually and sometimes dramatically as exploration and missionary zeal combined to push back frontiers. Towns developed and grew more sophisticated. An epoch which began in the desert, ended in the city.

Further reading

M. Barber, *The Two Cities: Medieval Europe 1050–1320* (Routledge, London, 1992).

R. Barber, *The Knight and Chivalry*, 2nd edn (Boydell, Woodbridge, 1995).

R. Barber and J. Barker, *The Tournament in England, 1100–1400* (Boydell, Woodbridge, 1986)

R. Bartlett, *The Making of Europe: Conquest, Colonisation and Cultural Change 950–1350* (Penguin, Harmondsworth, 1993).

R. Bartlett, *Medieval Panorama* (Thames & Hudson, London, 2001).

M. Bloch, *Feudal Society*, 2nd edn (Routledge & Kegan Paul, London, 1962).

P. Brown, *The Rise of Western Christendom* (Blackwell, Oxford, 1996).

P. Contamine, *War in the Middle Ages* (Blackwell, Oxford, 1985).

C. Dawson, *Religion and the Rise of Western Culture* (The Gifford Lectures: 1948–1949, London, 1950).

J. Evans, *The Flowering of the Middle Ages* (Thames & Hudson, London, 1985).

R. Fletcher, *The Quest for El Cid* (Oxford University Press, Oxford, 1991).

C. Frayling, *Strange Landscape* (BBC Books, London, 1995).

F. L. Ganshof, *Feudalism*, 3rd edn (Longman, London, 1964).

B. Hamilton, *Religion in the Medieval West* (Edward Arnold, London, 1986).

F. Heer, *The Medieval World: Europe, 1100–1350* (The New American Library. New York, 1962).

J. Le Goff, *Medieval Civilisation 400–1500* (Blackwell, Oxford, 1989).

P. Lineham and J. L. Nelson, *Medieval World* (Routledge, London, 2000).

B. H. Rosenwein, *A Short History of the Middle Ages* (Broadview Press, Ontario, 2002).

R. W. Southern, *The Making of the Middle Ages* (Arrow Books, London, 1959).

P. Wolfe, *The Awakening of Europe* (Penguin, Harmondsworth, 1968).

2

THE MONASTIC
WORLD

In Western Christendom the Christian Church was all-compassing. Through baptism men and women became an integral part of 'the people of God'. Within this Christian community the *ordo* of those who prayed was further set aside by either ordination or religious profession. The ordained clergy – bishops, priests, deacons and sub-deacons – who, with clerks, men dedicated to the church as full-time administrators or as aspirants to ordination, formed the hierarchical church in the Middle Ages. This group was complemented by numerous individuals, predominantly men but including many women, who were monks, friars, nuns or other religious. These individuals consecrated themselves to the search for God. The origins of the religious life go back at least to the third century of the Christian era when, following the end of the active persecution of Christians, some sought an ascetic life separate from the ordinary secular society. An attempt to recapture the aspirations and community of the first Christians, described in the *Acts of* the *Apostles* was always part of the impulse to this way of life.

Acts of the Apostles, *New Revised Standard Version* (1993)

Acts 2, 42–47

They devoted themselves to the apostles' teaching and fellowship, to the breaking of bread and prayers. Awe came upon everyone, because many wonders and signs were being done by the apostles. All who believed were together and had all things in common; they would sell their possessions and goods and distribute the proceeds to all, as they had need. Day by day, as they spent much time together in the temple, they broke bread at home and ate their food with glad and generous hearts, praising God and having the good-will of all people. And day by day the Lord added to their number those who were being saved.

Acts 4, 32–37

Now the whole group of those who believed were of one heart and soul, and no one claimed private ownership of any possessions, but everything they owned was held in common. With great power the apostles gave their testimony to the resurrection of the Lord Jesus, and great grace was upon them all. There was not a needy person among them, for as many as owned lands or houses sold them and brought the proceeds of what was sold. They laid it at the apostles' feet and it was distributed to each as any had need. There was a Levite, a native of Cyprus, Joseph, to whom the apostles gave the name Barnabas (which means 'son of encouragement'). He sold a field that belonged to him, then brought the money, and laid it at the apostles' feet.

There was, too, a tradition of individual endeavour which led some Christians to seek God in the desert, the margins of civilisation, as hermits. The word monk in its original meaning was a *solitary*. The lives of these desert fathers, as they were called (there were also desert mothers), inspired the religious life throughout the Middle Ages. Among the lives which were particularly influential were those of Antony of Egypt (251–356) and Martin of Tours (c. 316–397). Antony of Egypt, at the age of twenty, gave up his possessions to live among the local ascetics. Between 286 and 306 he lived in complete solitude before taking on the task of guiding the disciples who had gathered about him. Martin of Tours also lived solitary life before founding the first monastery in Gaul. He became Bishop of Tours in 372. Gradually religious rules, blueprints for living as a monk, were compiled, drawing deeply on the living tradition of monasticism. Rules existed for both hermits and cenobites, those living as a community. The rules of the Celtic monks reflected primitive simplicity and austerity.

ཻ 2.1 The Rule of Colmcille: a ninth-century ཻ Irish rule for Hermits

1 If your conscience does not allow you to live among men, then live alone in the vicinity of a great city.

2 Let your life be completely detached from the world, and follow the teaching of Christ and the gospels.

3 Whether you possess much or little in the way of food, drink or clothing, let it be retained with the permission of a senior. Let him have control of its disposition, for it is not becoming for a follower of Christ to be in any way superior to the nobility.

4 Let your hermitage be a very secure place with only one door.

5 Have a few devout men who will discuss God and the scriptures with you. Let them visit you on great feast-days, so that they may strengthen your devotion to the words and precepts of God.

6 Hold no converse with anyone who is given to idle or worldly gossip, or with anyone who grumbles about what he can neither prevent nor rectify. All the more should you have no dealings with a tattler carrying tales from friend to foe; simply give him your blessing and send him off about his business.

7 Let your servant be a God-fearing and discreet man who will always attend to your needs in a constant but restrained manner.

8 Cherish every practice of devotion greatly.

9 Be ready in mind for red martyrdom.

10 Be persevering and steadfast for white martyrdom.

11 Forgive every person from your heart.

12 Pray constantly for those who annoy you.

13 Be very constant in your prayers for the faithful departed, as if each dead person were a personal friend of yours.

14 The litanies should be sung standing.

15 Let your vigils be constant day by day, but always under the direction of another.

16 Your daily occupation should be threefold, namely, prayer, manual labour, and lectio.

17 Your manual labour should have a three-fold division. First, fill your own needs and those of the place where you live. Secondly, do your share of your brothers' work. Thirdly, help your neighbours by instruction, by writing, by making garments, or by providing for any other need of theirs that may arise. As the Lord says, 'No one should come before me empty-handed'.

18 Let everything be done in proper order for 'no one can win a crown without keeping all the rules of combat'.

19 Above and before all else practice almsgiving.

20 Do not eat until you are hungry.

21 Do not sleep until it is necessary.

22 Do not speak until necessity demands.

23 Out of compassion you should do without your due allowance of food and clothing so that you may share with your less fortunate brothers and with the poor in general.

24 Love God with all your heart and with all your strength.

25 Love your neighbour as you would yourself.

26 Be faithful to the commands of God at all times.

27 The extent of your prayer should be until tears come.

28 The measure of your work should be to labour until tears of exhaustion come.

29 The limit of your labour or of your genuflections, in the event that tears do not come, should be perspiration.

Source: U. Ó Maidín (trans.) *The Celtic Monk*
(Michigan, 1996) pp. 39–41

Among the seminal early rules were those of Basil, Pachomius and the so-called *Rule of the Master*.

ತಿ 2.2 *The Rule of the Master* ೕ

What should be the Nature of the Disciples' Obedience?

The Lord has replied through the master:

The first degree of humility is obedience without delay. But this kind is proper to the perfect, few in number, those who consider nothing more dear to them than Christ; because of the holy service they have vowed, for fear of hell, and for the sake of the treasures of eternal life, as soon as they hear something commanded by the superior they can tolerate no delay in conforming. It is of these that the Lord says: 'No sooner do they hear than they obey me'. And he likewise says to those who teach: 'Anyone who listens to you listens to me'. Such as these, therefore, immediately relinquishing their own concerns and abandoning their own will, disengaging their hands and leaving unfinished what they were doing, comply by their actions with the voice of the one who commands, falling into step with prompt obedience. Thus in one and the same moment, so to speak, the command issued by the superior and what is done by the disciples, the two together, occur without any delay, in the swiftness of the fear of God.

But this kind of obedience, proper to the few who are perfect, should not unduly alarm the souls of the weak and the indolent and make them despair, but, should inspire them to do likewise. So keeping in mind that among us there are assorted embodiments of misery, since a sluggish nature is the source of a great deal of laziness in some persons – for it is well known that the hearing of certain ones is dulled by insensibility of the ears, and we also note that the minds of some are immediately distracted and wander off into a jungle of thought – we therefore indulgently moderate the strictures of obedience on the part of the teachers. Accordingly, the master should not be irked at having to repeat his command to the disciples, as the Lord testified when, calling Abraham, he repeated his name a second time, saying: 'Abraham, Abraham'. By this repetition the Lord clearly showed us that one call is possibly not enough to ensure [his] being heard.

As regards questions, when the master's voice is twice directed to the disciples, it is only right to indulge by a repetition of the question those who do not reply, in such a that if the disciple remains silent at first he should not be held at fault, but it should be considered a mark of respect reserved for the master. In this reverence the virtuous disciple is credited with hesitating to break the silence he maintains in order not to overwhelm you with replies rushing from a glib tongue as soon as you state your question.

But as regards commands, if the master must repeat his order, however slow or negligent the hearers may be, when what was first said is repeated to them a second time, it is by all means proper that the second delay be interrupted by acts of obedience. If however there should be a third delay on the disciple's part – may it never happen! – it must be considered a fault, the perversity of contumacy.

It is right and proper to consider here the theme of the two ways, namely, the broad road which leads to perdition, and the narrow road which leads to life. On these two roads proceed the various types of human obedience. Thus, on the broad road go men of the world and sarabaite and gyrovague monks. These live alone or two or three together, without a superior, on an equal footing and moving about as they please. Alternating in authority, taking turns in commanding one another whatever each one wishes, safeguarding for themselves whatever they individually choose – since no one wants to be thwarted in his self-interest – such as these never banish dispute from themselves. Right after a violent quarrel these evilly-assembled men break up and wander off like a flock without a shepherd, dispersing in various directions, no doubt only to fall into the jaws of the wolf. It is not God who provides cells for them once again, but their self-will. Individually, on their own authority, each one for himself alone, they assume the title of abbot. And you find that there are more monasteries than monks.

One may be confident that such as these walk the broad road in that, while retaining the name monk, they live in the same way as do those in the world, distinguished from them only by having the tonsure. They give obedience to their desires instead of to God. Trusting their own judgement they think that what is evil is allowed to them; whatever they want they call holy, and whatever they do not want they consider forbidden. They deem it proper to think about providing for their body rather than for their soul, in other words, that they better than anyone else can be concerned about food, clothing, and footwear for themselves. They recklessly fancy themselves so secure as regards the account they will have to give of their soul that, whereas they are living as monks according to their own judgement without the guidance of superiors, they think that in their cell they are perfectly observant of every law and all the justice of God. If perchance some superior or other, in passing by, offers them some suggestions for their improvement and tells them that this solitary manner of living is not good for them, the advice as well as the very person of the teacher immediately displeases them. Unmoved, they do not promise to reform by agreeing with him and heeding him, but reply that they must live all alone, ignoring what the prophet said: 'Such are corrupt; they do abominable deeds', and that testimony of Solomon which says: 'There are ways which men think right, but whose end plunges into the depth of hell'.

Such as these therefore travel the broad way because wherever the foot of their desires leads them, they immediately consent to follow, and most willing indulgence is unhesitatingly at the service of whatever their lust craves. Breaking for themselves new paths of licentiousness and self-will without a master, they enlarge the way of their life by divers kinds of forbidden pleasures, and toward whatever place their delights wish to go, they direct their wanton and criminal steps. They never want to realise that for the creature man, death is stationed at the entrance of delight, and they bypass with unhearing ears what is said to them: 'Do not follow your lusts; restrain your desires'.

Those whom love urges on to eternal life, on the contrary, take the narrow way. Not living according to their own discretion or obeying their own desires and pleasures, but walking by the judgement and command of another, they not only exercise self-control in the aforesaid desires and pleasures and do not want to do their own will even if they could, but they also submit themselves to the authority of another. Living in monasteries, they wish to have an abbot over them and not bear this title themselves. Certainly such as these conform to what the Lord says: 'I have come not to do my own will, but to do the will of the one who sent me'. And not doing their own will, denying themselves for the sake of Christ, they follow God whithersoever the command of the abbot leads them. Furthermore, under the care of the abbot, not only are they not forced to worry about temporal necessities, that is, food, clothing and footwear, but solely by rendering obedience in all things to the master, they are made secure about the account they will have to give of their soul and about whatever else is profitable for both body and soul. This is so because, whether for good or for ill, what happens among the sheep is the responsibility of the shepherd, and he who gave orders is the one who will have to render an account when inquiry is made at the judgement, not he who carried out the orders, whether good or bad.

Now, it may be said that such as these travel the narrow way, because their own desires are never put into effect at all and they do not do what they wish. But bearing the yoke of another's judgement, they are restrained from going where their own pleasure would lead them, and what they themselves would choose to do or achieve is denied them by the master. In the monastery their will is daily thwarted for the sake of the Lord, and in the spirit of martyrdom they patiently endure whatever commands they receive to test them. In the monastery they will assuredly say to the Lord, with the prophet: 'For your sake we are being slain all the day; we are looked upon as sheep to be slaughtered'. And later on, at the judgement, they will likewise say to the lord: 'You tested us, God, you refined us like silver. You let us fall into the net. You laid heavy burdens on our backs. You have set men over our heads'. Therefore when they say, 'You have set men over our heads', it is evident that they are to have over them as God's representative a superior, whom they fear in the monastery. And continuing with what is stated, they will rightly say to the Lord again, this time in the next world: 'But now the ordeal by fire and water is over, and you allow us once more to draw breath', that is, 'We have gone through the thwarting of our own will and by serving in obedience we have come to the enjoyment of your love'. But obedience such as this will be acceptable to God and gratifying to men only if the thing commanded is done without fear, without apathy, without hesitation, without murmuring or protesting, because obedience offered to superiors is given to God, as the Lord says to our teachers: 'Anyone who listens to you listens to me', and elsewhere he says: 'No sooner do they hear than they obey me'. Obedience is such, therefore, if it is given with good will, because 'God loves a cheerful giver'. The disciple obeys with ill will if he reproaches not only us verbally but God inwardly about what he does in a bad mood. And even though he does what he was commanded, still it will not be acceptable to God, who sees that he is murmuring in his heart. To repeat, even though he does what he is told, but does it in a bad mood, he will get no reward for doing it, for God is watching his heart right now and finds in it the wretched disposition of one who acts in this way.

> Source: L. Eberle (trans.) *The Rule of the Master*
> (Michigan, 1977) pp. 119–115

The relationship between the *Rule of the Master* and the *Rule of St Benedict,* which owed much to the master, has been a continuing source of controversy in monastic historical studies. But there is no doubt that the Benedictine Rule, distinguished by its balance, moderation and brevity, was the most influential of the monastic rules in the West. Benedict (*c.* 480–*c.*550) was an Italian abbot who was a superior of monasteries at Subiaco and Montecassino. Benedict's abbot is, as the name implies, a father to his community, and the lifelong association of the monks in their 'school of the Lord's service' provides the setting for a self-contained religious life which can be sustained in hostile territory or trouble times.

ᘒ 2.3 *The Rule of St Benedict* ᘓ

Prologue

Hearken, my son, to the precepts of the master and incline the ear of thy heart, freely accept and faithfully fulfil the instructions of a loving father, that by the labour of obedience thou mayest return to him from whom thou hast strayed by the sloth of disobedience. To thee are my words now addressed, whosoever thou mayest be that renouncing thine own will to fight for the true King, Christ, dost take up the strong and glorious weapons of obedience.

And first of all, whatever good work thou undertakest, ask him with most instant prayer to perfect it, so that he who has deigned to count us among his sons may never be provoked by our evil conduct. For we must always so serve him with the gifts which he has given us, that he may never as an angry father disinherit his children, nor yet as a dread lord be driven by our sins to cast into everlasting punishment the wicked servants who would not follow him to glory.

Up with us then at last, for the Scripture arouseth us, saying: Now is the hour for us to rise from sleep (Rom. xiii II). Let us open our eyes to the divine light, and let us hear with attentive ears the warning that the divine voice crieth daily to us: Today if ye will hear his voice, harden not your hearts (Ps. xciv 8). And again: He that hath ears to hear, let him hear what the Spirit saith to the churches (Matt. xi 15; Apoc. ii 7). And what doth he say? Come, ye children, hearken unto me: I will teach you the fear of the Lord (Ps. xxxiii 12). Run while ye have the light of life, lest the darkness of death overtake you (I John xii 35). And the Lord, seeking his workman among the multitudes to whom he thus crieth, saith again: What man is he that desireth life and would fain see good days? (Ps. xxxiii 13). And if hearing him thou answer, 'I am he', God saith to thee: If thou wilt have true and everlasting life, keep thy tongue from evil and thy lips that they speak no guile. Turn away from evil and do good: seek after peace and pursue it (Ps. xxxiii 14–16). And when you have done these things, my eyes will be upon you and my ears open unto your prayers. And before you call upon me, I shall say to you, 'Lo, here I am'. What can be sweeter to us, dearest brethren, than this voice of our Lord inviting us? Behold in his loving mercy the Lord showeth us the way of life.

Let us, therefore, gird our loins with faith and the performance of good works, and following the guidance of the Gospel walk in his paths, so that we may merit to see him who has called us unto his kingdom. And, if we wish to dwell in the tabernacle of his kingdom, except we run thither with good deeds we shall not arrive. But let us ask the Lord with the prophet: Lord, who shall dwell in thy tabernacle, or who shall rest upon thy holy hill? (Ps. xiv 1). Then, brethren, let us hear the Lord answering and showing us the way to that tabernacle and saying: He that walketh without blemish and doth that which is right; he that speaketh truth in his heart, who hath used no deceit in his tongue, nor done evil to his neighbour, nor believed ill of his neighbour (Ps. xiv 1). He that taketh the evil spirit that tempteth him, and casteth him and his temptation from the sight of his heart, and bringeth him to naught; who graspeth his evil suggestions as they arise and dasheth them to pieces on the rock that is Christ. Such men as these, fearing the Lord, are not puffed up on account of their good works, but judging that they can do no good of themselves and that all cometh from God, they magnify the Lord's work in them, using the word of the prophet: Not unto us, O Lord, not unto us, but unto thy name give the glory (Ps. cxiii 9). So the apostle Paul imputed nothing of his preaching to himself, but said: By the grace of God I am what I am (1 Cor. xv 10). And again he saith: He that, glorieth, let him glory in the Lord. (2 Cor. x 17).

Wherefore the Lord also saith in the Gospel: He that heareth these my words and doth them, shall be likened to a wise man that built his house upon a rock. The floods came and the winds blew, and they beat upon that house, and it fell not, for it was founded upon a rock (Matt. vii 24, 25). Having given us these instructions, the Lord daily expects us to make our life correspond with his holy admonitions. And the days of our life are lengthened and a respite allowed us for this very reason, that we may amend our evil ways. For the Apostle saith: Knowest thou not that the patience of God inviteth thee to repentance? (Rom. i 4). For the merciful Lord saith: I will not the death of a sinner, but that he should be converted and live. (Ezech. xxxiii 11).

So, brethren, we have asked the Lord about the dwellers in his tabernacle and have heard what is the duty of him who would dwell therein; it remains for us to fulfil this duty. Therefore our hearts and bodies must be made ready to fight under the holy obedience of his commands; and let us ask God that he be pleased, where our nature is powerless, to give us the help of his grace. And if we would escape the pains of hell and reach eternal life, then must we — while there is still time, while we are in this body and can fulfil all these things by the light of this life — hasten to do now what may profit us for eternity.

Therefore must we establish a school of the Lord's service; in founding which we hope to ordain nothing that is harsh or burdensome. But if, for good reason, for the amendment of evil habit or the preservation of charity, there be some strictness of discipline, do not be at once dismayed and run away from the way of salvation, of which the entrance must needs be narrow. But, as we progress in our monastic life and in faith, our hearts shall be enlarged, and we shall run with unspeakable sweetness of love in the way of God's commandments; so that, never abandoning his rule but persevering in his teaching in the monastery until death, we shall share by patience in the sufferings of Christ, that we may deserve to be partakers also of his kingdom. Amen.

Chapter 2

What kind of Man the Abbot should be

An abbot who is worthy to rule a monastery should always remember what he is called and realise in his actions the name of a superior. For he is believed to be the representative of Christ in the monastery, and for that reason is called by a name of his, according to the words of the Apostle: Ye have received the spirit of the adoption of sons, whereby we cry Abba, Father (Rom. viii 15). Therefore the abbot ought not to teach, or ordain, or command anything which is against the law of the Lord; on the contrary, his commands and teaching should be infused into the minds of his disciples like the leaven of divine justice. Let the abbot remember always that at the dread Judgement of God there will be an examination of both these matters, of his teaching and of the obedience of his disciples. And let the abbot realise that the shepherd will have to answer for any lack of profit which the Father of the family may discover in his sheep. On the other hand, if the shepherd have spent all diligence on an unruly and disobedient flock and devoted his utmost care to the amending of its vicious ways, then he will be acquitted at the Judgement and may say to the Lord with the prophet: I have not hid thy justice within my heart: I have declared thy truth and thy salvation (Ps. xxxix 11) but they have despised and rejected me (Is. i. 3). And so at the last, for these sheep disobedient to his care, let death itself bring its penalty.

Therefore, when anyone has received the name of abbot, he ought to rule his disciples with a twofold teaching, displaying all goodness and holiness by deeds and by words, but by deeds rather than by words. To intelligent disciples let him expound the Lord's commandments in words; but to those of harder hearts and ruder minds let him show forth the divine precepts by his example. And whatever he has taught his disciples to be contrary to God's law, let him show by his example that it is not to be done, lest while preaching to others he should himself become a castaway, and lest God should some day say to him in his sin: Why dost thou repeat my commandments by rote, and boast of my covenant with thee? For thou hast hated to amend thy life and hast cast my words behind thee (Ps. xlix 16, 17). And again: Thou sawest the speck of dust in thy brother's eye and didst not see the beam in thy own (Matt. vii 3).

Let him not make any distinction of persons in the monastery. Let him not love one more than another, unless he find him better in good works and obedience. Let not a freeborn monk be put before one that was a slave, unless there be some other reasonable ground for it. But if the abbot, for just reason, think fit so to do, let him fix anyone's order as he will; otherwise let them keep their due places; because, whether slaves or freemen, we are all one in Christ, and have to serve alike in the army of the same Lord. For there is no respect of persons with God (Rom. ii 11). In this regard only are we distinguished in his sight, if we be found better than others in good works and humility. Therefore let the abbot show an equal love to all, and let the same discipline be imposed on all in accordance with their deserts.

For the abbot in his teaching ought always to observe the rule of the apostle, wherein he says: Reprove, persuade, rebuke (Tim. iv 2). He must adapt himself to circumstances, now using severity and now persuasion, displaying the rigour of a master or the loving kindness of a father. That is to say, that he must sternly rebuke the undisciplined and restless; but the obedient, meek, and patient, these he should exhort to advance in virtue. As for the negligent and rebellious, we warn him to reprimand and punish them. And let him not shut his eyes to the faults of offenders; but as soon as they begin to appear, let him, as he can, cut them out by the roots, mindful of the fate of Heli, the priest of Silo. Those of gentle disposition and good understanding should be punished, for the first and second time, by verbal admonition; but bold, hard, proud, and disobedient characters should be checked at the very beginning of their ill-doing by the rod and corporal punishment, according to the text: The fool is not corrected with words; (Prov. xviii 2; xxix 19) and again: Beat thy son with the rod and thou shalt deliver his soul from death (Prov. xxiii 14).

The abbot should always remember what he is and what he is called, and should know that to whom more is committed, from him more is required. Let him realise also how difficult and arduous a task he has undertaken, of ruling souls and adapting himself to many dispositions. One he must humour, another rebuke, another persuade, according to each one's disposition and understanding, and thus adapt and accommodate himself to all in such away, that he may not only suffer no loss in the sheep committed to him, but may even rejoice in the increase of a good flock.

Above all let him not have greater solicitude for fleeting, earthly, and perishable things, and so overlook or undervalue the salvation of the souls committed to him; but let him always remember that he has undertaken the government of souls and will have to give an account of them. And if he be tempted to complain of lack of means, let him remember the words: Seek ye first the kingdom of God and his approval, and all these things shall be yours without the asking (Matt. vi 33). And again: Those that fear him never go wanting (Ps. xxxiii 10). And let him know that he who has undertaken the government of souls, must prepare himself to render an account of them. And whatever number of brethren he knows he has under his care, let him regard it as certain that he will have to give the Lord an account of all these souls on the Day of Judgement, and certainly of his own soul also. And thus, fearing always the examination which the shepherd will have to face for the sheep entrusted to him, and anxious regarding the account which will have to be given for others; he is made solicitous for his own sake also; and while by his admonitions helping others to amend, he himself is cleansed of his faults.

> Source: J. McCann, *The Rule of St Benedict* (1952)
> pp. 6–13, 16–23

The Rule of St Benedict owed much to the encouragement of Gregory the Great, who became Benedict's first biographer, in his *Second Dialogue*.

ও 2.4 Gregory the Great, *Second Dialogue* ও

How St Benedict died in Christ

The same year in which he departed this life, he told the day of his holy death to his monks, some of which did live daily with him, and some dwelt far off, willing those that were present to keep it secret, and telling them that were absent by what token they should know that he was dead. Six days before he left this world, he gave order to have his sepulchre opened, and forthwith falling into an ague, he began with burning heat to wax faint, and when as the sickness daily increased, upon the sixth day he commanded his monks to carry him into the oratory, where he did arm himself with receiving the body and blood of our Saviour Christ; and having this weak body holden up twixt the hands of his disciples, he stood with his own lifted up to heaven, and as he was in that manner praying, he gave up the ghost. Upon which day two monks, one being in his cell, and the other far distant, had concerning him one and the self-same vision: for they saw all the way from the holy man's cell, towards the east even up to heaven, hung and adorned with tapestry, and shining with an infinite number of lamps, at the top whereof a man, reverently attired, stood and demanded if they knew who passed that way, to whom they answered saying, that they knew not. Then he spake unto them: 'This is the way,' quoth he, 'by which the beloved servant of God, Bennet, is ascended up to heaven.'

> Source: *The High History of Saint Benedict and*
> *his Monks, collated by a Monk of Douai Abbey*
> (1945) pp. 290–291

Gregory the Great sent Augustine of Canterbury (d. *c.* 604) to England in 597 and although there is no evidence that the Rule of Benedict itself reached England so early, it was the Anglo-Saxons, first in the court of Charlemagne, and later in the person of St Boniface, who popularised the Benedictine Rule. The long-term importance of the Rule is shown in many later medieval sources, and the Benedictine abbot as a man of action and initiative is very clearly shown in the chronicle of Bury St Edmund's Abbey, in England.

ᚲᚱ 2.5 The Election of Abbot Samson ᚱᚲ

After the death of Abbot Hugh, when a year and three months were gone, our lord the King sent letters to us, commanding that our Prior and twelve of the Convent, unanimously chosen by our whole body, should appear before him on an appointed day to elect an Abbot. On the day after we had received these letters we assembled in the chapterhouse to deal with the matter. First of all the King's letters were read before the Convent: after this we asked the Prior and charged him on the peril of his soul to nominate according to his conscience the twelve whom he should take with him, men whose life and character made it clear that they would refuse to stray from the right way. And he, granting our petition and inspired by the Holy Spirit, chose six from one side of the choir and six from the other, and satisfied us, not a voice being raised against his choice. From the right side there were Geoffrey of Fordham, Benedict, Master Denys, Master Samson the sub-sacrist, Hugh the third prior, and Master Hermer, at that time a novice: from the left William the Sacrist, Andrew, Peter of Brook, Roger the Cellarer, Master Ambrose, and Master Walter the physician. But one of us said, 'What will happen, if those thirteen, when they come before the King, are unable to agree in their choice of an Abbot?' And one made answer, 'This will be an everlasting reproach to us and to our Church.' Therefore a number of us were for electing an Abbot at home before the others departed, in order that by thus taking forethought there might be no disagreement in the presence of the King. But it seemed to us to be foolish and unseemly to do this without the King's assent, since we did not yet know whether we should be able to secure a free election from our lord the King. Samson the sub-sacrist, speaking in the spirit, said, 'Let us take a middle course that we may avoid peril on this side and on that. Let four confessors be chosen from the Convent and two from among the elder of our seniors, who are of good repute; and let them when they have looked upon the holy mysteries and laid their hands upon the Gospels, choose three men from the Convent whom they think best fitted for the office according to the Rule of St Benedict; and let them set down the names in writing and enclose what they have written under seal; and thus enclosed let it be consigned to those of us who are to go to the Court. And when we are come into the King's presence and have been assured of a free election, then at last let the seal be broken, and thus we shall ascertain who are the three whom we are to nominate before the King. If our lord the King refuse to grant us one of our own house, the seal shall be carried back unbroken and handed to the six that have been sworn, so that their secret shall, on peril of their souls, be hidden for ever.' To this counsel we all gave our assent: and four confessors were nominated, to wit

Eustace, Gilbert of Elveden, Hugh the third prior and Antony, and two others, Turstan and Ruald, both of them old men. This done, we went out singing '*Verba mea*', and the aforesaid six remained behind, having the Rule of St Benedict ready to hand; and as they carried out the business according to their instructions. While these six were thus busied, we held divers opinions concerning those that should be chosen, but every one of us was almost certain that Samson would be one of the three, when we considered his labours and the perils of death that he had faced when he journeyed to Rome to defend the possessions of our Church, and how he was haled away and fettered and imprisoned by Abbot Hugh because he spoke out for the common good, refusing to be bent to flattery, though he might be forced to hold his tongue. But after some delay, the Convent returned to the chapterhouse; and the seniors said that they had done as they were bidden. Then the Prior asked what should be done if the King refused to accept anyone of the three names that they had written; and he got the answer that we should accept anyone whom our lord the King was ready to accept, provided that he were a son of our Church. And to this also was added that if these thirteen brethren saw anything in that writing that needed correction, they should alter it according to God's will, by the common assent or counsel of them all. Samson the sub-sacrist, who sat at the Prior's feet, said, 'It is expedient for the sake of our Church that we should all swear upon the word of truth that, on whomsoever the choice should chance to fall, he should treat the Convent reasonably and refrain from changing obedientiaries without the consent of the Convent, or burdening the Sacrist or admitting any man as a monk without the good-will of the Convent.' And this we all of us granted, raising our hands in token of assent. It was provided that if our lord the King should desire to make Abbot one who was not of our Church, he should not be accepted by the thirteen save with the counsel of the brethren who remained at home.

On the morrow therefore those thirteen set out upon their journey to the Court. Last of them all went Samson, who had charge of their expenses, because he was sub-sacristan. Hung about his neck he carried a case containing the letters of the Convent, as though he were the sole servant of them all; and without any to squire him, he went forth on his way to the Court, carrying his frock tucked up on his arms and following his comrades afar off. On the way to the Court, as the brethren talked together, Samson said that it would be well that all of them should swear that whoso-ever were made Abbot, he should give back the Churches of the Convent's domain to provide for the entertainment of guests, to which all gave their assent save only the Prior who said, 'We have sworn enough: you may put such a burden on the Abbot that I for one should not care to have the abbacy'. And so on this occasion they took no oath; and it was well done, because, if the oath had been sworn, it would not have been kept. On the same day that the thirteen departed from us, William of Hastings, one of our brethren, said as we sat in the cloister, 'I know that we have one of our own folk as Abbot'. And when he was asked how he knew this, he said that he had seen in a vision, as he slept, a prophet clad in white raiment standing before the gate of the monastery, and that he had asked him in the name of the Lord whether we should have one of ourselves for Abbot. And the prophet replied, 'You shall have one of your own, but he shall raven among you like a wolf'. And the purport of the dream was fulfilled in part, since he that was to be Abbot was zealous to be feared rather than to be loved, as many of us said. And another brother was sitting with us,

Edmund by name, who asserted that Samson would be Abbot, and told us of a vision that he had seen the night before. He said that he had seen Roger the Cellarer and Hugh the third prior standing before the altar, and between them was Samson, towering above them from the shoulders upwards and wearing a long cloak that flowed down to his heels and was bound about his shoulders, and he stood with raised fists ready for a fight. And St Edmund arose from the feretory, as it seemed to him in his dreams and, as though some sickness was upon him, bared his feet and legs, and when someone drew near and would have covered his feet, the saint said, 'Draw not near; behold that man shall veil my feet'; and he pointed with his finger toward Samson. Now this is the interpretation of the dream. Inasmuch as he seemed like a fighter, it was foretold that the Abbot to be should live in toil, now contending with the Archbishop of Canterbury concerning the pleas of the crown, now against the knights of St Edmund concerning the payment of full scutage, now with the burgesses over encroachments in the market, now with the sokemen over the suits of the hundreds, wishing like a fighter to overcome his adversaries in battle, that he might reclaim the rights and liberties of his Church. As for the feet of the holy Martyr he veiled them, when he completed the towers of the church that were begun a hundred years before. Such were the dreams our brothers dreamed, which were forthwith bruited abroad, first through the cloister and next through the court, so that before evening it was said openly among the common people, 'He and he and he have been chosen, and one of them will be Abbot.'

But the Prior and the twelve with him, after much toil and delay, at length stood before the King at Waltham, a manor of the Bishop of Winchester, on the second Sunday in Lent. Our lord the King received them kindly and, declaring that he wished to act according to God's will and for the honour of the Church, he commanded the brethren by the mouth of his intermediaries, Richard Bishop of Winchester and Geoffrey the Chancellor, afterwards Archbishop of York, that they should nominate three of our Convent. Whereupon the Prior and the brethren went aside, as though to speak on this matter, and drew out the seal and broke it, and found the names in the following order: Samson the sub-sacrist, Roger the Cellarer and Hugh the third prior. Whereat the brothers who were of higher rank blushed. Moreover, all marvelled that the same Hugh was both elector and elect. But since they could not change the facts, by common consent they changed the order, putting Hugh first, because he was third prior, Roger the Cellarer second, and Samson third, making, on the face of it, the first last and the last first. But the King, after first enquiring whether those nominated were born in his realm and within whose domain, said that he did not know them and ordered that three others of the Convent should be nominated as well as those three. This being agreed, William the Sacrist said, 'Our Prior should be nominated because he is Our head.' This was readily allowed. Then said the Prior, 'William the Sacrist is a good man.' The same was said of Denys, and it was allowed. These being nominated without delay before the King, he marvelled saying, 'They have done this quickly; God is with them.' Afterwards the King demanded that for the honour of his realm they should nominate three more from other houses. Hearing this the brethren were afraid, suspecting guile. At length they agreed to name three, but on this condition that they should accept none of them without the counsel of those of the Convent who remained at home. And they nominated three: Master Nicholas of Wallingford, later and at the present time Abbot of

Malmesbury, Bertrand, Prior of St Faith, afterwards Abbot of Chertsey, and the Lord H. of St Neots, a monk of Bec, a man of great religion and very circumspect both in matters temporal and spiritual. This done, the King thanked them and gave orders that three out of the nine should be struck off the list, whereupon the three aliens were at once removed, to wit, the Prior of St Faith afterwards Abbot of Chertsey, Nicholas, monk of St Albans, afterwards Abbot of Malmesbury, and the Prior of St Neots. William the Sacrist withdrew of his own free will: two of the remaining five were struck off by order of the King, and then one of the three remaining, two only being left, namely the Prior and Samson. Finally the intermediaries of our lord the King whom I have mentioned above, were called in to take counsel with the brethren. And Denys, speaking for us all, began to commend the persons of the Prior and Samson, saying that both were literate, both good, both of praiseworthy life and of unblemished reputation; but always in the corner of his speech thrusting Samson forward, multiplying the words he uttered in his praise and saying that he was a man strict in his behaviour, stern in chastising transgressions, a hard worker, prudent in worldly business, and proved in divers offices. The Bishop of Winchester replied, 'We understand clearly what you mean; from your words we gather that your Prior seems to you to be somewhat slack and that you desire him whom you call Samson.' Denys replied, 'Both of them are good, but we should like, God willing, to have the better.' The Bishop made answer, 'Of two good men you must choose the better. Tell me openly, do you wish to have Samson?' And a number, making a majority, answered clearly, 'We want Samson', not a voice being raised against them, though some of set purpose said nothing, because they wished to offend neither the one nor the other. Samson then having been nominated in the presence of the King, and the latter having taken brief counsel with his advisers, all the rest were summoned, and the King said, 'You have presented Samson to me: I do not know him. If you had presented your Prior, I should have accepted him; for I have seen him and know him. But, as it is, I will do what you desire. But have a care; for by the very eyes of God, if you do ill, I will be at you.' He then asked the Prior, if he agreed to this and desired it. The Prior answered that he did desire it and that Samson was much more worthy of honour. The elect therefore fell at the King's feet and kissed them, then rose in haste, and in haste went to the altar with the brethren, singing 'Miserere mei, Deus', his head held high and his countenance unchanged. And when the King saw this, he said to those who stood by, 'By God's eyes, this elect thinks himself worthy to be the guardian of his Abbey.' When the news of this election reached the Convent, it gladdened all the cloister monks, or nearly all, and certain of the obedientiaries, but only a few. 'It is well,' said many, 'because it is well.' Others said, 'Nay, in truth we have all been deceived.' The elect, before he returned to us, received his benediction from the Lord Bishop of Winchester, who at the same time placed the mitre on his head and the ring upon his finger, saying, 'This is the dignity of the Abbots of St Edmund: it is long since I knew this.' The Abbot then, keeping three monks with him, sent all the rest home in advance, announcing that he would come to them on Palm Sunday, and charging some of them with the duty of providing all that was necessary for his feast. On his return journey a multitude of new kinsmen went to meet him, desiring to be taken into his service. But to all of them he made answer that he was content with the Prior's servants, and could not keep any others until he had consulted the Convent on the matter. But one knight he kept with him, an eloquent man and skilled in the law, not so much on account of his kinship, but for his usefulness, since he was accustomed to secular business. So being new in office he took him to be his helper in worldly disputes; for he had but now received the abbacy and was unused to such matters, as he himself protested, since before he became Abbot he was never in any place where gage and pledge were given. He was received by the Convent on Palm Sunday with all due honour and a procession as well.

Now the manner in which the Lord Abbot was received was thus. On the night before, he lay at Kent-ford, and we, taking advantage of the opportunity, as soon as we had left the chapterhouse, went out in solemn state to meet him at the gate of the cemetery, while the bells both within the choir and without all rang together. But he, surrounded as he was by a multitude of men, as soon as he saw the Convent, dismounted from his horse outside the threshold of the gate, and after causing his sandals to be taken off, was received barefoot within the gate, the Prior and the Sacrist walking on either side. We on our part sang the responses '*Benedictus Dominus*' from the office for Trinity Sunday and '*Martyri adhuc*' from the office for the Feast of St Edmund, and led the Abbot right up to the High Altar. This done, the organs and the bells were silent, and the Prior said the prayer '*Omnipotens sempiterne Deus miserere huic*', etc. over the Abbot lying prostrate. Then the Abbot made an oblation and kissed the feretory, after which he returned into the choir, and there Samson the Precentor took him by the hand and led him to the Abbot's seat at the west end of the choir, where (the Abbot still standing) the Precentor forthwith began to chant the '*Te deum laudamus*'; and while this was being sung the Abbot was kissed by the Prior and by the whole Convent in order. These things being accomplished, the Abbot went into the chapterhouse followed by the Convent and many others. And after we had said '*Benedicite*', he first gave thanks to the Convent, because they had, not according to his deserts but by the will of God, chosen him, the least of them all (as he said), to be their lord and shepherd; and after briefly asking them to pray for him, he turned to address the clerks and knights, asking them to advise him for the performance of the anxious duties of the governance committed to his care. And Wimer the Sheriff speaking for them all made answer saying, 'Aye, and we are ready to stand by you and give you counsel and to aid you in every way, as being our beloved lord, whom God has called for His own honour and for the honour of Edmund the holy Martyr.' Then the charters of the King concerning the donation of the abbacy were produced and read for all to hear. And after the Abbot had said a prayer beseeching God to care for him according to His grace, and all present had answered 'Amen', the Convent went to the first Mass. Then the Abbot, still barefoot, went to his lodgings, where he held his feast amid great rejoicing, more than a thousand dining with him.

Source: H. E. Butler (ed.) *The Chronicle of Jocelin of Brakelond* (1951) pp. 16–25

The Rule of St Augustine of Hippo also remained a standard text for medieval religious life. It is simpler even than St Benedict's Rule and provides a basis for a religious community which can be expanded according to local conditions or needs. Those who followed Augustine's Rule often lived as communities of canons regular (that is clerks following a common rule) either in town or country.

---

৪৯ 2.6 *The Rule of St Augustine* ৫৬

The Basic Ideal: Mutual Love Expressed in the Community of Goods
and in Humility

1   We urge you who form a religious community to put the following precepts into practice.
2   Before all else, live together in harmony (Ps. 67 (68): 7), being of one mind and one heart (Acts 4:32) on the way to God. For is it not precisely for this reason that you have come to live together?
3   Among you there can be no question of personal property. Rather, take care that you share everything in common. Your superior should see to it that each person is provided with food and clothing. He does not have to give exactly the same to everyone, for you are not all equally strong, but each person should be given what he personally needs. For this is what you read in the Acts of the Apostles: 'Everything they owned was held in common, and each one received whatever he had need of' (Acts 4:32; 4:35).
4   Those who owned possessions in the world should readily agree that, from the moment they enter the religious life, these things become the property of the community.
5   But those who did not have possessions ought not to strive in the religious community for what they could not obtain outside it. One must indeed have regard for their frailty by providing them with whatever they need, even if they were formerly so poor that they could not even afford the very necessities of life. They may not, however, consider themselves fortunate because they now receive food and clothing which were beyond their means in their earlier lives.
6   Nor should they give themselves airs because they now find themselves in the company of people whom they would not have ventured to approach before. Their hearts should seek the nobler things, not vain earthly appearances. If, in the religious life, rich people were to become humble and poor people haughty, then this style of life would seem to be of value only to the rich and not to the poor.
7   On the other hand, let those who appear to have had some standing in the world not look down upon their brothers who have entered the religious community from a condition of poverty. They ought to be more mindful of their life together with poor brothers than of the social status of their wealthy parents. And the fact that they have made some of their possessions available to the community gives them no reason to have a high opinion of themselves. Otherwise people would more easily fall prey to pride in sharing their riches with the community than they would have done if they had enjoyed them in the world. For while all vices manifest themselves in wrongdoing, pride lurks also in our good works, seeking

to destroy even them. What good does it do to distribute one's possessions to the poor and to become poor oneself; if giving up riches makes a person prouder than he was when he had a fortune?

8   You are all to live together, therefore, one in mind and one in heart (Acts 4:32), and honour God in one another, because each of you has become his temple (2 Cor. 6:16).

> Source: R. Canning (trans.) *The Rule of Saint Augustine* (1984) pp. 11–13

The gold standard provided by the rules was difficult to maintain and a drift towards complacency was a recurring trend in medieval monasticism with reform movements seeking continuing renewal. The eleventh and twelfth centuries witnessed an extraordinary diversity of such movements. Benedictinism was refined by the Cluniacs and the Cistercians. The abbey of Cluny in Burgundy, established at the beginning of the tenth century, became a model of liturgical practice and grandeur of architectural and artistic expression. The *Opus Dei*, the office of the monastic hours, the true work of God, became highlighted and proclaimed.

2.7 John of Salerno, *St Odo of Cluny*

They observed especially the custom of silence. At unsuitable times no one might speak or consort with another of the brethren in the cloister of the monastery, and on days when a twelve-lesson office was celebrated no one might speak in the cloister before chapter on the following day. Within the octaves of Christmas and Easter there was a strict silence day and night. This short silence, they said, signifies the eternal silence. When there was necessity to ask for anything they made various signs to each other, which grammarians I suppose would call the language of the fingers and eyes. This usage had developed to such an extent among them that, if they were without the use of their tongues, the signs, I think, would suffice to indicate everything necessary. But on ferial days and in the other octaves of the saints there was this arrangement. On ferial days in the day and night office together they sang one hundred and thirty-eight psalms, from which we subtract fourteen for the sake of their weaker brethren. But against this must be put the special prayers which our brethren say are seen to exceed the psalter and also the two Masses and litanies. At each of the canonical hours they knelt twice. During the other octaves which were mentioned, they sang seventy-five psalms only in the day and night Offices together, and they knelt once and rested twice. There are many other points which I think may be omitted lest they should weary the reader.

> Source: G. Sitwell (ed. and trans.) *St Odo of Cluny: being the Life of St Odo of Cluny by John of Salerno* (1958) p. 33

Citeaux, also in Burgundy, sought a simplification of the Cluniac ideals by an emphasis on manual labour (with *conversi* or lay brothers emerging for the first time) and on a stark simplicity. Citeaux (from which the term Cistercian comes) and Cluny were both distinguished by a centralisation which was not present in the early Benedictine monasteries which were effectively autonomous and can therefore be seen as the first religious orders. Cluny had a succession of great reforming abbots: Odo (879–942) elected abbot in 927, Odilo (962–1049) elected in 994, Hugh the Great (1024–1109) elected 1049 and Peter the Venerable (*c.* 1092–1156) elected in 1122. The Cistercians, in Bernard of Clairvaux (*c.* 1090–1153), had one of the dominant personalities of the Middle Ages.

---

৯ 2.8 Bernard of Clairvaux, *An Apologia* ৶ for Abbot William

---

Against Superfluity

viii, 16

It is said, and quite rightly, that the Cluniac way of life was instituted by holy Fathers; anxious that more might find salvation through it, they tempered the Rule to the weak without weakening the Rule. Far be it from me to believe that they recommended or allowed such an array of vanities or superfluities as I see in many religious houses. I wonder indeed how such intemperance in food and drink, in clothing and bedding, in horses and buildings can implant itself among monks. And it is the houses that pursue this course with thoroughgoing zeal, with full-blown lavishness, that are reputed the most pious and the most observant. They go so far as to count frugality avarice, and sobriety austerity, while silence is reputed gloom. Conversely, slackness is called discretion, extravagance liberality, chattering becomes affability, guffawing cheerfulness, soft clothing and rich caparisons are the requirements of simple decency, luxurious bedding is a matter of hygiene, and lavishing these things on one another goes by the name of charity. By such charity is charity destroyed, and this discretion mocks the very word. It is a cruel mercy that kills the soul while cherishing the body. And what sort of charity is it that cares for the flesh and neglects the spirit? What kind of discretion that gives all to the body and nothing to the soul? What kind of mercy that restores the servant and destroys the mistress? Let no one who has shown that sort of mercy hope to obtain the mercy promised in the Gospel by him who is the truth: 'Blessed are the merciful, for they shall receive mercy'. On the contrary, he can expect the sure and certain punishment which holy Job invoked with the full force of prophecy on those whom I call 'cruelly kind': 'Let him be no longer remembered, but let him be broken like a sterile tree'. The cause – and a sufficient cause for that most proper retribution – follows at once: 'He feeds the barren, childless woman and does no good to the widow'.

17

Such kindness is obviously disordered and irrational. It is that of the barren and
unfruitful flesh, which the Lord tells us profits nothing and Paul says will not inherit
the kingdom of God. Intent on satisfying our every whim it pays no heed to the Sage's
wise and warning words: 'Have mercy on your own soul and you will please God'.
That is indeed true mercy, and must perforce win mercy, since one pleases God by
exercising it. Conversely it is, as I said, not kindness but cruelty, not love but malev-
olence, not discretion but confusion to feed the barren woman and do no good to the
widow – in other words, to pander to the desires of the profitless flesh while giving
the soul no help in cultivating the virtues. For the soul is indeed bereaved in this life
of her heavenly Bridegroom. Yet she never ceases to conceive by the Holy Spirit and
bring forth immortal offspring, which, provided they are nurtured with diligent care,
will rightfully be heirs to an incorruptible and heavenly inheritance.

18

Nowadays, however, these abuses are so widespread and so generally accepted that
almost everyone acquiesces in them without incurring censure or even blame, though
motives differ. Some use material things with such detachment as to incur little or
no guilt. Others are moved by simple-mindedness, by charity or by constraint. The
first, who do as they are bidden in all simplicity, would be ready to act differently if
the bidding were different. The second kind, afraid of dissension in the community,
are led, not by their own pleasure, but by their desire to keep the peace. Lastly there
are those who are unable to stand out against a hostile majority that vociferously
defends such practices as pertaining to the Order and moves swiftly and forcibly to
block whatever judicious restrictions changes the former try to bring in.

ix, 19

Who would have dreamed, in the far beginnings of the monastic order, that monks
would have slid into such slackness? What a way we have come from the monks who
lived in Anthony's day! When one of them paid on occasion a brotherly call on
another, both were so avid for the spiritual nourishment they gained from the
encounter that they forgot their physical hunger would commonly pass the whole day
with empty stomachs but with minds replete. And this was the right order of precedence – to give priority to what is nobler in man's make-up; this was real discretion
– making greater provision for the more important part; this indeed true charity – to
tend with loving care the souls for love of whom Christ died.

   As for us, when we come together, to use the Apostle's words, it is not to eat the
Lord's supper. There is none who asks for heavenly bread and none who offers it.
Never a word about Scripture or salvation. Flippancy, laughter and words on the wind
are all we hear. At table our ears are as full of gossip as our mouths of festive fare,
and all intent on the former we quite forget to restrain our appetite.

**Source: P. Matarasso (ed. and trans.) *The Cistercian
World: Monastic Writings of the Twelfth Century*
(1993) pp. 48–50**

The Carthusians, named after their monastery at the Grande Chartreuse in the French Savoie, were inspired less by Benedict than by the eremitical ideal and were founded by Bruno (*c.* 1032–1101). The Carthusians, dedicated to a complete immersion in the contemplative life, remained a small group but were regarded as a true spiritual elite.

ᙓ 2.9 Guigo de Ponte, *On Contemplation* ᙚ

Chapter 24

How to keep busy outside the brief times of Contemplation permitted by Human Weakness

To put the matter briefly, vices stemming from carnal desire make war against the celibate life, and human weakness, as Gregory says, will not permit one to remain in contemplation for a long time. Thus it is necessary, lest one be ensnared by leisure, to keep busy with the things mentioned in the first stage (namely reading, prayer, meditation, etc.), or to do other good works, so that the devil may always find the servant of God busy. One should ask God for and, when received, practice the various virtues necessary to avoid idleness: charity, joy, peace, patience, forbearance, goodness, kindness, gentleness, faithfulness, modesty, self-control, chastity (Gal. 5:22–23). Would that we might show ourselves in all things to be ministers of God: in great patience, in tribulations, in times of need, in distresses, in beatings, in prison, in civil strife, in labours, in vigils, in fasts, in chastity, in knowledge, in forbearance, in sweetness, in the Holy Spirit, in unfeigned charity, in the word of truth, in the power of God, with the armour of righteousness on the right hand and on the left, . . . as sorrowful yet always rejoicing, . . . as having nothing yet possessing all things (2 Cor 6: 4–7, 10). And, as James, chapter one, says, The wisdom that comes from above is first chaste, then peaceable, modest, ready to be persuaded, agreeable to good things, full of mercy and good fruits, judging without dissimulation (Jas 3:17). These and similar things renew the spirit.

> **Source: D. D. Martin, *Carthusian Spirituality, the writings of Hugh of Balma and Guigo de Ponte* (New York, 1997) p. 249**

The Fourth Council of the Lateran (1215) attempted to regulate the number of religious orders and to bring them more closely into the institutional life of the Church. At the same time a number of more radical religious movements were developing which were intended to meet the new challenges provided by town life and heretical groups who claimed to have rediscovered apostolic simplicity. This was the context in which the various orders of friars were founded, men who emphasised fraternity over paternity, freedom of movement rather than stability, and complete poverty rather than communal ownership. The four principal orders of friars were the Augustinians, who adopted Augustine of Hippo's rule for a more mobile life; the Carmelites who grew from a fellowship of hermits on Mount Carmel into a recognised order; the Dominicans and the Franciscans. All four had an ideal of mendicancy: begging for a living. The Dominicans and Franciscans benefited from charismatic founders. Dominic, a Spanish canon regular, gathered around him a fraternity of preachers, known as the Blackfriars, who were in time to produce the most influential of medieval theologians, Thomas Aquinas (c. 1225–1274) and the personnel of the Inquisition. The Dominican constitutions were very representative, even democratic in their tone, and contrasted sharply with the monarchical character of Benedictinism. The Dominicans, too, emphasised preaching as against liturgical prayer.

৪৯ 2.10 The Early Dominicans ৪৯

I. The Characteristics of the Preacher's Job

The Nobility of the Preacher's Job

(2) To see what a noble job preaching is, we must notice that it is an apostolic job: it was for this job that the Lord chose the apostles. 'He appointed twelve to be with him and to be sent out to preach' (Mark 3:14).

It is also an angelic job. 'I saw a mighty angel, preaching with a loud voice' (Apoc. 5:2). And was he not preaching who said, 'See, I bring you good news of a great joy' (Luke 2:10)? And there is nothing surprising in angels being called preachers, since their mission is for the sake of those who are to inherit salvation, just as preachers are sent out for the salvation of men. Further, it is a divine job. God became man precisely to do this job. 'Let us go into the neighbouring villages and towns so that I may preach there too, because it was for this purpose that I came' (Mark 1:38).

Now, the apostles are the most outstanding of all the saints, the angels are the most outstanding of all creatures, and in all that exists, nothing is more outstanding than God. So a job which is apostolic, angelic and divine must indeed be outstanding!

(3) Another way of showing the nobility of the preacher's job depends on the privileged status of scripture. Scripture surpasses all other kinds of knowledge in three ways: in its source, in its content and in its purpose. In its source, because, whereas all other sciences were discovered by the mind of man (though not, of course, without the help of God), the knowledge contained in scripture was directly inspired by God. 'The holy men of God spoke under the inspiration of the Holy Spirit' (2 Pet. 1:21).

In its content, because other sciences are concerned either with the things of the mind, or with things of nature, or with things that derive from human free will; but scripture is concerned with the things of God, which infinitely transcend all these other things. This is why divine Wisdom, who bestowed this knowledge on men, says, 'Listen, for I am going to speak of great matters' (Prov. 8:6). And indeed she does speak of great matters, such as the Trinity and Unity of God, and the Incarnation of the Son of God, and there is nothing greater than these. In its purpose, because other sciences are designed to serve the ordering of temporal affairs (law, for example), or the needs of the body (medicine, for example), or to remedy intellectual ignorance (like the theoretical sciences); but scripture aims at the acquisition of eternal life. 'Whoever drinks of this water which I shall give him, it will become in him a fountain of living water, welling up to eternal life' (John 4:14). It says this because the water of divine wisdom points to and leads men to eternal life. And eternal life is nothing other than God himself, and so we may say that the purpose of this science is God himself. This is why sacred scripture is referred to as 'theology', from *theos* (God) and *logos* (word), because its words are from God, about God and directed to God. Now all proper preaching is woven out of just such words, and not from the words of other sciences. And since the value of a thing is greater if it is made out of more precious material – a golden cup is worth more than one made out of lead – how precious must preaching be, since it is formed from such outstanding material!

(4) Again, the philosophers say that man is the most worthy of all creatures; and of the two kinds of nature that he has, namely body and soul, the soul is the more worthy. And of the many things which the soul needs, some have little or nothing to do with salvation (learning, for instance), while others are directly relevant for salvation; and these latter are the more worthy. Now preaching is directed at man. 'Preach the gospel to the whole creation' (Mark 16:15), which means, 'To man', according to Gregory. And it is concerned with the soul, not the body. In response to Peter's preaching, it specifically says that 'about three thousand souls were added' (Acts 2:41), because it is souls that are sought by preaching. And what it seeks with regard to them is only what is relevant to salvation, which is why scripture says of an outstanding preacher, 'You shall go before the face of the Lord, to prepare his ways before him, to give to his people the knowledge of salvation' (Luke 1:76–77).

Now, the nobility of a job depends on the dignity and worth of its sphere of operation. A job done for a king is more noble than a job done for his horses, and a job done in a temple is more noble than one performed in the stables. So what a noble job it must be, which is concerned with the most worthy of all creatures, and with the more worthy part of that creature, and with the more worthy aspect of that part of the most worthy creature!

(5) So, if we bear in mind the exalted status of those to whom this job is assigned, and the excellence of its material, and the superiority of its sphere of operation, it should be obvious to us that this is a job of quite outstanding value.

Source: S. Tugwell (ed.) *Early Dominicans: Selected Writings* (New York, 1982) pp. 184–186

Francis of Assisi (1181–1226), the most popular of all medieval saints, turned his back on urban prosperity and proclaimed a joyful poverty and a close following of the passion of Christ. Franciscan spirituality, which produced its own great theologian in Bonaventure (1221–1274), contributed to the rise of a newly sensitive art and a free expression of religious language in the vernacular.

·· 2.11 St Bonaventure, from *The Twenty-five Injunctions* ··

Prologue

To Brother Peter, his beloved in Christ – and to all who, having put off the old man (cf. Eph. iv 22), strive to live with Christ and die to the world – from Brother Bonaventure, his brother in the Lord.

When, as we parted after our last meeting, you pressed me so earnestly, dear brother in the Lord, to visit you again as it were, by some little letters of spiritual advice, I felt at once, Brother, that in asking this of me, you were heaping coals of fire upon my head (cf. Prov. xxv 22: or Rom. xii 20). Still so lovingly insistent were you in your demands, and yet so suppliantly humble, that you so far prevailed over my proud aloofness as to win from me a promise to do as you wished. It were, indeed, more fitting for me to receive of you, than to offer you of mine, but the insistence of your devotion has prevailed, and I am become foolish (ii Cor. xii 11). As best I may, then, let me in some fashion make trial of what you urge me to; not indeed writing anything new, but rather setting down such points as, simple and plain though they be, I have tried to gather together for my own use, and with most of which you will be familiar already.

But before going further, we must – and I appeal herein, Carissime, to your love – we must convince ourselves that, since no one, as unquestioned experience teaches, can perfectly serve God till he quite wholly sever himself from the world, so we too, would we follow the Lord, our Saviour, must hearken to the words of His prophet and loose the bands of wickedness and undo the bundles that oppress (Isaias lviii 6), so that, being free from earthly occupations, we may with feet untrammelled follow the Redeemer; for, as the Apostle bears witness: No man being a soldier to God, entangleth himself with secular affairs (ii Tim. ii 4). Never, then, let us allow our heart to grow solicitous over any created thing, except in so far as it may help us the more earnestly to love God; for the manifold variety of transient things, unduly pondered on, not merely distracts the soul and breaks in on the restful tranquillity of a peaceful mind, but also gives rise to all sorts of disquieting and agitating imaginations, and renders the mind continually uneasy. But rather let us set aside completely the heavy burden of earthly affections, and press unhampered forward towards Him who invites us, in Whom lies the soul's most real refreshment, and that supreme peace, which surpasseth all understanding (Philipp. iv 7). Come to me – He says – all you that labour and are burdened, and I will refresh you (Math. xi 28). O Lord, of whom dost Thou stand in need? Why dost Thou call? What bond twixt Thee and us? O truly compassionate words – Come to me, and I will refresh you. O wonderful condescension of our God! O ineffable charity! Whoever did the like? When was a like thing heard of or seen? (Isaias lxvi 8). Come, He says, come to me, all, and learn of me; take up my yoke upon you and you shall find rest to your souls (cf. Math. xi 28, 29). O tenderest words, words most sweet, and of God most worthy; words more piercing than any two-edged sword (Heb. iv 12), tearing at the heart-strings of men, overflowing with sweetness, reaching unto the division of the soul and the spirit (ibid.). Arouse thyself, then, O Christian soul, before So gentle a love, So sweet a saviour, So tender a perfume. Truly, he Who perceives them not is sickly indeed, insensible even and nigh unto death. I beseech thee, O my soul, enkindle thy fervour, grow strong and grow rich, in the mercy of thy God, in the meekness of thy God, in the charity of thy spouse. Glow with the passionate ardour of thy Beloved, grow strong in loving Him, rich in feasting on Him. Let no man hinder thee from entering, holding, tasting. What seek we further, what are we to look for, what desire? In this One we have all good. But, alas! for our incredible folly, our lamentable weakness, our dreadful raving; for we are called to rest, and we pursue after labour; we are summoned to what may solace us, and we seek around for sorrow; we are promised joy and we crave for weeping. Miserable weakness, indeed, most miserable perversity! We are become as senseless things, lower even than mere craven images, having eyes, yet seeing not; ears, yet not hearing; reason, yet not discerning, holding bitter for sweet, and sweet for bitter (Isaias v 20). O God, how can we rectify such great perversity, how satisfy for so great an offence? Certainly, there are no latent tendencies thereto within us, but such as Thou hast placed there. Thou alone canst correct us, Thou alone satisfy for our sins, Thou Who alone knowest our frame (Psalm 102: 14), Who art our Salvation and our Redemption, and Who dost work only in those who, seeing the deep of their own misery, trust but in Thee as the One Who alone canst raise them up therefrom.

Since, then, he cares little to rise who knows not his proper state, let us lift up the eyes of our soul straight towards God, and see how prostrate we are lying now. Alive to our condition, let us lustily cry out to the Lord from the depths (Psalm 129: I), that He may stretch out towards us that helping hand of mercy which can never be shortened that it cannot save (Isaias lix I). Let us not, I beg, lose the confidence which hath a great reward (Heb. x 35). Let us go . . . with confidence to the throne of grace, receiving the end of our faith, even the salvation of our souls (Heb. iv 16: i Pet. i 9). Let there be no delaying amongst us, for Life is summoning us, Salvation awaits us, and our very anguish compels us to press on. What then are we doing? Why do we dally in sloth? Why do we plunge into entangling hindrances? Let us hasten therefore to enter in that rest (Heb. iv 11) of eternal delight. Where there are great things and unsearchable and wonderful things without number (Job v 9). Let Jerusalem, I beg you, come into your mind (Jerem. li 50). Let us sigh after our own country, stretch out our arms towards our mother (cf. Gal. iv 26). Let us enter into the powers of the Lord (Psalm 70: 16); let us gaze upon our gentle King reigning there and may our hearts soften before His tender mercies.

Let us with our whole heart render thanks to Him, Who, taking no account of our ingratitude, draws not away from us the kindliness of His mercy but gives to us the desire to run the way of His commandments (Psalm 118: 32), along which way, without the desire to, none can run. And this gift, indeed, is not to be weighed lightly, but rather highly esteemed, as one eminent among the prophets taught us when he declared his great desire, saying: My soul hath longed to desire in every time thy justifications (Psalm 118: 20).

Since this very desire grows weak at times, owing to our heedless tepidity and neglect, I have then thought it fitting to set down here certain injunctions calculated to awaken it, in which are made clear some things we should avoid, and others we should follow. Noting these daily, and joining thereto an affectionate resolve, we may resume our early vigour, and grow up untiringly in the virtues and graces of divine charity, till at length there comes to us in its fullness the Desire of the Eternal Hills (Gen. xlix 26). And of these injunctions eight are general ones, and the rest more special.

General Injunctions

Here, then, are certain well-established virtues, most profitable to beginners, real ladders of perfection, in the faithful use of which one may without any doubt ascend to the perfection of virtue and to the summit of heavenly glory; to wit, firstly, a well-intentioned unobtrusiveness in all one's words and actions; then to be taciturn, to be prompt in obeying, to be instant in prayer, to confess one's faults frankly and often, to give ready service, and lastly to shun unprofitable society. These are shining jewels, indeed, making the possessor thereof pleasing to God and to the Angels and to men. But when it pleased him who separated you from your mother's womb, and called you by his grace, to reveal his Son in you (cf. Gal. i 15, 16), drawing you out from the miserable bondage of Egypt into the liberty . . . of the children of God (Rom. viii 21), so that, as a new man (Eph. iv 24), you began to step out along that way of humility that lies twixt fear and love; so, as you ascend higher, but ever by this same path of humility, you may begin to practise yet nobler virtues, of which some are here set down.

> Source: D. Devas, *A Franciscan View of the Spiritual and Religious Life, being three treatises from the writing of Saint Bonaventure* (1922) pp. 125–132

☙ 2.12 St Francis of Assisi, *The Canticle of Brother Sun* ❧

Most High, all-powerful, good Lord, Yours are the praises, the glory, the honour, and all blessing.
To You alone, Most High, do they belong, and no man is worthy to mention your name.
Praised be You, my lord, with all your creatures, especially Brother Sun, Who is the day and through whom You give us light.
And he is beautiful and radiant with great splendour; and bears a likeness of You, Most High One.
Praised be you, my Lord, through Sister Moon and the stars, in heaven you formed them clear and precious and beautiful.
Praised be You, my Lord, through Brother Wind, and through the air, cloudy and serene, and every kind of weather through which you give sustenance to your creatures.

Praised be You, my Lord, through Sister Water, which is very useful and humble and precious and chaste.

Praised be You, my Lord, through Brother Fire, through whom you light the night and he is beautiful and playful and robust and strong.

Praised be you, my Lord, through our Sister Mother Earth, who sustains and governs us, and who produces varied fruits with coloured flowers and herbs.

Praised be you, my Lord, through those who give pardon for your love and bear infirmity and tribulation.

Blessed are those who endure in peace for by You, Most High, they shall be crowned.

Praised be You, my Lord, through our Sister Bodily Death, from whom no living man can escape.

Woe to those who die in mortal sin. Blessed are those whom death will find in Your most holy will, for the second death shall do them no harm.

Praise and bless my Lord and give Him thanks and serve Him with great humility.

> Source: For context and writings see M. A. Habig (ed.) *St Francis of Assisi: Writings and early biography* (Chicago, 1983)

❧ 2.13 *The Rule of St Francis* (1223) ☙

Chapter 1

In the name of the Lord begins the life of the Friars Minor

The Rule and life of the Friars Minor is this, namely, to observe the Holy Gospel of our Lord Jesus Christ by living in obedience, without property, and in chastity. Brother Francis promises obedience and reverence to his holiness Pope Honorius and his lawfully elected successors and to the Church of Rome. The other friars are bound to obey Brother Francis and his successors.

Chapter 2

Of those who wish to take up this life and how they are to be received

If anyone wants to profess our Rule and comes to the friars, they must send him to their provincial minister, because he alone, to the exclusion of others, has permission to receive friars into the Order. The ministers must carefully examine all candidates on the Catholic faith and the sacraments of the Church. If they believe all that the Catholic faith teaches and are prepared to profess it loyally, holding by it steadfastly to the end of their lives, and if they are not married; or if they are married and their wives have already entered a convent or after taking a vow of chastity have by the authority of the bishop of the diocese been granted this permission; and the wives are of such an age that no suspicion can arise concerning them: let the ministers tell them what the holy Gospel says (Mt. 19: 21), that they should go and sell all that belongs to them and endeavour to give it to the poor. If they cannot do this, their good will is sufficient.

The friars and their ministers must be careful not to become involved in the temporal affairs of newcomers to the Order, so that they may dispose of their goods freely, as God inspires them. If they ask for advice, the ministers may refer them to some God-fearing persons who can advise them how to distribute their property to the poor.

When this has been done, the ministers should clothe the candidates with the habit of probation, namely, two tunics without a hood, a cord and trousers, and a caperon reaching to the cord, unless the ministers themselves at any time decide that something else is more suitable. After the year of the novitiate, they should be received to obedience, promising to live always according to this life and Rule. It is absolutely forbidden to leave the Order, as his holiness the Pope has laid down. For the Gospel tells us, No one, having put his hand to the plough and looking back, is fit for the kingdom of God (Lk. 9: 62).

The friars who have already vowed obedience may have one tunic with a hood and those who wish may have another without a hood. Those who are forced by necessity may wear shoes. All the friars are to wear poor clothes and they can use pieces of sack-cloth and other material to mend them, with God's blessing. I warn all the friars and exhort them not to condemn or look down on people whom they see wearing soft or gaudy clothes and enjoying luxuries in food or drink; each one should rather condemn and despise himself.

Chapter 3

Of the Divine Office and fasting, and how the friars are to travel about the world

The clerics are to recite the Divine Office according to the rite of the Roman Curia, except the psalter; and so they may have breviaries. The lay brothers are to say twenty-four *Our Fathers* for Matins and five for Lauds; for Prime, Terce, Sext, and None, for each of these, they are to say seven; for Vespers twelve and for Compline seven. They should also say some prayers for the dead.

All the friars are to fast from the feast of All Saints until Christmas. Those who voluntarily fast for forty days after Epiphany have God's blessing, because this is the period our Lord sanctified by his holy fast (cf. Mt. 4: 2). However, those who do not wish to do so, should not be forced to it. All the friars are bound to keep the Lenten fast before Easter, but they are not bound to fast at other times, except on Fridays. However, in case of manifest necessity, they are not obliged to corporal fasting.

And this is my advice, my counsel, and my earnest plea to my friars in our Lord Jesus Christ that, when they travel about the world, they should not be quarrelsome or take part in disputes with words (cf. 2 Tim. 2: 14) or criticise others; but they should be gentle, peaceful, and unassuming, courteous and humble, speaking respect-fully to everyone, as is expected of them. They are forbidden to ride on horseback, unless they are forced to it by manifest necessity or sickness. Whatever house they enter, they should first say, 'Peace to this house' (Lk. 10: 5), and in the words of the Gospel they may eat what is set before them (Lk. 10: 8).

Chapter 4

The friars are forbidden to accept money
I strictly forbid all the friars to accept money in any form, either personally or through an intermediary. The ministers and superiors, however, are bound to provide carefully for the needs of the sick and the clothing of the other friars, by having recourse to spiritual friends, while taking into account differences of place, season, or severe climate, as seems best to them in the circumstances. This does not dispense them from the prohibition of receiving money in any form.

Chapter 5

The manner of working
The friars to whom God has given the grace of working should work in a spirit of faith and devotion and avoid idleness, which is the enemy of the soul without however extinguishing the spirit of prayer and devotion, to which every temporal consideration must be subordinate. As wages for their labour they may accept anything necessary for their temporal needs, for themselves or their brethren, except money in any form. And they should accept it humbly as is expected of those who serve God and strive after the highest poverty.

Chapter 6

**That the friars are to appropriate nothing for themselves; on seeking alms;
and on the sick friars**
The friars are to appropriate nothing for themselves, neither a house, nor a place, nor anything else. As strangers and pilgrims (1 Pet. 2: 11) in this world, who serve God in poverty and humility, they should beg alms trustingly. And there is no reason why they should be ashamed, because God made himself poor for us in this world. This is the pinnacle of the most exalted poverty, and it is this, my dearest brothers, that has made you heirs and kings of the kingdom of heaven – poor in temporal things, but rich in virtue. This should be your portion, because it leads to the land of the living. And to this poverty, my beloved brothers, you must cling with all your heart, and wish never to have anything else under heaven, for the sake of our Lord Jesus Christ.

Wherever the friars meet one another, they should show that they are members of the same family. And they should have no hesitation in making known their needs to one another. For if a mother loves and cares for her child in the flesh, a friar should certainly love and care for his spiritual brother all the more tenderly. If a friar falls ill, the others are bound to look after him as they would like to be looked after themselves.

Chapter 7

Of the penance to be imposed on friars who fall into sin
If any of the friars, at the instigation of the enemy, fall into mortal sin, they must have recourse as soon as possible, without delay, to their provincial ministers, if it is

a sin for which recourse to them has been prescribed for the friars. If the ministers are priests, they should impose a moderate penance on such friars; if they are not priests, they should see that a penance is imposed by some priest of the Order, as seems best to them before God. They must be careful not to be angry or upset because a friar has fallen into sin, because anger or annoyance in themselves or in others makes it difficult to be charitable.

Chapter 8

The election of the Minister General of the Order and the Pentecost Chapter
The friars are always bound to have a member of the Order as Minister General, who is the servant of the whole fraternity, and they are strictly bound to obey him. At his death the provincial ministers and the custodes are to elect a successor at the Pentecost Chapter, at which the provincial ministers are bound to assemble in the place designated by the Minister General. This chapter should be held once every three years, or at a longer or shorter interval, if the Minister General has so ordained.

If at any time it becomes clear to all the provincial ministers and custodes that the Minister General is incapable of serving the friars and can be of no benefit to them, they who have the power to elect must elect someone else as Minister General.

After the Pentecost Chapter, the provincial ministers and custodes may summon their subjects to a chapter in their own territory once in the same year, if they wish and it seems worthwhile.

Chapter 9

Of preachers
The friars are forbidden to preach in any diocese, if the bishop objects to it. No friar should dare to preach to the people unless he has been examined and approved by the Minister General of the Order and has received from him the commission to preach.

Moreover, I advise and admonish the friars that in their preaching, their words should be examined and chaste. They should aim only at the advantage and spiritual good of their listeners, telling them briefly about vice and virtue, punishment and glory, because our Lord himself kept his words short on earth.

Chapter 10

On admonishing and correcting the friars
The ministers, who are the servants of the other friars, must visit their subjects and admonish them, correcting them humbly and charitably, without commanding them anything that is against their conscience or our Rule. The subjects, however, should remember that they have renounced their own wills for God's sake. And so I strictly command them to obey their ministers in everything that they have promised God and is not against their conscience and our Rule. The friars who are convinced that they cannot observe the Rule spiritually, wherever they may be, can and must have recourse to their ministers. The ministers, for their part, are bound to receive them kindly and charitably, and be so sympathetic towards them that the friars can speak and deal with them as employers with their servants. That is the way it ought to be; the ministers should be the servants of all the friars.

With all my heart, I beg the friars in our Lord Jesus Christ to be on their guard against pride, boasting, envy, and greed, against the cares and anxieties of this world, against detraction and complaining. Those who are illiterate should not be anxious to study. They should realise instead that the only thing they should desire is to have the spirit of God at work within them, while they pray to him unceasingly with a heart free from self interest. They must be humble, too, and patient in persecution or illness, loving those who persecute us by blaming us or bringing charges against us, as our Lord tells us, Love your enemies, pray for those who persecute and calumniate you (Mt. 5: 44). Blessed are those who suffer persecution for justice' sake, for theirs is the kingdom of heaven (Mt. 5: 10). He who has persevered to the end will be saved (Mt. 10: 22).

Chapter 11

The friars are forbidden to enter the monasteries of nuns
I strictly forbid all the friars to have suspicious relationships or conversations with women. No one may enter the monasteries of nuns, except those who have received special permission from the Apostolic See. They are forbidden to be sponsors of men or women lest scandal arise amongst or concerning the friars.

Chapter 12

Of those who wish to go among the Saracens and other unbelievers
If any of the friars is inspired by God to go among the Saracens or other unbelievers, he must ask permission from his provincial minister. The ministers, for their part, are to give permission only to those whom they see are fit to be sent.

The ministers, too, are bound to ask the Pope for one of the cardinals of the holy Roman Church to be governor, protector, and corrector of this fraternity, so that we may be utterly subject and submissive to the Church. And so, firmly established in the Catholic faith, we may live always according to the poverty, and the humility, and the Gospel of our Lord Jesus Christ, as we have solemnly promised.

> **Source: M. A. Habig (ed.) *St Francis of Assisi:***
> ***Writings and early biography* (Chicago, 1983)**
> pp. 57–64

At the end of the period with the gradual clericalisation of the Church, which meant that most religious were ordained to the priesthood, the distinction between the various orders could be blurred. Priesthood and clerical status could obscure inspiration and identity, but throughout the Middle Ages the monastic and religious way of life remained a vocation which was characteristic of its period.

Further reading

P. Brown, *The Lives of the Saints* (1981).

J. Burton, *Monastic and Religious Orders in Britain* (Cambridge University Press, Cambridge, 1994).

D. H. Farmer (ed.) *Oxford Dictionary of Saints*, 3rd edn (Oxford University Press, Oxford, 1992).

W. M. Johnston (ed.) *Encyclopaedia of Monasticism*, 2 vols (Fitzroy Dearborn, London, 2000).

D. Knowles, *The Monastic Order in England* (Cambridge University Press, Cambridge, 1940).

J. R. H. Moorman, *A History of the Franciscan Order* (Oxford University Press, Oxford, 1962).

THE WORLD
OF THE PAPACY

The survival of the papacy into the modern world is an unusual example of a medieval institution which remains remarkably intact. Papal Rome is now, at a physical level, largely a creation of the Renaissance and Baroque periods, but many of its institutions, and especially the claims of papal authority, were developed in the Middle Ages. The Bishop of Rome, as successor to St Peter, and (from the twelfth century, Vicar of Christ) was the most powerful churchman in Christendom and temporal Lord of the Papal States, the most coherent political territory in medieval Italy. The title Pope (*papa*) emphasised the pope's paternal role; another, pontiff (*pontifex maximus*), his priestly dignity; and yet another, 'servant of the servants of God' (*servus servorum Dei*) his responsibility for the whole people of God. The keys on the Papal Arms emphasised the authority he had from Peter, to whom Christ had given the 'Keys of the Kingdom of Heaven', and his distinctive headgear, the *tiara*, his role as king as well as bishop. He combined in his person the roles of priest and king and, although the reality of papal power often fell far short of its pretensions, the papacy was a force for unity. Papal origins are obscure, but from an early date the Pope claimed special authority among the bishops of the Church and, through the Donation of Constantine, a real succession to the imperial hegemony of the Roman Empire. The relationship, and the relative authority of Pope and Emperor was to be one of the critical conflicts of the Middle Ages, not so much a dispute between Church and State as a contest between the respective rights of *regnum* (earthly rule) and *sacerdotium* (princely power). The idea of 'the two powers' had been articulated by Pope Gelasius I (492–496) and a number of the great Popes of the early Medieval Church, notably Leo the Great (440–461) and Gregory the Great (590–604), considered the papal office.

❧ 3.1 *The Donation of Constantine (c. 750)* ☙

In the name of the holy and undivided Trinity, Father, the Son and the Holy Spirit. The Emperor Caesar Flavius Constantinus in Christ Jesus . . . to the most holy and blessed father of fathers, Silvester Bishop of the Roman city and Pope; and to all his successors, the pontiffs, who shall sit in the chair of blessed Peter to the end of time . . .

And so the first day after my reception of the mystery of Holy Baptism and the cure of my body from the filthiness of leprosy I understood that there is no other God than the Father, the Son and the Holy Spirit, whom most blessed Silvester, the Pope, preaches, a Trinity in unity and Unity in trinity. For all the gods of the nations, whom I have hitherto worshipped, are shown to be demons, the works of men's hands. And the same venerable father told us clearly how great power in heaven and earth our Saviour gave to His Apostle, blessed Peter, when in answer to questioning He found him faithful and said: 'Thou art Peter, and upon this rock I will build My Church; and the gates of hell shall not prevail against it.' Attend, ye mighty, and incline the ear of your heart to what the good Lord and Master gave in addition to His disciple when He said: 'I will give unto thee the keys of the kingdom of heaven, and whatsoever thou shalt bind on earth shall be bound in heaven, and whatsoever thou shalt loose on earth shall be loosed in heaven.' And when I learned these things at the mouth of the blessed Silvester, and found that I was wholly restored to health by the beneficence of blessed Peter himself . . . we decree that he shall have rule as well over the principal sees, Antioch, Alexandria, Constantine and Jerusalem, as also over all the churches of God in all the world. And the pontiff who for the time being presides over that most holy Roman Church shall be the highest and chief of all priests in the whole world, and according to his decision shall all matters be settled which shall be taken in hand for the service of God or the confirmation of the faith of Christians.

> Source: H. Bettenson (trans.) *Documents of the Christian Church* (Oxford, 1950) pp. 136–140.

3.2 Letter to Emperor Anastasius I from Pope Gelasius I, on the proper relationship between imperial and priestly powers

---

Two there are, august emperor, by which this world is chiefly ruled, the sacred authority of the priesthood and the royal power. Of these the responsibility of the priests is more weighty in so far as they will answer for the kings of men themselves at the divine judgement. You know, most clement son, that, although you take precedence over all mankind in dignity, nevertheless you piously bow the neck to those who have charge of divine affairs and seek from them the means of your salvation, and hence you realise that, in the order of religion, in matters concerning the reception and right administration of the heavenly sacraments, you ought to submit yourself rather than rule, and that in these matters you should depend on their judgement rather than seek to bend them to your will. For if the bishops themselves, recognising that the imperial office was conferred on you by divine disposition, obey your laws so far as the sphere of public order is concerned lest they seem to obstruct your decrees in mundane matters, with what zeal, I ask you, ought you to obey those who have been charged with administering the sacred mysteries? Moreover, just as no light risk attends pontiffs who keep silent in matters concerning the service of God, so too no little danger threatens those who show scorn – which God forbid – when they ought to obey. And if the hearts of the faithful should be submitted to all priests in general who rightly administer divine things, how much more should assent be given to the bishop of that see which the Most High wished to be pre-eminent over all priests, and which the devotion of the whole church has honoured ever since. As Your Piety is certainly well aware, no one can ever raise himself by purely human means to the privilege and place of him whom the voice of Christ has set before all, whom the church has always venerated and held in devotion as its primate. The things which are established by divine judgement can be assailed by human presumption; they cannot be overthrown by anyone's power. It happened before the coming of Christ that certain men, though still engaged in carnal activities, were symbolically both kings and priests, and sacred history tells us that Melchisedek was such a one. The Devil also imitated this among his own people, for he always strives in a spirit of tyranny to claim for himself what pertains to divine worship, and so pagan emperors were called supreme pontiffs. But when He came who was true king and true priest, the emperor no longer assumed the title of priest, nor did the priest claim the royal dignity – though the members of Him who was true king and true priest, through participation in his nature, may be said to have received both qualities in their sacred nobility so that they constitute a race at once royal and priestly. For Christ, mindful of human frailty, regulated with an excellent disposition what pertained to the salvation of his people. Thus he distinguished between the offices of both powers according to their own proper activities and separate dignities, wanting his people to be saved by healthful humility and not carried away again by human pride, so that Christian emperors would need priests for attaining eternal life and priests would avail themselves of imperial regulations in the conduct of temporal affairs. In this fashion spiritual activity would be set apart from worldly encroachments and the 'soldier of God' would not be involved in secular affairs, while on the other hand he who was involved in secular affairs would not seem to preside over divine matters. Thus the humility of each order would be preserved, neither being exalted by the subservience of the other, and each profession would be especially fitted for its appropriate functions.

> **Source: B. Tierney, *The Crisis of Church and State,***
> ***1050–1300* (New Jersey, 1964) pp. 13–15**

ཞ❧ 3.3 Petrine Primacy ❧

Gregory the Great to Eulogius, bishop of Alexandria

Your most sweet Holiness has spoken much in your letter to me about the chair of Saint Peter, prince of the apostles, saying that he himself now sits on it in the persons of his successors, . . . and, indeed, I gladly accepted all that was said, inasmuch as he has spoken to me about Peter's chair who occupies Peter's chair. Although special honour to me in no way delights me, I greatly rejoice because you, Most Holy One, have given to yourself what you have bestowed on me. For who can be unaware that the holy Church has been made firm in the strength of the prince of the apostles, who derived his name from the firmness of his spirit, so that he was called *Petrus,* which comes from *petra.* And to him it is said by the voice of Truth: 'I will give you the keys of the Kingdom of Heaven.' And again it is said to him: 'When you are converted, strengthen your brothers.' And once more: 'Simon, son of Jonah, do you love Me? Then feed My sheep.' It follows from this that although there are many apostles, so far as primacy is concerned, the see of the prince of the apostles alone has grown strong in authority, which in three places is one see. For Peter himself exalted the see in which he deigned to reside and end his life on earth. Peter himself honoured the see to which he sent his disciple as evangelist. Peter himself strengthened the see in which, although he would leave it, he sat for seven years. Because it is the see of one, and one see over which by Divine Authority three bishops now preside, whatever good I hear of you I impute to myself. If you believe anything good of me, impute this to your merits, because we are one in Him who says: 'That they all may be one, as You, Father, are in Me and I in You, and that they may be one in Us.'

Source: A. J. Andrea, *The Medieval Record*
(Boston, 1997) pp. 116–117

ਿ 3.4 Leo the Great (440–461) on Petrine theory ਿ

Column (Col.) 628

Our Lord Jesus Christ, the Saviour of the world, caused his truth to be promulgated through the apostles. And while this duty was placed on all the apostles, the Lord made St Peter the head of them all, that from him as from their head his gifts should flow out into all the body. So that if anyone separates himself from St Peter he should know that he has no share in the divine blessing.

Col. 656

If any dissensions in regard to church matters and the clergy should arise among you, we wish you to settle them and report to us all the terms of the settlement, so that we may confirm all your just and reasonable decisions.

Col. 995

Constantinople has its own glory and by the mercy of God has become the seat of the empire. But secular matters are based on one thing, ecclesiastical matters on another. For nothing will stand which is not built on the rock which the Lord laid in the foundation . . . Your city is royal, but you cannot make it apostolic.

Col. 1081

You will learn with what reverence the bishop of Rome treats the rules and canons of the church if you read my letters by which I resisted the ambition of the patriarch of Constantinople, and you will see also that I am the guardian of the catholic faith and of the decrees of the church fathers.

Col. 991

On this account the holy and most blessed pope, Leo, the head of the universal church, with the consent of the holy synod, endowed with the dignity of St Peter, who is the foundation of the church, the rock of the faith, and the door-keeper of heaven, through us, his vicars, deprived him of his rank as bishop, etc.

Col. 615

And because we have the care of all the churches, and the Lord, who made Peter the prince of the apostles, holds us responsible for it, etc.

Col. 881

Believing that it is reasonable and just that as the holy Roman church, through St Peter, the prince of the apostles, is the head of all the churches of the whole world, etc.

Col. 147

This festival should be so celebrated that in my humble person he should be seen and honoured who has the care over all the shepherds and the sheep committed to him, and whose dignity is not lacking in me, his heir, although I am unworthy.

Source: O. J. Thatcher, E. H. McNeal (trans.) *A Source Book for Mediaeval History* (New York, 1905) No. 35, pp. 85–86

The coronation of Charlemagne on Christmas Day 800 symbolised the growing interdependence of papacy and German Empire but it was the citizens of Rome who often dominated individual popes and their election. In the tenth century the papacy sank to a low condition only to be revived in the eleventh century, first at the instigation of the German emperors, afterwards under the aegis of a line of great reforming popes beginning with Leo IX (1049–1054) and culminating in Gregory VII (1073–1085), formerly Archdeacon Hildebrand and instigator of the Gregorian reform. This was the heart of contention in the struggle between pope and emperor known as the Investiture Contest on account of the dispute about who had the authority to invest or appoint bishops and church dignitaries. Gregory VII wanted an end to all royal control of bishops and a free church. He died in exile upholding his beliefs, having humbled the German Henry IV into submission at Canossa in Northern Italy.

৪৺ 3.5 The Letter of Henry IV to Gregory VII ৶৭
(24 January 1076)

Henry, king not through usurpation but through the holy ordination of God, to Hildebrand, at present not pope but false monk. Such greeting as this hast thou merited through thy disturbances, inasmuch as there is no grade in the church which thou hast omitted to make a partaker not of honour but of confusion, not of benediction but of malediction. For, to mention few and especial cases out of many, not only hast thou not feared to lay hands upon the rulers of the holy church, the anointed of the Lord – the archbishops, namely, bishops and priests – but thou hast trodden them under foot like slaves ignorant of what their master is doing. Thou hast won favour from the common herd by crushing them; thou hast looked upon all of them as knowing nothing, upon thy sole self, moreover, as knowing all things. This knowledge, however, thou hast used not for edification but for destruction; so that with reason we believe that St Gregory, whose name thou hast usurped for thyself, was prophesying concerning thee when he said: 'The pride of him who is in power increases the more, the greater the number of those subject to him; and he thinks that he himself can do more than all.' And we, indeed, have endured all this, being eager to guard the honour of the apostolic see; thou, however hast understood our humility to be fear, and hast not, accordingly, shunned to rise up against the royal power conferred upon us by God, daring to threaten to divest us of it. As if we had received our kingdom from thee! As if the kingdom and the empire were in thine and not in God's hand! And this although our Lord Jesus Christ did call us to the kingdom, did not, however, call thee to the priesthood. For thou hast ascended by the following steps. By wiles, namely, which the profession of monk abhors, thou hast achieved money; by money, favour; by the sword, the throne of peace. And from the throne of peace thou hast disturbed peace, inasmuch as thou hast armed subjects against those in authority over them; inasmuch as thou, who wert not called, hast taught that our bishops called of God are to be despised; inasmuch as thou hast usurped for laymen the ministry over their priests, allowing them to depose or condemn those whom they themselves had received as teachers from the hand of God through the laying on of hands of the bishops. On me also who, although unworthy to be among the anointed, have nevertheless been anointed to the kingdom, thou hast lain thy hand; me who – as the tradition of the holy Fathers teaches, declaring that I am not to be deposed for any crime unless, which God forbid, I should have strayed from the faith – am subject to the judgment of God alone. For the wisdom of the holy fathers committed even Julian the apostate not to themselves, but to God alone, to be judged and to be deposed. For himself the true pope, Peter, also exclaims: 'Fear God, honour the king.' But thou who dost not fear God, dost dishonour in me his appointed one. Wherefore St Paul, when he has not spared an angel of Heaven if he shall have preached otherwise, has not excepted thee also who dost teach otherwise upon earth. For he says: 'If anyone, either I or an angel from Heaven, should preach a gospel other than that which has been preached to you, he shall be damned. Thou, therefore, damned by this curse and by the judgment of all our bishops and by our own, descend and relinquish the apostolic chair which thou hast usurped. Let another ascend the throne of St Peter, who shall not practise violence under the cloak of religion, but shall teach the sound doctrine of St Peter. I Henry, king by the grace of God, do say unto thee, together with all our bishops: Descend, descend, to be damned throughout the ages.

Source: E. F. Henderson (ed. and trans.) *Select Historical Documents of the Middle Ages* (1925) pp. 372–373

3.6 Gregory VII's first excommunication and deposition of Henry IV (22 February 1076)

O St Peter, chief of the apostles, incline to us, I beg, thy holy ears, and hear me thy servant whom thou hast nourished from infancy, and whom, until this day, thou hast freed from the hand of the wicked, who have hated and do hate me for my faithfulness to thee. Thou, and my mistress the mother of God, and thy brother St Paul are witnesses for me among all the saints that thy holy Roman church drew me to its helm against my will; that I had no thought of ascending thy chair through force, and that I would rather have ended my life as a pilgrim than, by secular means, to have seized thy throne for the sake of earthly glory. And therefore I believe it to be through thy grace and not through my own deeds that it has pleased and does please thee that the Christian people, who have been especially committed to thee, should obey me. And especially to me, as thy representative and by thy favour, has the power been granted by God of binding and loosing in Heaven and on earth. On the strength of this belief therefore, for the honour and security of thy church, in the name of Almighty God, Father, Son and Holy Ghost, I withdraw, through thy power and authority, from Henry the king, son of Henry the emperor, who has risen against thy church with unheard of insolence, the rule over the whole kingdom of the Germans and over Italy. And I absolve all Christians from the bonds of the oath which they have made or shall make to him; and I forbid anyone to serve him as king. For it is fitting that he who strives to lessen the honour of thy church should himself lose the honour which belongs to him. And since he has scorned to obey as a Christian, and has not returned to God whom he had deserted – holding intercourse with the excommunicated; practising manifold iniquities; spurning my commands which, as thou dost bear witness, I issued to him for his own salvation; separating himself from thy church and striving to rend it – I bind him in thy stead with the chain of the anathema. And, leaning on thee, I so bind him that the people may know and have proof that thou art Peter, and above thy rock the Son of the Living God hath built His church, and the gates of Hell shall not prevail against it.

Source: Henderson, *Select Historical Documents*, pp. 376–377

Gregory, bishop, servant of the servants of God, to all the archbishops, bishops, dukes, counts, and other princes of the German kingdom, defenders of the Christian faith, greeting and apostolic benediction.

Since you have made common cause with us and shared our perils in the recent controversy, we have thought it only right that you should be informed of the recent course of events, how king Henry came to Italy to do penance, and how we were led to grant him absolution.

According to the agreement made with your representatives we had come to Lombardy and were there awaiting those whom you were to send to escort us into your land. But after the time set was already passed, we received word that it was at that time impossible to send an escort, because of many obstacles that stood in the way, and we were greatly exercised at this and in grave doubt as to what we ought to do. In the meantime we learned that the king was approaching. Now before he entered Italy he had sent to us and had offered to make complete satisfaction for his fault, promising to reform and henceforth to obey us in all things, provided we would give him our absolution and blessing. We hesitated for some time, taking occasion in the course of the negotiations to reprove him sharply for his former sins. Finally he came in person to Canossa, where we were staying, bringing with him only a small retinue and manifesting no hostile intentions. Once arrived, he presented himself at the gate of the castle, barefoot and clad only in wretched woollen garments, beseeching us with tears to grant him absolution and forgiveness. This he continued to do for three days, until all those about us were moved to compassion at his plight and interceded for him with tears and prayers. Indeed, they marvelled at our hardness of heart, some even complaining that our action savoured rather of heartless tyranny than of chastening severity. At length his persistent declarations of repentance and the supplications of all who were there with us overcame our reluctance, and we removed the excommunication from him and received him again into the bosom of the holy mother church. But first he took the oath which we have subjoined to this letter, the abbot of Cluny, the countess Mathilda, the countess Adelaide, and many other ecclesiastic and secular princes going surety for him. Now that this arrangement has been reached to the common advantage of the church and the empire, we purpose coming to visit you in your own land as soon as possible. For, as you will perceive from the conditions stated in the oath, the matter is not to be regarded as settled until we have held consultation with you. Therefore we urge you to maintain that fidelity and love of justice which first prompted your action. We have not bound to anything, except that we assured the king that he might depend upon us to aid him in everything that looked to his salvation and honour.

Source: O. J. Thatcher, E. H. McNeal (trans.) *A Source Book for Mediaeval History* (New York, 1905) No. 80, pp. 158–159

3.8 The *Dictatus Papae*

1 That the Roman church was founded by God alone.
2 That the Roman pontiff alone can with right be called universal.
3 That he alone can depose or reinstate bishops.
4 That, in a council, his legate, even if a lower grade, is above all bishops, and can pass sentence of deposition against them.
5 That the pope may depose the absent.
6 That, among other things, we ought not to remain in the same house with those excommunicated by him.
7 That for him alone is it lawful, according to the needs of the time, to make new laws, to assemble together new congregations, to make an abbey of a canonry; and, on the other hand, to divide a rich bishopric and unite the poor ones.
8 That he alone may use the imperial insignia.
9 That of the pope alone all princes shall kiss the feet.
10 That his name alone shall be spoken in the churches.
11 That this is the only name in the world.
12 That it may be permitted to him to depose emperors.
13 That he may be permitted to transfer bishops if need be.
14 That he has power to ordain a clerk of any church he may wish.
15 That he who is ordained by him may preside over another church, but may not hold a subordinate position; and that such a one may not receive a higher grade from any bishop.
16 That no synod shall be called a general one without his order.
17 That no chapter and no book shall be considered canonical without his authority.
18 That a sentence passed by him may be retracted by no one; and that he himself, alone of all, may retract it.
19 That he himself may be judged by no one.
20 That no one shall dare to condemn one who appeals to the apostolic chair.
21 That to the latter should be referred the more important cases of every church.
22 That the Roman church has never erred; nor will it err to all eternity, the Scripture bearing witness.
23 That the Roman pontiff, if he have been canonically ordained, is undoubtedly made a saint by the merits of St Peter; St Ennodius, bishop of Pavia, bearing witness, and many holy fathers agreeing with him. As is contained in the decrees of St Symmachus the pope.
24 That, by his command and consent, it may be lawful for subordinates to bring accusations.
25 That he may depose and reinstate bishops without assembling a synod.
26 That he who is not at peace with the Roman church shall not be considered catholic.
27 That he may absolve subjects from their fealty to wicked men.

Source: Henderson, *Select Historical Documents*, pp. 366–367

Conflict between the two powers remained characteristic of the papal world of the high Middle Ages and Rome remained throughout a dangerous place and the papal office itself something of a poisoned chalice as the only English Pope, Adrian IV (1154–1159), made clear:

ᘓ 3.9 *The Pope's Body* ᘐ

Who can doubt that the pope is the servant of servants? I call as a Witness Our Lord Adrian (may it please God that his years be happy ones!). He used to say that no one is more wretched than the Roman pontiff, no condition more unhappy than his. Even had he no other problems, the weight of his duties alone would overwhelm him. He confided to me that he had found so many cares in the cathedral of Peter that by comparison all his earlier troubles seemed like joyful moments and happy times. He used to declare, moreover, that the see of Rome is a prickly Seat; that the papal mantle is covered everywhere with thorns and is heavy enough to crush, wear down, and break even the strongest shoulders; and lastly, that if the crown and the tiara seem to shine, it is because they burn like fire. And he added that were it not for fear of opposing the decision of God, he would have preferred never to have left his native England, where he might have lived forever hidden in the cloister of the Blessed Rufus, rather than face so many anxieties. While he was still living I questioned him directly, and someone with personal experience can be believed. He repeated to me many times that his rise from being a simple cloistered cleric through so many offices to the papal throne had added nothing to the happiness and serenity of his earlier life. But because whenever I was with him his grace wished that nothing should be hidden from my eyes, I will use his own words: 'The Lord has always beat me between the anvil and the hammer. But now, if it please Him, may He raise up with His right hand the burden that He has imposed upon my infirmity; Since for me it has become unbearable.'

> **Source: Paravicini-Bagliani (trans.)** *The Pope's Body*
> (2000) p. 14

The conflict in England between Henry II and his archbishop, Thomas Becket, over the freedom of the Church provided a vivid local example of the regnum/sacerdotium conflict and provided, in 1170, a martyr to the cause.

҈ 3.10 Edward Grim, *Vita S. Thomae Cantuariensis* ҈ *Archiepiscopi et Martyris*

After the monks had retreated within the precincts of the church, the four knights came following hard on their heels with rapid strides. They were accompanied by a certain subdeacon called Hugh, armed with malice like their own, appropriately named Mauclere, being one who showed no reverence either to God or his saints, as be proved by his subsequent action. As soon as the archbishop entered the monastic buildings, the monks ceased the vespers, which they had already begun to offer to God, and ran to meet him, glorifying God for that they saw their father alive and unharmed, when they had heard he was dead. They also hastened to ward off the foe from the slaughter of their shepherd by fastening the bolts of the folding doors giving access to the church. But Christ's doughty champion turned to them and ordered the doors to be thrown open, saying, 'It is not meet to make a fortress of the house of prayer, the Church of Christ, which, even if it be not closed, affords sufficient protection to its children; by suffering rather than by fighting shall we triumph over the enemy; for we are come to suffer, not to resist.' Straightway these sacrilegious men, with drawn swords, entered the house of peace and reconciliation, causing no little horror to those present by the mere sight of them and the clash of their armour. All the onlookers were in tumult and consternation, for by this time those who had been singing vespers had rushed up to the scene of death. In a spirit of mad fury the knights called out, 'Where is Thomas Becket, traitor to the king and the realm?' When he returned no answer, they cried out the more loudly and insistently, 'Where is the archbishop?' At this quite undaunted, as it is written, 'The righteous shall be bold as a lion and without fear', he descended from the steps, whither he had been dragged by the monks through their fear of the knights, and in a perfectly clear voice answered, 'Lo! here am I, no traitor to the king, but a priest. What do you seek from me?' And whereas he had already told them that he had no fear of them, he now added, 'Behold, I am ready to suffer in His Name who redeemed me by His Blood. Far be it from me to flee from your swords, or to depart from righteousness.' Having thus said, he turned aside to the right, under a pillar, having on one side the altar of the blessed Mother of God, Mary ever-Virgin, on the other, that of the holy confessor, Benedict, by whose example and prayers, having crucified the world and its lusts, he endured whatsoever the murderers did to him with such constancy of soul, as if he were no longer in the flesh. The murderers pursued him. 'Absolve', they cried, 'and restore to communion those whom you have excommunicated, and the functions of their office to the others who have been suspended.' He answered, 'There has been no satisfaction made, and I will not absolve them.' 'Then you shall die this instant', they cried, 'and receive your desert.' 'I, too,' said he, 'am ready to die for my Lord, that in my blood the Church may obtain peace and liberty; but in the name of Almighty God I forbid you to harm any of my men, whether clerk or lay.' Thus did the noble martyr provide piously for his followers, and prudently for himself, in that no one standing near should be hurt nor the innocent oppressed, lest any serious mishap befalling any that stood by him should dim the lustre of his glory as his soul sped up to Christ. Most fitting was it that the soldier-martyr should follow in the footsteps of his Captain and Saviour, who, when the wicked sought to take him, said, 'If ye seek me, let these go their way.'

Then they made a rush at him and laid sacrilegious hands upon him, pulling and dragging him roughly and violently, endeavouring to get him outside the walls of the church and there slay him, or bind him and carry him off prisoner, as they afterwards confessed was their intention. But as he could not easily be moved from the pillar, one of them seized hold of him and clung to him more closely. The archbishop shook him off vigorously, calling him a pandar and saying, 'Touch me not, Reginald; you owe me fealty and obedience; you are acting like a madman, you and your accomplices.' All aflame with a terrible fury at this rebuff, the knight brandished his sword against that consecrated head. 'Neither faith', he cried, 'nor obedience do I owe you against my fealty to my lord the king.' Then the unconquered martyr understood that the hour was approaching that should release him from the miseries of this mortal life, and that the crown of immortality prepared for him and promised by the Lord was already nigh at hand. Whereupon, inclining his head as one in prayer and joining his hands together and uplifting them, he commended his cause and that of the Church to God and St Mary and the blessed martyr, St Denys. Scarce had he uttered the words than the wicked knight, fearing lest he should be rescued by the people and escape alive, leapt suddenly upon him and wounded the sacrificial lamb of God in the head, cutting off the top of the crown which the unction of the sacred chrism had dedicated to God, and by the same stroke he almost cut off the arm of him who tells the story. For he, when all the others, both monks and clerks had fled, steadfastly stood by the saintly archbishop and held his arms around him, till the one he opposed to the blow was almost severed. Behold the simplicity of the dove, the wisdom of the serpent in this martyr who presented his body to the strikers that he might preserve his head, that is to say, his soul and the Church, unharmed, nor would he take any forethought or employ any stratagem against those who slay the body whereby he might escape. O worthy shepherd, who gave himself so boldly to the wolves, in order that his flock might not be torn to pieces! Because he had cast away the world, the world in seeking to crush him unconsciously exalted him.

Next he received a second blow on the head, but still he stood firm and immovable. At the third blow he fell on his knees and elbows, offering himself a living sacrifice and saying in a low voice, 'For the Name of Jesus and the protection of the Church I am ready to embrace death.' But the third knight inflicted a terrible wound as he lay prostrate. By this stroke the sword was dashed against the pavement and the crown of his head, which was large, was separated from the head in such a way that the blood white with the brain and the brain no less red from the blood, dyed the floor of the cathedral with the white of the lily and the red of the rose, the colours of the Virgin and Mother and of the life and death of the martyr and confessor. The fourth knight warded off any who sought to intervene, so that the others might with greater freedom and licence perpetrate the crime. But the fifth — no knight he, but that same clerk who had entered with the knights — that a fifth blow might not be wanting to the martyr who in other things had imitated Christ, placed his foot on the neck of the holy priest and precious martyr and, horrible to relate, scattered the brains and blood about the pavement, crying out to the others, 'Let us away, knights; this fellow will rise no more.'

In all his sufferings the illustrious martyr displayed an incredible steadfastness. Neither with hand nor robe, as is the manner of human frailty, did he oppose the fatal stroke. Nor when smitten did he utter a single word, neither cry nor groan, nor any sound indicative of pain. But he held motionless the head which he had bent to meet the uplifted sword until, bespattered with blood and brains, as though in an attitude of prayer, his body lay prone on the pavement, while his soul rested in Abraham's bosom.

> Source: D. C. Douglas and G. W. Greenaway, *English Historical Documents* (1953) pp. 765–768

Through a developing bureaucracy the papal claims to *plenitudo potestatis* (a fullness of power) and to the status of a universal ordinary (bishop above all other bishops) continued to develop. In the central Middle Ages the papal *curia* became a powerhouse of inter-national talent, the cardinals emerged as the Pope's sole electors, and the Canon Law of the Church grew in sophistication and influence. The Pope's status was being continually enhanced. St Bernard wrote to his fellow Cistercian, Pope Eugenius III, on the subject:

---

৯ 3.11 St Bernard to Eugenius III: Letter 205 ৯

3

When I think of the heights to which you have been lifted up, I fear a fall. When I think of your great dignity, I look down into the jaws of the gulf that yawns below you. When I ponder on the honour which is yours, I fear the danger which is at hand. I do not think that the words 'Man when he is honoured does not remember what he is' refer so much to the time as to the cause and mean that honours blind the judge-ment of a man, so that he forgets that he is human.

4

You chose to be the last in the household of God, you took the bottom seat at his feast, but now your Host has said, 'Friend, go up higher'. So you have gone up on high. But do not let that make you high-minded, lest when it is too late it should befall you to cry out, 'I shrink before thy vengeful anger, so low thou hast brought me, who didst once lift me up so high'. You have been called to hold a high posi-tion, but not a safe one; a sublime position, but not a secure one. How terrible, how very terrible is the place you hold! The place where you stand is holy ground. It is the place of Peter, the place of the Prince of the Apostles, the very place where his feet have stood. It is the place of him whom the Lord made master of his house-hold and chief over all his possessions. He is buried there in that very place to watch over you and bear witness against you if your feet should ever stray from the path of righteousness. Happy was the church when still young, when still in her cradle, to be entrusted to care of such a shepherd, of such a nurse, and to be taught to trample earthly things under foot by the example of one who would sully his fingers with no gifts and who could say with a clear conscience and a pure heart: 'Silver and gold have I none' . . .

6

Who will grant me before I die to see the Church as she was in the days of old when the Apostles let down their nets to catch not gold and silver but the souls of men? How I hope that you will inherit the words as well as the office of him who said: 'Silver and gold have I none'. What words of thunder! What magnificent and virtuous words! At the very sound of them all those who hate Sion are shamed and turned back in confusion. This is what your mother looks for from you and longs for with all her heart. This is what the sons of your mother, both young and old, hope and sigh for, so that every tree your father has not planted may be torn down with your own hands. You have been set up over peoples and kingdoms for this purpose, to pull up and to destroy. Many said when they heard of your election: 'Now the axe is laid to the tree'. Many said in their hearts: 'At home the flowers have begun to blossom, the pruning time has come'; the dead branches will be cut away so that those which are left may bear more abundant fruit.

7

Have courage and be of good heart. You hold your enemies by the neck; claim for yourself with a strong hand and a firm purpose the land which your omnipotent father has allotted to you above that of your brothers, the land he took from the Amorite with his sword and bow. But in all your actions remember that you are human, and have the fear of him who 'Strikes awe into the hearts of princes' ever before your eyes. How many are the deaths of Roman Pontiffs which your own eyes have seen in a short time! Let the sudden and sure deaths of your predecessors be a warning to you. Let the short span of their power remind you of how short is the time allotted to you. Remember, by constant meditations amidst the blandishments of your fleeting glory, that your last end will come. Without any doubt you too will follow to the grave those men you have followed to the throne.

> Source: B. Scott James (trans.) *The Letters of*
> *St Bernard of Clairvaux*, 2nd edn (Stroud, 1998)
> pp. 278–280

Rome was emerging as Christendom's highest court of appeal. Such developments reached their apogee under the person of Innocent III (1198–1216).

౸ 3.12 King John renders homage and fealty to ౸⸱
Innocent III (1214)

Innocent, Bishop, servant of the servants of God, to his well-beloved son in Christ, John illustrious king of the English, and to his legitimate free-born heirs for ever.

The King of kings and Lord of lords, Jesus Christ, a priest for ever after the order of Melchisedech, has so established in the Church His kingdom and His priesthood that the one is a kingdom of priests and the other a royal priesthood, as is testified by Moses in the Law and by Peter in his Epistle; and over all He has set one whom He has appointed as His Vicar on earth, so that, as every knee is bowed to Jesus, of things in heaven, and things in earth, and things under the earth, so all men should obey his Vicar and strive that there may be one fold and one shepherd. All secular kings for the sake of God so venerate this Vicar, that unless they seek to serve him devotedly they doubt if they are reigning properly. To this, dearly beloved son, you have paid wise attention; and by the merciful inspiration of Him in whose hand are the hearts of kings which He turns whithersoever He wills, you have decided to submit in a temporal sense yourself and your kingdom to him to whom you knew them to be spiritually subject, so that kingdom and priesthood, like body and soul, for the great good and profit of each, might be united in the single person of Christ's Vicar. He has deigned to work this wonder, who being alpha and omega has caused the end to fulfil the beginning and the beginning to anticipate the end, so that those provinces which from of old have had the Holy Roman Church as their proper teacher in spiritual matters should now in temporal things also have her as their peculiar sovereign. You, whom God has chosen as a suitable minister to effect this, by a devout and spontaneous act of will and on the general advice of your barons have offered and yielded, in the form of an annual payment of a thousand marks, yourself and your kingdoms of England and Ireland, with all their rights and appurtenances, to God and to SS Peter and Paul His apostles and to the Holy Roman Church and to us and our successors, to be our right and our property – as is stated in your official letter attested by a golden seal, the literal tenor of which is as follows:
'John, by the grace of God king of England, lord of Ireland, duke of Normandy and Aquitaine, count of Anjou, to all the faithful of Christ who may see this charter, greeting in the Lord.
By this charter attested by our golden seal we wish it to be known to you all that, having in many things offended God and Holy Church our mother and being therefore in the utmost need of divine mercy and possessing nothing but ourselves and our kingdoms that we can worthily offer as due amends to God and the Church, we desire to humble ourselves for the sake of Him who for us humbled Himself even unto death; and inspired by the grace of the Holy Spirit – not induced by force nor compelled by fear, but of our own good and spontaneous will and on the general advice of our barons – we offer and freely yield to God, and to SS Peter and Paul His apostles, and to the Holy Roman Church our mother, and to our lord Pope Innocent III

and his catholic successors, the whole kingdom of England and the whole kingdom of Ireland with all their rights and appurtenances for the remission of our sins and the sins of our whole family, both the living and the dead. And now, receiving back these kingdoms from God and the Roman Church and holding them as feudatory vassal, in the presence of our venerable father, lord Nicholas, bishop of Tusculum, legate of the Apostolic See, and of Pandulf, subdeacon and member of household to our lord the Pope, we have pledged and sworn our fealty henceforth to our lord aforesaid, Pope Innocent, and to his catholic successors, and to the Roman Church, in the terms hereinunder stated; and we have publicly paid liege homage for the said kingdoms to God, and to the Holy Apostles Peter and Paul, and to the Roman Church, and to our lord aforesaid, Pope Innocent III, at the hands of the said legate who accepts our homage in place and instead of our said lord, the Pope; and we bind in perpetuity our successors and legitimate heirs that without question they must similarly render fealty and acknowledge homage to the Supreme Pontiff holding office at the time and to the Roman Church. As a token of this our perpetual offering and concession we will and decree that out of the proper and special revenues of our said kingdoms, in lieu of all service and payment which we should render for them, the Roman Church is to receive annually, without prejudice to the payment of Peter's pence, one thousand marks sterling – five hundred at the feast of St Michael and five hundred at Easter – that is, seven hundred for the kingdom of England and three hundred for the kingdom of Ireland, subject to the maintenance for us and our heirs of our jurisdiction, privileges, and regalities. Desiring all these terms, exactly as stated, to be forever ratified and valid, we bind ourselves and our successors not to contravene them; and if we or any of our successors shall presume to contravene them, then, no matter who he be, unless on due warning he come to his senses, let him lose the title to the kingdom, and let this document of our offer and concession remain ever valid.

I, John, by grace of God king of England and lord of Ireland, will from this hour hence-forward be faithful to God and Saint Peter and the Roman Church and my lord Pope Innocent III and his catholic successors. I will not take part in deed, word, agreement, or plan whereby they should lose life or limb or be treacherously taken prisoners; any injury to them, if aware of it, I will prevent and will check if I can; and otherwise, I will notify them as soon as possible, or inform a person whom I can trust without fail to tell them; any counsel they have entrusted to me either person-ally or by envoys or by letter I will keep secret, nor will I wittingly divulge it to anyone to their disadvantage. I will help in maintaining and defending, to the utmost of my power, against all men, the patrimony of Saint Peter, and particularly the kingdom of England and the kingdom of Ireland. So help me God and the Holy Gospels of God whereon I swear.

To prevent any questioning of these terms at any time in the future, and for the greater surety of our offer and concession, we have caused this charter to be made and to be sealed with our golden seal; and as tribute for this the first year we pay a thou-sand marks sterling to the Roman Church by the hand of the said legate.

Witnessed by his lordship Stephen archbishop of Canterbury, and by their lord-ships William bishop of London, Peter bishop of Winchester, Eustace bishop of Ely, and Hugh bishop of Lincoln, and by our Chancellor, Walter de Gray, our brother William earl of Salisbury, Ranulf earl of Chester, William Marshal earl of Pembroke, William earl of Ferrers, Saer earl of Winchester, Robert de Ros, William Briwerre, Peter FitzHerbert, Matthew FitzHerbert, and Brian de Lisle our steward.

By the hand of Master Richard Marsh archdeacon of Richmond and Northumberland, at St Paul's London, the third of October AD 1213, in the fifteenth year of our reign.

This offer and concession so piously and wisely made we regard as acceptable and valid, and we take under the protection of Saint Peter and of ourselves your person and the persons of your heirs together with the said kingdoms and their appurtenances and all other goods which are now reasonably held or may in future be so held: to you and to your heirs, according to the terms set out above and by the general advice of our brethren, we grant the said kingdoms in fief and confirm them by this privilege, on condition that any of your heirs on receiving the crown will publicly acknowledge this as a fief held of the Supreme Pontiff and of the Roman Church, and will take an oath of fealty to them. Let no man, therefore, have power to infringe this document of our concession and confirmation, or presume to oppose it. If any man dare to do so, let him know that he will incur the anger of Almighty God and of SS Peter and Paul, His apostles.'

> Source: C. R. Cheney and W. H. Semple, *Selected Letters of Pope Innocent III Concerning England* (Edinburgh, 1953) pp. 177–182

Among the instruments used by medieval popes to extend their power was the calling of a General Council of the Church and Innocent III was responsible for calling the Fourth Council of the Lateran which represented the high point of papal concilliar control. The Lateran was the Pope's Cathedral Church and principal Roman palace of the Middle Ages.

3.13 Lateran IV (1215)

The Creed, The Church, The Sacraments, and Transubstantiation (Canon 1)

We firmly believe and openly confess that there is only one true God, eternal and immense, omnipotent, unchangeable, incomprehensible, and ineffable, Father, Son and Holy Ghost; three Persons indeed but one essence, substance, or nature absolutely simple; the Father (proceeding) from no one, but the Son from the Father only, and the Holy Ghost equally from both, always without beginning and end. The Father begetting, the Son begotten, and the Holy Ghost proceeding; consubstantial and coequal, co-omnipotent and co-eternal, the one principle of the universe, Creator of all things invisible and visible, spiritual and corporeal, who from the beginning of time and by His omnipotent power made from nothing creatures both spiritual and corporeal, angelic, namely, and mundane, and then human, as it were, common, composed of spirit and body. The devil and the other demons were indeed created by God good by nature but they became bad through themselves; man, however, sinned at the suggestion of the devil. This Holy Trinity in its common essence undivided and in personal properties divided, through Moses, the holy prophets, and other servants gave to the human race at the most opportune intervals of time the doctrine of salvation. And finally, Jesus Christ, the only begotten Son of God made flesh by the entire Trinity, conceived with the co-operation of the Holy Ghost of Mary ever Virgin, made true man, composed of a rational soul and human flesh, one Person in two natures pointed out more clearly the way of life. Who according to His divinity is immortal and impassible, according to His humanity was made passible and mortal, suffered on the cross for the salvation of the human race, and being dead descended into hell, rose from the dead, and ascended into heaven. But He descended in soul, arose in flesh, and ascended equally in both; He will come at the end of the world to judge the living and the dead and will render to the reprobate and to the elect according to their works. Who all shall rise with their own bodies which they now have that they may receive according to their merits, whether good or bad, the latter eternal punishment with the devil, the former eternal glory with Christ.

There is one universal Church of the faithful, outside of which there is absolutely no salvation. In which there is the same priest and sacrifice, Jesus Christ, whose body and blood are truly contained in the sacrament of the altar under the forms of bread and wine; the bread being changed (*transsubstantiatis*) by divine power into the body, and the wine into the blood, so that to realise the mystery of unity we may receive of Him what He has received of us. And this sacrament no one can effect except the priest who has been duly ordained in accordance with the keys of the Church, which Jesus Christ Himself gave to the Apostles and their successors.

But the sacrament of baptism, which by the invocation of each Person of the Trinity, namely, of the Father, Son, and Holy Ghost, is effected in water, duly conferred on children and adults in the form prescribed by the Church by anyone whatsoever, leads to salvation. And should anyone after the reception of baptism have fallen into sin, by true repentance he can always be restored. Not only virgins and those practising chastity, but also those united in marriage, through the right faith and through works pleasing to God, can merit eternal salvation.

Source: Schroder *Disciplinary Decrees,*
pp. 237–239

ॐ 3.14 On the abuse and the validation of relics (Canon 62) ॐ

From the fact that some expose for sale and exhibit promiscuously the relics of saints, great injury is sustained by the Christian religion. That this may not occur hereafter, we ordain in the present decree that in the future old relics may not be exhibited outside of a vessel or exposed for sale. And let no one presume to venerate publicly new ones unless they have been approved by the Roman pontiff. In the future prelates shall not permit those who come to their churches *causa venerationis* to be deceived by worthless fabrications or false documents as has been done in many places for the sake of gain. We forbid also that seekers (*quaestores*) of alms, some of whom, misrepresenting themselves, preach certain abuses, be admitted, unless they exhibit genuine letters either of the Apostolic See or of the diocesan bishop, in which case they may not preach anything to the people but what is contained in those letters.

Source: Schroder, *Disciplinary Decrees*, pp. 286–287

Boniface VIII (1294–1303) overreached himself and gave to the papacy in his bull *Unam Sanctum* (1302) rights and powers which were impossible to impose.

3.15 *Unam Sanctum*

We are compelled, our faith urging us, to believe and to hold – and we do firmly believe and simply confess – that there is one holy catholic and apostolic church, outside of which there is neither salvation nor remission of sins; her Spouse proclaiming it in the canticles: 'My dove, my undefiled is but one, she is the choice one of her that bare her', which represents one mystic body, of which body the head is Christ; but of Christ, God. In this church there is one Lord, one faith and one baptism. There was one ark of Noah, indeed, at the time of the flood, symbolising one church; and this being finished in one cubit had, namely, one Noah as helmsman and commander. And, with the exception of this ark, all things existing upon the earth were, as we read, destroyed. This church, moreover, we venerate as the only one, the Lord saying through His prophet: 'Deliver my soul from the sword, my darling from the power of the dog.' He prayed at the same time for His soul – that is, for Himself the Head, and for His body – which body, namely, he called the one and only church on account of the unity of the faith promised, of the sacraments, and of the love of the church. She is that seamless garment of the Lord which was not cut but which fell by lot. Therefore of this one and only church there is one body and one head – not two heads as if it were a monster – Christ, namely, and the vicar of Christ, St Peter, and the successor of Peter. For the Lord Himself said to Peter, Feed my sheep. My sheep, He said, using a general term, and not designating these or those particular sheep; from which it is plain that He committed to Him all His sheep. If, then, the Greeks or others say that they were not committed to the care of Peter and his successors, they necessarily confess that they are not of the sheep of Christ; for the Lord says, in John, that there is one fold, one shepherd and one only. We are told by the word of the gospel that in this His fold there are two swords – a spiritual, namely, and a temporal. For when the apostles said 'Behold here are two swords' – when, namely, the apostles were speaking in the church – the Lord did not reply that this was too much, but enough. Surely he who denies that the temporal sword is in the power of Peter wrongly interprets the word of the Lord when He says: 'Put up thy sword in its scabbard'. Both swords, the spiritual and the material, therefore, are in the power of the church; the one, indeed, to be wielded for the church, the other by the church; the one by the hand of the priest, the other by the hand of kings and knights, but at the will and sufferance of the priest. One sword, moreover, ought to be under the other, and the temporal authority to be subjected to the spiritual. For when the apostle says 'there is no power but of God, and the powers that are of God are ordained', they would not be ordained unless sword were under sword and the lesser one, as it were, were led by the other to great deeds. For according to St Dionysius the law of divinity is to lead the lowest through the intermediate to the highest things. Not therefore, according to the law of the universe, are all things reduced to order equally and immediately; but the lowest through the intermediate, the intermediate through the higher. But that the spiritual exceeds any earthly power in dignity and nobility we ought the more openly to confess the more spiritual things excel temporal ones. This also is made plain to our eyes from the giving of tithes, and the benediction and the sanctification; from the acceptation of this same power, from the control over those same things. For, the truth bearing witness, the spiritual power has to establish the earthly power, and to judge it if it be not good. Thus concerning the church and the ecclesiastical power is verified the prophecy of Jeremiah: 'See, I have this day set thee over the nations and over the kingdoms', and the other things which follow. Therefore if the earthly power err it shall be judged by the spiritual power; but if the lesser spiritual power err, by the greater. But if the greatest, it can be judged by God alone, not by man, the apostle bearing witness. A spiritual man judges all things, but he himself is judged by no one. This authority, moreover, even though it is given to man and exercised through man, is not human but rather divine, being given by divine lips to Peter and founded on a rock for him and his successors through Christ himself whom he has confessed; the Lord himself saying to Peter: 'Whatsoever thou shalt bind', etc. Whoever, therefore, resists this power thus ordained by God, resists the ordination of God, unless he makes believe, like the Manichean, that there are two beginnings. This we consider false and heretical, since by the testimony of Moses, not 'in the beginnings', but 'in the beginning' God created the Heavens and the earth. Indeed we declare, announce and define, that it is altogether necessary to salvation for every human creature to be subject to the Roman pontiff, The Lateran, November, 14th, in our 8th year. As a perpetual memorial of this matter.

> Source: Henderson *Select Historical Documents*,
> pp. 435–437

In the later Middle Ages the papacy was increasingly at the mercy of the politics of Italian particularism which chipped away at its internationalism, and of the growing force of conciliarism which intensified supreme authority in the Church not in the person of the Pope but in a general council of the Church's bishops.

 The Council of Constance (1414–1417)

This holy Council of Constance . . . declares, first that it is lawfully assembled in the Holy Spirit, that it constitutes a General Council, representing the Catholic Church, and that therefore it has authority immediately from Christ; and that all men, of every rank and condition, including the Pope himself, are bound to obey it in matters concerning the Faith, the abolition of the schism, and the reformation of the Church of God in its head and members. Secondly it declares that any one, of any rank and condition, who shall contumaciously refuse to obey the orders, decrees, statutes or instructions, made or to be made by this holy Council, or by any other lawfully assembled general council . . . shall, unless he comes to a right frame of mind, be subjected to fitting penance and punished appropriately: and, if need be, recourse shall be had to the other sanctions of the law.

Source: Bettenson *Christian Church*, p. 189

&» 3.17 Marsilius of Padua «§

Chapter II

In which are explicitly inferred certain conclusions which follow necessarily from the results set forth in the first two discourses. By heeding these conclusions, rulers and subjects can more easily attain the end aimed at by this book. Of the conclusions to be inferred, we shall place this one first:

1. For the attainment of eternal beatitude it is necessary to believe in the truth of only the divine or canonic Scripture, together with its necessary consequences and the interpretations of it made by the common council of the believers, if these have been duly propounded to the person concerned. The certainty of this is set forth in, and can be obtained from, Discourse II, Chapter XIX, paragraphs 2 to 5.

2. Doubtful sentences of divine law, especially on those matters which are called articles of the Christian faith, as well as on other matters belief in which is necessary for salvation, must be defined only by the general council of the believers, or by the weightier multitude or part thereof; no partial group or individual person, of what-ever status, has the authority to make such definitions. The certainty of this is to be had in Discourse II, Chapter XX, paragraphs 4 to 13.

3. The evangelic Scripture does not command that anyone be compelled by temporal pain or punishment to observe the commands of divine law: Discourse II, Chapter IX, paragraphs 3 to 10.

4. For eternal salvation it is necessary to observe only the commands of the evan-gelic law, and their necessary consequences, and the dictates of right reason as to what should be done and not done; but not all the commands of the Old Law: Discourse II, Chapter IX, paragraph 10 to the end.

5. No mortal can dispense with the commands or prohibitions of the divine or evangelic law; only the general councillor the faithful human legislator, and not any partial group or individual person, of whatever status, can prohibit things which are permitted by that law, by obliging transgressors of this prohibition to incur guilt

or punishment for the status of the present or of the future world: Discourse I, Chapter XII, paragraph 9; Discourse II, Chapter IX, paragraph I, and Chapter XXI, paragraph 8.

6. Only the whole body of citizens, or the weightier part thereof, is the human legislator: Discourse I, Chapters XII and XIII.

7. The decretals or decrees of the Roman or any other pontiffs, collectively or distributively, made without the grant of the human legislator, bind no one to temporal pain or punishment: Discourse I, Chapter XII; Discourse II, Chapter XXVIII, paragraph 29.

8. Human laws can be dispensed with only by the human legislator or by someone else acting by its authority: Discourse I, Chapter XII, paragraph 9.

9. An elective ruler, or any other official, is dependent only upon election by the body having the authority therefore, and needs no other confirmation or approval: Discourse I, Chapter XII, paragraph 9; Discourse II, Chapter XXVI, paragraphs 4 to 7

10. The election of any elective ruler or other official, especially if such office carries coercive force, depends upon the expressed will of the legislator alone: Discourse I, Chapter XII; Chapter XV, paragraphs 2 to 4.

11. The supreme government in a city or state must be only one in number: Discourse I, Chapter XVII.

12. Only the faithful ruler in accordance with the laws or approved customs has the authority to appoint persons to the offices of the state and to determine their quality and number, as well as all other civil affairs: Discourse I, Chapter XII; Chapter XV, paragraphs 4 and 10.

13. No ruler, and still less any partial group or individual person of whatever status, has plenitude of control or power over the individual or civil acts of other persons without the determination of the mortal legislator: Discourse I, Chapter XI; Discourse II, Chapter XXIII, paragraphs 3 to 5.

14. A bishop or priest, as such, has no rulership or coercive jurisdiction over any clergyman or layman, even if the latter be a heretic: Discourse I, Chapter XV, paragraphs 2 to 4; Discourse 11, Chapters IV, V, IX, and X, paragraph 7.

15. Only the ruler by authority of the legislator has coercive jurisdiction over the person and property of every individual mortal person, of whatever status, and of every group of laymen or clergymen: Discourse I, Chapters XV and XVII; Discourse II, Chapters IV, V, and VIII.

16. No bishop or priest or group of them is allowed to excommunicate anyone without authorisation by the faithful legislator: Discourse II, Chapter VI, paragraphs 11 to 4; Chapter XXI, paragraph 9.

17. All bishops are of equal authority immediately through Christ, nor can it be proved by divine law that there is any superiority or subjection among them in spiritual or in temporal affairs: Discourse II, Chapters XV and XVI.

18. By divine authority, accompanied by the consent or concession of the faithful human legislator, the other bishops, collectively or distributively, can excommunicate the Roman bishop and exercise other authority over him, just as conversely: Discourse II, Chapter VI, paragraphs 11 to 14; Chapters XV and XVI.

19. No mortal being can give a dispensation with respect to marriages prohibited by divine law, while those prohibited by human law pertain only to the authority of the legislator or of him who rules through the legislator: Discourse I, Chapter XII, paragraph 9; Discourse II, Chapter XXI, paragraph 8.

20. Only the faithful legislator has the authority to legitimise illegitimate children so that they may succeed to their inheritances and receive other civil and ecclesiastic offices and benefits: same passages as immediately above.

21. It pertains only to the faithful legislator to exercise coercive judgment with regard to candidates for church orders and their qualifications, and no priest or bishop is allowed to promote anyone to these orders without authorization by this legislator: Discourse I, Chapter XV, paragraphs 2, 3 and 4; Discourse II, Chapter XVII, paragraphs 8 to 16.

22. Only the ruler in accordance with the laws of the believers has the authority to regulate the number of churches or temples, and of the priests, deacons and other officials who are to minister therein: same passages as immediately above.

23. Only by the authority of the faithful legislator can and should separable church offices be bestowed and taken away, and similarly benefices and other things established for religious purposes: Discourse I, Chapter XV, paragraphs 2 and 4; Discourse II, Chapter XVII, paragraphs 16 to 18; Chapter XXI, paragraphs 11 to 15.

24. No bishops, as such, collectively or distributively, have the authority to appoint notaries or other civil public officials: Discourse I, Chapter XV, paragraphs 2, 3 and 10; Discourse II, Chapter XXI, paragraph 15.

25. No licence for the public teaching or practice of any art or discipline can be bestowed by any bishop, collectively or distributively, as such; but this pertains only to the legislator, at least the faithful one, or to the ruler by its authority: same passages as immediately above.

26. Persons appointed to the diaconate or priesthood, and others who are irrevocably dedicated to God, must be given preference in church offices and benefices over persons who are not thus dedicated: Discourse 11, Chapter XIV, paragraphs 6 to 8.

27. Ecclesiastic temporal goods which remain over and above the needs of priests and other gospel ministers and of the helpless poor, and which are not needed for divine worship, can lawfully, in accordance with divine law, be used in whole or in part by the legislator for the common or public welfare or defence: Discourse I, Chapter XV, paragraph 10; Discourse 11, Chapter XVII, paragraph 16; Chapter XXI, paragraph 14.

28. All temporal goods which have been set aside for religious purposes or for deeds of mercy, such as legacies bequeathed for overseas crossing to resist the infidels, or for the redemption of captives, or for the support of the helpless poor, and for other similar purposes, are to be distributed only by the ruler in accordance with the designation of the legislator and the intention of the donor: same passages as immediately above.

29. Only the faithful legislator has the authority to grant exemption to any group or religious body, and to approve or institute such exemption: Discourse I, Chapter XV, paragraphs 2, 3, 4 and 10; Discourse II, Chapter XVII, paragraphs 8 to 16; Chapter XXI, paragraphs 8 and 15.

30. Only the ruler in accordance with the designation of the human legislator has the authority to exercise coercive judgment over all heretics, criminals, and other persons subject to temporal pain or punishment; to inflict on them penalties in person, to exact penalties in property, and to dispose of these latter penalties: Discourse I, Chapter XV, paragraphs 6 to 9; Discourse II, Chapter VIII, paragraphs 2 and 3; and Chapter X.

31. No one who is subject and obligated to someone else by lawful oath can be released by any bishop or priest without reasonable cause, which cause is to be judged

by the faithful legislator by a judgment in the third sense; and the opposite of this is contrary to sound doctrine: Discourse 11, Chapters VI and VII; and Chapter XXVI, paragraphs 13 to 16.

32. Only the general council of all the faithful has the authority to designate a bishop or any metropolitan church highest of all, and to deprive or depose them from such position: Discourse II, Chapter XXII, paragraphs 9 to 12.

33. Only the faithful legislator, or the ruler by its authority in communities of believers may assemble through coercive power a general or partial council of priests, bishops, and other believers; and if a council is assembled in a different way, then decisions made therein have no force or validity, and no one is obliged under temporal or spiritual guilt or punishment to observe such decisions: Discourse I, Chapter XV, paragraphs 2, 3 and 4; Chapter XVII; Discourse II, Chapter VIII, paragraph 6 to the end; and Chapter XXI, paragraphs 2 to 8.

34. Fasts and prohibitions of food must be imposed only by the authority of the general council of believers, or of the faithful legislator; if divine law does not prohibit the practice of mechanical arts or the teaching of disciplines on any day, then these can be forbidden only by the aforesaid council or legislator, and only the faithful legislator or the ruler by its authority can enforce the observance of such prohibitions by temporal pain or punishment: Discourse I, Chapter XV, paragraphs 2,3,4, and 8; Discourse II, Chapter XII paragraph 8.

35. The canonisation and worship of anyone as a saint must be established and ordained only by the general council: Discourse II, Chapter XXI, paragraph 8.

36. Only the general council of believers has the authority to make decrees forbidding bishops, priests, and other temple ministers to have wives, as well as other ordinances with regard to church practice; and such decrees may be dispensed with only by that group or person to whom the authority for this has been given by the aforesaid council: same passages as immediately above.

37. From the coercive jurisdiction granted to a bishop or priest a litigant may always appeal to the legislator or to the ruler by its authority: Discourse I, Chapter XV, paragraphs 2 and 3; Discourse II, Chapter XXII, paragraph II.

38. A person who is to maintain the evangelical perfection of supreme poverty can have no chattels in his power without the firm intention of selling them as soon as possible and giving the price received to the poor; of no thing, movable or immovable, can he have the ownership or power, that is, with the intention of laying claim to that thing before a coercive judge from anyone who seizes or wishes to seize it: Discourse II, Chapter XIII, paragraphs 22 and 30; Chapter XIV, paragraph 14.

39. Communities and individuals are obliged by divine law to contribute, so far as they can, the food and clothing which are needed, at least on each successive day, by the bishops and others who minister the gospel to them; but they are not obliged to give tithes or anything else over and above the needs of the aforesaid ministers: Discourse II, Chapter XIV, paragraphs 6 to 11.

40. The faithful legislator, or the ruler by its authority in a province subject to it, can compel bishops and other gospel ministers, who have been provided with sufficient food and clothing, to perform the divine functions and to minister the ecclesiastic sacraments: Discourse I, Chapter XV, paragraphs 2, 3 and 4; Discourse II, Chapter VIII, paragraph 6 to the end; Chapter XVII, paragraph 12.

41. Appointments of the Roman bishop and of any other ecclesiastic or temple ministers in accordance with divine law to separable ecclesiastic offices, as well as suspensions and removals therefrom because of delict, must be effected only by the

faithful legislator, or the ruler by its authority, or the general council of the believers: Discourse I, Chapter XV, paragraphs 2, 3, 4 and 10; Discourse II, Chapter XVII, paragraphs 8 to 16; Chapter XXII, paragraphs 9 to 13.

42. We might infer many other useful conclusions which necessarily follow from the first two discourses; but let us be content with those deduced above, because they afford a ready and sufficient entering wedge for cutting away the afore-mentioned pestilence and its cause, and also for the sake of brevity.

Source: A. Gewirth (trans.) *Marsilius of Padua: the Defender of Peace* (New York, 1967) pp. 426–431

The manipulation of the great powers led to a period when the papacy was exiled to Avignon in the South of France and when it was sometimes not clear as to which of the several papal claimants were truly pope, accusing each of being anti-pope.

૩ 3.18 Catherine of Siena to Gregory XI outlining her policy ૩ for the return of the papacy to Rome

In the Name of Jesus Christ crucified and of sweet Mary:

Most holy and reverend sweet father in Christ sweet Jesus: your poor unworthy daughter Catherine, servant and slave of the servants of Jesus Christ, writes to your Holiness in His precious Blood, with desire to see you so strong and persevering in your holy resolve that no contrary wind can hinder you, neither devil nor creature. For it seems that your enemies are disposed to come, as Our Saviour says in His holy gospel, in sheep's raiment, looking like lambs, while they are ravening wolves. Our Saviour says that we should be on our guard against such. Apparently, sweet father, they are beginning to approach you in writing; and beside writing, they announce to you the coming of the author, saying that he will arrive at your door when you know it not. The man sounds humble when he says, 'If it is open to me, I will enter and we will reason together'; but he puts on the garment of humility only that he may be believed. And the virtue in which pride cloaks itself is really boastful.

So far as I have understood, this person has treated your Holiness in this letter as the devil treats the soul, who often, under colour of virtue and compassion, injects poison into it. And he uses this device especially with the servants of God, because he sees that he could not deceive them with open sin alone. So it seems to me that this incarnate demon is doing who has written you under colour of compassion and in holy style, for the letter purports to come from a holy and just man, and it does come from wicked men, counsellors of the devil, who cripple the common good of the Christian congregation and the reform of Holy Church, self-lovers, who seek only their own private good. But you can soon discover, father, whether it came from that just man or not. And it seems to me that, for the honour of God, you must investigate.

So far as I can understand, I do not think the man a servant of God, and his language does not so present him – but the letter seems to me a forgery. Nor does he who wrote it understand his trade very well. He ought to put himself to school – he seems to have known less than a small child.

Notice, now, most Holy Father: he has made his first appeal to the tendency that he knows to be the chief frailty in man, and especially in those who are very tender and pitiful in their natural affections, and tender to their own bodies – for such men as these hold life dearer than any others. So he fastened on this point from his first word. But I hope, by the goodness of God, that you will pay more heed to His honour and the safety of your own flock than to yourself, like a good shepherd, who ought to lay down his life for his sheep.

Next, this poisonous man seems on the one hand to commend your return to Rome, calling it a good and holy thing; but, on the other hand, he says that poison is prepared for you there; and he seems to advise you to send trustworthy men to precede you, who will find the poison on the tables – that is, apparently, in bottles, ready to be administered by degrees, either by the day, or the month, or the year. Now I quite agree with him that poison can be found – for that matter, as well on the tables of Avignon or other cities as on those of Rome: and prepared for administration slowly, by the month, or the year, or in large quantities, as may please the purchaser: it can be found everywhere. So he would think it well for you to send, and delay your return for this purpose; he proposes that you wait till divine judgment fall by this means on those wicked men who, it would seem, according to what he says, are seeking your death. But were he wise, he would expect that judgment to fall on himself, for he is sowing the worst poison that has been sown for a long time in Holy Church, inasmuch as he wants to hinder you from following God's call and doing your duty. Do you know how that poison would be sown? If you did not go, but sent, as the good man advises you, scandal and rebellion, spiritual and temporal, would be stirred up – men finding a lie in you, who hold the Seat of Truth. For since you have decided on your return and announced it, the scandal and bewilderment and disturbance in men's hearts would be too great if they found that it did not happen. Assuredly he says the truth: he is as prophetic as Caiphas when he said: 'It is necessary for one man to die that the people perish not.' He did not know what he was saying, but the Holy Spirit, who spoke the truth by his mouth, knew very well – though the devil did not make him speak with this intention. So this man is likely to be another Caiphas. He prophesies that if you send, men will find poison. Truly so it is; for were your sins so great that you stayed and they went, your confidants will find poison bottled in their hearts and mouths, as was said. And not only enough for one day, but it would last the month and the year before it was digested. Much I marvel at the words of this man, who commends an act as good and holy and religious, and then wants this holy act to be given up from bodily fear! It is not the habit of the servants of God ever to be willing to give up a spiritual act or work on account of bodily or temporal harm, even should life itself be spent: for had they done thus, none of them would have reached his goal. For the perseverance of holy and good desire into good works, is the thing which is crowned, and which merits glory and not confusion. Therefore I said to you, Reverend Father, that I desired to see you firm and stable in your good resolution (since on this will follow the pacification of your rebellious sons and the reform of Holy Church) and also to see you fulfil the desire felt by the servants of God, to behold you raise the standard of the most holy Cross against the infidels. Then can you minister the Blood of the

Lamb to those wretched infidels: for you are cupbearer of that Blood, and hold the keys of it.

Alas, father, I beg you, by the love of Christ crucified, that you turn your power to this swiftly, since without your power it cannot be done. Yet I do not advise you, sweet father, to abandon those who are your natural sons, who feed at the breasts of the Bride of Christ, for bastard sons who are not yet made lawful by holy baptism. But I hope, by the goodness of God, that if your legitimate sons walk with your authority, and with the divine power of the sword of holy Writ, and with human force and virtue, these others will turn to Holy Church the Mother, and you will legalise them. It seems as if this would be honour to God, profit to yourself, honour and exaltation to the sweet Bride of Christ Jesus, rather than to follow the foolish advice of this just man, who propounds that it would be better for you and for other ministers of the Church of God to live among faithless Saracens than among the people of Rome and Italy.

I am pleased by the commendable hunger that he has for the salvation of the infidels, but I am not pleased that he wishes to take the father from his lawful sons, and the shepherd from the sheep gathered in the fold. I think he wants to treat you as the mother treats the child when she wants to wean him: she puts something bitter on her bosom, that he may taste the bitterness before the milk, so that he may abandon the sweet through fear of the bitter; because a child is more easily deluded by bitterness than by anything else. So this man wants to do to you, suggesting to you the bitterness of poison and of great persecution, to delude the childishness of your weak sensuous love, that you may leave the milk through fear: the milk of grace, which follows on your sweet return. And I beg of you, on behalf of Christ crucified, that you be not a timorous child, but manly. Open your mouth, and swallow down the bitter for the sweet. It would not befit your holiness to abandon the milk for the bitterness. I hope by the infinite and inestimable goodness of God, that if you choose He will show favour to both us and to you; and that you will be a firm and stable man, unmoved by any wind or illusion of the devil, or counsel of devil incarnate, but following the will of God and your good desire, and the counsel of the servants of Jesus Christ crucified.

I say no more. I conclude that the letter sent to you does not come from that servant of God named to you, and that it was not written very far away; but I believe that it comes from very near, and from the servants of the devil, who have little fear of God. For in so far as I might believe that it came from that man, I should not hold him a servant of God unless I saw some other proof. Pardon me, father, my over-presumptuous speech. Humbly I ask you to pardon me and give me your benediction. Remain in the holy and sweet grace of God. I pray His infinite Goodness to grant me the favour soon, for His honour, to see you put your feet beyond the threshold in peace, repose, and quiet of soul and body. I beg you, sweet father, to grant me audience when it shall please your Holiness, for I would find myself in your presence before I depart. The time is short: therefore, wherever it may please you, I wish that it might be soon. Sweet Jesus, Jesus Love.

Source: V. D. Scudder, *Saint Catherine of Siena as Seen in her Letters* (1905) pp. 181–185

The papacy was battered throughout the Middle Ages and its entanglement in the defence of the Papal States and the politics of the Germans and the Normans as well as with its own city life, darkened the lives of many popes. Yet, at its ideological centre, the papacy encapsulated the medieval ideal of the primacy of the spiritual and the ultimate freedom of the Church from the restrictions of the state.

Further reading

F. Barlow, *Thomas Becket* (Guild Publishing, London, 1986).

D. A. Bellenger and S. Fletcher, *Princes of the Church: The English Cardinals* (Sutton, Stroud, 2001).

E. Duffy, *Saints and Sinners: A History of the Popes* (Yale University Press/SC4, London, 1997).

J. N. D. Kelly, *The Oxford Dictionary of Popes* (Oxford, University Press, Oxford, 1986).

C. Morris, *The Papal Monarchy: The Western Church from 1050 to 1250* (Clarendon Press, Oxford, 1989).

I. S. Robinson, *The Papacy 1073–1198: Continuity and Innovation* (Cambridge University Press, Cambridge, 1990).

R. W. Southern, *Western Society and the Church in the Middle Ages* (Penguin, Harmondsworth, 1970).

W. Ullmann, *A Short History of the Papacy in the Middle Ages* (Methuen, London, 1972).

4

THE WORLD
OF THE CRUSADES

The Crusades, beginning at the end of the eleventh century and continuing throughout the Middles Ages, showed Christendom at its most united and most complex. The word crusade (French, *croisade*) means 'taking the cross' and in its simplest definition a crusade was a holy war launched at the invitation of the Pope and generally directed towards the Holy Land. Pilgrimage was a characteristically medieval activity: visiting the sites and tombs of the saints, 'the very special dead', as a way of celebrating holy lives and expiating sins. The Crusades were to an extent an armed pilgrimage; a response, in their immediate origin, to the military might of the Seljurk Turks' threatening of the holy places.

The context of the Crusades casts light on many aspects of medieval life. They are part of the economic expansionism of western Europe, a reflection of the process by which Europeans made contact in the Middle Ages with much of the inhabited world, preparing the way for the voyages of discovery of the Renaissance. They showed, too, the growing strength of Islam, stemming from the teachings of the Prophet Mahomet (570–632), which was establishing a power base in the southern Mediterranean, and posing a threat to the Eastern Christian Church centred at Byzantium (or Constantinople). The Eastern and Western parts of Christendom were in long-term dispute and the Crusades revealed the growing hostility of Christendom to all outsiders. It provided an opportunity for the Reform Papacy to flex its muscles and promote the reunification of the Church. It provided, too, a partial solution to the problems of a growing population and a distraction to the feudal disputes and knightly wars raging in western Europe, a problem already addressed by the Church in the tenth-century *Peace of God* and the eleventh-century *Truce of God*.

4.1 *The Truce of God* (1042)

From the hour of vespers on Wednesday until sunrise on Monday let there reign a settled peace and an enduring truce between all Christians, friends and enemies, neighbours and strangers, so that for these four days and five nights at all hours there may be safety for all men, so that they can devote themselves to business without fear of attack. Let those who, having pledged themselves to the truce, break it, be excommunicated, accursed, and abominated, now and forever, unless they repent and make amends. Whosoever shall kill a man on a day of truce shall be banished and driven out of the country, and shall make his way into exile at Jerusalem.

Source: J. Evans, *Monastic Life at Cluny, 910–1157*
(Oxford, 1931) pp. 22–23

Approaches had been made by the Eastern Empire to Pope Gregory VII to give military support to beleaguered Byzantium, but it was Urban II, in 1095, who set the agenda for the Crusade in his sermon preached at Clermont in France which survives in many versions.

৪ঙ 4.2 Urban II's sermon ও৯

Fulcher of Chartres (1059–c. 1127)

'Most beloved brethren: Urged by necessity, I, Urban, by the permission of God chief bishop and prelate over the whole world, have come into these parts as an ambassador with a divine admonition to you, the servants of God. I hoped to find you as faithful and as zealous in the service of God as I had supposed you to be. But if there is in you any deformity or crookedness contrary to God's law, with divine help I will do my best to remove it. For God has put you as stewards over His family to minister to it. Happy indeed will you be if He finds you faithful in your stewardship. You are called shepherds; see that you do not act as hirelings. But be true shepherds, with your crooks always in your hands. Do not go to sleep, but guard on all sides the flock committed to you. For if through your carelessness or negligence a wolf carries away one of your sheep, you will surely lose the reward laid up for you with God. And after you have been bitterly scourged with remorse for your faults, you will be fiercely overwhelmed in hell, the abode of death. For according to the Gospel you are the salt of the earth. But if you fall short in your duty, how, it may be asked, can it be salted? O how great the need of salting! It is indeed necessary for you to correct with the salt of wisdom this foolish people which is so devoted to the pleasures of this world, lest the Lord, when He may wish to speak to them, find them putrefied by their sins, unsalted and stinking. For if He shall find worms, that is, sins, in them, because you have been negligent in your duty, He will command them as worthless to be thrown into the abyss of unclean things. And because you cannot restore to Him His great loss, He will surely condemn you and drive you from His loving presence. But the man who applies this salt should be prudent, provident, modest, learned, peaceable, watchful, pious, just, equitable, and pure. For how can the ignorant teach others? How can the licentious make others modest? And how can the impure make others pure? If anyone hates peace, how can he make others peaceable? Or if anyone has soiled his hands with baseness, how can he cleanse the impurities of another? We read also that if the blind lead the blind, both will fall into the ditch. But first correct yourselves, in order that, free from blame, you may be able to correct those who are subject to you. If you wish to be the friends of God, gladly do the things which you know will please Him. You must especially let all matters that pertain to the church be controlled by the law of the church. And be careful that simony does not take root among you, lest both those who buy and those who sell [church offices] be beaten with the scourges of the Lord through narrow streets and driven into the place of destruction and confusion. Keep the church and the clergy in all its grades entirely free from the secular power. See that the tithes that belong to God are faithfully paid from all the produce of the land; let them not be sold or withheld. If anyone seizes a bishop let him be treated as an outlaw. If anyone seizes or robs monks, or clergymen, or nuns, or their servants, or pilgrims, or merchants, let him be anathema. Let robbers and incendiaries and all their accomplices be expelled from the church and anathematised. If a man who does not give a part of his goods as alms is punished with the damnation of hell, how should he be punished who robs another of his goods? For thus it happened to the rich man in the Gospel; for he was not punished because he had stolen the goods of another, but because he had not used well the things which were his.

'You have seen for a long time the great disorder in the world caused by these crimes. It is so bad in some of your provinces, I am told, and you are so weak in the administration of justice, that one can hardly go along the road by day or night without being attacked by robbers; and whether at home or abroad, one is in danger of being despoiled either by force or fraud. Therefore it is necessary to re-enact the truce, as it is commonly called, which was proclaimed a long time ago by our holy fathers. I exhort and demand that you, each, try hard to have the truce kept in your diocese. And if anyone shall be led by his cupidity or arrogance to break this truce, by the authority of God and with the sanction of this council he shall be anathematised.'

After these and various other matters had been attended to, all who were present, clergy and people, gave thanks to God and agreed to the Pope's proposition. They all faithfully promised to keep the decrees. Then the Pope said that in another part of the world Christianity was suffering from a state of affairs that was worse than the one just mentioned. He continued:

'Although, O sons of God, you have promised more firmly than ever to keep the peace among yourselves and to preserve the rights of the Church, there remains still an important work for you to do. Freshly quickened by the divine correction, you must apply the strength of your righteousness to another matter which concerns you as well as God. For your brethren who live in the East are in urgent need of your help, and you must hasten to give them the aid which has often been promised them. For, as the most of you have heard, the Turks and Arabs have attacked them and have conquered the territory of Romania as far west as the shore of the Mediterranean and the Hellespont, which is called the Arm of St George. They have occupied more and more of the lands of those Christians, and have overcome them in seven battles. They have killed and captured many, and have destroyed the churches and devastated the empire. If you permit them to continue thus for awhile with impunity, the faithful of God will be much more widely attacked by them. On this account I, or rather the *Lord, beseech you as Christ's heralds* to publish this everywhere and to persuade all people of whatever rank, foot-soldiers and knights, poor and rich, to carry aid promptly to those Christians and to destroy that vile race from the lands of our friends. I say this to those who are present; it is meant also for those who are absent. Moreover, Christ commands it.

'All who die by the way, whether by land or by sea, or in battle against the pagans, shall have immediate remission of sins. This I grant them through the power of God with which I am invested. O what a disgrace if such a despised and base race, which worships demons, should conquer a people which has the faith of omnipotent God and is made glorious with the name of Christ! With what reproaches will the Lord overwhelm us if you do not aid those who, with us, profess the Christian religion! Let those who have been accustomed unjustly to wage private warfare against the faithful now go against the infidels and end with victory this war which should have been begun long ago. Let those who, for a long time, have been robbers, now become knights. Let those who have been fighting against their brothers and relatives now fight in a proper way against the barbarians. Let those who have been serving as mercenaries for small pay now obtain the eternal reward. Let those who have been wearing themselves out in both body and soul now work for a double honour. Behold! On this side will be the sorrowful and poor, on that, the rich; on this side, the enemies of the Lord, on that, his friends. Let those who go not put off the journey, but rent their lands and collect money for their expenses; and as soon as winter is over and spring comes, let them eagerly set out on the way with God as their guide.'

Robert the Monk

In 1095 a great council was held in Auvergne, in the city of Clermont. Pope Urban II, accompanied by cardinals and bishops, presided over it. It was made famous by the presence of many bishops and princes from France and Germany. After the council had attended to ecclesiastical matters, the Pope went out into a public square, because no house was able to hold the people, and addressed them in a very persuasive speech, as follows: 'O race of the Franks, O people who live beyond the mountains, O people loved and chosen of God, as is clear from your many deeds, distinguished over all other nations by the situation of your land, your Catholic faith, and your regard for the holy Church, we have a special message and exhortation for you. For we wish you to know what a grave matter has brought us to your country. The sad news has come from Jerusalem and Constantinople that the people of Persia, an accursed and foreign race, enemies of God, a generation that set not their heart aright, and whose spirit was not steadfast with God, have invaded the lands of those Christians and devastated them with the sword, rapine, and fire. Some of the Christians they have carried away as slaves, others they have put to death. The churches they have either destroyed or turned into mosques. They desecrate and overthrow the altars. They circumcise the Christians and pour the blood from the circumcision on the altars or in the baptismal fonts. Some they kill in a horrible way by cutting open the abdomen, taking out a part of the entrails and tying them to a stake; they then beat them and compel them to walk until all their entrails are drawn out and they fall to the ground. Some they use as targets for their arrows. They compel some to stretch out their necks and then they try to see whether they can cut off their heads with one stroke of the sword. It is better to say nothing of their horrible treatment of the women. They have taken from the Greek empire a tract of land so large that it takes more than two months to walk through it. Whose duty is it to avenge this and recover that land, if not yours? For to you more than to other nations the Lord has given the military spirit, courage, agile bodies, and the bravery to strike down those who resist you. Let your minds be stirred to bravery by the deeds of your forefathers, and by the efficiency and greatness of Charles the Great, and of Louis his son, and of the other kings who have destroyed Turkish kingdoms, and established Christianity in their lands. You should be moved especially by the holy grave of our Lord and Saviour which is now held by unclean peoples, and by the holy places which are treated with dishonour and irreverently befouled with their uncleanness.

'O bravest of knights, descendants of unconquered ancestors, do not be weaker than they, but remember their courage. If you are kept back by your love for your children, relatives, and wives, remember what the Lord says in the Gospel: "He that loveth father or mother more than me is not worthy of me"; and "everyone that hath forsaken houses, or brothers, or sisters, or father, or mother, or wife, or children, or lands for my name's sake, shall receive a hundred-fold and shall inherit everlasting life." Let no possessions keep you back, no solicitude for your property. Your land is shut in on all sides by the sea and mountains, and is too thickly populated. There is not much wealth here, and the soil scarcely yields enough to support you. On this account you kill and devour each other, and carry on war and mutually destroy each other. Let your hatred and quarrels cease, your civil wars come to an end, and all your dissensions stop. Set out on the road to the holy sepulchre, take the land from that wicked people, and make it your own. That land which, as the Scripture says, is flowing with milk and honey, God gave to the children of Israel. Jerusalem is the best of all lands; more fruitful than all others, as it were a second Paradise of delights. This land our Saviour made illustrious by his birth, beautiful with his life, and sacred with his suffering; He redeemed it with his death and glorified it with his tomb. This royal city is now held captive by her enemies, and made pagan by those who know not God. She asks and longs to be liberated and does not cease to beg you to come to her aid. She asks aid especially from you because, as I have said, God has given more of the military spirit to you than to other nations. Set out on this journey and you will obtain the remission of your sins and be sure of the incorruptible glory of the Kingdom of Heaven.'

When Pope Urban had said this and much more of the same sort, all who were present were moved to cry out with one accord, 'It is the will of God, it is the will of God.' When the Pope heard this he raised his eyes to heaven and gave thanks to God, and, commanding silence with a gesture of his hand, he said: 'My dear brethren, today there is fulfilled in you that which the Lord says in the Gospel, "Where two or three are gathered together in my name, there am I in the midst." For unless the Lord God had been in your minds you would not all have said the same thing. For although you spoke with many voices, nevertheless it was one and the same thing that made you speak. So I say unto you, God, who put those words into your hearts, has caused you to utter them. Therefore let these words be your battle cry, because God caused you to speak them. Whenever you meet the enemy in battle, you shall all cry out, "It is the will of God, it is the will of God." And we do not command the old or weak to go, or those who cannot bear arms. No women shall go without their husbands, or brothers, or proper companions, for such would be a hindrance rather than a help, a burden rather than an advantage. Let the rich aid the poor and equip them to fighting and take them with them. Clergymen shall not go without the consent of their bishop, for otherwise the journey would be of no value to them. Nor will this pilgrimage be of any benefit to a layman if he goes without the blessing of his priest. Whoever therefore shall determine to make this journey and shall make a vow to God and shall offer himself as a living sacrifice, holy, acceptable to God, shall wear a cross on his brow or on his breast. And when he returns after having fulfilled his vow he shall wear the cross on his back. In this way he will obey the command of the Lord, "Whosoever doth not bear his cross and come after me is not worthy of me".'

When these things had been done, while all prostrated themselves on the earth and beat their breasts, one of the cardinals, named Gregory, made confession for

them, and they were given absolution for all their sins. After the absolution, they
received the benediction and the permission to go home.

Source: O. J. Thatcher, E. H. McNeal (trans.)
A Source Book for Mediaeval History (New York,
1905) pp. 514–521

Urban's sermon, improved by the telling of the Chroniclers, set off the First Crusade in 1097
and led eventually, in 1099, to the capture of Jerusalem by the knights of Christendom.

4.3 The capture of Jerusalem, by an unknown soldier in the army of the Norman Bohemond of Taranto

We attacked the city on Monday (13 June) so fast and furiously that it would have
been taken, if only the ladders had been ready. As it is, we destroyed the lesser wall
and set a ladder against the main wall, and some knights climbed up and attacked
the Saracen defenders with swords and spears. Many of our men, but more of theirs,
found death there.

During this siege we could get no bread for ten days, when a carrier from our ships
arrived; and we suffered from such a burning thirst that we had to trudge up to six
miles in fearful danger to water our horses and other animals. The Pool of Siloam, at
the foot of Mount Sion, relieved us, but the water was sold to us at too high a price.
. . . The Saracens were laying traps for our people and poisoning the cisterns and
springs. They killed and cut in pieces all of us they could find; they hid their animals
in caves and ravines.

Our lords were planning to attack the city with the aid of machines, so that we
could enter it and worship the sepulchre of our Saviour. They built two wooden
castles and many other machines. Duke Godfrey and Count Raymond each
constructed a castle equipped with contrivances, built with wood fetched from afar.

When the Saracens saw our people building these machines, they fortified the city
amazingly, strengthening the defences of the towers overnight. Then our lords,
finding that the weakest side of the city was on the east, got our wooden castle and
machines moved there during Saturday night. They set them up at dawn and through
Sunday, Monday and Tuesday fitted out the castle and manned it. In the southern
sector Count Raymond of Saint-Giles prepared his appliance. By this time we were
suffering so much from thirst that a man could not buy enough water to quench it
even for a denier.

On Wednesday and Thursday we fiercely attacked the city from all sides. But
before the assault the bishops and priests exhorted us in their sermons to make a
procession around the walls of Jerusalem to the glory of God, coupled with prayers,
alms and fasts.

Early in the morning of Friday, we launched a concerted attack on the city but
were not able to damage it and this surprised us and filled us with fear. Then, as the

hour approached when our Lord Jesus Christ consented to suffer the agony of the cross for us, those of our knights who were posted in the wooden castle – Duke Godfrey, his brother Count Eustace and others – fought furiously, and one of our knights, named Litold, got to the top of the wall. As soon as he reached it, the defenders all fled from the walls through the city, and our men pursued and smote them, cutting them down and killing them as far as the Temple of Solomon, where there was such a slaughter that our men waded ankle deep in blood.

Count Raymond on his side had led his army and wooden castle near the wall to the south, but between wall and castle ran a ditch. It was announced that any who carried three stones into the ditch should have a denier, and this took three days and nights to fill, when the castle was brought close to the wall. The defenders fought hard against our men, using fire and stones. The Count, hearing that the Franks were inside the city, shouted to his men, 'What are you waiting for? All the Franks are already inside!'

The governor commanded the Tower of David, but surrendered to the Count and opened the gate where the pilgrims used to pay tribute. Once inside the city our pilgrims pursued the Saracens right up to the Temple of Solomon, slaughtering all the way. There the Saracens joined up their forces and fought our people most furiously all through that day, so that the whole Temple flowed with their blood. After crushing the pagans our men captured the Temple and a great number of men and women, whom they killed or spared as they thought fit. A large group of the pagans of both sexes had taken refuge on the roof, and Tancred and Gaston of Béarn gave them their banners. Soon the crusaders were running all over the city, seizing gold, silver, horses and mules, and plundering the houses, which were crammed with treasures.

Then, full of gladness, weeping for joy, our people went to worship the Sepulchre of our Saviour Jesus and pay their thanks to him. Next morning they climbed to the roof of the Temple, attacked both the men and women of the Saracens and, drawing swords, cut off their heads. Some threw themselves down from the roof. When he saw this, Tancred was filled with indignation . . . .

Orders were given that all the dead Saracens should be thrown out of the city because of the horrible stench, for almost the whole city was filled with their corpses. The living Saracens dragged out the dead, and heaped them almost as high as the houses in front of the gates. No one had ever seen, no one had ever heard of such a butchery of pagans; funeral pyres were set up like milestones – God alone knows how many.

> **Source: D. Ayerst and A. Fisher, *Records of**
> ***Christianity*, pp. 114–117**

Disputes among the crusading nations were present from the beginning as also were popular crusading movements based on enthusiastic piety and rabble-rousing. Alongside the Knights Crusade of 1097–1099 there ran a parallel Crusade inspired by preachers like Peter the Hermit.

4.4 Guibert, Abbot of Nogent (1053–1124)

As far as I know, Peter came from the city of Amiens. He lived as a hermit in a monk's habit somewhere in the north of France and when he left there — for what purpose I do not know — we saw him going through towns and cities under the pretext of preaching. He was surrounded by greater crowds, received richer gifts, and was more famed and praised for holiness than anyone I can remember. From the riches he received he gave generously to the poor, and reclaimed prostitutes by providing them — not without dowries — with husbands. With amazing authority he everywhere restored peace and concord in place of strife. All he did or said was accepted as little short of divine. Folk went so far as to pull hairs from his mule as relics — not because they loved truth but because it was something new. He wore a plain woollen shirt with a hood and over this an ankle-length sleeveless cloak, and his feet were bare. He lived on wine and fish and seldom or never ate bread.

Such a burning zeal inflamed the poor that no one paused to consider his lack of means, nor if it was wise to leave his house, vineyards or fields, but each sold his best goods for a price less than if he had been a prisoner in cruel captivity and forced to get himself a quick ransom . . . you could hear of seven sheep sold for five deniers, an astonishing example of the sudden and unexpected drop in all values . . .

You could see astounding things which could only make you laugh: poor people shoeing their oxen as though they were horses, harnessing them to two-wheeled carts, on which they piled their few provisions and small children and led them away. And when these little children saw a castle or a town, they were eager to know whether that was the Jerusalem they were going to.

Though the Apostolic See appealed especially to the Frankish nation, there was almost no Christian people who did not pour out in force and try to join the Franks and share their dangers, thinking that they owed God a like allegiance. You could see crowds of Scots, who were savages at home, unskilled in the arts of war, bare-legged, wearing cloaks of shaggy skins, with their provisions slung in sacks over their shoulders, hurrying from their mist-shrouded homeland. Many, whose arms are absurd compared with ours, came to offer us the aid of their faith and vows. God is my witness that I heard of men who had landed at one of our ports from some barbarous nation unknown to me, who spoke a language so unknown that no one could understand them. They laid their fingers over one another in the form of a cross, to show by signs instead of words that they wished to further the cause of faith.

Source: D. Ayerst and A. Fisher, *Records of Christianity*, pp. 111–113

Following the capture of Jerusalem, a Latin kingdom was established in the city and European colonists settled in the Holy Land. The later Crusades, increasingly unsuccessful, were often aimed at maintaining this tenuous presence. The Second (1147–1149), Third (1189–1192) and Fourth (1202–1204) Crusades showed the tenacity of the movement but also revealed the tendency to violence and disagreement between the combatants. While the freedom of access to the Holy Places remained a priority the identity of the enemy became more ambiguous. Jews made an easy target and the Crusades, too, were increasingly hostile to the Greek Christians.

4.5 Geoffroy de Villehardouin: *The Conquest of Constantinople*

Now the Greeks, who were very disloyal, still nourished treachery in their hearts. They perceived at that time that the Franks were so scattered over the land that each had his own matters to attend to. So they thought they could the more easily betray them. They took envoys therefore privily, from all the cities in the land, and sent them to Johannizza, the King of Wallachia and Bulgaria, who was still at war with them as he had been aforetime. And they told Johannizza they would make him emperor, and give themselves wholly to him, and slay all the Franks. So they swore that they would obey him as their lord, and he swore that he would defend them as though they were his own people. Such was the oath sworn.

Uprising of the Greeks at Demotica and Adrianople: Their Defeat at Arcadiopolis

At that time there happened a great misfortune at Constantinople, for Count Hugh of St Paul, who had long been in bed, sick of the gout, made an end and died; and this caused great sorrow, and was a great mishap, and much was he bewept by his men and by his friends. He was buried with great honour in the church of our Lord St George of Mangana.

Now Count Hugh in his lifetime had held a castle called Demotica, which was very strong and rich, and he had therein some of his knights and sergeants. The Greeks, who had made oath to the King of Wallachia that they would kill and betray the Franks, betrayed them in that castle, and slaughtered many and took many captive. Few escaped, and those who escaped went flying to a city called Adrianople, which the Venetians held at that time.

Not long after, the Greeks in Adrianople rose in arms; and such of our men as were therein, and had been set to guard it, came out in great peril, and left the city. Tidings thereof came to the Emperor Baldwin of Constantinople, who had but few men with him, he and Count Lewis of Blois. Much were they then troubled and dismayed. And thenceforth, from day to day, did evil tidings begin to come to the that everywhere the Greeks were rising, and that wherever the Greeks found F occupying the land, they killed them.

And those who had left Adrianople, the Venetians and the others wh came to a city called Tzurulum, that belonged to the Emperor Bal found William of Blanvel, who kept the place for the emper comfort that he gave them, and because he accompanied the he could, they turned back to a city, some twelve leagues di which belonged to the Venetians, and they found it empty. put a garrison there.

On the third day the Greeks of the land gathered together, and came at the break of dawn before Arcadiopolis; and then began, from all sides, an assault, great and marvellous. The Franks defended themselves right well, and opened their gates, and issued forth, attacking vigorously. As was God's will, the Greeks were discomfited, and those on our side began to cut them down and to slay them, and then chased them for a league, and killed many, and captured many horses and much other spoil.

So the Franks returned with great joy to Arcadiopolis, and sent tidings of their victory to the Emperor Baldwin, in Constantinople, who was much rejoiced thereat. Nevertheless they dared not hold the city of Arcadiopolis, but left it on the morrow, and abandoned it, and returned to the city of Tzurulum. Here they remained in very great doubt, for they misdoubted the Greeks who were in the city as much as those who were without, because the Greeks in the city had also taken part in the oath sworn to the King of Wallachia, and were bound to betray the Franks. And many there were who did not dare to abide in Tzurulum, but made their way back to Constantinople.

Then the Emperor Baldwin and the Doge of Venice, and Count Lewis took counsel together, for they saw they were losing the whole land. And they settled that the emperor should tell his brother Henry, who was at Adramittium, to abandon whatsoever conquests he had made, and come to their succour. Count Lewis, on his side, sent to Payen of Orleans, and Peter of Bracieux, who were at Lopadium, and to all the people that were with them, telling them to leave whatsoever conquests they had made, save Piga only, that lay on the sea, where they were to set a garrison – the smallest they could – and that the remainder were to come to their succour.

The emperor directed Macaire of Sainte-Menehould, and Matthew of Wallincourt, and Robert of Ronsoi, who had some hundred knights with them in Nicomedia, to leave Nicomedia and come to their succour.

By command of the Emperor Baldwin, Geoffry of Villehardonim, Marshal of Champagne and of Roumania, issued from Constantinople, with Manasses of l'Isle, and with as many men as they could collect, and these were few enough, seeing that all the land was being lost. And they rode to the city of Tzurulum, which is distant a three days' journey. There they found William of Blanvel, and those that were with him, in very great fear, and much were these reassured at their coming. At that place they remained four days. The Emperor Baldwin sent after Geoffry the Marshal as many as he could, of such people as were coming into Constantinople, so that on the fourth day there were at Tzurulum eighty knights.

Then did Geoffry the Marshal move forward, and Manasses of l'Isle, and their people, and they rode on, and came to the city of Arcadiopolis, and quartered themselves therein. There they remained a day, and then moved to a city called Bulgaropolis. The Greeks had avoided this city and the Franks quartered themselves therein. The following day they rode to a city called Neguise, which was very fair and strong, and well furnished with all good things. And they found that the Greeks had abandoned it, and were all gone to Adrianople. Now Adrianople was distant nine French leagues, and therein were gathered all the great multitude of the Greeks. And the Franks decided that they should wait where they were till the coming of the Emperor Baldwin.

ow does this book relate a great marvel: for Renier of Trit, who was at Finepopolis, od nine days' journey from Constantinople, with at least one hundred and twenty nts, was deserted by Renier his son, and Giles his brother, and James of Bondies, who was his nephew, and Achard of Verdun, who had his daughter to wife. And they had taken some thirty of his knights, and thought to come to Constantinople; and they had left him, you must know, in great peril. But they found the country raised against them, and were discomfited; and the Greeks took them, and afterwards handed them over to the King of Wallachia, who had their heads cut off. And you must know that they were but little pitied by the people, because they had behaved in such evil sort to one whom they were bound to treat quite otherwise.

And when the other knights of Renier de Trit saw that he was thus abandoned by those who were much more bound to him than themselves, they felt the less shame, and some eighty together left him, and departed by another way. So Renier of Trit remained among the Greeks with very few men, for he had not more than fifteen knights at Philippopolis and Stanimac – which is a very strong castle which he held, and where he was for a long time besieged.

Source: F. Marzials (trans.) *Joinville and Villehardouin,*
Chronicles of the Crusades (1908) pp. 87–91

As early as 1204 the Crusaders sacked Byzantium.

4.6 An account of the sack and the desecration of Hagia Sophia, 1204

3

How shall I begin to tell of the deeds wrought by these nefarious men! Alas, the images, which ought to have been adored, were trodden under foot! Alas, the relics of the holy martyrs were thrown into unclean places! Then was seen what one shudders to hear, namely, the divine body and blood of Christ was spilled upon the ground or thrown about. They snatched the precious reliquaries, thrust into their bosoms the ornaments which these contained, and used the broken remnants for pans and drinking cups – precursors of Antichrist, authors and heralds of his nefarious deeds which we momentarily expect. Manifestly, indeed, by that race then, just as formerly, Christ was robbed and insulted and His garments were divided by lot; only one thing was lacking, that His side, pierced by a spear, should pour rivers of divine blood on the ground.

Nor can the violation of the Great Church be listened to with equanimity. For the sacred altar, formed of all kinds of precious materials and admired by the whole world, was broken into bits and distributed among the soldiers, as was all the other sacred wealth of so great and infinite splendour.

When the sacred vases and utensils of unsurpassable art and grace and rare material, and the fine silver, wrought with gold, which encircled the screen of the tribunal and the *ambo*, of admirable workmanship, and the door and many other ornaments, were to be borne away as booty, mules and saddled horses were led to the very sanctuary of the temple. Some of these which were unable to keep their footing on the splendid and slippery pavement, were stabbed when they fell, so that the sacred pavement was polluted with blood and filth.

4

Nay more, a certain harlot, a sharer in their guilt, a minister of the furies, a servant of the demons, a worker of incantations and poisonings, insulting Christ, sat in the patriarch's seat, singing an obscene song and dancing frequently. Nor, indeed, were these crimes committed and others left undone, on the ground that these were of lesser guilt, the others of greater. But with one consent all the most heinous sins and crimes were committed by all with equal zeal. Could those, who showed so great madness against God Himself, have spared the honourable matrons and maidens or the virgins consecrated to God? Nothing was more difficult and laborious than to soften by prayers, to render benevolent, these wrathful barbarians, vomiting forth bile at every unpleasing word, so that nothing failed to inflame their fury. Whoever attempted it was derided as insane and a man of intemperate language. Often they drew their daggers against any one who opposed them at all or hindered their demands. No one was without a share in the grief. In the alleys, in the streets, in the temples, complaints, weeping, lamentations, grief, the groaning of men, the shrieks of women, wounds, rape, captivity, the separation of those most closely united. Nobles wandered about ignominiously, those of venerable age in tears, the rich in poverty. Thus it was in the streets, on the corners, in the temple, in the dens, for no place remained unassailed or defended the suppliants. All places everywhere were filled full of all kinds of crime. Oh, immortal God, how great the afflictions of the men, how great the distress!

> Source: *Translations and Reprints from Original Sources of European History* (Philadelphia, 1894–1900) III, 1 (v. 3), pp. 15–16

Some Western leaders sought accommodation with the followers of Islam, notably Frederick II, the most cosmopolitan of monarchs.

4.7 Letter of Frederick II to Henry II of England (1279)

Frederick, by the grace of God, the august emperor of the Romans, king of Jerusalem and Sicily, to his well-beloved friend Henry, king of the English, health and sincere affection.

Let all rejoice and exult in the Lord, and let those who are correct in heart glorify Him, who, to make known His power, does not make boast of horses and chariots, but has now gained glory for Himself, in the scarcity of His soldiers, that all may know and understand that He is glorious in His majesty, terrible in His magnificence, and wonderful in His plans on the sons of men, changing seasons at will, and bringing the hearts of different nations together; for in these few days, by a miracle rather than by strength, that business has been brought to a conclusion, which for a length of time past many chiefs and rulers of the world amongst the multitude of nations, have never been able till now to accomplish by force, however great, nor by fear.

Not, therefore, to keep you in suspense by a long account, we wish to inform your holiness, that we, firmly putting our trust in God, and believing that Jesus Christ, His Son, in whose service we have so devotedly exposed our bodies and lives, would not abandon us in these unknown and distant countries, but would at least give us wholesome advice and assistance for His honour, praise, and glory, boldly in the name set forth from Acre on the fifteenth day of the month of November last past and arrived safely at Joppa, intending to rebuild the castle at that place with proper strength, that afterwards the approach of the holy city of Jerusalem might be not only easier, but also shorter and more safe for us as well as for all Christians. When, therefore, we were, in the confidence of our trust in God, engaged at Joppa, and superintending the building of the castle and the cause of Christ, as necessity required and as was our duty, and whilst all our pilgrims were busily engaged in these matters, several messengers often passed to and fro between us and the sultan of Babylon; for he and another sultan, called Xaphat, his brother, were with a large army at the city of Gaza, distant about one day's journey from us; in another direction, in the city of Sichen, which is commonly called Neapolis, and situated in the plains, the sultan of Damascus, his nephew, was staying with an immense number of knights and soldiers also about a day's journey from us and the Christians.

And whilst the treaty was in progress between the parties on either side of the restoration of the Holy Land, at length Jesus Christ, the Son of God, beholding from on high our devoted endurance and patient devotion to His cause, in His merciful compassion of us, at length brought it about that the sultan of Babylon restored to us the holy city, the place where the feet of Christ trod, and where the true worshippers adore the Father in spirit and in truth. But that we may inform you of the particulars of this surrender each as they happened, be it known to you that not only is the body of the aforesaid city restored to us, but also the whole of the country extending from thence to the sea-coast near the castle of Joppa, so that for the future pilgrims will have free passage and a safe return to and from the sepulchre; provided, however, that the Saracens of that part of the country, since they hold the temple in great veneration, may come there as often as they choose in the character of pilgrims, to worship according to their custom, and that we shall henceforth permit them to come, however, only as many as we may choose to allow, and without arms, nor are they to dwell in the city, but outside, and as soon as they have paid their devotions they are to depart. Moreover, the city of Bethlehem is restored to us, and all the country between Jerusalem and that city; as also the city of Nazareth, and all the country between Acre and that city; the whole of the district of Turon, which is very extensive, and very advantageous to the Christians; the city of Sidon, too, is given up to us with the whole plain and its appurtenances, which will be the more acceptable to the Christians the more advantageous it has till now appeared to be to the Saracens, especially as there is a good harbour there, and from there great quantities of arms and necessaries might be carried to the city of Damascus, and often from Damascus to Babylon. And although according to our treaty we are allowed to rebuild the city of Jerusalem in as good state as it has ever been, and also the castles of Joppa, Cesarea,

Sidon, and that of St Mary of the Teutonic order, which the brothers of that order have begun to build in the mountainous district of Acre, and which it has never been allowed the Christians to do during any former truce; nevertheless the sultan is not allowed, till the end of the truce between him and us, which is agreed on for ten years, to repair or rebuild any fortresses or castles.

And so on Sunday, the eighteenth day of February last past, which is the day on which Christ, the Son of God, rose from the dead, and which, in memory of His resurrection, is solemnly cherished and kept holy by all Christians in general throughout the world, this treaty of peace was confirmed by oath between us. Truly then on us and on all does that day seem to have shone favourably, in which the angels sing in praise of God, 'Glory to God on high, and on earth peace, and good-will toward men.' And in acknowledgement of such great kindness and of such an honour, which, beyond our deserts and contrary to the opinion of many, God has mercifully conferred on us, to the lasting renown of His compassion, and that in His holy place we might personally offer to Him the burnt offering of our lips, be it known to you that on the seventeenth day of the month of March of this second indiction, we, in company with all the pilgrims who had with us faithfully followed Christ, the Son of God, entered the holy city of Jerusalem, and after worshipping at the holy sepulchre, we, as being a Catholic emperor, on the following day, wore the crown, which Almighty God provided for us from the throne of His majesty, when of His especial grace, He exalted us on high amongst the princes of the world; so that whilst we have supported the honour of this high dignity, which belongs to us by right of sovereignty, it is more and more evident to all that the hand of the Lord hath done all this; and since His mercies are over all His works, let the worshippers of the orthodox faith henceforth know and relate it far and wide throughout the world, that He, who is blessed for ever, has visited and redeemed His people, and has raised up the horn of salvation for us in the house of His servant David. And before we leave the city of Jerusalem, we have determined magnificently to rebuild it, and its towers and walls, and we intend so to arrange matters that, during our absence, there shall be no less care and diligence used in the business, than if we were present in person. In order that this our present letter may be full of exultation throughout, and so a happy end correspond with its happy beginning, and rejoice your royal mind, we wish it to be known to you our ally, that the said sultan is bound to restore to us all those captives whom he did not in accordance with the treaty made between him and the Christians deliver up at the time when he lost Damietta some time since, and also the others who have been since taken.

Given at the holy city of Jerusalem, on the seventeenth day of the month of March, in the year of our Lord one thousand two hundred and twenty-nine.

Source: J. A. Giles (trans.) *Roger of Wendover, Flowers of History: Comprising the History of England from the Descent of the Saxons to AD 1235*, 2 vols (1849) Vol. II, pp. 522–524

However, the Latin Patriarch, in 1221, made it clear that Frederick's *détente* was not in concert with the crusading idea.

ɞ 4.8 Letter from Gerold, Patriarch of Jerusalem, to ઝ All the Faithful (1229)

Gerold, patriarch of Jerusalem, to all the faithful – greeting.

If it should be fully known how astonishing, nay rather, deplorable, the conduct of the emperor has been in the eastern lands from beginning to end, to the great detriment of the cause of Jesus Christ and to the great injury of the Christian faith, from the sole of his foot to the top of his head no common sense would be found in him. For he came, excommunicated, without money and followed by scarcely forty knights, and hoped to maintain himself by spoiling the inhabitants of Syria. He first came to Cyprus and there most discourteously seized that nobleman J. of Ibelin and his sons, whom he had invited to his table under pretext of speaking of the affairs of the Holy Land. Next the king, whom he had invited to meet him, he retained almost as a captive. He thus by violence and fraud got possession of the kingdom.

After these achievements he passed over into Syria. Although in the beginning he promised to do marvels, and although in the presence of the foolish he boasted loudly, he immediately sent to the sultan of Babylon to demand peace. This conduct rendered him despicable in the eyes of the sultan and his subjects, especially after they had discovered that he was not at the head of a numerous army, which might have to some extent added weight to his words. Under the pretext of defending Joppa, he marched with the Christian army towards that city, in order to be nearer the sultan and in order to be able more easily to treat of peace or obtain a truce. What more shall I say? After long and mysterious conferences, and without having consulted any one who lived in the country, he suddenly announced one day that he had made peace with the sultan. No one saw the text of the peace or truce when the emperor took the oath to observe the articles which were agreed upon. Moreover, you will be able to see clearly how great the malice was and how fraudulent the tenor of certain articles of the truce which we have decided to send to you. The emperor, for giving credit to his word, wished as a guarantee only the word of the sultan, which he obtained. For he said, among other things, that the holy city was surrendered to him. He went thither with the Christian army on the eve of the Sunday when *Oculi mei* is sung. The Sunday following, without any fitting ceremony and although excommunicated, in the chapel of the sepulchre of our Lord, to the manifest prejudice of his honour and of the imperial dignity, he put the diadem upon his forehead, although the Saracens still held the temple of the Lord and Solomon's temple, and although they proclaimed publicly as before the law of Mohammed – to the great confusion and chagrin of the pilgrims.

This same prince, who had previously very often promised to fortify Jerusalem, departed in secrecy from the city at dawn on the following Monday. The Hospitallers and the Templars promised solemnly and earnestly to aid him with all their forces and their advice, if he wanted to fortify the city, as he had promised. But the emperor, who did not care to set affairs right, and who saw that there was no certainty in what had been done, and that the city in the state in which it had been surrendered to him could be neither defended nor fortified, was content with the name of surrender, and on the same day hastened with his family to Joppa. The pilgrims who had entered Jerusalem with the emperor, witnessing his departure, were unwilling to remain behind.

The following Sunday when *Laetare Jerusalem* is sung, he arrived at Acre. There in order to seduce the people and to obtain their favour, he granted them a certain privilege. God knows the motive which made him act thus, and his subsequent conduct will make it known. As, moreover, the passage was near, and as all pilgrims, humble and great, after having visited the Holy Sepulchre, were preparing to with-draw, as if they had accomplished their pilgrimage, because no truce had been concluded with the sultan of Damascus, we, seeing that the holy land was already deserted and abandoned by the pilgrims, in our council formed the plan of retaining soldiers, for the common good, by means of the alms given by the king of France of holy memory.

When the emperor heard of this, he said to us that he was astonished at this, since he had concluded a truce with the sultan of Babylon. We replied to him that the knife was still in the wound, since there was not a truce or peace with the sultan of Damascus, nephew of the aforesaid sultan and opposed to him, adding that even if the sultan of Babylon was unwilling, the former could still do us much harm. The emperor replied, saying that no soldiers ought to be retained in his kingdom without his advice and consent, as he was now king of Jerusalem. We answered to that, that in the matter in question, as well as in all of a similar nature, we were very sorry not to be able, without endangering the salvation of our souls, to obey his wishes, because he was excommunicated. The emperor made no response to us, but on the following day he caused the pilgrims who inhabited the city to be assembled outside by the public crier, and by special messengers he also convoked the prelates and the monks. Addressing them in person, he began to complain bitterly of us, by heaping up false accusations. Then turning his remarks to the venerable master of the Templars he publicly attempted to tarnish severely the reputation of the latter, by various vain speeches, seeking thus to throw upon others the responsibility for his own faults which were now manifest, and adding at last, that we were maintain-ing troops with the purpose of injuring him. After that he ordered all foreign soldiers, of all nations, if they valued their lives and property, not to remain in the land from that day on, and ordered count Thomas, whom he intended to leave as bailiff of the country, to punish with stripes any one who was found lingering, in order that the punishment of one might serve as an example to many. After doing all this he withdrew, and would listen to no excuse or answers to the charges which he had so shamefully made. He determined immediately to post some cross-bowmen at the gates of the city, ordering them to allow the Templars to go out but not to return. Next he fortified with cross-bows the churches and other elevated positions, and especially those which commanded the communications between the Templars and ourselves. And you may be sure that he never showed as much animosity and hatred against Saracens.

For our part, seeing his manifest wickedness, we assembled all the prelates and all the pilgrims, and menaced with excommunication all those who should aid the emperor with their advice or their services against the Church, the Templars, the other monks of the holy land, or the pilgrims.

The emperor was more and more irritated, and immediately caused all the passages to be guarded more strictly, refused to allow any kind of provisions to be brought to us or to the members of our party, and placed everywhere cross-bowmen and archers, who attacked severely us, the Templars and the pilgrims. Finally to fill the measure of his malice, he caused some Dominicans and Minorites who had come on Palm Sunday to the proper places to announce the Word of God, to be torn from the pulpit, to be thrown down and dragged along the ground and whipped throughout the city, as if they had been robbers. Then seeing that he did not obtain what he had hoped from the above-mentioned siege, he treated of peace. We replied to him that we would not hear of peace until he sent away the cross-bowmen and other troops, until he had returned our property to us, until finally he had restored all things to the condition and freedom in which they were on that day when he entered Jerusalem. He finally ordered what we wanted to be done, but it was not executed. Therefore we placed the city under interdict.

The emperor, realising that his wickedness could have no success, was unwilling to remain any longer in the country. And, as if he would have liked to ruin everything, he ordered the cross-bows and engines of war, which for a long time had been kept at Acre for the defence of the Holy Land, to be secretly carried onto his vessels. He also sent away several of them to the sultan of Babylon, as his dear friend. He sent a troop of soldiers to Cyprus to levy heavy contributions of money there, and, what appeared to us more astonishing, he destroyed the galleys which he was not able to take with him. Having learned this, we resolved to reproach him with it, but shunning the remonstrance and the correction, he entered a galley secretly, by an obscure way, on the day of the Apostles St Philip and St James, and hastened to reach the island of Cyprus, without saying adieu to any one, leaving Joppa destitute; and may he never return!

Very soon the bailiffs of the above-mentioned sultan shut off all departure from Jerusalem for the Christian poor and the Syrians, and many pilgrims died thus on the road.

This is what the emperor did, to the detriment of the Holy Land and of his own soul, as well as many other things which are known and which we leave to others to relate. May the merciful God deign to soften the results! Farewell.

> Source: *Translations and Reprints from Original Sources of European History* (Philadelphia, 1894–1900) I, 4, (vi. 2) pp. 27–31

The ideal crusader king was probably Louis IX, St Louis.

---

৫ 4.9 Preparations for a crusade (1244–1248) ৩

XXIV

1244. After these things aforesaid it befell, as God willed, that a great sickness laid hold on the King in Paris, whereby he was in such evil case that, as they tell, one of the ladies who tended him wished to draw the sheet over his face, and said that he was dead. And another lady, that was the other side the bed, would not suffer it; but said that the soul was still in his body. And as he heard the contention of these two ladies, Our Lord worked upon him and straightway gave him health; for before he had been dumb and could not speak. And so soon as he was able to speak, he asked that they should give him the Cross, which they did. When the Queen, his mother heard tell that speech had come back to him she was in such great joy as might be. And when she knew that he had taken the Cross, as he himself used to tell, she grieved as much as if she saw him dead. After he had taken the Cross, so too did Robert Count of Artois, Alfonse Count of Poitiers, Charles Count of Anjou, who was after King of Sicily, all three brothers of the King; and Hugh Duke of Burgundy took the Cross, William Count of Flanders, brother of Count Guy of Flanders now lately dead, the good old Hugh Count of Saint Pol, my lord Walter his nephew, who bore himself passing well oversea, and would have been of much avail had he lived. And there took the Cross likewise the Count of La Marche and my lord Hugh the Black his son, the Count of Sarrebruck, my lord Gobert of Apremont his brother, in whose company I, John, Lord of Joinville, crossed the sea in a ship that we hired, for we were cousins; and we crossed all told twenty knights, of whom he had command over nine and I over nine.

XXV

1248. At Easter, in the year of grace in which our age stood at a thousand two hundred and forty-eight, did I summon my men and my vassals to Joinville; and on the eve of that Easter, when all the folk that I had summoned had come, was born my son John, Lord of Ancerville, by my first wife, who was sister to the Count of Grandpre. All that week did we dance and make holiday, for my brother, the Lord of Vaucouleurs, and all the other rich men who were present, gave feasts one after the other on the Monday, the Tuesday, the Wednesday, and the Thursday.

On the Friday I said to them: 'My lords, I am going away beyond the seas, and I know not if I shall return. Come forward; and if I have done you wrong in aught, I will right it, one by one, as my custom is to any that has aught to ask of me or of my folk.' So I made matters right with each, according to the opinion of all the common people of my land; and so that I should have no weight with them, I went from the council and accepted whatsoever they rehearsed without debate. Since I was not of a mind to take away any money to which I had no right, I went to Metz in Lorraine to leave great part of my lands in pawn. And I would have you know that on the day that I left our country to go to the Holy Land I did not hold five hundred crowns a year in land, for Madam my mother yet lived; and so went I forth at the head of nine knights and with two others that were knights banneret. These things do I recount to you, because if God had not succoured me, Who never failed me, I should scarcely have had enough for so long as the space of six years that I tarried in the Holy Land.

At the time I was making ready to go, John, Lord of Apremont, and Count of Sarrebruck in right of his wife, sent to me and told me that he had all his affairs set in order to go oversea, at the head of nine knights; and asked me if I were willing that we should hire a ship between us; and I consented thereto; and his folk and mine hired a ship at Marseilles.

XXVI

The King summoned all his barons to Paris and made them take an oath that they would do fealty and give loyalty to his children, if aught befell him on the way. He asked it of me likewise; but I would take no oath for I was not his liegeman.

As I went thither, I found three men that a clerk had slain, dead on a wagon; and they told me that they were taking them to the King. When I heard this, I sent a squire of mine after them to know what had befallen. And my squire whom I sent said that the King, when he came out of chapel, went into the foreporch to see the dead men, and asked the Provost of Paris how it had chanced.

And the Provost told him that the dead were three of his sergeants of the Châtelet, and that they used to go through the streets outside the walls to steal from folk. And he said to the King that 'they found this clerk that ye see here, and took from him all his habit. The clerk went in naught but his shirt into his house, and took his crossbow, and had a child bring him his falchion. When he saw the sergeants he cried out to them and told them that they were to die there. The clerk bent his bow and drew it, and struck one of them through the heart; and the two took to flight; and the clerk took the falchion that the child held, and gave them chase by the light of the moon that was clear and full. One thought to pass behind a hedge in a garden, and the clerk struck him with the falchion,' said the Provost, 'and cut off all his leg in such wise that it held only by the boot, as ye see. The clerk took up the chase of the other, who thought to get into a strange house, where the folk were not yet abed; and the clerk struck him with the falchion on the head, so that he split it to the teeth, as ye may see,' said the Provost to the King. 'Sir,' said he, 'the clerk displayed his deed to the neighbours in the street, and then he went to put himself in your prison; and, Sir, I have brought him to you, that ye may do your will with him; and here he is.'

'Sir Clerk,' said the King, 'ye have lost your priesthood by your prowess; and for your prowess I will keep you in my pay, and ye shall come with me oversea. And I would have you know that I do this unto you because I wish that my people should see that I will not uphold them in their evildoings.' When the people that were assembled there heard this, they cried upon Our Lord and prayed that God should give him good life and long and bring him back in joy and health.

XXVII

After these things I came back into our country and we arranged, the Count of Sarrebruck and I, that we should send our baggage in wagons to Auxonne, to be put on the Saône, to go to Aries from the Saône to the Rhone.

Source: N. de Wailly and J. Evans (trans.) *Joinville, The History of St Louis* (Oxford, 1938) pp. 33–36

Seen from the Arab point of view the Franks (as the Crusaders under French leadership were called) not only fell far short of the kingly, chivalric ideal but also showed signs of local assimilation.

---

২৯ 4.10 An appreciation of the Frankish character: ২৯ Usmah ibn Munqidh, *The Book of Reflections*

A Frank Domesticated in Syria Abstains from Eating Pork

Among the Franks are those who have become acclimatised and have associated long with the Muslims. These are much better than the recent comers from the Frankish lands. But they constitute the exception and cannot be treated as a rule. Here is an illustration. I dispatched one of my men to Antioch on business. There was in Antioch at that time al-Ra'is Theodoros Sophianos, to whom I was bound by mutual ties of amity. His influence in Antioch was supreme. One day he said to my man, 'I am invited by a friend of mine who is a Frank. You should come with me so that you may see their fashions.' My man related the story in the following words:

> I went along with him and we came to the home of a knight who belonged to the old category of knights who came with the early expeditions of the Franks. He had been by that time stricken off the register and exempted from service, and possessed in Antioch an estate on the income of which he lived. The knight presented an excellent table, with food extraordinarily clean and delicious. Seeing me abstaining from food, he said, 'Eat, be of good cheer! I never eat Frankish dishes, but I have Egyptian women cooks and never eat except their cooking. Besides, pork never enters my home.'
>
> I ate, but guardedly, and after that we departed. As I was passing in the market place, a Frankish woman all of a sudden hung to my clothes and began to mutter words in their language, and I could not understand what she was saying. This made me immediately the centre of a big crowd of Franks. I was convinced that death was at hand. But all of a sudden that same knight approached. On seeing me, he came and said to that woman, 'What is the matter between you and this Muslim?' She replied, 'This is he who has killed my brother Hurso.' This Hurso was a knight in Afamiyah who was killed by someone of the army of Hamah. The Christian knight shouted at her saying, 'This is a bourgeois [i.e. a merchant] who neither fights nor attends a fight.' He also yelled at the people who had assembled, and they all dispersed. Then he took me by the hand and went away. Thus the effect of that meal was my deliverance from certain death.

> **Source: P. K. Hitti (trans.) *The Memoirs of An Arab–Syrian Gentleman* (Beirut, 1964) pp. 163–164**

The Crusades led to the formation of a number of religious orders which combined military and monastic ideals. The Knights of the Hospital of St John of Jerusalem, the Hospitallers, dating from First Crusade, were established to assist sick pilgrims. The Knights of the Temple or Templars, founded in 1118, were more warlike, dedicated to protecting pilgrims. Their rule of life owed its inspiration to St Bernard of Clairvaux who was an eloquent advocate of the Crusades.

---

৪৯ 4.11 *The Rule of the Order of the Knights Templar* ৵৪

How the Brothers Form the Line of March

156. When the convent wishes to ride, the brothers should not saddle up, nor load the baggage, nor mount, nor move from their places unless the Marshal has the order called or commands it; but tent pegs, empty flasks, the camping axe, the camping rope and fishing net may be put on the horses before the order to load the baggage is given. And if any brother wishes to speak to the Marshal he should go to him on foot, and when he has spoken to him he should return to his place; and he should not leave his place before the order to mount is given, for as long as his companions are in camp.

157. When the Marshal has the order to mount called, the brothers should look over their campsite so that nothing of their equipment is left behind, and then they should mount and go quietly with their troop, at a walk or amble, their squires behind them, and position themselves in the line of march if they find an empty place for themselves and their equipment; and if he does not find it empty, he may ask the brother who has taken it, who may give it to him if he wishes, but need not if he does not wish to. And when they have joined the line of march, each brother should give his squire and his equipment a place in front of him. And if it is night-time, he should keep silent except for any important task, and then he should go quietly and in silence within the line of march until the next day when they have heard or said prime, in the manner which is established in the house, and for as long as the camp lasts. The brother who has joined the line of march may give the place in front of him to another who has not joined it, but no one should give up the place behind him; and then neither of these two brothers, neither the one who gave the place nor the one who took it in this way, may give it to another in front or behind.

158. And if two brothers wish to talk to one another, the one in front should go to the one behind in such a way that their equipment is in front of them; and when they have spoken, each should return to his troop. And if any brother rides beside the line of march for his own purposes, he should come and go downwind; for if he went upwind, the dust would harm and annoy the line of march. And if anything happens so that a brother cannot nor knows how to join his troop, one of the brothers should give him a place in front of him until daylight, and then he should return to his troop as best and as quickly as he can. And this also applies to the squires. And no brother should ride beside the line of march, nor two, nor three, nor four or more, either for pleasure or to speak, rather they should go behind their equipment and each one keep to his troop quietly and in silence.

159. No brother should leave his troop to water his horses or for anything else, without permission; and if they pass by running water in peaceful territory, they may water their horses if they wish; but they may not endanger the line of march. And if they pass by water whilst on reconnaissance, and the Standard Bearer passes by without watering his horses, they should not do so without permission; and if the Standard Bearer stops to water his horses, they may do likewise without permission. And if the alarm is raised in the line of march, the brothers who are near the shout may mount their horses and take up their shields and lances, and keep calm and await the Marshal's order; and the others should go towards the Marshal to hear his command.

160. When there is war and the brothers are lodged in an inn or established in camp, and the alarm is raised, they should not leave without permission, until the banner is taken out; and when it is taken out they should all follow it as soon as possible, and they should not arm or disarm without permission; and if they are lying in ambush or guarding pasture, or somewhere they are reconnoitring, or they are going from one place to another, they should not remove bridle or saddle or feed their horses without permission.

How the Brothers should go in a Squadron

161. When they are established in squadrons, no brother should go from one squadron to another, nor mount his horse nor take up his shield or lance without permission; and when they are armed and they go in a squadron, they should place their squires with lances in front of them, and those with horses behind them, in such a way that the Marshal or the one who is in his place commands; no brother should turn his horse's head towards the back to fight or shout, or for anything else, while they are in a squadron.

162. If any brother wishes to try out his horse to learn what needs to be done for it or if there is anything to adjust to do with the saddle or saddle cloth, he may mount up to leave for a while without permission, and then return quietly and in silence to his squadron; and if he wishes to take his shield and lance, he should have permission; and whoever wishes to protect his head with his iron coif may do so without permission; but he may not take it off. No brother may charge or leave the ranks without permission.

163. And if it happens by chance that any Christian acts foolishly, and any Turk attacks him in order to kill him, and he is in peril of death, and anyone who is in that area wishes to leave his squadron to help him, and his conscience tells him that he can assist him, he may do so without permission, and then return to his squadron quietly and in silence. And if he otherwise charges or leaves the squadron, justice will be done even as far as going on foot to the camp and taking from him all that may be taken from him except his habit.

Source: J. M. Upton-Ward, *The Rule of the Templars* (Woodbridge, 1992) pp. 58–59

Other religious congregations, including the Teutonic Knights, had begun in the Holy Land but were later more fully involved in the Prussian and Baltic areas as part of the Northern Crusades.

ঌ 4.12 Helmond of Bosnan, *Chronica Slavorum* ঌ

Because God gave plentiful aid and victory to our leader and the other princes, the Slavs have been everywhere crushed and driven out. A people strong and without number have come from the bounds of the ocean and taken possession of the territories of the Slavs. They have built cities and churches and have grown in riches beyond all estimation.

> **Source: R. A. Fletcher, *The Conversion of Europe: from Paganism to Christianity*, 371–1386 AD (1997) p. 484**

ঌ✦ঌ

The crusading ideal was adjusted to include many adventures which were only marginally religious. They revealed the gradual process of 'conversion' from paganism to Christianity and the cultural dominance of Latin Christendom. A *locus classicus* of such 'crusading' activity was the Iberian peninsular which had been under Islamic domination from the early years of the eighth century until the second half of the thirteenth; the Islamic emirate of Granada remained independent if somewhat precarious until 1492. The centuries of *reconquista* (reconquest) have formed the core of Spanish medieval historiography, but as with all aspects of 'crusading' history a simple narrative approach conceals the realities of conversion tactics and cultural domination.

The Crusades left a profound impact on medieval literature through the writings of the troubadours and the refinement of the chivalric tradition. They contributed to the development of the military architecture of the period in such great castles as Krak des Chevaliers. The name is still given to good causes. In general, however, since the Enlightenment the Crusades have had a bad name. To the eighteenth-century philosopher, David Hume, they were 'the most signal and most durable monuments of human folly that has yet appeared in any age or nation', while his contemporary Edward Gibbon saw them as having 'checked rather than forwarded the maturity of Europe'. To Stephen Runciman, the twentieth-century historian of the Crusades, the Crusades were a disaster: 'high ideals were besmirched by cruelty and greed, enterprise and endurance by a blind and narrow self-righteousness; and the Holy War itself was nothing more than a long act of intolerance in the name of God, which is the sin against the Holy Ghost'. A more recent commentator, Jonathon Riley-Smith (*The Crusades: a Brief History*, p. 257) attempts to penetrate medieval mentality by quoting as a conclusion to his own history of the Crusades a short passage from the Dominican Humbert of Romans, a preacher of the Crusades, writing in the 1270s:

The aim of Christianity is not to fill the earth, but to fill heaven. Why should one worry if the number of Christians is lessened in the world by deaths endured for God? By this kind of death people make their way to heaven who perhaps would never reach it by another road.

Further reading

E. Christiansen, *The Northern Crusade, the Baltic and the Catholic Frontier* (Macmillan, London, 1980).

P. Constantine, *War in the Middle Ages* (Blackwell, Oxford, 1984).

A. J. Forey, *The Military Orders from the Twelfth to the Early Fourteenth Centuries* (Macmillan Education, Basingstoke, 1992).

B. Hamilton, *The Crusades* (Sutton, Stroud, 1998).

D. W. Lomax, *The Reconquest of Spain* (Longman, London, 1978).

J. Prawer, *The Latin Kingdom of Jerusalem: Europe's Colonisation in the Middle Ages* (Weidenfeld & Nicolson, London, 1972).

J. Richard, *The Crusades* (Cambridge University Press, Cambridge, 1999).

J. Riley-Smith, *The Crusades: a Short History* (Yale University Press, New Haven, 1987).

J. Riley-Smith, *Atlas of the Crusades* (Times Books, London, 1991).

J. Riley-Smith, *Oxford Illustrated History of the Crusades* (Oxford University Press, Oxford, 1995).

S. Runciman, *A History of the Crusades*, 3 vols (Cambridge University Press, Cambridge, 1951–54).

R. C. Smail, *Crusading Warfare, 1097–1193* (Cambridge University Press, Cambridge, 1994).

८ 5 ৯

THE WORLD OF
THE FEUDAL KINGDOMS

The concept of feudalism conceals from view the shifting alliances and boundaries which make it very difficult to draw a map of medieval Europe. The feudal reality was less a system than a series of traditional relationships based on service in exchange for land which tried to provide a place for everyone and to ensure that everyone was in their place. National identity slowly emerged but throughout the Middle Ages was overshadowed by the search for a continental hegemony tied up with the idea of a Catholic Western Holy Roman Empire which remained most of the time an aspiration rather than a reality.

The coronation of the Frankish king Charlemagne on Christmas Day 800, an event which has been variously interpreted, gave papal sanction to imperial pretensions.

---

८ 5.1 The Roman Council of 800 AD ৯

Since the title of emperor had become extinct among the Greeks and a woman claimed the imperial authority, it seemed to Pope Leo and to all the holy fathers who were present at the council and to the rest of the Christian people that Charles, king of the Franks, ought to be named emperor, for he held Rome itself where the Caesars were always wont to reside and also other cities in Italy, Gaul and Germany. Since almighty God had put all these places in his power it seemed fitting to them that, with the help of God, and in accordance with the request of all the Christian people, he should hold this title. King Charles did not wish to refuse their petition, and, humbly submitting himself to God and to the petition of all the Christian priests and people, he accepted the title of emperor on the day of the nativity of our Lord Jesus Christ and was consecrated by Pope Leo.

The coronation ceremony

On the day of the nativity of our Lord Jesus Christ all came together again in the same basilica of blessed Peter the apostle. And then the venerable and holy pontiff, with his own hands, crowned [Charles] with a most precious crown. Then all the faithful Romans, seeing how he loved the holy Roman church and its vicar and how he defended them, cried out with one voice by the will of God and of St Peter, the key-bearer of the kingdom of heaven, 'To Charles, most pious Augustus, crowned by God, great and peace-giving emperor, life and victory.' This was said three times before the sacred tomb of blessed Peter the apostle, with the invocation of many saints, and he was instituted by all as emperor of the Romans. Thereupon, on that same day of the nativity of our Lord Jesus Christ, the most holy bishop and pontiff anointed his most excellent son Charles as king with holy oil.

Source: B. Tierney, *The Crisis of Church, 1050–1300* (1964) pp. 22–23

The papacy, through the forged document known as the Donation of Constantine, claimed the right to make emperors.

ৡ 5.2 The Donation of Constantine ৻

To the holy apostles, my lords the most blessed Peter and Paul, and through them also to blessed Silvester, our father, supreme pontiff and universal pope of the city of Rome, and to the pontiffs, his successors, who to the end of the world shall sit in the seat of blessed Peter, we grant and by this present we convey our imperial Lateran palace, which is superior to and excels all palaces in the whole world; and further the diadem, which is the crown of our head; and the mitre; as also the superhumeral, that is, the stole which usually surrounds our imperial neck; and the purple cloak and the scarlet tunic and all the imperial robes; also the rank of commanders of the imperial cavalry . . . And we decree that those most reverend men, the clergy of various orders serving the same most holy Roman Church, shall have that eminence, distinction, power and precedence, with which our illustrious senate is gloriously adorned; that is, they shall be made patricians and consuls. And we ordain that they shall also be adorned with other imperial dignities. Also we decree that the clergy of the sacred Roman Church shall be adorned as are the imperial officers . . .

Wherefore that the pontifical crown should not be made of less repute, but rather that the dignity of a more than earthly office and the might of its glory should be yet further adorned – lo, we convey to the oft-mentioned and most blessed Silvester, universal pope, both our palace, as preferment, and likewise all provinces, palaces and districts of the city of Rome and Italy and of the regions of the West; and, bequeathing them to the power and sway of him and the pontiffs, his successors, we do (by means of fixed imperial decision through this our divine, sacred and authoritative sanction) determine and decree that the same be placed at his disposal, and do lawfully grant it as a permanent possession to the holy Roman Church.

Wherefore we have perceived that our empire and the power of our government should be transferred and removed to the regions of the East and that a city should be built in our name in the best place in the province of Byzantium and our empire there established; for it is not right that an earthly emperor should have authority there, where the rule of priests and the head of the Christian religion have been established by the Emperor of heaven . . .

Given at Rome, 30 March, when our lord Flavius Constantinus Augustus, for the fourth time, and Galliganus, most illustrious men, were consuls.

Source: H. Bettenson (trans.) *Documents of the Christian Church* (1993) pp. 141–142

Einhard's life of Charlemagne, written before 840, is heavily influenced by Suetonius' life of the Roman Emperors and, like so many medieval biographies, is reflective of the baptised classicism which characterised so much of medieval learning. The description of the Frankish king's private life emphasises the characteristics of the good king without losing sight of the man himself.

ও 5.3 Einhard the Monk ও

The Emperor was strong and well built. He was tall in stature, but not excessively so, for his height was just seven times the length of his own feet. The top of his head was round, and his eyes were piercing and unusually large. His nose was slightly longer than normal, he had a fine head of white hair and his expression was gay and good-humoured. As a result, whether he was seated or standing, he always appeared masterful and dignified. His neck was short and rather thick, and his stomach a trifle too heavy, but the proportions of the rest of his body prevented one from noticing these blemishes. His step was firm and he was manly in all his movements. He spoke distinctly, but his voice was thin for a man of his physique. His health was good, except that he suffered from frequent attacks of fever during the last four years of his life, and towards the end he was lame in one foot . . .

He spent much of his time on horseback and out hunting, which came naturally to him, for it would be difficult to find another race on earth who could equal the Franks in this activity. He took delight in steam baths at the thermal springs, and loved to exercise himself in the water whenever he could. He was an extremely strong swimmer and in this sport no one could surpass him. It was for this reason that he built his palace at Aachen and remained continuously in residence there during the last years of his life and indeed until the moment of his death . . .

He wore the national dress of the Franks . . . He hated the clothes of other countries, no matter how becoming they might be, and he would never consent to wear them . . . On ordinary days his dress differed hardly at all from that of the common people. He was moderate in his eating and drinking, and especially so in drinking; for he hated to see drunkenness in any man, and even more so in himself and his friends. All the same, he could not go long without food, and he often used to complain that fasting made him feel ill. He rarely gave banquets and these only on high feast days, but then he would invite a great number of guests. His main meal of the day was served in four courses, in addition to the roast meat which his hunters used to bring in on spits and which he enjoyed more than any other food. During his meal he would listen to a public reading or some other entertainment. Stories would be recited for him, or the doings of the ancients told again. He took great pleasure in the books of Saint Augustine and especially . . . *The City of God.*

He was so sparing in his use of wine and every other beverage that he rarely drank more than three times in the course of his dinner. In summer, after his midday meal, he would eat some fruit and take another drink; then he would remove his shoes and undress completely, just as he did at night, and rest for two or three hours. During the night he slept so lightly that he would wake four or five times and rise from his bed . . . Moreover, if the Count of the Palace told him that there was some dispute which could not be settled without the Emperor's personal decision, he would order the disputants to be brought in there and then, hear the case as if he were sitting in tribunal and pronounce a judgement. If there was any official business to be transacted on that day, or any order to be given to one of his ministers, he would settle it at the same time.

He spoke easily and fluently, and could express with great clarity whatever he had to say. He was not content with his own mother tongue, but took the trouble to learn foreign languages . . .

He paid the greatest attention to the liberal arts; and he had great respect for men who taught them, bestowing high honours upon them. When he was learning the rules of grammar he received tuition from Peter the Deacon of Pisa . . . Under him the Emperor spent much time and effort in studying rhetoric, dialectic and especially astrology. He applied himself to mathematics and traced the course of the stars with great attention and care. He also tried to learn to write . . . but, although he tried very hard, he had begun too late in life and he made little progress.

Charlemagne practised the Christian religion with great devotion and piety, for he had been brought up in this faith since earliest childhood. This explains why he built a cathedral of such great beauty at Aachen . . .

As long as his health lasted he went to church morning and evening with great regularity, and also for early morning Mass, and the late night hours. He took the greatest pains to ensure that all church ceremonies were performed with the utmost dignity . . . He donated so many sacred vessels made of gold and silver, and so many priestly vestments, that when service time came even those who opened and closed the doors . . . had no need to perform their duties in their everyday clothes.

He made careful reforms in the way in which the psalms were chanted and the lessons read. He was himself quite an expert at both of these exercises, but he never read the lesson in public and he would sing only with the rest of the congregation and then in a low voice.

He was most active in relieving the poor and in that form of really disinterested charity . . . He gave alms not only in his own country and in the kingdom over which he reigned, but also across the sea in Syria, Egypt, Africa, Jerusalem, Alexandria and Carthage. Wherever he heard that Christians were living in want, he took pity on their poverty and sent them money regularly . . .

Charlemagne cared more for the church of the holy Apostle Peter in Rome than for any other sacred and venerable place. He poured into its treasury a vast fortune in gold and silver coinage and in precious stones. He sent so many gifts to the Pope that it was impossible to keep count of them. Throughout the whole period of his reign nothing was ever nearer to his heart than that . . . the city of Rome should regain its former proud position. His ambition was not merely that the church of Saint Peter should remain safe and protected thanks to him, but that by means of his wealth it should be more richly adorned and endowed than any other church.

Source: L. Thorpe (trans.) *The Life of Charlemagne* (1970) pp. 63–71 (Translation © Professor Lewis Thorpe, 1969)

Charlemagne's 'empire', for all its talk of *renovatio* and renaissance, was short-lived and in 843 by the Treaty of Verdun it was divided into three: France and Germany, destined to be the most powerful of the medieval 'feudal' states formed the western and eastern parts, while the central part remained volatile and disputed.

The French state stabilised in the central Middle Ages and was characterised by a strong monarchy. The fourteen Capetian kings (called after Hugh Capet, the first) who reigned between 987 and 1324 showed how the longevity of a dynasty could cement the state. Among the most notable of the kings were Philip II, known as Augustus (1180–1223), master of the legal and practical niceties of kingship, and Louis IX, Saint Louis (1226–1270), crusader, Christian monarch and exemplar.

৪ৡ 5.4 Expedition to Sidon: July 1253–February 1254 ৶ৡ

CX

29 June 1253

When the King had completed the fortress of the town of Jaffa, he took counsel that he should go to fortify anew the city of Sidon, that the Saracens had overthrown. He set out to go thither on the feast day of the Apostles Saint Peter and Saint Paul, and the King and his host lay before the castle of 'Arsûf, that is very strong. That night the King summoned his people, and told them that if they agreed, he would go to take a city of the Saracens that is called Naplous, which city the ancient Scriptures call Samaria. The Templars and the Hospitallers and the barons of the land answered him with one consent, that it was well to essay to take the city; but they in no wise agreed that he should go there in person, because if aught befell him, all the land would be lost. And he said that never would he let them go thither if he went not in person with them. And so this emprise went no farther, since the lords of the land would not agree that he should go thither.

By day's marches we came to the sands of Acre, where we pitched camp, the King and the host. Thither in that place came to me a troop of many people from Great Armenia, that were going on pilgrimage to Jerusalem, having paid a great toll to the Saracens that guided them. By an interpreter that knew their language and ours, they begged me that I would show them the saintly King. I went to the King where he sate in a pavilion, leaning against the pole of the pavilion; and he sate on the sand, without carpet or any other thing under him. I said to him: 'Sir, there is without a band of many folk from Great Armenia, that are going to Jerusalem, and they pray me, Sir, that I have them shown the saintly King; but I have no wish yet to kiss your bones.' And he laughed aloud and told me to go to fetch them; and so I did. And when they had seen the King, they commended him to God, and the King them.

On the morrow the host lay at a place that is called Passe-Poulain, which is to say the Colt's Crossing, where there is very good water wherewith they water the plant whence sugar cometh. When we were lodged there, one of my knights said to me: 'Sir', said he, 'now have I lodged you in a fairer place than ye were in yesterday.' The other knight that had chosen the place before, leapt up all dismayed, and said to him aloud: 'Ye are over bold when ye speak of a matter that I have done.' And he leapt upon him and seized him by the hair. And I arose and struck him with my fist between the shoulders, and he let go; and I said to him: 'Now out of my house; for (as God may help me!) with me shall ye not be again.' The knight went away mourning much and brought to me my lord Giles the Black, the Constable of France; and he, by reason of the great repentance that he saw that the knight felt for the folly he had done, begged me, as instantly as he might, that I would take him back into my household. And I answered that I would not take I him back unless the Legate would absolve me from mine oath. They went to the Legate and told him the tale; and the Legate answered them that he could not absolve me, because the oath was reasonable; for the knight had well deserved it. And these things do I make clear to you, that ye may keep yourselves from taking an oath; that it is not fitting to take reasonably; for, as the Wise Man saith: 'Whoso sweareth easily, easily forsweareth himself'.

CXI

On the morrow the King went to lie before the city of Sur, that is called Tyre in the Bible. There the King summoned the men of substance of the host, and asked counsel of them whether it would be well that he should go to take the city of Bâniyâs before he went to Sidon. We all advised that it was well that the King should send some of his people thither; but no man counselled that he should go there in person; and with much ado did men turn him from it. It was agreed thus, that the Count of Eu should go, and my lord Philip of Montfort, the lord of Tyre, my lord Giles the Black, Constable of France, my lord Peter the Chamberlain, the Master of the Temple and his Order, and the Master of the Hospital and his brethren likewise.

We armed ourselves at nightfall, and came a little after daybreak into a plain that is before the city that is called Bâniyâs; and the ancient Scripture calleth it Caesarea Philippi. In this city riseth a fountain that men call Jor; and among the plains that surround the city riseth another very fair fountain that is called Dan. Now so it is, that when the two streams of these two fountains meet together, men call the river Jordan, wherein God was baptised.

By consent of the Templars and of the Count. of Eu, of the Hospital and of the barons of the land there present, it was agreed that the King's squadron (in which squadron I then was, since the King had kept the forty knights that were in my squadron with him), and my lord Geoffrey of Sargines, the noble knight, likewise, should get between the castle and the city; and the lords of the land should enter the city on the left hand, and the Hospital on the right, and the Temple should get into the city straight ahead by the way that we had come. We set forth until we were come nigh the city, and found that the Saracens that were in the town had discomfited the men-at-arms of the King and had driven them forth out of the town. When I saw this, I went to the men of worth that were with the Count of Eu, and said to them: 'My lords, if ye go not whither we are ordered, between the castle and the town, the Saracens will slay our men that have gone into the city.' The going thither was passing perilous; for the place whither we were to go was very parlous in that there were three double dry walls to cross, and the slope was so steep that a horse could hardly stand thereon; and the hillock that we were to make for was held by great plenty of Turks on horseback. As I spake to them, I saw that our foot-soldiers were breaking down the walls. When I saw this, I said to them with whom I was speaking, that orders had been given that the King's squadron should go thither where the Turks were; and since those were the orders I would go. I made my way, I and my two knights, towards them that were breaking down the walls, and saw that a mounted man-at-arms had thought to cross the wall, and that his horse had fallen on his body. When I saw this, I dismounted and took my horse by the bridle. When the Turks saw us coming, as God would, they left the place whither we were to go. From this place where the Turks had been a sheer rock went down into the city.

When we had got there and the Turks had gone thence, the Saracens that were in the city were discomfited and left the town to our people without dispute. As I stood there, the Master of the Temple heard tell that I was in danger, and came thither uphill towards me. While I was standing at the top of the hill, the Germans that were in the squadron of the Count of Eu followed me; and when they saw the Turks on horseback that were flying towards the castle, they set out to go after them; and I said to them: 'My lords, ye do not well; for we are here where we have been ordered to be, and ye go beyond your orders.'

CXII

The castle that standeth above the city is called Subayba, and standeth full half a league up in the mountains of Lebanon; and the foothill that goeth up to the castle is strewn with great rocks as big as chests. When the Germans saw that it was folly to pursue, they came back to the rear. When the Saracens saw this, they made at them on foot, and gave them great blows with their maces from above the rocks, and tore away the housings of their horses.

When our men-at-arms that were with us saw the mischief, they began to be dismayed; and I told them that if they went thence I would have them cast forth out of the King's pay for ever afterwards. And they said to me: 'Sir, the lots have fallen uneven between us; for ye are on horseback, if ye fly; and we are on foot, and the Saracens will slay us.' And I said to them: 'Sirs, I give you my word that I will not fly; for I will stay afoot with you.' I dismounted and sent my horse to be with the Templars, that were a good crossbow-shot behind.

As the Germans came back, the Saracens struck a knight of mine, that was called my lord John of Bussey, with a quarrel through the throat; and he fell dead just before me. My lord Hugh of Ecot, who had proved himself worthy in the Holy Land, and was his uncle, said to me: 'Sir, come help us to bring in my nephew down the hill.' 'An ill turn will he do', said I, 'that helpeth you therein: for ye have gone up there without my orders; and if ill hath befallen you therefrom, it is with good reason. Take him down to the town ditch, for I will not go hence until they send for me back.'

When my lord John of Valenciennes heard of the plight in which we were, he went to my lord Oliver of Termes and to those other chieftains of Languedoc, and said to them: 'My lords, I beg and command you, in the King's name, that ye lend me your aid to seek the Seneschal.' As he endeavoured thus, my lord William of Beaumont came to him and said to him: 'Ye labour for naught, for the Seneschal is dead.' And he answered: 'Dead or alive, I will bring tidings of him to the King.' Then he set out and came towards us, where we were up on the hill; and when he was come to us, he sent word to me to come to speak with him; and so I did.

Then Oliver of Termes said to me that we were in great peril in that place; for if we went down by the way that we had come, we could not do it without great loss, for the hillside was too steep, and the Saracens would leap down upon our bodies: 'But if ye would give heed to me, I will deliver you without loss.' And I told him that he should devise what he would, and I would do it. 'I will tell you', said he, 'how we may escape. We will go', said he, 'all along this slope as if we were going towards Damascus; and the Saracens that are there will think that we mean to take them in the rear. And when we are in the plains, we will set spur to our horses round the city and we shall have crossed the brook before they can reach us; and so shall we do them great hurt; for we will set fire to this threshed grain that is lying about in the fields.'

We did even as he devised; and he had them take canes such as men make flutes of, and had live coals put therein, and set them in the grain. And thus God led us back into safety by the counsel of Oliver of Termes. And know ye that when we came to the lodging where our people were, we found them all disarmed; for there was never a man that had taken heed for us. So we came back on the morrow to Sidon, where was the King.

> **Source: N. de Wailly and J. Evans (trans.)** *Joinville,*
> *The History of St Louis* (1938) pp. 170–176

French monarchical power had a tendency to move towards an 'absolutism' made possible by the French royal dominance in land-ownership, the real basis of power in the Middle Ages, and the concentration of land in the fertile Ile-de-France. This enabled France, politically and demographically less strong than Germany, in the eleventh and twelfth centuries, to become the centre of so many intellectual, artistic and religious movements.

In the period after the Carolingians the Germans began to show their ability as soldiers and colonists; in the tenth and eleventh centuries European political leadership was predominately German. The Ottonians and Hohenstaufens combined ambition with a determination to enhance a German imperial idea. The German kings used the Church to enhance royal power but the reformed papacy turned on its erstwhile political patrons especially following the pontificate of Gregory VII and, in the short term, the papacy emerged as the victor in the Investiture Contest. Frederick I of Hohenstaufen, called Barbarossa (*c.* 1152–1190), reinforced the power of the German king, but his continuing preoccupation with Italian and papal affairs (the German kings provided the military might for papal authority) compelled him to make increasing concessions to the German princes. Otto of Freising (*c.* 1115–1158), Frederick's chronicler uncle, brings out these preoccupations in his account of the early years of Frederick's reign.

---

৪৯ 5.5 The deeds of Frederick Barbarossa ৩৯

---

i

In the year 1800 since the founding of the City, but 1154 [1152] from the incarnation of the Lord, the most pious King Conrad departed this life in the springtime, on the fifteenth day before the Kalends of March – that is, on the Friday following Ash Wednesday – in the city of Bamberg, as has been said. Wonderful to relate, it was possible to bring together the entire company of the princes, as into a single body, in the town of Frankfort, from the immense extent of the transalpine kingdom (as well as certain barons from Italy), by the third [fourth] day before the Nones of March . . . When the chief men took counsel together there concerning the choice of a prince . . . finally Frederick, duke of the Swabians, the son of Duke Frederick, was sought by all. By the favour of all he was raised to the rank of king.

ii

The explanation of this support, the reason for so unanimous an agreement upon that person, was, as I recall, as follows. There have been hitherto in the Roman world, within the borders of Gaul and Germany, two renowned families: one that of the Henrys of Waiblingen, the other that of the Welfs of Altdorf. The one was wont to produce emperors, the other great dukes. These families, eager for glory as is usually the case with great men, were frequently envious of each other and often disturbed the peace of the state. But by the will of God, providing for the peace of his people in time to come, it came about that Duke Frederick, the father of this Frederick, who was a descendant of one of the two families (that is, of the family of the kings), took to wife a member of the other, namely, the daughter of Henry, duke of the Bavarians, and by her became the father of the Frederick who rules at the present time. The princes, therefore, considering not merely the achievements and the valour of the youth already so frequently mentioned, but also this fact, that being a member of both families, he might . . . link these two separate walls, decided to select him as head of the realm. They foresaw that it would greatly benefit the state if so grave and so long-continued a rivalry between the greatest men of the empire for their own private advantage might by this opportunity and with God's help be finally lulled to rest. So it was not because of dislike for King Conrad, but . . . in the interest of a universal advantage that they preferred to place this Frederick ahead of Conrad's son . . . who was still a little child. By reason of such considerations and in this way the election of Frederick was celebrated.

iii

When, therefore, all the princes who had thronged to that place had been bound by oath of fealty and homage, the king with a few men whom he considered suitable for the purpose, having dismissed the rest in peace, took ship, amid great rejoicing, on the fifth day of the week. He sailed by the Main and the Rhine, and disembarked at the royal seat at Sinzig. There taking horse, he came the next Saturday to Aachen. On the following day . . . he was escorted by the bishops from the palace to the church of the blessed Mary ever virgin. With the greatest applause of all who were present, he was crowned by Arnold, archbishop of Cologne, the others assisting, and was seated on the throne of the realm of the Franks that was placed in that same church by Charles the Great. Not a few marvelled that in so short a space of time not only had so great a throng of princes and of nobles of the kingdom flocked together, but that some also had arrived from western Gaul, whither the report of this event was supposed not yet to have arrived . . . On the same day and in the same church the bishop-elect of Munster . . . was consecrated by those same bishops who consecrated the king. So it was believed that the Highest King and Priest was actually participating in the present rejoicing: and this was the sign, that in one church one day beheld the anointing of the two persons who alone are sacramentally anointed according to the ordinance of the New and of the Old Testament, and are rightly called the anointed of Christ the Lord.

iv

When all that pertains to the dignity of the crown had been duly performed, the prince retired to the private apartments of the palace and summoned the more prudent and powerful of the assembled nobles. After consulting them concerning the condition of the state, he arranged to have ambassadors sent to the Roman pontiff, Eugenius, to the City, and to all Italy, to carry the tidings of his elevation to the rank of king. Therefore, Hillin, archbishop-elect of Trier, and Eberhard, bishop of Bamberg, prudent and learned men, were sent. Then the prince advanced upon the lower regions of the Rhine, to punish the people of Utrecht for the arrogance which, as has previously been related, they had shown toward his uncle Conrad. After he had punished them by the imposition of a fine and confirmed Herman as bishop, moving back up the Rhine he celebrated holy Easter at Cologne. Thence he passed through Westphalia and entered Saxony.

v

In the kingdom of the Danes there arose at that time a serious controversy concerning the rule, between the two kinsmen Peter . . . and Knut. The king summoned them before him and held a great assembly in *Martinopolis*, a city of Saxony which is also called Merseburg, with a large number of princes. The aforesaid young men came there and humbly yielded themselves to his command. Their case is said finally to have been settled by the judgement or advice of the chief men as follows: that Knut . . . should abdicate the royal title by surrendering his sword – for it is the custom of the court that kingdoms are bestowed by the prince or taken back again by the sword, provinces by the military standard – but that Peter, receiving the royal power at the sovereign's hand, should be bound to him by fealty and homage. So the crown of the realm was placed on his head by the hand of the prince, on Whit-Sunday, and he himself, wearing the crown, bore the sword of the king who marched in state wearing his crown. Waldemar, also, who was a member of the same family, received a certain duchy of Denmark.

vi

. . . The king, having brought all matters in Saxony into good order and inclined to his own will all the princes of that province, entered Bavaria and wore his crown in Regensburg, the metropolis of that duchy, at the festival of the apostles, in the monastery of St Emmeram; for the cathedral had burned down, together with certain quarters of the city. The ambassadors sent to the City, to Pope Eugenius, and to the other cities of Italy returned to that same diet with glad tidings. There indeed did the prince, having displayed a strong will in arranging all to his satisfaction within the confines of his empire, think to display abroad a stout arm. He wished to declare war on the Hungarians and to bring them under the might of the monarchy. But being for certain obscure reasons unable to secure the assent of the princes in this matter, and thus being powerless to put his plans into effect, he postponed them until a more opportune time.

vii

However, though all was prospering in his kingdom, the most serene prince was indeed very anxious to end without bloodshed that dispute over the duchy of Bavaria between his own relatives, that is, Duke Henry, his paternal uncle, and Duke Henry, his maternal uncle's son. (For the latter was the son of the former Duke Henry of Bavaria, whom King Conrad had compelled to remain in Saxony after he had been outlawed, as has been told elsewhere. His duchy he had bestowed first upon Leopold, the son of Margrave Leopold, and then upon this Henry, the younger Leopold's brother.) The king, therefore, to decide the aforesaid strife by judicial decree or by his counsel, appointed for them a diet at the city of Würzburg in autumn, during the month of October. Inasmuch as the one (that is, the son of Duke Henry) appeared there and the other absented himself, the latter was summoned again and again.

At that same diet exiles from Apulia, whom Roger had driven out from their native land . . . cast themselves . . . at the feet of the prince. Both because of the affliction of these people and that he might receive the crown of empire, it was solemnly agreed that an expedition into Italy should be undertaken . . .

ix

Now the king, when he wore the crown in Bamberg the following Easter, had with him two cardinals, namely, the priest Bernard and the deacon Gregory, sent by the apostolic see for the deposing of certain bishops. So, while celebrating the next Whitsunday at Worms, he deposed through the instrumentality of the same cardinals Henry, archbishop of the see of Mainz . . . and replaced him by his chancellor, Arnold, through election by certain of the clergy and people who had come thither. To the aforesaid court came the dukes previously mentioned, the two Henrys, contending for the duchy of Bavaria, as has been said. But as the one alleged that he had not been summoned in proper form, the matter could not there reach a due conclusion. Moreover, the same cardinals with the permission of the prince likewise removed Burchard of Eichstädt, a man weighed down by years, giving as their reason his inefficiency. And when, after this, they were thinking of passing sentence upon the archbishop of Magdeburg and certain others they were prevented by the prince and bidden to return home . . .

xi

At about the same time . . . the princes and the leading men of Bavaria were called together by the king at Regensburg. But nothing could be settled there with reference to the blessing of peace in that province, on account of the strife between the two dukes. Now the king, because he had been separated from his wife by legates of the apostolic see not long before, on the ground of consanguinity, was negotiating for another marriage. Both on this account and for the overthrow of William of Sicily, who had recently succeeded his deceased father, Roger, the enemy of both empires, he arranged to send ambassadors to Manuel, emperor of the Greeks. And so, by the advice of his chief men, that mission was undertaken by Anselm, bishop of Havelberg, and Alexander, once count of Apulia, but expelled by Roger with other nobles of that same province under suspicion of seeking the throne.

Then, in the following month . . . both the dukes . . . attended the prince's judgement seat in the city of Speyer. But the case was postponed, because the one for the second time claimed that he had not been summoned in due legal form. Frederick had now striven for almost two years to terminate the strife between the two princes so close to him, as has been said, by blood relationship. Therefore, being at length moved by the insistence of the one who desired to return to the land he had inherited from his father, from which he had long been debarred, Frederick was compelled to make an end of the matter because of the imminent task of the expedition in which he needed that same youth as a knight and companion of his journey. Accordingly, holding court at Goslar, a town of Saxony, he summoned both dukes by issuing edicts. Since the one came and the other absented himself, the duchy of Bavaria was there by decision of the princes, adjudged to the former, that is, to Duke Henry of Saxony. After this the prince, betaking himself from Saxony into Bavaria and thence proceeding through Swabia, in the third year of his reign assembled a military force on the plains of the river Lech, the boundary of Bavaria, opposite the city of Augsburg, in order to enter Italy. This was at about the beginning of the month of October, almost two years having elapsed since the expedition had first been vowed. Nor, by the judgement recently proclaimed against so great a prince of the empire and the no little murmuring of other princes arising therefrom, was it possible to distract the illustrious spirit from so great a deed, but disregarding all those things that were behind, and entrusting himself to God, he pressed on to the things that were before. Therefore after crossing the passes of the Alps and passing through Brixen and the valley of the Trent, he encamped on the plains of Verona, near Lake Garda. When he was there taking counsel with his princes concerning their further advance, he determined he must first of all win the favour of the Prince of Heaven. In short, the army, being unable on its passage through the mountain barriers to find things necessary for the support of life, on account of the barrenness of the country, while suffering great want (a thing that is always very grievous for troops) had violated certain holy places. To atone for this – although they seemed to have the aforesaid excuse of necessity – the king ordered a collection to be taken from the entire army. He decided that the not inconsiderable sum of money thus amassed should be taken back by certain holy men to the two bishops (of Trent, that is, and of Brixen) and divided among the various places of the saints which had suffered loss. Thus he provided nobly for the common good, fulfilling nobly a leader's task. For being about to enter upon very great undertakings, he decided that before all else he must placate the Ruler and Creator of all, without Whom nothing is well begun, nothing successfully completed, and that His wrath must be averted from his people.

xii

Then, breaking camp, Frederick halted in the month of November on the plain of Roncaglia, on the Po, not far from Piacenza.

> Source: C. C. Mierow (ed.) *Otto of Freising,*
> *The Deeds of Frederick Barbarossa* (1994)
> pp. 115–131

Frederick II, elected emperor in 1211, was constantly threatened by the power of nobles, and was secure only in his maternal inheritance in Sicily where he lived. Much of his reign was occupied with confrontations with the papacy and with the emerging Lombard league in Northern Italy. His legacy to his family was not a positive one; war and papal enmity were a heady mix which was to lead to the end of the Hohenstaufens in 1268.

Later medieval German history is increasing about *particularism* in Germany and *communalism* in the Empire's Italian lands. The *Golden Bull* of the Emperor Charles IV established the electoral process of the Empire and confirmed the authority of the German princes.

ᢊ 5.6 The *Golden Bull* of the Emperor Charles IV, 1356 AD ᢊ

In the name of the holy and indivisible Trinity felicitously amen. Charles the Fourth, by favour of the divine mercy emperor of the Romans, always august, and king of Bohemia; as a perpetual memorial of this matter. Every kingdom divided against itself shall be desolated. For its princes have become the companions of thieves. Wherefore God has mingled among them the spirit of dizziness, that they may grope in midday as if in darkness; and He has removed their candlestick from out of His place, that they may be blind and leaders of the blind. And those who walk in darkness stumble; and the blind commit crimes in their hearts which come to pass in time of discord. Tell us, pride, how would'st thou have reigned over Lucifer if thou had'st not had discord to aid thee? Tell us, hateful Satan, how would'st thou have cast Adam out of Paradise if thou had'st not divided him from his obedience? Tell us, luxury, how would'st thou have destroyed Troy, if thou had'st not divided Helen from her husband? Tell us, wrath, how would'st thou have destroyed the Roman republic had'st thou not, by means of discord, spurred on Pompey and Caesar with raging swords to internal conflict? Thou, indeed, oh envy, hast, with impious wickedness, spued with the ancient poison against the Christian empire which is fortified by God, like to the holy and indivisible Trinity, with the theological virtues of faith, hope, and charity; whose foundation is happily established above in the very kingdom of Christ. Thou hast done this, like a serpent, against the branches of the empire and its nearer members; so that, the columns being shaken, thou mightest subject the whole edifice to ruin. Thou hast often spread discord among the seven electors of the holy empire, through whom, as through seven candlesticks throwing light in the unity of a septiform spirit, the holy empire ought to be illuminated. Inasmuch as we, through the office by which we possess the imperial dignity, are doubly – both as emperor and by the electoral right which we enjoy – bound to put an end to future danger of discords among the electors themselves, to whose number we, as king of Bohemia are known to belong: we have promulgated, decreed and recommended for ratification, the subjoined laws for the purpose of cherishing unity among the electors, and of bringing about a unanimous election, and of closing all approach to the aforesaid detestable discord and to the various dangers which arise from it. This we have done in our solemn court at Nuremberg, in session with all the electoral princes, ecclesiastical and secular, and amid a numerous multitude of other princes, counts, barons, magnates, nobles and citizens; after mature deliberation, from the fullness of our imperial power; sitting on the throne of our imperial majesty, adorned with the imperial bands, insignia and diadem; in the year of our Lord 1356, in the

9th Indiction, on the 4th day before the Ides of January, in the 10th year of our reign as king, the 1st as emperor.

2. *Concerning the election of a king of the Romans*

1. After, moreover, the oft-mentioned electors or their envoys shall have entered the city of Frankfort, they shall, straightway on the following day at dawn, in the church of St Bartholomew the apostle, in the presence of all of them, cause a mass to be sung to the Holy Spirit, that the Holy Spirit himself may illumine their hearts and infuse the light of his virtue into their senses; so that they, armed with his protection, may be able to elect a just, good and useful man as king of the Romans and future emperor, and as a safeguard for the people of Christ. After such mass has been performed all those electors or their envoys shall approach the altar on which that mass has been celebrated, and there the ecclesiastical prince electors, before the gospel of St John: 'In the beginning was the word', which must there be placed before them, shall place their hands with reverence upon their breasts. But the secular prince electors shall actually touch the said gospel with their hands. And all of them, with all their followers, shall stand there unarmed. And the archbishop of Mainz shall give to them the form of the oath, and he together with them, and they, or the envoys of the absent ones, together with him, shall take the oath in common as follows:

2. 'I, archbishop of Mainz, arch-chancellor of the holy empire throughout Germany, and prince elector, do swear on this holy gospel of God here actually placed before me, that I, through the faith which binds me to God and to the holy Roman empire, do intend by the help of God, to the utmost extent of my discretion and intelligence, and in accordance with the said faith, to elect one who will be suitable, as far as my discretion and discernment can tell, for a temporal head of the Christian people, that is, a king of the Romans and prospective emperor. And my voice and vote, or said election, I will give without any pact, payment, price, or promise, or whatever such things may be called. So help me God and all the saints.'

3. Such oath having been taken by the electors or their envoys in the aforesaid form and manner, they shall then proceed to the election. And from now on they shall not disperse from the said city of Frankfort until the majority of them shall have elected a temporal head for the world and for the Christian people; a king, namely, of the Romans and prospective emperor. But if they shall fail to do this within thirty days, counting continuously from the day when they took the aforesaid oath: when those thirty days are over, from that time on they shall live on bread and water, and by no means leave the aforesaid city unless first through them, or the majority of them, a ruler or temporal head of the faithful shall have been elected, as was said before.

4. Moreover after they, or the majority of them, shall have made their choice in that place, such election shall in future be considered and looked upon as if it had been unanimously carried through by all of them, no one dissenting. And if anyone of the electors or their aforesaid envoys should happen for a time to be detained and to be absent or late, provided he arrive before the said election has been consummated, we decree that he shall be admitted to the election in the stage at which it was at the actual time of his coming. And since by ancient approved and laudable custom what follows has always been observed inviolately, therefore we also do establish and decree by the plenitude of the imperial power that he who shall have, in the aforesaid manner, been elected king of the Romans, shall, directly after such election shall have been held, and before he shall attend to any other cases or matters by virtue of his

imperial office, without delay or contradiction, confirm and approve, by his letters and seals, to each and all of the elector princes, ecclesiastical and secular, who are known to be the nearer members of the holy empire, all their privileges, charters, rights, liberties, ancient customs, and also their dignities and whatever they shall have obtained and possessed from the empire before the day of the election. And he shall renew to them all the above after he shall have been crowned with the imperial adornments. Moreover, the elected king shall make such confirmation to each prince elector in particular, first as king, then, renewing it, under his title as emperor; and, in these matters, he shall be bound by no means to impede either those same princes in general or any one of them in particular, but rather to promote them with his favour and without guile.

5. In a case, finally, where three prince electors in person, or the envoys of the absent ones, shall elect as king of the Romans a fourth from among themselves or from among their whole number an elector prince, namely, who is either present or absent: we decree that the vote of that person who has been elected, if he shall be present, or of his envoys if he shall chance to be absent, shall have full vigour and shall increase the number of those electing, and shall constitute a majority like that of the other prince electors.

5. *Concerning the right of the count palatine and also of the duke of Saxony*

Whenever, moreover, as has been said before, the throne of the holy empire shall happen to be vacant, the illustrious count palatine of the Rhine, arch-steward of the holy empire, the right hand of the future king of the Romans in the districts of the Rhine and of Swabia and in the limits of Franconia, ought, by reason of his principality or by privilege of the county palatine, to be the administrator of the empire itself, with the power of passing judgements, of presenting to ecclesiastical benefices, of collecting returns and revenues and investing with fiefs, of receiving oaths of fealty for and in the name of the holy empire. All of these acts, however, shall, in due time, be renewed by the king of the Romans who is afterwards elected, and the oaths shall be sworn to him anew. The fiefs of princes are alone excepted, and those which are commonly called banner-fiefs: the conferring of which, and the investing, we reserve especially for the emperor or king of the Romans alone. The count palatine must know, nevertheless, that every kind of alienation or obligation of imperial possessions, in the time of such administration, is expressly forbidden to him. And we will that the illustrious king of Saxony, arch-marshall of the holy empire, shall enjoy the same right of administration in those places where the Saxon jurisdiction prevails, under all the modes and conditions that have been expressed above.

And although the emperor or king of the Romans, in matters concerning which he is called to account, has to answer before the count palatine of the Rhine and prince elector – as is said to have been introduced by custom – nevertheless the count palatine shall not be able to exercise that right of judging otherwise than in the imperial court, where the emperor or king of the Romans shall be present.

Among those innumerable cares for the well-being of the holy empire over which we, by God's grace, do happily reign – cares which daily try our heart – our thoughts are chiefly directed to this: that union, desirable and always healthful, may continually flourish among the prince electors of the holy empire, and that the hearts of those men may be preserved in the concord of sincere charity, by whose timely care the disturbances of the world are the more easily and quickly allayed, the less error creeps in among them, and the more purely charity is observed, obscurity being removed and the rights of each one being clearly defined. It is, indeed, commonly known far and wide; and clearly manifest, as it were, throughout the whole world, that those illustrious men the king of Bohemia and the count palatine of the Rhine, the duke of Saxony and the margrave of Brandenburg, have – the one by reason of his kingdom, the others of their principalities – together with the ecclesiastical princes their co-electors, their right, vote and place in the election of the king of the Romans and prospective emperor. And, together with the spiritual princes, they are considered and are the true and lawful prince electors of the holy empire. Lest, in future, among the sons of these same secular prince electors, matter for scandal and dissension should arise: concerning the above right, vote and power, and the common welfare be thus jeopardised by dangerous delays, we, wishing by God's help to wholesomely obviate future dangers, do establish with imperial authority and decree, by the present ever-to-be-valid law, that when these same secular prince electors, or any of them, shall die, the right, vote and power of thus electing shall, freely and without the contra-diction of anyone, devolve on his first born, legitimate, lay son; but, if he be not living, on the son of this same first born son, if he be a layman. If, however, such first born son shall have departed from this world without leaving male legitimate lay heirs, by virtue of the present imperial edict, the right, vote and aforesaid power of electing shall devolve upon the elder lay brother descended by the true paternal line, and thence upon his first born lay son. And such succession of the first born sons, and of the heirs of these same princes, to their right, vote and power, shall be observed in all future time; under such rule and condition, however, that if a prince elector, or his first born or eldest lay son, should happen to die leaving male, legitimate, lay heirs who are minors, then the eldest of the brothers of that elector, or of his first born son, shall be their tutor and administrator until the eldest of them shall have attained legitimate age. Which age we wish to have considered, and we decree that it shall be considered, eighteen full years in the case of prince electors; and, when they shall have attained this, the guardian shall straightway be obliged to resign to them completely, together with his office, the right, vote and power, and all that these involve. But if any such principality should happen to revert to the holy empire, the then emperor or king of the Romans should and may so dispose of it as of a possession which has lawfully devolved upon himself and the empire. Saving always the privileges, rights and customs of our kingdom of Bohemia concerning the election, through its subjects, of a king in case of a vacancy. For they have the right of electing the king of Bohemia; such election to be made according to the contents of those privileges obtained from the illustrious emperors or kings of the Romans, and according to long observed custom; to which privileges we wish to do no violence by an imperial edict of this kind. On the contrary we decree that, now and in all future time, they shall have undoubted power and validity as to all their import and as to their form.

9. *Concerning mines of gold, silver and other specie*

We establish by this ever-to-be-valid decree, and of certain knowledge do declare that our successors the kings of Bohemia, also each and all future prince electors, ecclesi-astical and secular, may justly hold and lawfully possess – with all their rights without exception, according as such things can be, or usually have been possessed – all the gold and silver mines and mines of tin, copper, lead, iron and any other kind of metal, and also of salt: the king, those which have been found, and which shall at any future time be found, in the aforesaid kingdom and the lands and dependencies of that kingdom, and the aforesaid electors in their principalities, lands, domains and dependencies. And they may also have the Jew taxes and enjoy the tolls which have been decreed and assigned to them in the past, and whatever our progenitors the kings of Bohemia of blessed memory, and these same prince electors and their progenitors and predecessors shall have legally possessed until now; as is known to have been observed by ancient custom, laudable and approved, and sanctioned by the lapse of a very long period of time.

11. Concerning the immunity of the prince electors

We also decree that no counts, barons, nobles, feudal vassals, knights of castles, followers, citizens, burghers – indeed, no male or female subjects at all of the Cologne, Mainz and Treves churches, whatever their standing, condition or dignity – could in past times, or may or can in future be summoned at the instance of any plaintiff whatsoever, beyond the territory and boundaries and limits of these same churches and their dependencies, to any other tribunal or the court of any other person than the archbishops of Mainz, Treves and Cologne and their judges. And this we find was the observance in the past. But if, contrary to our present edict, one or more of the aforesaid subjects of the Treves, Mainz or Cologne churches should chance to be summoned, at the instance of anyone whatever, to the tribunal of anyone beyond the territory, limits or bounds of the said churches or of anyone of them, for any criminal, civil or mixed case, or in any matter at all; they shall not in the least be compelled to appear or respond. And we decree that the summons, and the proceedings, and the provisional and final sentences already sent or passed, or in future to be sent or passed against those not appearing, by such extraneous judges, furthermore their ordinances, and the carrying out of the above measures, and all things which might come to pass, be attempted or be done through them or anyone of them, shall be void of their own accord. And we expressly add that no count, baron, noble, feudal vassal, knight of a castle, citizen, peasant – no person, in short, subject to such churches or inhabiting the lands of the same, whatever be his standing, dignity or condition – shall be allowed to appeal to any other tribunal from the proceedings, the provisional and final sentences, or the ordinances – or the putting into effect of the same – of such archbishops and their churches, or of their temporal officials, when such proceedings, sentences or ordinances shall have been, or shall in future be held, passed or made against him in the court of the archbishops or of the aforesaid officials. Provided that justice has not been denied to those bringing plaint in the courts of the aforesaid archbishops and their officials. But appeals against this statute shall not, we decree, be received; we declare them null and void. In case of defect of justice, however, it is allowed to all the aforementioned persons to appeal, but only to the imperial court and tribunal or directly to the presence of the judge presiding at the time in the imperial court. And, even in case of such defect, those to whom justice has been denied may not appeal to any other judge, whether ordinary or delegated. And whatever shall have been done contrary to the above shall be void of its own accord. And, by virtue of this our present imperial law, we will that this statute be fully extended, under all the preceding forms and conditions, to those illustrious men the count palatine of the Rhine, the duke of Saxony, the margrave of Brandenburg, the secular or lay prince electors, their heirs, successors and subjects.

12. *Concerning the coming together of the princes*

In view of the manifold cares of state with which our mind is constantly distracted, after much consideration our sublimity has found that it will be necessary for the prince electors of the holy empire to come together more frequently than has been their custom, to treat of the safety of that same empire and of the world. For they, the solid bases and immovable columns of the empire, according as they reside at long distances from each other, just so are able to report and confer concerning the impending defects of the districts known to them, and are not ignorant how, by the wise counsels of their providence, they may aid in the necessary reformation of the same. Hence it is that, in the solemn court held by our highness at Nuremburg together with the venerable ecclesiastical and illustrious secular prince electors, and many other princes and nobles, we, having deliberated with those same prince electors and followed their advice, have seen fit to ordain, together with the said prince electors, ecclesiastical as well as secular, for the common good and safety: that these same prince electors, once every year, when four weeks, counting continuously from the Easter feast of the Lord's resurrection, are past, shall personally congregate in some city of the holy empire; and that when next that date shall come round, namely, in the present year, a colloquium, or court, or assembly of this kind, shall be held by us and these same princes in our imperial city of Metz. And then, and henceforth on any day of an assembly of this kind, the place where they shall meet the following year shall be fixed upon by us with their counsel. And this our ordinance is to endure just so long as it may be our and their good pleasure. And, so long as it shall endure, we take them under our imperial safe conduct when going to, remaining at, and also returning from said court. Moreover, lest the transactions for the common safety and peace be retarded, as is sometimes the case, by the delay and hindrance of diversion or the excessive frequenting of feasts, we have thought best to ordain, by concordant desire, that henceforth, while the said court or congregation shall last, no one may be allowed to give general entertainments for all the princes. Special ones, however, which do not impede the transaction of business, may be permitted in moderation.

15. *Concerning conspiracies*

Furthermore we reprobate, condemn, and of certain knowledge declare void, all conspiracies, detestable and frowned upon by the sacred laws and conventicles, or unlawful assemblies in the cities and out of them, and associations between city and city, between person and person or between a person and a city, under pretext of clientship, or reception among the citizens, or of any other reason; furthermore the confederations and pacts – and the usage which has been introduced with regard to such things, which we consider to be corruption rather than any thing else – which cities or persons, of whatever dignity, condition or standing, shall have thus far made and shall presume to make in future, whether among themselves or with others, without the authority of the lords whose subjects or serving-men they are, those same lords being expressly excluded. And it is clear that such are prohibited and declared void by the sacred laws of the divine emperors our predecessors. Excepting alone those confederations and leagues which princes, cities and others are known to have formed among themselves for the sake of the general peace of the provinces and lands. Reserving these for our special declaration, we ordain that they shall remain in full vigour until we shall decide to ordain otherwise concerning them. And we decree that, henceforth, each individual person who, contrary to the tenor of the present decree, and of the ancient law issued regarding this, shall presume to enter into such confederations, leagues, conspiracies and pacts, shall incur, besides the penalty of that law, a mark of infamy and a penalty of ten pounds of gold. But a city or community similarly breaking this our law shall, we decree, by the act itself incur the penalty of a hundred pounds of gold, and also the loss and privation of the imperial liberties and privileges; one half of such pecuniary penalty to go to the imperial fisc, the other to the territorial lord to whose detriment the conspiracies, etc., were formed.

17. *Concerning challenges of defiance*

We declare that those who, in future, feigning to have just cause of defiance against any person, unseasonably challenge them in places where they do not have their domicile, or which they do not inhabit in common, cannot with honour inflict any harm through fire, spoliation or rapine, on the challenged ones. And, since fraud and deceit should not shelter anyone, we establish by the present ever-to-be-valid decree that challenges of this kind, thus made, or in future to be made by anyone against any lords or persons to whom they were previously bound by companionship, familiarity or any honest friendship, shall not be valid; nor is it lawful, under pretext of any kind of challenge, to invade anyone through fire, spoliation or rapine, unless the challenge, three natural days before, shall have been intimated personally to the challenged man himself, or publicly in the place where he has been accustomed to reside, where full credibility can be given, through suitable witnesses, to such an intimation. Whoever shall presume otherwise to challenge anyone and to invade him in the aforesaid manner, shall incur, by the very act, the same infamy as if no challenge had been made; and we decree that he be punished as a traitor by his judges, whoever they are, with the lawful punishments.

We prohibit also each and every unjust war and feud, and all unjust burnings, spoliations and rapines, unlawful and unusual tolls and escorts, and the exactions usually extorted for such escorts, under the penalties by which the sacred laws prescribe that the foregoing offences, and any one of them, are to be punished.

18. *Letter of intimation*

To you, illustrious and magnificent prince, lord margrave of Brandenburg, archchamberlain of the holy empire, our co-elector and most dear friend, we intimate by these presents the election of the king of the Romans, which is about to take place on account of rational causes. And, as a duty of our office, we duly summon you to said election, bidding you within three months, counting continuously, from such and such a day, yourself, or in the person of one or more envoys or procurators having sufficient mandates, to be careful and come to the rightful place, according to the form of the holy laws issued concerning this, ready to deliberate, negotiate and come to an agreement with the other princes, yours and our co-electors, concerning the election of a future king of the Romans and, by God's favour, future emperor. And be ready to remain there until the full consummation of such election, and otherwise to act and proceed as is found expressed in the sacred laws carefully promulgated concerning this. Otherwise, notwithstanding your or your envoys' absence, we, together with our other co-princes and co-electors, shall take final measures in the aforesaid matters, according as the authority of those same laws has sanctioned.

20. *Concerning the unity of the electoral principalities and of the rights connected with them*

Since each and all the principalities, by virtue of which the secular prince electors are known to hold their right and vote in the election of the king of the Romans and prospective emperor, are so joined and inseparably united with such right of election, also with the offices, dignities and other rights connected with each and every such principality and dependent from it, that the right, vote, office and dignity, and all other privileges belonging to each of these same principalities may not devolve upon any other than upon him who is recognized as possessing that principality itself, with all its lands, vassalages, fiefs and domains, and all its appurtenances: we decree, by the present ever-to-be-valid imperial edict, that each of the said principalities, with the right and vote and duty of election, and with all other dignities, rights and appurtenances concerning the same, ought so to continue and to be, indivisibly and for all time, united and joined together, that the possessor of any principality ought also to rejoice in the quiet and free possession of its right, vote and office, and dignity, and all the appurtenances that go with it, and to be considered prince elector by all. And he himself, and no one else, ought at all times to be called in and admitted by the other prince electors, without any contradiction whatever, to the election and to all other transactions to be carried on for the honour or welfare of the holy empire. Nor, since they are and ought to be inseparable, may any one of the said rights, etc., be divided from the other, or at any time be separated, or be separately demanded back, in court or out of it, or distrained, or, even by a decision of the courts, be separated; nor shall anyone obtain a hearing who claims one without the other. But if, through error or otherwise, anyone shall have obtained a hearing, or proceedings, judgment, sentence or any thing of the kind shall have taken place, or shall chance in any way to have been attempted, contrary to this our present decree: all this, and all consequences of such proceedings, etc., and of any one of them, shall be void of their own accord.

21. *Concerning the order of marching, as regards the archbishops*

Inasmuch as we saw fit above, at the beginning of our present decrees, fully to provide for the order of seating of the ecclesiastical prince electors in council, and at table and elsewhere, whenever, in future, an imperial court should chance to be held, or the prince electors to assemble together with the emperor or king of the Romans as to which order of seating we have heard that in former times discussions often arose: so, also, do we find it expedient to fix, with regard to them, the order of marching and walking. Therefore, by this perpetual imperial edict, we decree that, as often as, in an assembly of the emperor or king of the Romans and of the aforesaid princes, the emperor or king of the Romans shall be walking, and it shall happen that the insignia are carried in front of him, the archbishop of Treves shall walk in a direct diametrical line in front of the emperor or king, and those alone shall walk in the middle space between them, who shall happen to carry the imperial or royal insignia. When, however, the emperor or king shall advance without those same insignia, then that same archbishop shall precede the emperor or king in the aforesaid manner, but so that no one at all shall be in the middle between them; the other two archiepiscopal electors always keeping their places – as with regard to the seating above explained, so with regard to walking – according to the privilege of their provinces.

22. *Concerning the order of proceeding of the prince electors, and by whom the insignia shall be carried*

In order to fix the order of proceeding, which we mentioned above, of the prince electors in the presence of the emperor or king of the Romans when he is walking, we decree that, so often as, while holding an imperial court, the prince electors shall, in the performance of any functions or solemnities, chance to walk in procession with the emperor or king of the Romans, and the imperial or royal insignia are to be carried: the duke of Saxony, carrying the imperial or royal sword, shall directly precede the emperor or king, and shall place himself in the middle, between him and the archbishop of Treves. But the count palatine, carrying the imperial orb, shall march in the same line on the right side, and the margrave of Brandenburg, bearing the sceptre, on the left side of the same duke of Saxony. But the king of Bohemia shall directly follow the emperor or king himself, no one intervening.

23. *Concerning the benedictions of the archbishops in the presence of the emperor*

Furthermore, so often as it shall come to pass that the ceremony of the mass is celebrated in the presence of the emperor or king of the Romans and that the archbishops of Mainz, Treves and Cologne, or two of them, are present, in the confession which is usually said before the mass, and in the presenting of the gospel to be kissed, and in the blessing to be said after the Agnus Dei, also in the benedictions to be said after the end of the mass, and also in those said before meals, and in the thanks to be offered after the food has been partaken of, the following order shall be observed among them, as we have seen fit to ordain by their own advice: namely, on the first day each and all of these shall be done by the first of the archbishops, on the second, by the second, on the third, by the third. But we will that first, second and third shall be understood in this case, according as each one of them was consecrated at an earlier or later date. And, in order that they may mutually make advances to each other with worthy and becoming honour, and may give an example to others of mutual respect, he whose turn it is according to the aforesaid, shall, without regard to that fact, and with charitable intent, invite the other to officiate; and, not till he has done this, shall he proceed to perform the above, or any of the above functions.

28

Moreover the imperial or royal table ought so to be arranged that it shall be elevated above the other tables in the hall by a height of six feet. And at it, on the day of a solemn court, shall sit no one at all except alone the emperor or king of the Romans.

But the seat and table of the empress or queen shall be prepared to one side in the hall, so that that table shall be three feet lower than the imperial or royal table, and as many feet higher than the seats of the prince electors; which princes shall have their seats and tables at one and the same altitude among themselves. Within the imperial place of session tables shall be prepared for the seven prince electors, ecclesiastical and secular, three, namely, on the right, and three others on the left, and the seventh directly opposite the face of the emperor or king, as has above been more clearly defined by us in the chapter concerning the seating and precedence of the prince electors; in such wise, also, that no one else, of whatever dignity or standing he may be, shall sit among them or at their table.

Moreover it shall not be allowed to any one of the aforesaid secular prince electors, when the duty of his office has been performed, to place himself at the table prepared for him so long as anyone of his fellow prince electors has still to perform his office. But when one or more of them shall have finished their ministry, they shall pass to the tables prepared for them, and, standing before them, shall wait until the others have fulfilled the aforesaid duties; and then, at length, one and all shall place themselves at the same time before the tables prepared for them.

29

We find, moreover, from the most renowned accounts and traditions of the ancients that, from time immemorial, it has been continuously observed, by those who have felicitously preceded us, that the election of the king of the Romans and future emperor should be held in the city of Frankfort, and the first coronation in Aix, and that his first imperial court should be celebrated in the town of Nuremburg. Wherefore, on sure grounds, we declare that the said usages should also be observed in future, unless a lawful impediment should stand in the way of them or any one of them. Whenever, furthermore, any prince elector, ecclesiastical or secular, detained by a just impediment, and not able to come when summoned to the imperial court, shall send an envoy or procurator, of whatever dignity or standing, that envoy, although, according to the mandate given him by his master, he ought to be admitted in the place of him who sends him, shall, nevertheless, not sit at the table or in the seat intended for him who sent him.

Moreover, when those matters shall have been settled which were at that time to be disposed of in any imperial or royal court, the master of the court shall receive for himself the whole structure or wooden apparatus of the imperial or royal place of session, where the emperor or king of the Romans shall have sat with the prince electors to hold his solemn court, or, as has been said, to confer fiefs on the princes.

31

Inasmuch as the majesty of the holy Roman empire has to wield the laws and the government of diverse nations distinct in customs, manner of life, and in language, it is considered fitting, and, in the judgment of all wise men, expedient, that the prince electors, the columns and sides of that empire, should be instructed in the varieties of the different dialects and languages: so that they who assist the imperial sublimity in relieving the wants of very many people, and who are constituted for the sake of keeping watch, should understand, and be understood by, as many as possible. Wherefore we decree that the sons, or heirs and successors of the illustrious prince electors, namely of the king of Bohemia, the count palatine of the Rhine, the duke of Saxony and the margrave of Brandenburg – since they are expected in all likelihood to have naturally acquired the German language, and to have been taught it from their infancy – shall be instructed in the grammar of the Italian and Slavic tongues, beginning with the seventh year of their age; so that, before the fourteenth year of their age, they may be learned in the same according to the grace granted them by God. For this is considered not only useful, but also, from the aforementioned causes, highly necessary, since those languages are wont to be very much employed in the service and for the needs of the holy empire, and in them the more arduous affairs of the empire are discussed. And, with regard to the above, we lay down the following mode of procedure to be observed: it shall be left to the option of the parents to send their sons, if they have any – or their relatives whom they consider as likely to succeed themselves in their principalities – to places where they can be taught such languages, or, in their own homes, to give them teachers, instructors, and fellow youths skilled in the same, by whose conversation and teaching alike they may become versed in those languages.

Source: E. F. Henderson, *Select Historical Documents of the Middle Ages* (1925) pp. 220–261

The eastward expansion of Germany continued throughout the Middle Ages and often owed as much to dogged peasant colonists as it did to king-emperors preoccupied with power games.

5.7 Frederick, Archbishop of Hamburg: Charter of Privileges

---

1. In the name of the holy and undivided Trinity, Frederick, by the grace of God bishop of Hamburg, to all the faithful in Christ, gives a perpetual benediction. We wish to make known to all the agreement which certain people living this side of the Rhine, who are called Hollanders, have made with us.
2. These men came to us and earnestly begged us to grant them certain lands in our bishopric which are uncultivated, swampy, and useless to our people. We have consulted our subjects about this and, considering that this would be profitable to us and to our successors, have granted their request.
3. The agreement was made that they should pay us every year one denarius for every hide of land. We have thought it necessary to determine the dimensions of the hide, in order that no quarrel may hereafter arise about it. The hide shall be 720 royal rods long and thirty royal rods wide. We also grant them the streams which flow through this land.
4. They agreed to give the tithe according to our decree, that is, every eleventh sheaf of grain, every tenth lamb, every tenth pig, every tenth goat, every tenth goose, and a tenth of the honey and of the flax. For every colt they shall pay a denarius on St Martin's day, and for every calf an obol. [a penny]
5. They promised to obey me in all ecclesiastical matters according to the decrees of the holy fathers, the canonical law, and the practice in the diocese of Utrecht.

6.   They agreed to pay every year two marks for every 100 hides for the privilege of holding their own courts for the settlement of all their differences about secular matters. They did this because they feared they would suffer from the injustice of foreign judges. If they cannot settle the more important cases they shall refer them to the bishop. And if they take the bishop with them for the purpose of deciding one of their trials, they shall provide for his support as long as he remains there by granting him one-third of all the fees arising from the trial; and they shall keep the other two-thirds.

7.   We have given them permission to found churches wherever they may wish on these lands. For the support of the priests who shall serve God in these churches we grant a tithe of our tithes from these parish churches. They promised that the congregation of each of these churches should endow their church with a hide for the support of their priest. The names of the men who made this agreement with us are: Henry, the priest, to whom we have granted the aforesaid churches for life; and the others are laymen, Helikin, Arnold, Hiko, Fordolt, and Referic. To them and to their heirs after them we have granted the aforesaid land according to the secular laws and to the terms of this agreement

> **Source: O. J. Thatcher, E. H. McNeal (trans.) *A Source Book for Mediaeval History* (1905) pp. 572–573**

The medieval period was not static either in its geographical certainties or in the character of its government and mentality. In some places expansion meant coming to terms with cultural diversity. This was certainly the case with Spain where the reconquest of the Iberian peninsular from the Moslems formed both an abiding national myth and a richly eclectic culture. Regional traditions and customs were formalised by the charter (*fuero*) which established a body of regulations and rules. The *fuero* of Cuenca was granted to this prosperous town sometime between 1189 and 1190 by King Alfonso who gave 'to all inhabitants of the city of Cuenca and to their successors, Cuenca itself with all its district; that is to say, with its mountains, springs, grass, rivers, saltworks, and mines of silver, iron, or other metal'. [p. 29]

ࢭ 5.8 *The Fuero of Cuenca*, Spain ࢩ

---

32 *Concerning the Bathhouse and the Testimony of Women*

Men may use the common bathhouses on Tuesdays, Thursdays, and Saturdays. Women may enter on Mondays and Wednesdays. Jews enter on Fridays and Sundays. No one, neither woman nor man, pays more than a halfpenny entry fee. Servants and children of residents enter free of charge. If a man enters any part of the bathhouse premises on the women's day for bathing, he is liable to a fine of ten gold coins. He pays the same fine for spying on women in the bath on those days. However, if a woman should enter a bathhouse on a day reserved for men or be found there at night, and because of this the woman is publicly dishonoured or harmed in some way, she has no right to bring charges of a kind sufficient to exile the offending man. On the other hand, if a man commits these acts against a woman on the women's bathing day or steals her clothing, he will be thrown from the cliffs of the town. Officials can gather testimony from women at the bathhouse, the bakehouse, at the fountain and river, and also at the spinners' and weavers' workplaces. Female witnesses should be wives or daughters of residents of the town.

If a Christian intrudes in a bathhouse on the Jewish bathing day or if a Jew intrudes on the Christian bathing days, resulting in either person attacking or killing the other, no formal accusations will be accepted from either of the persons or their relatives.

The bathhouse manager provides bathers with all bathing necessities, such as water and the like. Failing to provide these necessities will make the manager liable for a fine of ten *solidi*, five to be paid to the Master of the Marketplace and five to the complainant. Anyone stealing bathhouse equipment will have his ears cut off; if bathers' belongings are worth a total of ten *mencales* or more, then the thief shall be thrown off the town cliffs.

30 He who injures someone with an egg

Whoever injures someone with an egg, with a *butello*, or with a water-melon, or with any other thing that can dirty him should pay ten *aurei* if the plaintiff can prove it; but if not, he should clear himself with two of four named from his parish and he should be believed.

> Source: J. F. Powers (trans.) *The Code of Cuenca: Municipal Law on the Twelfth-Century Castilian Frontier* (2000) pp. 40–41, 91

Sicily, in Muslim hands until the end of the eleventh century, was conquered by the Normans and was consolidated by them as part of an increasingly united southern Italy, an empire in the sun, in the early twelfth century. It was beset with conflicts with the papacy and with the ambitions of the Germans and Byzantines as well as with internal dissension. Nonetheless, it provides an excellent example of the eclectic and diverse character of the medieval secular state.

⮞ 5.9 Romuald of Salerno, *Chronicon sive Annales*, 1153–1169 ⮜

King Roger possessed his realm in peace and tranquillity. Since in neither peace nor war did he know how to be idle, he ordered a very beautiful palace to be built at Palermo, in which he constructed a chapel floored in astonishing stone, which he covered with a gilded roof, and endowed and beautified with various ornaments. And so that this great man should at no time be without the pleasures afforded by either land or water, he had a large quantity of earth excavated and removed at a place which was called Favara, and there created a delightful lake which he ordered to be stocked with different types of fish, brought from many different regions. He had another beautiful and splendid palace constructed next to this lake. He had some of the hills and woods which are round about Palermo enclosed with a stone wall, and ordered a delightful and well-stocked park made, planted with all sorts of trees, and in it he had deer, roebucks and wild boars kept. And he had a palace built in this park to which he ordered water to be brought by underground pipes from a particularly clear spring. So this wise and careful man enjoyed these pleasures as the nature of the season suggested. For in winter, and in Lent because of its profusion of fish, he lived at the Favara palace; while in the summer he made the fiery season's heat bearable at the park, and diverted his mind from the strain of his many cares by enjoying a moderate amount of hunting. And although the king himself was possessed of great wisdom, intelligence and judgement, he also gathered men of good sense of different classes from the various parts of the earth and made them partners in his decisions. For he brought George, a man of mature wisdom, foresight and care, from Antioch, and made him great admiral, and through his advice and prudence he obtained many victories on land and sea. He appointed learned and prudent clerics, Guarin and Robert, in succession as his chancellor. And if he could find honest and wise men, whether from his own land or born elsewhere, laymen or clerics, he ordered them to be at his side, and promoted them to honours and riches as each man's status suggested. Finally he made Maio, a young man originating from Bari, who was both fluent of speech and prudent and careful, first *scrinarius,* then vice-chancellor and eventually chancellor. He created many new counts in his kingdom, and had the city of Cefalu built, in which he had the splendid and beautiful church of the Holy Saviour constructed at his own expense, to which he made the city subject and assigned its service. Towards the end of his life, allowing secular matters to be neglected and delayed, he laboured in every conceivable way to convert Jews and Muslims to the faith of Christ, and endowed converts with many gifts and resources. He ordered the church of St Nicholas, Messina, to be built, in large part at his own expense, although it could not be completed in his lifetime. He had a silver panel, made at his own expense, placed before the altar of St Matthew in Salerno as a memorial to his name, and every time he came to Salerno from Sicily he customarily offered one or two precious cloths to the Salernitan church. But since it is impossible to remain for very long at the summit, and as punishment for the sins of the whole kingdom, after so many victories and successes the most glorious King Roger died of a fever at Palermo and was buried in the cathedral of that city, in the fifty-eighth year of his life, the second month and fifth day, on the 27th of February, in the twenty-fourth year of his reign, in the year from the Lord's Incarnation 1152, first of the indiction. King Roger was large of stature, corpulent, leonine of face, somewhat hoarse of voice; wise, far-seeing, careful, subtle of mind, great in counsel, preferring to use his intelligence rather than force. He was very concerned to gain money, hardly very prodigal in expending it, fierce in public but in private kindly, generous with honours and rewards to those faithful to him, but inflicting injuries and punishments on those disloyal. He was more feared than loved by his subjects, dreaded and feared by the Greeks and Muslims.

Source: G. A. Loud, T. Wiedemann (trans.) *The History of the Tyrants of Sicily by 'Hugo Falcandus' 1154–1169* (1998) pp. 219–221

Further reading

D. Abulafia, *Frederick II: A Medieval Ruler* (Allen Lane, London, 1988).

B. Arnold, *Medieval Germany, 500–1700* (Macmillan, Basingstoke, 1997).

G. Barraclough, *The Origins of Modern Germany* (Blackwell, Oxford, 1966).

J. Dunrabin, *France in the Making 1043–1180* (Oxford University Press, Oxford, 1985).

R. Fawtier, *The Capetian Kings of France* (Macmillan, London, 1964).

H. Fuhrmann, *Germany in the High Middle Ages* (Cambridge University Press, Cambridge, 1986).

J. Gillingham, *The Angevin Empire* (Edward Arnold, London, 1984).

E. M. Hallam, *Capetian France* (Longman, London, 1980).

J. Larner, *Italy in the Age of Dante and Petrach* (Longman, London, 1980).

K. J. Leyser, *Medieval Germany and its Neighbours* (Hambledon, London, 1982).

J. Le Patourel, *The Norman Empire* (Clarendon Press, Oxford, 1976).

D. Matthew, *The Norman Kingdom of Sicily* (Cambridge University Press, Cambridge, 1992).

T. Reuter, *Germany in the Early Middle Ages, 800–1056* (Longman, London, 1991).

S. Reynolds, *Kingdoms and Communities in Western Europe*, 2nd edn (Clarendon Press, Oxford, 1997).

D. Waley, *The Italian City Republics* (Weidenfeld & Nicolson, London, 1969).

THE ENGLISH POLITICAL
WORLD

Medieval England was the product of a series of conquests and settlements which began with the Anglo-Saxons and ended with the Normans. Its unity as a kingdom was forged slowly and its identity reflected many aspects of its component parts. Bede the Venerable set his classic account of the *Ecclesiastical History of the English People* (731) in the context of Britain's geographical position.

꒒ꞏ 6.1 Bede the Venerable ꞏ꒤

Chapter 1

Britain, once called Albion, is an island of the ocean and lies to the north-west, being opposite Germany, Gaul, and Spain, which form the greater part of Europe, though at a considerable distance from them. It extends 800 miles to the north, and is 200 miles broad, save only where several promontories stretch out further and, counting these, the whole circuit of the coast line covers 4,875 miles. To the south lies Belgic Gaul, from which the city called *Rutubi Portus* is the nearest port for travellers. Between this and the closest point in the land of the Morini, *Gessoriacum*, is a crossing of fifty miles or, as some writers have it, 450 *stadia*. Behind the island, where it lies open to the boundless ocean, are the Orkney islands. The island is rich in crops and in trees, and has good pasturage for cattle and beasts of burden. It also produces vines in certain districts, and has plenty of both land and waterfowl of various kinds. It is remarkable too for its rivers, which abound in fish, particularly salmon and eels, and for copious springs. Seals as well as dolphins are frequently captured and even whales; besides these there are various kinds of shellfish, among which are mussels, and enclosed in these there are often found excellent pearls of every colour, red and purple, violet and green, but mostly white. There is also a great abundance of whelks, from which a scarlet-coloured dye is made, a most beautiful red which neither fades through the heat of the sun nor exposure to the rain; indeed the older it is the more beautiful it becomes. The land possesses salt springs and warm springs and from them flow rivers which supply hot baths, suitable for all ages and both sexes, in separate places and adapted to the needs of each. For water, as St Basil says, acquires the quality of heat when it passes through certain metals, so that it not only becomes warm but even scalding hot. The land also has rich veins of metal, copper, iron, lead and silver. It produces a great deal of excellent jet, which is glossy black and burns when put into the fire and, when kindled, it drives away serpents; when it is warmed by rubbing it attracts whatever is applied to it, just as amber does. The country was once famous for its twenty-eight noble cities as well as innumerable fortified places equally well guarded by the strongest of walls and towers, gates and locks. Because Britain lies almost under the North Pole, it has short nights in summer, so that often at midnight it is hard for those who are watching to say whether it is evening twilight which still lingers, or whether morning dawn has come, since the sun at night returns to the east through the regions towards the north without passing far below the horizon. For this reason the summer days are extremely long. On the other hand the winter nights are also of great length, namely eighteen hours, doubtless because the sun has then departed to the region of Africa. In summer too the nights are extremely short; so are the days in winter, each consisting of six standard equinoctial hours, while in Armenia, Macedonia, Italy, and other countries in the same latitude the longest day or night consists of fifteen hours and the shortest of nine. At the present time, there are five languages in Britain, just as the divine law is written in five books, all devoted to seeking out and setting forth one and the same kind of wisdom, namely the knowledge of sublime truth and of true sublimity. These are the English, British, Irish, Pictish, as well as the Latin languages; through the study of the scriptures, Latin is in general use among them all. To begin with, the inhabitants of the island were all Britons, from whom it receives its name; they sailed to Britain, so it is said, from the land of Armorica, and appropriated to themselves the southern part of it. After they had got possession of the greater part of the island, beginning from the south, it is related that the Pictish race from Scythia sailed out into the ocean in a few warships and were carried by the wind beyond the furthest bounds of Britain, reaching Ireland and landing on its northern shores. There they found the Irish race and asked permission to settle among them but their request was refused. Now Ireland is the largest island of all next to Britain, and lies to the west of it. But though it is shorter than Britain to the north, yet in the south it extends far beyond the limits of that island and as far as the level of North Spain, though a great expanse of sea divides them. The Picts then came to this island, as we have said, by sea and asked for the grant of a place to settle in. The Irish answered that the island would not hold them both; 'but', said they, 'we can give you some good advice as to what to do. We know of another island not far from our own, in an easterly direction, which we often see in the distance on clear days. If you will go there, you can make a settlement for yourselves; but if anyone resists you, make use of our help.' And so the Picts went to Britain and proceeded to occupy the northern parts of the island, because the Britons had seized the southern regions. As the Picts had no wives, they asked the Irish for some; the latter consented to give them women, only on condition that, in all cases of doubt, they should elect their kings from the female royal line rather than the male; and it is well known that the custom has been observed among the Picts to this day. In course of time Britain received a third tribe in addition to the Britons and the Picts, namely the Irish. These came from Ireland under their leader Reuda, and won lands among the Picts either by friendly treaty or by the sword. These they still possess. They are still called Dalreudini after this leader, *Dal* in their language signifying a part.

Ireland is broader than Britain, is healthier and has a much milder climate, so that snow rarely lasts there for more than three days. Hay is never cut in summer for winter use nor are stables built for their beasts. No reptile is found there nor could a serpent survive; for although serpents have often been brought from Britain, as soon as the ship approaches land they are affected by the scent of the air and quickly perish.

In fact almost everything that the island produces is efficacious against poison. For instance we have seen how, in the case of people suffering from snake-bite, the leaves of manuscripts from Ireland were scraped, and the scrapings put in water and given to the sufferer to drink. These scrapings at once absorbed the whole violence of the spreading poison and assuaged the swelling. The island abounds in milk and honey, nor does it lack vines, fish, and birds. It is also noted for the hunting of stags and roe deer. It is properly the native land of the Irish; they emigrated from it as we have described and so formed the third nation in Britain in addition to the Britons and the Picts. There is a very wide arm of the sea which originally divided the Britons from the Picts. It runs far into the land from the west. Here there is to this day a very strongly fortified British town called Alcluith [Dumbarton]. The Irish whom we have mentioned settled to the north of this arm of the sea and made their home there.

> **Source: B. Colgrave and R. A. B. Mynors (eds)**
> ***Venerable Bede, Ecclesiastical History of the English***
> ***People*** **(1979) pp. 16–21, © Oxford University Press,**
> **1969. Reprinted from** ***Bede's Ecclesiastical History of***
> ***the English People*,** **edited by Bertram Colgrave and**
> **R. A. B. Mynors (1969) by permission of Oxford**
> **University Press.**

The Anglo-Saxon kingdoms vied for hegemony and the predominance of the southern kingdom of Wessex owed much to the unifying effect of Viking incursions. If there was an English Charlemagne, Alfred is the most likely candidate, at least according to his biographer.

ৡ 6.2 Asser: *Of the deeds of Alfred* ৶

---

81. Yet, all the while, the King, amid his wars, and the constant hindrances of his worldly duties, yea, and the attacks of the Heathen, and his own daily attacks of illness, never slacked nor stayed in his tendance on the helm of the kingdom, and in his practice of all wood-craft; nor yet in his teaching of all his goldsmiths, and his craftsmen, and his falconers, and his huntsmen; nor in his construction of buildings, stately and costly beyond all the elder wont, by new plans of his own; nor in his recitation of Saxon books; nor, most of all, in himself learning by heart Saxon songs, with all diligence and to the utmost of his power, and bidding others do the like.

82. Nor yet slacked he ever in attendance at Divine Service. Daily, to wit, heard he Mass, and certain psalms and prayers, and the Day Hours and the Night Hours. And by night too, as we have said, was he wont to haunt the churches, unbeknown to all his folk, for prayer.

83. Great too was his diligence, and great his bounty, in his alms-deeds which he did, both toward them of his own land and toward incomers from all nations. Kind of speech, above all, was he, beyond compare, and free of wit toward all men. And with all his mind did he throw himself into the seeking out of things unknown.

84. And of their own free will did many Franks, Frisians, Gauls, Heathens, Britons, Scots, and Armoricans, bow them to his sway, high-born alike and low-born; and all of them, in his own worthy wise, did he rule, and love, and honour, even as his own folk, and enriched them with place and profit.

85. Unto Divine Scripture was he ever ready and careful to hearken, and that his own home-born folk should read it him; yet would he join in prayer with outlanders no less, if need arose thereof.

86. His Bishops, moreover, and churchmen of every order, and his Thanes, and his Lords, and his Counsellors also, and all his Household loved he with wondrous love. And their sons, too, who were brought up in the Royal Household, loved he even as his own, and slacked not by day nor yet by night, in himself setting them in every good way, and imbuing them with culture and the like.

87. Yet (as if in all this he found no comfort) would he, day and night, sadly bewail him, to the Lord, and to all near and dear unto him, with many a sigh and moan (as though he felt no grief either of body or soul save this only), that Almighty God had made him to lack Divine Wisdom and Culture. And herein was he even as the pious Solomon, richest and wisest of all Hebrew kings, who made light of earthly wealth and glory, and asked wisdom from God first. And thus, moreover, found he both – wisdom, to wit, and earthly glory; even as it is written, 'Seek ye first the Kingdom of God and his righteousness, and all these things shall be added unto you.'

88. But God, Who ever beholdeth the inmost heart, by Whose holy inspiration we think those things that be good, by Whose bountiful guiding are performed the same; Who doth put into our minds good desires, never save for this, that He may bring the same to good effect, by His abundant mercy; He stirred up the heart of Alfred, by no outward means, but by His own inward working; even as it is written: 'I will hearken what the Lord God will say within me' (Psalm lxxxiv).

89. Fellow-workers, also, of his good purpose, who might help him in the wisdom he longed for, the attaining of his heart's desire, would he get him whensoever he could. And thus, like as the cunning bee riseth early in the summer morning from the cells of the hive, and cleaveth swiftly the pathless air, and settleth on many a divers plant – moss, or fruit, or flowret – and proveth that which pleaseth her most, and beareth it back home, with all foresight, so sought he from abroad that which he had not at home, that is, in his own realm.

Source: E. Conybeare, *Alfred in the Chronicles* (1900) pp. 104–106

In the creation of an English identity the search for an 'ideal king' was never far from the chronicler's attention and in the monkish Edward the Confessor, the penultimate Anglo-Saxon monarch, later kings found something of that ideal.

≈ 6.3 Edward the Confessor ≈

When by God's gracious mercy there came for the English, who had suffered so long under the yoke of the barbarians, the jubilee of their redemption, that Earl Godwin, whom I have already mentioned, took the lead in urging that they should admit their king to the throne that was his by right of birth; and since Godwin was regarded as a father by all, he was gladly heard in the witenagemot. And so, amid the festive joy of all the people, earls and bishops were sent to fetch him. By these he was brought back safely, by those acknowledged with alacrity; and before he was raised to the royal throne he was consecrated God's anointed at Christ Church, Canterbury. Everywhere he was acclaimed with loyal undertakings of submission and obedience. Now that the kingdom was settled under its native rule there was rejoicing by all, and at this turn of events they offered thanksgivings to the King most High. And not only the English, to whom this favour had been shown by heaven, but indeed the whole of Gaul on account of its close kinship rejoiced with them; and its kings, gladdened by the report, hastened to send by their ambassadors friendly greetings and to seek the friendship of such a king together with the boon of peace. First the Emperor of the Romans himself, Henry, who besides had married Edward's sister Gunnhild, delighted to learn that Edward had been enthroned in his ancestral seat, dispatched ambassadors to confirm their amity, sent gifts to be bestowed with imperial generosity, and, as befitted these great lords of the earth, offered and asked for peace and friendship for him and his vassals. Also the king of the Franks, another Henry, a close kinsman by blood of the king of the English, much pleased with the news, made with him through ambassadors a treaty welcome to the friends of both. Even the king of the Danes, although separated by the immense distance of the intervening ocean, with ambassadors exhausted by their long travels on land and sea, entreated his peace and love, chose him as a father, submitted himself to him in all things as a son, and by the order of the English king affirmed this agreement by oath and confirmed it with hostages. Moreover, all the other nobles of those kings and all the most powerful dukes and princes approached him with their ambassadors, made him their friend and lord for them and theirs, and put their fealty and service in his hands. To each of these according to his rank were sent from the king royal gifts, and, so that no generosity, however bountiful, of any king or prince whatsoever should ever equal these gifts, Edward, the most fair and noble of English kings, made them for these same Frankish princes in the form of either annual or perpetual grants. Indeed, at the start of his reign he was vouchsafed so much renown and favour by that, with all Britain, together with the jagged islands of the adjacent kingdoms and monarchies, settling down in the calm of peace, there seemed to have been renewed in him that grant of heavenly favour, by which David, after a martial reign, repressed the terrors of war, and presented to his son Solomon, who followed him on the throne of glory, a rule of peace, so that, with all counter movements completely destroyed, he lived in mercy, ruled his people with kindness, and overflowed more abundantly in the general glory and riches of the world than all the other kings of the earth.

And not to omit his attitude and appearance, he was a very proper figure of a man – of outstanding height, and distinguished by his milky white hair and beard, full face and rosy cheeks, thin white hands, and long translucent fingers; in all the rest of his body he was an unblemished royal person. Pleasant, but always dignified, he walked with eyes down-cast, most graciously affable to one and all. If some cause aroused his temper, he seemed as terrible as a lion, but he never revealed his anger by railing. To all petitioners he would either grant graciously or graciously deny, so that his gracious denial seemed the highest generosity. In public he carried himself as a true king and lord; in private with his courtiers as one of them, but with royal dignity unimpaired. He entrusted the cause of God to his bishops and to men skilled in canon law, warning them to act according to the case, and he ordered his secular judges, princes, and palace lawyers to distinguish equitably, so that, on the one hand, righteousness should have royal support, and, on the other, evil, wherever it appeared, its just condemnation. This goodly king abrogated bad laws, with his witan established good ones, and filled with joy all that Britain over which by the grace of God and hereditary right he ruled.

> Source: F. Barlow (ed. and trans.) *The Life of King Edward Who Rests at Westminster* (1962) pp. 9–13, © Frank Barlow, 1962, 1992. Reprinted from *The Life of King Edward Who Rests at Westminster*, edited and translated by Frank Barlow (2nd edn 1992) by permission of Oxford University Press.

A pivotal event like the Norman Conquest of 1066 was given full attention by contemporary historians and not least by the *Anglo Saxon Chronicle*.

ᢒ 6.4 *The Anglo-Saxon Chronicle* ᢒ

AD 1066

This year came Harold the king from York to Westminster, at that Easter which was after the midwinter upon which the king died; and Easter was then on this day, viz. the 16th of the kalends of May. Then was there seen all over England such a token in the heavens as no man had ever seen before. Some men said that it was the star Cometa, which some persons call the hairy star, and it appeared first on the eve Litania Major on the 8th of the kalends of May, and so shone all the seven nights. And soon thereafter came Tostig the earl from beyond sea into Wight, with as great a fleet as he might procure; and there they rendered to him as well money as provisions. And king Harold, his brother, gathered as great a ship army and also a land army as no king here on [this] land before had done, because it was intimated to him that William the bastard would come hither and win this land, just as it afterwards happened. And in the meanwhile came earl Tostig into the Humber with sixty ships;

and Eadwine the earl came with a land force and drove him out. And the butse-carls forsook him and went to Scotland with twelve vessels; and Harold, king of Norway, met him there with three hundred ships, and Tostig submitted to him and became his homager. And then both of them went into the Humber until they came to York; and there Eadwine the earl, and Morkere the earl, his brother, fought against them, but the North-men had the victory.

Then it was told to Harold, king of the English, that this had thus happened, and this fight was on the vigil of St Matthew. Then came Harold, our king, on the North-men unawares, and encountered them beyond York, at Steinford-bridge, with a great army of English folk: and there during the day there was a very strong fight on both sides. There was slain Harold Harfager and earl Tostis; and the North-men who there remained were put to flight, and the English from behind slew them furiously, until some of them came to their ships. Some were drowned, and some also were burned, and so in different ways destroyed that few were left; and the English had possession of the place of slaughter. The king then gave his protection to Olaf, the son of the king of the Norsemen, and to their bishop, and to the earl of Orkney, and to all those who were left in the ships; and they then went up to our king, and swore oaths that they would ever keep peace and friendship towards this land, and the king let them go home with twenty-four ships. These two general battles were fought within five days. Then came William, earl of Normandy, to Pevensey, on the eve of the mass of St Michael, and as soon as they had arrived they built at the town of Hastings. This was then intimated to king Harold, and he then gathered a large army, and came against him at the Hoar Apple-tree, and William came against him unawares before his people were put in array. But the king nevertheless very boldly fought against him along with those men who would support him; and there was there great slaughter made on either side. There was slain king Harold and earl Leofwine his brother, and earl Gyrth his brother, and many good men; and the French had possession of the place of slaughter, entirely as God permitted for the sins of the people. Adred, the archbishop, and the citizens of London, wished them to have Eadgar, child, as king, as was his undoubted hereditary right; and Edwine and Morkere promised him that they would fight along with him. But just in proportion as it ought to have been the forwarder, so was it from day to day the later and the worse, so that at the last it entirely passed away. This fight was done on the day of pope Calixtus. And earl William went again to Hastings, and waited there [to ascertain] whether the people would submit to him. And when he perceived that the people would not come to him, he went up with all the army which remained to him, and that which afterwards had come, from over sea to him, and he harried all that district which he passed over, until that he came to Berkhampstead. And there came to meet him archbishop Ealdred, and Eadgar, child, and earl Eadwine, and earl Morkere, and all the best men of London, and submitted then of necessity, when the greatest harm had been done; and this was great folly that they had not done so sooner, since God would not better it for our sins; and they gave him pledges and swore oaths to him and he promised them that he would be to them a faithful lord; nevertheless in the meanwhile they harried all that they passed over. Then on midwinter's day Ealdred, archbishop, consecrated him as king at Westminster, and he pledged him with Christ's book, and moreover swore, before he would place the crown on his head, that he would rule this nation as well as any king before him had done at the best, provided they [the people] would be faithful to him. Yet he nevertheless laid a very heavy tribute upon the people; and afterwards, during Lent, he went over the sea to

Normandy, and took with him Stigand, the archbishop, and abbot Aegelnath, of Glastonbury, and Eadgar, child, and earl Eadwine, and earl Morkere, and earl Waeltheof, and many other good men of England. And bishop Oda and earl William remained here behind, and they built castles wide throughout the nation, and oppressed the poor people, and ever after it grew worse exceedingly. May the end be good when God will.

> Source: J. Stevenson (ed. and trans.) *The Church Historians of England*, 5 vols (1858) Vol. 2, pp. 117–119

The reign of William the Conqueror has an unusually wide range of documentation including the visual representations of the *Bayeux Tapestry* which depicts not only scenes of battle but also much else besides. The Domesday Book of 1086 presents a detailed snapshot of England as it was at the end of the Conqueror's reign and compares it to the time of King Edward the Confessor, before 1066. A royal survey prepared for tax purposes, it provides details of many English communities in the eleventh century.

৪ 6.5 Wells, Somerset ৩

VI. *The Land of the Bishop Giso of Wells*

The Bishop of Wells holds WELLE [Wells]. He held [it] at the time of King Edward and paid geld for 50 hides. There is land for 60 ploughs. Of this [land] are in demesne 8 hides where are 6 ploughs and 6 serfs and [there are] 20 villeins and 14 bordars with 15 ploughs and 6 hides. There are 2 riding-horses and 22 beasts, and 30 swine and 150 sheep and 24 she-goats. There are 4 mills paying 30 shillings, and 300 acres of meadow. Pasture 3 leagues long and 1 league broad. Wood [land] 2 leagues long and 2 furlongs broad and 3 leagues of moor. It is worth 30 pounds for the use (*ad opus*) of the bishop.

Of that land of the same manor the canons of S Andrew hold 14 hides. They have there in demesne 6 hides and 6 ploughs and 8 serfs and [there are] 16 villeins and 12 bordars with 8 ploughs and 8 hides. There are 2 riding-horses and 12 beasts and 10 swine and 100 sheep. There are 2 mills paying 50 pence. It is worth 12 pounds.

Of that land of the same manor Fastrad holds of the bishop 6 hides, which two thegns held who could not be separated from the church. Richard [holds] 5 hides. Erneis [holds] 5 hides, which a thegn held who could not be separated from the church. There are in demesne 11 hides and 6 ploughs and 10 serfs and [there are] 17 villeins and 16 bordars with 11 ploughs and 5 hides. There are 2 riding-horses and 40 beasts and 62 swine and 500 sheep. There are 2 mills paying 10 shillings. Between them all it is worth 13 pounds.

Of that land of the same manor Fastrad holds of the bishop 2 hides. Ralf [holds] 2 hides. These 4 hides are part of the bishop's demesne. There [are] in demesne

3 hides and 2 ploughs and 3 serfs and [there are] 5 villeins and 5 bordars with 1 plough and 1 hide. There are 10 beasts and 6 swine and 50 sheep and 30 she-goats. There is a mill paying 7 shillings and 6 pence. Total value 70 shillings. Of the same 50 hides the wife of Manasseh holds 2 hides, but not of the bishop. It is worth 20 shillings.

Besides these 50 hides the bishop has 2 hides which never paid geld at the time of King Edward. Alward 'Crocco' and Edric hold [them] of the bishop. They are worth 30 shillings.

> Source: W. Page (ed.) *A History of Somerset*, 5 vols
> (1911) Vol. 1, pp. 455–456 [altered]

---

৪৯ 6.6 Stratton on the Fosse, Somerset ৪৯

---

43. William of Monceaux also holds Stratton (on the Fosse) from the Bishop [of Coustances). Alfwold held it before 1066 from Glastonbury Church; he could not be separated from it. It paid tax for 3 hides. Land for 3 ploughs. In lordship 2 ploughs; 3 slaves; 2½ hides.

5 villagers and 6 smallholders with 1½ ploughs and ½ hide.

A mill which pays 5s.; meadow, 20 acres; pasture, 4 furlongs in both length and width; woodland 3 furlongs long and 2 furlongs wide. 1 cob; 10 cattle; 27 unbroken mares; 21 pigs; 317 sheep; 43 goats.

The value was 50s.; now £4.

> Source: C. and F. Thorne (eds) *Domesday Book:*
> *Somerset* (1980) 5.43 88 c, d; 8.38 90d, 91a

The surviving public records of the English state allow an insight into the institutions which were so characteristic of medieval constitutions. The structures of shire and justice gradually built up over the medieval centuries and particularly in the critical eleventh and twelfth centuries witnessed a fully working administrative and legal system which was distinguished by continuity as well as change.

---

৪৯ 6.7 Report of a trial held on Pinnenden Heath ৪৯
(1072 or 1075/76)

In the time of the great King William, who conquered England by his arms and subjected it to his sway, it happened that Odo, bishop of Bayeux, who was the brother of that king came to England some time before Lanfranc, archbishop of Canterbury. He established himself in the county of Kent very strongly and exercised great power therein. Moreover, because in those days there was no one in that shire who could resist so powerful a magnate, he attached to himself many men of the archbishopric of Canterbury, and seized many of the customary rights which pertained to it. These he annexed wrongfully to his own lordship. Not long afterwards, the aforesaid Lanfranc, who was then abbot of Caen, himself came to England by the command of the king, and by the grace of God was made archbishop of Canterbury and primate of the realm of England. When the archbishop had resided here for some time he discovered that his church lacked many of its ancient possessions and that these had been dissipated or alienated through the negligence of his predecessors. He therefore diligently collected accurate information, and then, hastening to the king, he energetically stated his case. The king thereupon gave orders that the whole shire court should meet without delay, and that there should be brought together not only all the Frenchmen in the county, but also and more especially those English who were well acquainted with the traditional laws and customs of the land. This assembly met in due course at Pinnenden. At this trial very many question were raised between the archbishop and the bishop of Bayeux relating both to the ownership of particular estates and also to the legal customs of the country; and at the same time many opinions were mooted concerning the customary rights to which the king and the archbishop were respectively entitled. So numerous indeed were the matters in dispute that all the business could not be transacted in one day, and for that reason the court of the shire was held in continuous session for three whole days at this place. During these three days Lanfranc, the archbishop, proved his title to many lands which were then held by men of the bishop . . .

In this pleas the archbishop not only proved his right to these and other lands; he also vindicated afresh the liberties of his church and the customary jurisdiction which was entitled to exercise, to wit: sake and sake, toll and team, flymenafyrrmth, grithbryce, forsteal, hamfare and infangenthef, with all other customs like to these and less than these, on land and water, in woods and ways and meadows, within city and without, within borough and without, and everywhere in the land. And verdict was passed in his favour by all the worthy and wise men who were present, and by the whole court of the shire . . . In the presence of all these men, it was further fully proved that the king of the English could claim in all the lands of the church of Canterbury no customary dues save only three. If any men of the archbishop are arrested in the act either of digging up the royal roads which lead from city to city, or of felling trees so close to those roads that an obstruction is caused, then shall they fall under jurisdiction of the king's officer, whether they have previously given surety or not, and they shall be fined by him according to justice. The third custom concerns any man who commits homicide or any felonious act on the king's highway; if caught in the act and arrested forthwith, he shall be punished by the king; if however he is not caught in the act but, being suspected, absconds without giving any surety, the king shall have no jurisdiction over him . . . When the king heard the judgement given in this plea, and had been made aware of those who ratified it, and when he had learnt the many reasons which could be adduced in support of it, he gave thanks, and joyfully confirmed the judgement with the assent of all his magnates, and ordered that it should be steadfastly and completely upheld. Wherefore this has been written down so that it may in the future be kept in perpetual remembrance, and so that those who shall thereafter succeed to the church of Christ in Canterbury may know of it; and may be aware of the rights they hold from God in the same church; and may have knowledge of what things the kings and magnates of the realm may exact from them.

Source: D. C. Douglas and G. W. Greenaway, *English Historical Documents* (1953) pp. 449–451

An English version of feudalism was revealed in the reign of the Conqueror.

੬> 6.8 Writ of Summons to the Feudal Host (*c.* 1072) <੬

William, king of the English, to Æthelwig, abbot of Evesham, greeting.

I order you to summon all those who are subject to your administration and jurisdiction that they bring before me at Clarendon on the Octave of Pentecost all the knights they owe me duly equipped. You, also, on that day, shall come to me, and bring with you fully equipped those 5 knights which you owe me in respect of your abbacy.

Witness Eudo the steward. At Winchester.

Source: D. C. Douglas and G. W. Greenaway, *English Historical Documents* (1953) p. 895

੬> 6.9 An Early Enfeoffment on the Land of the Abbey <੬
of Bury St Edmunds (1066–1087)

Be it known to all of you that Peter, a knight of king William, will become the feudal man of St Edmund and of Baldwin the abbot, by performing the ceremony of homage. He will do this by permission of the king and with the consent of the monks, and in return for the service which will here be stated, saving always the fealty which he owes to the king, the fief having been freely received except for the six royal forfeitures. Peter promises that he will serve on behalf of the abbot within the kingdom with 3 or 4 knights at their own expense if he has been previously summoned by the king and the abbot to take part in the earlier or later levies of the king's host. If he is bidden to plead on the abbot's behalf at any place within the kingdom, they shall likewise bear their own expense. But if the abbot shall take him anywhere else, then the expense of his service shall be borne by the abbot. Besides this, he shall equip a knight for service without or within the kingdom where and when the abbot shall require to have this knight as his own retainer. This is the description of the fee. The land of Edric the blind with 14 freemen and as many peasants; Wulfmaer the priest and his land with 3 freemen; . . .

Source: D. C. Douglas and G. W. Greenaway, *English Historical Documents* (1953) pp. 896–897

≋ 6.10 A grant of land to be held by military service made ≋ by Robert Losinga, Bishop of Hereford (1085)

This privilege Robert, bishop of the church of Hereford, ordered to be recorded as agreed between him and Roger, son of Walter, concerning certain land which is called 'Hamme', and those things which pertain to it. This land belongs to the church of Holy Mary, the Mother of God, and St Ethelbert the martyr; and previously the said bishop held this land as his own demesne and for the sustenance of the church. This land the aforesaid knight, to wit, Roger, asked from the bishop through his friends, and he offered money in respect of it. But the bishop, by the counsel of his vassals, gave him this same land in return for a promise that he would serve the bishop with 2 knights as his father did whenever the need arose. This also was part of the contract: that the men of the bishop belonging to King's Hampton and Hereford, and to the estates pertaining thereto, should be at liberty to take timber from the wood for the use of the bishop as often as it should be needed for fuel or for repairing houses; and the pigs of these manors should feed in the same wood. This refers to the men belonging to the bishop. And this contract enjoins that if Roger becomes a monk, or dies, neither his mother nor his wife nor his sons nor his brothers nor any of his kinsfolk shall have rights in the aforesaid land, but let the bishop receive whatever in the estate may be to the profit of holy Church, and his men shall receive the same without any contradiction whatsoever. This instrument was executed in the year of the Incarnation of our Lord 1085, it being the eighth Indication.

Source: D. C. Douglas and G. W. Greenaway, *English Historical Documents* (1953) p. 897

Documents of all kinds proliferate in the central Middle Ages, reflecting a growing sophistication of legal forms. Letters became a common form in England; not in the form of correspondence but in the form of a writ – a written command given by one person to another. Judicial writs dating from the reign of Henry II provide an example of standardised royal documentation.

6.11 Concerning the laws and customs of the Kingdom of England (c. 1190)

Book I, 5–6

When anyone complains to the lord king or his justices concerning his fee or free tenement, if the case is such that it ought to be, or the lord king is willing that it should be, tried in the king's court, then the complainant shall have the following writ of summons:

The writ for making the first summons
The king to the sheriff greeting. Command N. to render to R. justly and without delay, one hide of land in such-and-such a vill, which the said R. complains that the aforesaid N. is withholding from him. If he does not do so, summon him by good summoners to be before me or my justices on the day after the Octave of Easter, to show why he has not done so. And have there the summoners and this writ.

Book XIII, 2–3

When anyone dies seised of a free tenement, if he was seised in his demesne as of fee, then his heir can lawfully claim the seisin which his ancestor had, and if he is of full age he shall have the following writ:

The writ of mort d'ancestor
The king to the sheriff greeting. If G. the son of O. gives you security for prosecuting his claim, then summon by good summoners twelve free and lawful men from the neighbourhood of such-and-such a vill to be before me or my justices on a certain day, ready to declare on oath if O. the father of the aforesaid G. was seised of his demesne as of his fee of one virgate of land in that vill on the day he died, whether he died after my first coronation, and whether G. is his next heir. And meanwhile let them view the land; and you are to see that their names are endorsed on this writ. And summon by good summoners R., who holds the land, to be there then to hear the recognition. And have there the summoners and this writ.

> Source: G. D. G. Hall (trans.) *The Treatise on the Laws and Customs of the Realm of England Commonly Called Glanvill* (1965) pp. 5, 149

Royal power was sometimes challenged. The continuing conflict between *regnum* and *sacerdotium* provided a wealth of employment for the clerks responsible for the drafting of writs, charters and other documents. Such conflicts reached their climax in the dispute between Henry II and his archbishop of Canterbury and erstwhile Chancellor, Thomas Becket, which led to the martyrdom of 1170. This event is recorded in the numerous surviving lives of Becket, noted already in chapter three, and in the legal documents which attempted to define the respective boundaries of ecclesiastical and civil authority.

---

๒๐ 6.12 *The Assize of Clarendon* (1166) from ๙ช
Roger of Howden, *Chronica*

Here begins the Assize of Clarendon made by King Henry II with the assent of the archbishops, bishops, abbots, earls and barons of all England.

1   In the first place the aforesaid King Henry, on the advice of all his barons, for the preservation of peace, and for the maintenance of justice, has decreed that inquiry shall be made throughout the several counties and throughout the several hundreds through twelve of the more lawful men of the hundred and through four of the more lawful men of each vill upon oath that they will speak the truth, whether there be in their hundred or vill any man accused or notoriously suspect of being a robber or murderer or thief, or any who is a receiver of robbers or murderers or thieves, since the lord king has been king. And let the justices inquire into this among themselves and the sheriffs among themselves.

2   And let anyone, who shall be found, on the oath of the aforesaid, accused or notoriously suspect of having been a robber or a murderer or thief, or a receiver of them, since the lord king has been king, be taken and put to the ordeal of water, and let him swear that he has not been a robber or murderer or thief, or receiver of them since the lord king has been king, to the value of 5 shillings, so far as he knows.

3   And if the lord of the man, who has been arrested, or his steward or his vassals shall claim him by pledge within the third day following his capture, let him be released on bail with his chattels until he himself shall stand his trial.

4   And when a robber or murderer or thief or receiver of them has been arrested through the aforesaid oath, if the justices are not about to come speedily enough into the county where they have been taken, let the sheriffs send word to the nearest justice by some well-informed person that they have arrested such men, and the justice shall send back word to the sheriffs informing them where they desire the men to be brought before them; and let the sheriffs bring them before the justices. And together with them let the sheriffs bring from the hundred and the vill, where they have been arrested, two lawful men to bear the record of the county and of the hundred as to why they have been taken, and there before the justice let them stand trial.

5   And in the case of those who have been arrested through the aforesaid oath of the assize, let no man have court of justice or chattels save the lord king in his court in the presence of his justices; and the lord king shall have all their chattels. But in the case of those who have been arrested otherwise than by this oath, let it be as is customary and due.

6   And let the sheriffs, who have arrested them, bring them before the justice without any other summons than that they have from him. And when robbers or murderers or thieves, or receivers of them, who have been arrested through the oath or otherwise, are handed over to the sheriffs, let them receive them immediately and without delay . . .

14   Moreover, the lord king wills that those who shall be tried by the law and absolved by the law, if they have been of ill repute and openly and disgracefully

spoken of by the testimony of many and that of the lawful men, shall abjure the king's land . . .

17   And if any sheriff shall send word to another sheriff that men have fled from his county, on account of robbery or murder or theft or the harbouring of them, or on account of outlawry or of a change concerning the king's forest, let him (the second sheriff) arrest them; and even if he knows of himself or through others that such men have fled into his county, let him arrest them and guard them until he has taken safe pledges for them.

18   And let all the sheriffs cause a record to be made of all fugitives who have fled from their counties; and let them do this before the county courts and carry the names of those therein before the justices, when next they come to them, so that these men may be sought throughout England, and their chattels may be seized for the needs of the king.

19   And the lord king wills that from the time the sheriffs shall receive the summons of the itinerant justices to present themselves before them, together with the men of the county, they shall assemble them and make inquiry for all who have newly come into their counties since this assize; and they shall send them away under pledge to attend before the justices, or they shall keep them in custody until the justices come to them, and then they shall present them before the justices.

20   Moreover, the lord king forbids monks or canons or any religious house to receive any men of the lower orders as a monk or a canon or a brother, until it be known of what reputation he is, unless he shall be sick unto death.

21   Moreover, the lord king forbids anyone in all England to receive in his land or in his soke or in a house under him any of that sect of renegades [Cathari] who were branded and excommunicated at Oxford . . .

And the lord king wills that this assize shall be kept in his realm so long as it shall please him.

> Source: D. C. Douglas and G. W. Greenaway, *English Historical Documents* (1953) p. 407–410

Disputes between ruling elites were not confined to those between kings and clerics. The subtle distinction between strong monarchy and tyranny was a fine one and with a skilled operator like King John the nobility sought definition. *Magna Carta* of 1215, frequently re-issued and refined afterwards, provided less a Charter of Liberties than a framework for mutual co-existence.

৯৯ 6.13 *Magna Carta*, 1215 ৯৯

John, by the grace of God king of England, lord of Ireland, duke of Normandy and Aquitaine, and count of Anjou: to the archbishops, bishops, abbots, earls, barons, justiciars, foresters, sheriffs, stewards, serving men, and to all his bailiffs and faithful subjects, greeting. Know that we, by the will of God and for the safety of our soul, and of the souls of all our predecessors and our heirs, to the honour of God and for the exaltation of the holy church and the bettering of our realm: by the counsel of our venerable fathers Stephen archbishop of Canterbury, primate of all England and cardinal of the holy Roman church; of Henry archbishop of Dublin; of the bishops William of London, Peter of Winchester, Jocelin of Bath and Glastonbury, Hugh of Lincoln, Walter of Worcester, William of Coventry and Benedict of Rochester; of master Pandulf, subdeacon and of the household of the lord pope; of brother Aymeric, master of the knights of the Temple in England; and of the noble men, William Marshall earl of Pembroke, William earl of Salisbury, William earl of Warrenne, William earl of Arundel, Alan de Galway constable of Scotland, Warin FitzGerold, Peter FitzHerbert, Hubert de Burgh seneschal of Poitiers, Hugo de Neville, Matthew son of Herbert, Thomas Basset, Alan Basset, Philip d'Aubigni, Robert de Roppelay, John Marshall, John son of Hugo, and others of our faithful subjects:

1. First of all have granted to God, and, for us and for our heirs forever, have confirmed, by this our present charter, that the English church shall be free and shall have its rights intact and its liberties uninfringed upon. And thus we will that it be observed. As is apparent from the fact that we, spontaneously and of our own free will, before discord broke out between ourselves and our barons, did grant and by our charter confirm – and did cause the lord pope Innocent III. to confirm – freedom of elections, which is considered most important and most necessary to the church of England. Which charter both we ourselves shall observe, and we will that it be observed with good faith by our heirs forever. We have also granted to all free men of our realm, on the part of our-selves and our heirs forever, all the subjoined liberties, to have and to hold, to them and to their heirs, from us and from our heirs

2. If any one of our earls or barons, or of others holding from us in chief through military service, shall die; and if, at the time of his death, his heir be of full age and owe a relief: he shall have his inheritance by paying the old relief; – the heir, namely, or the heirs of an earl, by paying one hundred pounds for the whole barony of an earl; the heir or heirs of a baron, by paying one hundred pounds for the whole barony; the heir or heirs of a knight, by paying one hundred shillings at most for a whole knight's fee; and he who shall owe less shall give less, according to the ancient custom of fees.

3. But if the heir of any of the above persons shall be under age and in wardship, – when he comes of age he shall have his inheritance without relief and without fine.

4. The administrator of the land of such heir who shall be under age shall take none but reasonable issues from the land of the heir, and reasonable customs and services and this without destruction and waste of men or goods. And if we shall have committed the custody of any such land to the sheriff or to any other man who ought to be responsible to us for the issues of it, and he cause destruction or waste to what is in his charge: we will fine him, and the land shall be handed over to two lawful and discreet men of that fee who shall answer to us, or to him to whom we shall have referred them, regarding those issues. And if we shall have given or sold to any one the custody of any such land, and he shall have caused destruction or waste to it – he shall lose that custody, and it shall be given to two lawful and discreet men of that fee, who likewise shall answer to us, as has been explained.

5. The administrator, moreover, so long as he may have the custody of the land, shall keep in order, from the issues of that land, the houses, parks, warrens, lakes, mills, and other things pertaining to it. And he shall restore to the heir when he comes to full age, his whole land stocked with ploughs and wainnages, according as the time of the wainnage requires and the issues of the land will reasonably permit.

6. Heirs may marry without disparagement; so, nevertheless, that, before the marriage is contracted, it shall be announced to the relations by blood of the heir himself.

7. A widow, after the death of her husband, shall straightway, and without difficulty, have her marriage portion and her inheritance, nor shall she give any thing in return for her dowry, her marriage portion, or the inheritance which belonged to her, and which she and her husband held on the day of the death of that husband. And she may remain in the house of her husband, after his death, for forty days; within which her dowry shall be paid over to her.

8. No widow shall be forced to marry when she prefers to live without a husband; so, however, that she gives security not to marry without our consent, if she hold from us, or the consent of the lord from whom she holds, if she hold from another.

9. Neither we nor our bailiffs shall seize any revenue for any debt, so long as the chattels of the debtor suffice to pay the debt; nor shall the sponsors of that debtor be distrained so long as that chief debtor has enough to pay the debt. But if the chief debtor fail in paying the debt, not having the wherewithal to pay it, the sponsors shall answer for the debt. And, if they shall wish, they may have the lands and revenues of the debtor until satisfaction shall have been given them for the debt previously paid for him; unless the chief debtor shall show that he is quit in that respect towards those same sponsors.

10. If any one shall have taken any sum, great or small, as a loan from the Jews, and shall die before that debt is paid – that debt shall not bear interest so long as the heir, from whomever he may hold, shall be under age. And if the debt fall into our hands, we shall take nothing save the chattel contained in the deed.

11. And if any one dies owing a debt to the Jews, his wife shall have her dowry, and shall restore nothing of that debt. But if there shall remain children of that dead man, and they shall be under age, the necessaries shall be provided for them according to the nature of the dead man's holding; and, from the residue, the debt shall be paid, saving the service due to the lords. In like manner shall be done concerning debts that are due to others besides Jews.

12. No scutage or aid shall be imposed in our realm unless by the common counsel of our realm; except for redeeming our body, and knighting our eldest son, and marrying once our eldest daughter. And for these purposes there shall only be given a reasonable aid. In like manner shall be done concerning the aids of the city of London.

13. And the city of London shall have all its old liberties and free customs as well by land as by water. Moreover we will and grant that all other cities and boroughs, and towns and ports, shall have all their liberties and free customs.

14. And, in order to have the common counsel of the realm in the matter of assessing an aid otherwise than in the aforesaid cases, or of assessing a scutage – we shall cause, under seal through our letters, the archbishops, bishops, abbots, earls, and greater barons to be summoned for a fixed day – for a term, namely, at least forty days distant – and for a fixed place. And, moreover, we shall cause to be summoned in general, through our sheriffs and bailiffs, all those who hold of us in chief. And in all those letters of summons we shall express the cause of the summons. And when a summons has thus been made, the business shall be proceeded with on the day appointed according to the counsel of those who shall be present, even though not all shall come who were summoned.

15. We will not allow any one henceforth to take an aid from his freemen save for the redemption of his body, and the knighting of his eldest son, and the marrying, once, of his eldest daughter; and, for these purposes, there shall only be given a reasonable aid.

16. No one shall be forced to do more service for a knight's fee, or for another free holding, than is due from it.

17. Common pleas shall not follow our court but shall be held in a certain fixed place.

18. Assizes of novel disseisin, of mort d'ancestor, and of darrein presentment shall not be held save in their own counties, and in this way: we, or our chief justice, if we shall be absent from the kingdom, shall send two justices though each county four times a year; they, with four knights from each county, chosen by the county, shall hold the aforesaid assizes in the county, and on the day and at the place of the county court.

19. And if on the day of the county court the aforesaid assizes can not be held, a sufficient number of knights and free tenants, from those who were present at the county court on that day, shall remain, so that through them the judgements may be suitably given, according as the matter may have been great or small.

20. A freeman shall only be amerced for a small offence according to the measure of that offence. And for a great offence he shall be amerced according to the magnitude of the offence, saving his way of living; and a merchant, in the same way, saving his merchandise. And a villein, in the same way, if he fall under our mercy, shall be amerced saving his wainnage. And none of the aforesaid fines shall be imposed save upon oath of upright men from the neighbourhood.

21. Earls and barons shall not be amerced save through their peers, and only according to the measure of the offence.

22. No clerk shall be amerced for his lay tenement except according to the manner of the other persons aforesaid; and not according to the amount of his ecclesiastical benefice.

23. Neither a town nor a man shall be forced to make bridges over the rivers, with the exception of those who, from of old and of right ought to do it.

24. No sheriff, constable, coroners, or other bailiffs of ours shall hold the pleas of our crown.

25. All counties, hundreds, wapentakes and tithings – our demesne manors being excepted – shall continue according to the old farms, without any increase at all.

26. If any one holding from us a lay fee shall die, and our sheriff or bailiff can show our letters patent containing our summons for the debt which the dead man owed to us – our sheriff or bailiff may be allowed to attach and enroll the chattels of the dead man to the value of that debt, through view of lawful men; in such way, however, that nothing shall be removed thence until the debt is paid which was plainly owed to us. And the residue shall be left to the executors that they may carry out the will of the dead man. And if nothing is owed to us by him, all the chattels shall go to the use prescribed by the deceased, saving their reasonable portions to his wife and children.

27. If any freeman shall have died intestate his chattels shall be distributed through the hands of his near relatives and friends, by view of the church; saving to any one the debts which the dead man owed him.

28. No constable or other bailiff of ours shall take the corn or other chattels of any one except he straightway give money for them, or can be allowed a respite in that regard by the will of the seller.

29. No constable shall force any knight to pay money for castle-ward if he be willing to perform that ward in person, or – he for a reasonable cause not being able to perform it himself – through another proper man. And if we shall have led or sent him on a military expedition, he shall be quit of ward according to the amount of time during which, through us, he shall have been in military service.

30. No sheriff nor bailiff of ours, nor any one else, shall take the horses or carts of any freeman for transport, unless by the will of that freeman.

31. Neither we nor our bailiffs shall take another's wood for castles or for other private uses, unless by the will of him to whom the wood belongs.

32. We shall not hold the lands of those convicted of felony longer than a year and a day; and then the lands shall be restored to the lords of the fiefs.

33. Henceforth all the weirs in the Thames and Medway, and throughout all England, save on the sea-coast, shall be done away with entirely.

34. Henceforth the writ which is called Praecipe shall not be served on any one for any holding so as to cause a free man to lose his court.

35. There shall be one measure of wine throughout our whole realm, and one measure of ale and one measure of corn – namely, the London quart; –and one width of dyed and russet and hauberk cloths – namely, two ells below the selvage. And with weights, moreover, it shall be as with measures.

36. Henceforth nothing shall be given or taken for a writ of inquest in a matter concerning life or limb; but it shall be conceded gratis, and shall not be denied.

37. If any one hold of us in fee-farm, or in socage or in burkage, and hold land of another by military service, we shall not, by reason of that fee-farm, or socage, or burkage, have the wardship of his heir or of his land which is held in fee from another. Nor shall we have the wardship of that fee-farm, or socage, or burkage unless that fee-farm owe military service. We shall not, by reason of some petit-serjeanty which some one holds of us through the service of giving us knives or arrows or the like, have the wardship of his heir or of the land which he holds of another by military service.

38. No bailiff, on his own simple assertion, shall henceforth put any one to his law, without producing faithful witnesses in evidence.

39. No freeman shall be taken, or imprisoned, or disseised, or outlawed, or exiled, or in any way harmed – nor will we go upon or send upon him – save by the lawful judgement of his peers or by the law of the land.

40. To none will we sell, to none deny or delay, right or justice.

41. All merchants may safely and securely go out of England, and come into England, and delay and pass through England, as well by land as by water, for the purpose of buying and selling, free from all evil taxes, subject to the ancient and right customs – save in time of war, and if they are of the land at war against us. And if such be found in our land at the beginning of the war, they shall be held, without harm to their bodies and goods, until it shall be known to us or our chief justice how the merchants of our land are to be treated who shall, at that time, be found in the land at war against us. And if ours shall be safe there, the others shall be safe in our land.

42. Henceforth any person, saving fealty to us, may go out of our realm and return to it, safely and securely, by land and by water, except perhaps for a brief period in time of war, for the common good of the realm. But prisoners and outlaws are excepted according to the law of the realm; also people of a land at war against us, and the merchants, with regard to whom shall be done as we have said.

43. If any one hold from any escheat – as from the honour of Wallingford, Nottingham, Boulogne, Lancaster, or the other escheats which are in our hands and are baronies and shall die, his heir shall not give another relief, nor shall he perform for us other service than he would perform for a baron if that barony were in the hand of a baron; and we shall hold it in the same way in which the baron has held it.

44. Persons dwelling without the forest shall not henceforth come before the forest justices, through common summonses, unless they are impleaded or are the sponsors of some person or persons attached for matters concerning the forest.

45. We will not make men justices, constables, sheriffs, or bailiffs, unless they are such as know the law of the realm, and are minded to observe it rightly.

46. All barons who have founded abbeys for which they have charters of the kings of England, or ancient right of tenure, shall have, as they ought to have, their custody when vacant.

47. All forests constituted as such in our time shall straightway be annulled; and the same shall be done for river banks made into places of defence by us in our time.

48. All evil customs concerning forests and warrens, and concerning foresters and warreners, sheriffs and their servants, river banks and their guardians, shall straightway be inquired into in each county, through twelve sworn knights from that county, and shall be eradicated by them, entirely, so that they shall never be renewed, within forty days after the inquest has been made; in such manner that we shall first know about them, or our justice if we be not in England.

49. We shall straightway return all hostages and charters which were delivered to us by Englishmen as a surety for peace or faithful service.

50. We shall entirely remove from their bailiwicks the relatives of Gerard de Athycs, so that they shall henceforth have no bailiwick in England: Engelard de Cygnes, Andrew Peter and Guy de Chanceaux, Guy de Cicogné, Geoffrey de Martigny and his brothers, Philip Mark and his brothers, and Geoffrey his nephew, and the whole following of them.

51. And straightway after peace is restored we shall remove from the realm all the foreign soldiers, crossbowmen, servants, hirelings, who may have come with horses and arms to the harm of the realm.

52. If any one shall have been disseised by us, or removed, without a legal sentence of his peers, from his lands, castles, liberties or lawful right, we shall straightway restore them to him. And if a dispute shall arise concerning this matter it shall be settled according to the judgement of the twenty-five barons who are mentioned below as sureties for the peace. But with regard to all those things of which any one was, by king Henry our father or king Richard our brother, disseised or dispossessed without legal judgement of his peers, which we have in our hand or which others hold, and for which we ought to give a guarantee: we shall have respite until the common term for crusaders. Except with regard to those concerning which a plea was moved, or an inquest made by our order, before we took the cross. But when we return from our pilgrimage, or if, by chance, we desist from our pilgrimage, we shall straightway then show full justice regarding them.

53. We shall have the same respite, moreover, and in the same manner, in the matter of showing justice with regard to forests to be annulled and forests to remain, which Henry our father or Richard our brother constituted; and in the matter of wardships of lands which belong to the fee of another – wardships of which kind we have hitherto enjoyed by reason of the fee which some one held from us in military service; – and in the matter of abbeys founded in the fee of another than ourselves – in which

the lord of the fee may say that he has jurisdiction. And when we return, or if we desist from our pilgrimage, we shall straightway exhibit full justice to those complaining with regard to these matters.

54. No one shall be taken or imprisoned on account of the appeal of a woman concerning the death of another than her husband.

55. All fines imposed by us unjustly and contrary to the law of the land, and all amercements made unjustly and contrary to the law of the land, shall be altogether remitted, or it shall be done with regard to them according to the judgement of the twenty-five barons mentioned below as sureties for the peace, or according to the judgement of the majority of them together with the aforesaid Stephen archbishop of Canterbury, if he can be present, and with others whom he may wish to associate with himself for this purpose. And if he can not be present, the affair shall nevertheless proceed without him; in such way that, if one or more of the said twenty-five barons shall be concerned in a similar complaint, they shall be removed as to this particular decision, and, in their place, for this purpose alone, others shall be substituted who shall be chosen and sworn by the remainder of those twenty-five.

56. If we have disseised or dispossessed Welshmen of their lands or liberties or other things without legal judgement of their peers, in England or in Wales – they shall straightway be restored to them. And if a dispute shall arise concerning this, then action shall be taken upon it in the March through judgement of their peers – concerning English holdings according to the law of England, concerning Welsh holdings according to the law of Wales, concerning holdings in the March according to the law of the March. The Welsh shall do likewise with regard to us and our subjects.

57. But with regard to all those things of which any one of the Welsh was, by king Henry our father or king Richard our brother, disseised or dispossessed without legal judgement of his peers, which we have in our hand or which others hold, and for which we ought to give a guarantee: we shall have respite until the common term for crusaders. Except with regard to those concerning which a plea was moved, or an inquest made by our order, before we took the cross. But when we return from our pilgrimage, or if, by chance, we desist from our pilgrimage, we shall straightway then show full justice regarding them, according to the laws of Wales and the aforesaid districts.

58. We shall straightway return the son of Llewelin and all the Welsh hostages, and the charters delivered to us as surety for the peace.

59. We shall act towards Alexander king of the Scots regarding the restoration of his sisters, and his hostages, and his liberties and his lawful right, as we shall act towards our other barons of England; unless it ought to be otherwise according to the charters which we hold from William, his father, the former king of the Scots. And this shall be done through judgement of his peers in our court.

60. Moreover all the subjects of our realm, clergy as well as laity, shall, as far as pertains to them, observe, with regard to their vassals, all these aforesaid customs and liberties which we have decreed shall, as far as pertains to us, be observed in our realm with regard to our own.

61. Inasmuch as, for the sake of God, and for the bettering of our realm, and for the more ready healing of the discord which has arisen between us and our barons, we have made all these aforesaid concessions – wishing them to enjoy for ever entire and firm stability, we make and grant to them the following security: that the barons, namely, may elect at their pleasure twenty-five barons from the realm, who ought, with all their strength, to observe, maintain and cause to be observed, the peace and

privileges which we have granted to them and confirmed by this our present charter. In such wise, namely, that if we, or our justice, or our bailiffs, or any one of our servants shall have transgressed against any one in any respect, or shall have broken some one of the articles of peace or security, and our transgression shall have been shown to four barons of the aforesaid twenty-five: those four barons shall come to us, or, if we are abroad, to our justice, showing to us our error; and they shall ask us to cause that error to be amended without delay. And if we do not amend that error, or, we being abroad, if our justice do not amend it within a term of forty days from the time when it was shown to us or, we being abroad, to our justice: the aforesaid four barons shall refer the matter to the remainder of the twenty-five barons, and those twenty-five barons, with the whole land in common, shall distrain and oppress us in every way in their power – namely, by taking our castles, lands and possessions, and in every other way that they can, until amends shall have been made according to their judgement. Saving the persons of ourselves, our queen and our children. And when amends shall have been made they shall be in accord with us as they had been previously. And whoever of the land wishes to do so, shall swear that in carrying out all the aforesaid measures he will obey the mandates of the aforesaid twenty-five barons, and that, with them, he will oppress us to the extent of his power. And, to any one who wishes to do so, we publicly and freely give permission to swear; and we will never prevent any one from swearing. Moreover, all those in the land who shall be unwilling, themselves and of their own accord, to swear to the twenty-five barons as to distraining and oppressing us with them: such ones we shall make to swear by our mandate, as has been said. And if any one of the twenty-five barons shall die, or leave the country, or in any other way be prevented from carrying out the afore-said measures – the remainder of the aforesaid twenty-five barons shall choose another in his place, according to their judgement, who shall be sworn in the same way as the others. Moreover, in all things entrusted to those twenty-five barons to be carried out, if those twenty-five shall be present and chance to disagree among them-selves with regard to some matter, or if some of them, having been summoned, shall be unwilling or unable to be present: that which the majority of those present shall decide or decree shall be considered binding and valid, just as if all the twenty-five had consented to it. And the aforesaid twenty-five shall swear that they will faithfully observe all the foregoing, and will cause them to be observed to the extent of their power. And we shall obtain nothing from any one, either through ourselves or through another, by which any of those concessions and liberties may be revoked or diminished. And if any such thing shall have been obtained, it shall be vain and invalid, and we shall never make use of it either through ourselves or through another.

62. And we have fully remitted to all, and pardoned, all the ill-will, anger and rancour which have arisen between us and our subjects, clergy and laity, from the time of the struggle. Moreover we have fully remitted to all, clergy and laity, and – as far as pertains to us – have pardoned fully all the transgressions committed, on the occasion of that same struggle, from Easter of the sixteenth year of our reign until the re-establishment of peace. In witness of which, moreover, we have caused to be drawn up for them letters patent of lord Stephen, archbishop of Canterbury, lord Henry, archbishop of Dublin, and the aforesaid bishops and master Pandulf, regarding that surety and the aforesaid concessions.

63. Wherefore we will and firmly decree that the English church shall be free, and that the subjects of our realm shall have and hold all the aforesaid liberties, rights

and concessions, duly and in peace, freely and quietly, fully and entirely, for themselves and their heirs, from us and our heirs, in all matters and in all places, forever, as has been said. Moreover it has been sworn, on our part as well as on the part of the barons, that all these above mentioned provisions shall be observed with good faith and without evil intent. The witnesses being the above mentioned and many others. Given through our hand, in the plain called Runnimede between Windsor and Stanes, on the fifteenth day of June, in the seventeenth year of our reign.

Source: E. F. Henderson (ed. and trans.) *Select Historical Document of the Middle Ages* (1925) pp. 135–148

The 'liberties' of the English people exemplified in the Magna Carta, together with the Common Law tradition, with its emphasis on precedence rather than precept, and its related institutions like the jury system, were to have a profound impact on the jurisprudence not only of modern England but on the United States. The Middle Ages, as barbaric as they may have appeared to the leaders of the Enlightenment, were the quarry from which English and American institutions were hewn. That quarry was dug deep in English history and its elements included much of Roman and Canon Law but its character was suited to the realities of medieval life. These realities were often unpleasant. The dynastic problems that beset the English monarchy in the later Middle Ages particularly in the fifteenth century, which resulted in the prolonged Wars of the Roses, led to much conflict and bloodshed.

6.14 Proclamation of Henry Tudor
22 and 23 August 1485

And moreover, the king ascertaineth you that Richard duke of Gloucester, late called King Richard, was slain at a place called Sandeford, within the shire of Leicester, and brought dead off the field unto the town of Leicester, and there was laid openly, that every man might see and look upon him. And also there was slain upon the same field, John late duke of Norfolk, John late earl of Lincoln, Thomas, late earl of Surrey, Francis Viscount Lovell, Sir Walter Devereux, Lord Ferrers, Richard Radcliffe, knight, Robert Brackenbury, knight, with many other knights, squires and gentlemen, of whose souls God have mercy.

Source: P. L. Hughes and J. P. Larkin (eds) *Tudor Royal Proclamations: Vol. I. The Early Tudors 1485–1553* (1964) p. 3.

The king's central role in medieval society was leading his people into battle and much opportunity was available for heroism in the prolonged fighting against France known as the Hundred Years War.

৪৯ 6.15 The Battle of Crecy (1346) ৬৩

The Englishmen, who were in three battles lying on the ground to rest them, as soon as they saw the Frenchmen approach, they rose upon their feet fair and easily without any haste and arranged their battles. The first, which was the prince's battle, the archers there stood in manner of a herse and the men of arms in the bottom of the battle. The earl of Northampton and the earl of Arundel with the second battle were on a wing in good order, ready to comfort the prince's battle, if need were.

The lords and knights of France came not to the assembly together in good order, for some came before and some came after in such haste and evil order, that one of them did trouble another. When the French king saw the Englishmen, his blood changed, and said to his marshals: 'Make the Genoways go on before and begin the battle in the name of God and Saint Denis.' There were of the Genoways crossbows about a fifteen thousand, but they were so weary of going afoot that day a six leagues armed with their crossbows, that they said to their constables: 'We be not well ordered to fight this day, for we be not in the case to do any great deed of arms: we have more need of rest.' These words came to the earl of Alençon, who said: 'A man is well at ease to be charged with such a sort of rascals, to be faint and fail now at most need.' Also the same season there fell a great rain and a clipse with a terrible thunder, and before the rain there came flying over both battles a great number of crows for fear of the tempest coming. Then anon the air began to wax clear, and the sun to shine fair and bright, the which was right in the Frenchmen's eyes and on the Englishmen's backs. When the Genoways were assembled together and began to approach, they made a great [shout] and cry to abash the Englishmen, but they stood still and stirred not for all that: then the Genoways again the second time made another leap and a fell cry, and stept forward a little, and the Englishmen removed not one foot: thirdly, again they lept and cried, and went forth till they came within shot; then they shot fiercely with their crossbows. Then the English archers stept forth one pace and let fly their arrows so wholly [together] and so thick, that it seemed snow. When the Genoways felt the arrows piercing through heads arms and breasts, many of them cast down their crossbows and did cut their strings and returned discomfited. When the French king saw them fly away, he said: 'Slay these rascals, for they shall let and trouble us without reason.' Then ye should have seen the men at arms dash in among them and killed a great number of them: and ever still the Englishmen shot whereas they saw thickest press; the sharp arrows ran into the men of arms and into their horses, and many fell, horse and men, among the Genoways, and when they were down, they could not relieve again, the press was so thick that one overthrew another. And also among the Englishmen there were certain rascals that went afoot with great knives, and they went in among the men of arms, and slew and murdered many as they lay on the ground, both earls, barons, knights, and squires, whereof the king of England was after displeased, for he had rather they had been taken prisoners. The valiant king of Bohemia called Charles of Luxembourg, son to the noble emperor Henry of Luxembourg, for all that he was nigh blind, when he understood the order of the battle, he said to the about him: 'Where is the lord Charles my son?' His men said: 'Sir we cannot tell; we think he be fighting.' Then he said: 'Sirs, ye are my men, my companions and friends in this journey: I require you bring me so far forward, that I may strike one stroke with my sword.' They said they would do his commandment, and to the intent that they should not lose him in the press, they tied all their reins of their bridles each to other and set the king before to accomplish his desire, and so they went on their enemies. The lord Charles of Bohemia his son, who wrote himself king of Almaine and bare the arms, he came in good order to the battle; but when he saw that the matter went awry on their party, he departed, I cannot tell you which way. The king his father was so far forward that he strake a stroke with his sword, yea and more than four, and fought valiantly and so did his company; and they adventured themselves so forward, that they were there all slain; and the next day they were found in the place about the king, and all their horses tied each to other. Then the second battle of the Englishmen came to succour the prince's battle, the which was time, for they had as then much ado and they with the prince sent a messenger to the king, who was on a little windmill hill. Then the knight said to the king: 'Sir, the earl of Warwick and the earl of Oxford, sir Raynold Cobham and other, such as be about the prince your son, are fiercely fought withal and are sore handled; wherefore they desire you that you and your battle will come and aid them; for if the Frenchmen increase, as they doubt they will, your son and they shall have much ado.' Then the king said: 'Is my son dead or hurt or on the earth felled?' 'No, sir,' quoth the knight, 'but he is hardly matched; wherefore he hath need of your aid.' 'Well,' said the king, 'return to him and to them that sent you hither, and say to them that they send no more to me for any adventure that falleth, as long as my son is alive: and also say to them that they suffer him this day to win his spurs; for if God be pleased, I will this journey be his and the honour thereof, and to them that be about him.'

Source: G. C. Macaulay (ed.), Lord Berners (trans.)
The Chronicles of Froissart (1904) pp. 104–105, 201

ৡৢ 6.16 The English in the 1370s ৢৡ

About the space of a month or more was the prince of Wales before the city of Limoges, and there was neither assault nor scrimmish, but daily they mined. And they within knew well how they were mined, and made a countermine there against to have destroyed the English miners; but they failed of their mine. And when the prince's miners saw how the countermine against them failed, they said to the prince: 'Sir, whensoever it shall please you we shall cause a part of the wall to fall into the dikes, whereby ye shall enter into the city at your ease without any danger.' Which words pleased greatly the prince, and said: 'I will that tomorrow betimes ye shew forth and execute your work.' Then the miners set fire into their mine, and so the next morning, as the prince had ordained, there fell down a great pane of the wall and filled the dikes, whereof the Englishmen were glad and were ready armed in the field to enter into the town. The foot-men might well enter at their ease, and so they did and ran to the gate and beat down the fortifying gate and barriers, for there was no defence against them: it was done so suddenly that they of the town were not ware thereof. Then the prince, the duke of Lancaster, the earl of Cambridge, the earl of Pembroke, sir Guichard d'Angle and all the other with their companies entered into the city, and all other foot-men, ready apparelled to do evil, and to pill and rob the city, and to slay men, women and children, for so it was commanded them to do. It was great pity to see the men, women and children that kneeled down on their knees before the prince for mercy; but he was so inflamed with ire, that he took no heed to them, so that none was heard, but all put to death, as they were met withal, and such as were nothing culpable. There was no pity taken of the poor people, who wrought never no manner of treason, yet they bought it dearer than the great personages, such as had done the evil and trespass. There was not so hard a heart within the city of Limoges, and if he had any remembrance of God, but that wept piteously for the great mischief that they saw before their eyes: for more than three thousand men, women and children were slain and beheaded that day, God have mercy on their souls, for I trow they were martyrs.

> **Source: G. C. Macaulay (ed.), Lord Berners (trans.)**
> *The Chronicles of Froissart* (1904) p. 201

The war with France was the beginning of a national myth which was to find its focus in the history plays of Shakespeare. It was also suggested in the development of the Arthurian legend which became one of the most enduring literary themes in English literature, capturing a lost chivalric idyll.

৪৯ 6.17 The Legend of King Arthur ৬৯

Chapter XIV

How the eleven kings with their host fought against Arthur and his host, and many great feats of the war
Then King Arthur and King Ban and King Bors, with their good and trusty knights, set on them so fiercely that they made them overthrow their pavilions on their heads, but the eleven kings, by manly prowess of arms, took a fair champaign, but there was slain that morrowtide ten thousand good men's bodies. And so they had afore them a strong passage, yet were they fifty thousand of hardy men. Then it drew toward day. Now shall ye do by mine advice, said Merlin unto the three kings: I would that King Ban and King Bors, with their fellowship of ten thousand men, were put in a wood here beside, in an ambushment, and keep them privy, and that they be laid or the light of the day come, and that they stir not till ye and your knights have fought with them long. And when it is daylight, dress your battle even afore them and the

passage, that they may see all your host, for then will they be the more hardy, when they see you but about twenty thousand men, and cause them to be the gladder to suffer you and your host to come over the passage. All the three kings and the whole barons said that Merlin said passingly well, and it was done anon as Merlin had devised. So on the morn, when either host saw other, the host of the north was well comforted. Then to Ulfius and Brastias were delivered three thousand men of arms, and they set on them fiercely in the passage, and slew on the right hand and on the left hand that it was wonder to tell.

When that the eleven kings saw that there was so few a fellowship did such deeds of arms, they were ashamed and set on them again fiercely; and there was Sir Ulfius's horse slain under him, but he did marvellously well on foot. But the Duke Eustace of Cambenet and King Clariance of Northumberland, were alway grievous on Ulfius. Then Brastias saw his fellow fared so withal he smote the duke with a spear, that horse and man fell down. That saw King Clariance and returned unto Brastias, and either smote other so that horse and man went to the earth, and so they lay long astonied, and their horses' knees brast to the hard bone. Then came Sir Kay the seneschal with six fellows with him, and did passing well. With that came the eleven kings, and there was Griflet put to the earth, horse and man, and Lucas the butler, horse and man, by King Brandegoris, and King Idres, and King Agwisance. Then waxed the medley passing hard on both parties. When Sir Kay saw Griflet on foot, he rode on King Nentres and smote him down, and led his horse unto Sir Griflet, and horsed him again. Also Sir Kay with the same spear smote down King Lot, and hurt him passing sore. That saw the King with the Hundred Knights, and ran unto Sir Kay and smote him down, and took his horse, and gave him King Lot, whereof he said gramercy. When Sir Griflet saw Sir Kay and Lucas the butler on foot, he took a sharp spear, great and square, and rode to Pinel, a good man of arms, and smote horse and man down, and then he took his horse, and gave him unto Sir Kay. Then King Lot saw King Nentres on foot, he ran unto Melot de la Roche, and smote him down, horse and man, and gave King Nentres the horse, and horsed him again. Also the King of the Hundred Knights saw King Idres on foot; then he ran unto Gwimiart de Bloi, and smote him down, horse and man, and gave King Idres the horse, and horsed him again; and King Lot smote down Clariance de la Forest Savage, and gave the horse unto Duke Eustace. And so when they had horsed the kings again they drew them, all eleven kings, together, and said they would be revenged of the damage that they had taken that day. The meanwhile came in Sir Ector with an eager countenance, and found Ulfius and Brastias on foot, in great peril of death, that were foul defoiled under horse-feet. Then Arthur as a lion, ran unto King Cradelment of North Wales, and smote him through the left side, that the horse and the king fell down; and then he took the horse by the rein, and led him unto Ulfius, and said, Have this horse, mine old friend, for great need hast thou of horse. Gramercy, said Ulfius. Then Sir Arthur did so marvellously in arms, that all men had wonder. When the King with the Hundred Knights saw King Cradelment on foot, he ran unto Sir Ector, that was well horsed, Sir Kay's father, and smote horse and man down, and gave the horse unto the king, and horsed him again. And when King Arthur saw the king ride on Sir Ector's horse, he was wroth and with his sword he smote the king on the helm, that a quarter of the helm and shield fell down, and so the sword carved down unto the horse's neck, and so the king and the horse fell down to the ground. Then Sir Kay came unto Sir Morganore, seneschal with the King of the Hundred Knights, and smote him down, horse and man, and led the horse unto his father, Sir Ector; then

Sir Ector ran unto a knight, knight Lardans, and smote horse and man down, and led the horse unto Sir Brastias, that great need had of an horse, and was greatly defoiled. When Brastias beheld Lucas the butler, that lay like a dead man under the horses' feet, and ever Sir Griflet did marvellously for to rescue him, and there were always fourteen knights on Sir Lucas; then Brastias smote one of them on the helm, that it went to the teeth, and he rode to another and smote him, that the arm flew into the field. Then he went to the third and smote him on the shoulder, that shoulder and arm flew in the field. And when Griflet saw rescues, he smote a knight on the temples, that head and helm went to the earth, and Griflet took the horse of that knight, and led him unto Sir Lucas, and bade him mount upon the horse and revenge his hurts. For Brastias had slain a knight to-fore and horsed Griflet. . . .

Chapter XVII

Yet more of the same battle, and how it was ended by Merlin
When Sir Arthur and King Ban and Bors beheld them and all their knights, they praised them much for their noble cheer of chivalry, for the hardiest fighters that ever they heard or saw. With that, there dressed them a forty noble knights, and said unto the three kings, they would break their battle; . . . all these knights rode on afore with spears on their thighs, and spurred their horses mightily as the horses might run. And the eleven kings with part of their knights rushed with their horses as fast as they might with their spears, and there they did on both parties marvellous deeds of arms. So came into the thick of the press, Arthur, Ban, and Bors, and slew down right on both hands, that their horses went in blood up to the fetlocks. But ever the eleven kings and their host was ever in the visage of Arthur. Wherefore Ban and Bors had great marvel, considering the great slaughter that there was, but at the last they were driven aback over a little river. With that came Merlin on a great black horse, and said unto Arthur, Thou hast never done! Hast thou not done enough? of three score thousand this day hast thou left alive but fifteen thousand, and it is time to say Ho! For God is wroth with thee, that thou wilt never have done; for yonder eleven kings at this time will not be overthrown, but an thou tarry on them any longer, thy fortune will turn and they shall increase. And therefore withdraw you unto your lodging, and rest you as soon as ye may, and reward your good knights with gold and with silver, for they have well deserved it; there may no riches be too dear for them, for of so few men as ye have, there were never men did more of prowess than they have done today, for ye have matched this day with the best fighters of the world. That is truth, said King Ban and Bors. Also said Merlin, withdraw you where ye list, for this three year I dare undertake they shall not dere you; and by then ye shall hear new tidings. And then Merlin said unto Arthur, These eleven kings have more on hand than they are ware of, for the Saracens are landed in their countries, more than forty thousand, that burn and slay, and have laid siege at the castle Wandesborow, and make great destruction; therefore dread you not this three year. Also, sir, all the goods that be gotten at this battle, let it be searched, and when ye have it in your hands, let it be given freely unto these two kings, Ban and Bors, that they may reward their knights withal; and that shall cause strangers to be of better will to do you service at need. Also you be able to reward your own knights of your own goods whensomever it liketh you. It is well said, quoth Arthur, and as thou hast devised, so shall it be done. When it was delivered to Ban and Bors, they gave the goods as freely to their knights as freely as it was given to them. Then Merlin took

his leave of Arthur and of the two kings, for to go and see his master Bleise, that dwelt in Northumberland; and so he departed and came to his master, that was passing glad of his coming; and there he told how Arthur and the two kings had sped at the great battle, and how it was ended, and told the names of every king and knight of worship that was there. And so Bleise wrote the battle word by word, as Merlin told him, how it began, and by whom, and in likewise how it was ended, and who had the worse. All the battles that were done in Arthur's days Merlin did his master Bleise do write; also he did do write all the battles that every worthy knight did of Arthur's court.

After this Merlin departed from his master and came to King Arthur, that was in the castle of Bedegraine, that was one of the castles that stand in the forest of Sherwood. And Merlin was so disguised that King Arthur knew him not, for he was all befurred in black sheep-skins, and a great pair of boots, and a bow and arrows, in a russet gown, and brought wild geese in his hand, and it was on the morn after Candlemas day; but King Arthur knew him not. Sir, said Merlin unto the king, will ye give me a gift? Wherefore, said King Arthur, should I give thee a gift, churl? Sir, said Merlin, ye were better to give me a gift that is not in your hand than to lose great riches, for here in the same place where the great battle was, is great treasure hid in the earth. Who told thee so, churl? said Arthur. Merlin told me so, said he. Then Ulfius and Brastias knew him well enough, and smiled. Sir, said these two knights, it is Merlin that so speaketh unto you. Then King Arthur was greatly abashed, and had marvel of Merlin, and so had King Ban and King Bors, and so they had great disport at him. So in the meanwhile there came a damosel that was an earl's daughter: his name was Sanam, and her name was Lionors, a passing fair damosel; and so she came thither for to do homage, as other lords did after the great battle. And King Arthur set his love greatly upon her, and so did she upon him, and the king had ado with her, and gat on her a child: his name was Borre, that was after a good knight, and of the Table Round. Then there came word that the King Rience of North Wales made great war on King Leodegrance of Cameliard, for the which thing Arthur was wroth, for he loved him well, and hated King Rience, for he was alway against him. So by ordinance of the three kings that were sent home unto Berwick, all they would depart for dread of King Claudas; and Phariance, and Antemes, and Gratian, and Lionses [of] Payarne, with the leaders of those that should keep the kings' lands.

Source: Sir Thomas Malory, *Le Morte D'Arthur*, 2 vols
(1903) Vol. 1, pp. 20–33

Further reading

R. Bartlett, *England Under the Norman and Angevin Kings 1075–1225* (Clarendon Press, Oxford, 2000).

M. Clanchy, *England and its Rulers*, 2nd edn (Blackwell, Oxford, 1998).

R. Davies, *Domination and Conquest: the Experience of Ireland, Scotland and Wales 1100–1300* (Cambridge University Press, Cambridge, 1990).

J. C. Holt, *Magna Carta*, 2nd edn (Cambridge University Press, Cambridge, 1992).

7

THE WORLD
OF THE OUTSIDER

The outsider is often seen as a modern concept, a typical archetype of the twentieth and twenty-first centuries, where the intervention of an outsider or alien can be seen as either sinister or helpful. The outsider as rebel, even a rebel without a cause, is now a stock character of fiction. In the Middle Ages life could be difficult if one did not fall into one of the accepted *ordines*. Yet alternative worlds did exist, and have their paradigm in the margins of medieval manuscripts with their grotesques and celebration of misrule. Some members of society – runaway monks, escaped serfs, hardened criminals – lived outside of the normal law and formed a genuine alternative society, and one celebrated in the Robin Hood ballads which proliferated in late medieval England.

7.1 Royal letters detailing local conditions in Nottingham, Derbyshire and Leicestershire

---

Through outlaws, robbers, thieves and malefactors, mounted and on foot ... wandering by day and night, so many and great homicides and robberies were done that no one with a small company could pass through those parts without being taken and killed or spoiled of his goods ... and no religious or other person could pass without being taken and spoiled of his goods.

Source: J. C. Holt, *Robin Hood* (1983) pp. 97–98

The most obvious group of medieval outsiders in Christendom were non-Christians: Muslims, Jews and Pagans. Beyond Iberia Muslims were few and identifying true 'pagans' (or even the survival of paganism) is notoriously difficult. The medieval Jewish community, however, is well documented and its history throws light, too, on the attitudes and mentality of 'mainstream' Christendom to all outsiders. Medieval Jews were segregated but persecuted only intermittently. In the medieval world the Jews had a unique and unfavourable legal status which restricted them to their own sections of town and identified them by their clothing. From the later twelfth century they had for a while the monopoly of lending which made them both indispensable and hated. The ambiguous attitudes of the Church towards the Jews gave way, especially when the Crusades focused attention on the Passion of Christ, to popular persecution.

---

৪ 7.2 St Augustine ৪ও

But the Jews who rejected Him, and slew Him (according to the needfulness of His death and resurrection), after that were miserably spoiled by the Romans, under the domination of strangers, and dispersed over the face of the whole earth. For they are in all places with their testament, to show that we have not forged those prophecies of Christ, which many of them considering, both before His passion and after His resurrection, believed in Him; and they are the remnant that are saved through grace. But the rest were blind, as the psalm says: 'Let their table be made a snare unto them, and their prosperity their ruin: let their eyes be blinded that they see not, and make their loins alway to tremble.' For in refusing to believe our scriptures, their own (which they read with blindness) are fulfilled upon them.

Some may say that the sibyl's prophecies which concern the Jews are but fictions of the Christians. But that suffices us which we have from the books of our enemies, which we acknowledge in that they preserve it for us against their wills, themselves and their books being dispersed as far as God's Church is extended and spread, in every corner of the world, as that prophecy of the psalm, which they themselves do read, foretells them. 'My merciful God will prevent me. God will let me see my desire upon mine enemies. Slay them not, lest my people forget it, but scatter them abroad with Thy power.' Here did God show mercy to His Church, even by the Jews His enemies, because, as the apostle says, 'through their fall cometh salvation to the Gentiles'. And therefore He slew them not, that is, He left them their name of Jews still, although they be the Romans' slaves, lest their utter dissolution should make us forget the law of God concerning this testimony of theirs. So it were nothing to say, 'Slay them not', but that He adds, 'Scatter them abroad': for if they were not dispersed throughout the whole world with their scriptures, the Church would lack their testimonies concerning those prophecies fulfilled in our Messiah.

Source: R. V. G. Tasker (ed.), J. Healey (trans.)
The City of God, 2 vols (1945) Vol. 2, pp. 220–221

---

৪ 7.3 Letter of Bernard of Clairvaux to the English people ৪ও
when he was promoting the Second Crusade (1146)

The Jews are not to be persecuted, killed, or even expelled. Ask all who know the Holy Scriptures about the prophecies concerning the Jews in the Psalms. 'God has informed me about my enemies, says the church: do not kill them, lest my people will be forgotten.' The Jews are for us like the living words of the Holy Scriptures, because they forever remind us of the Passion of the Lord. For that reason they have been dispersed in all directions so that they may, while bearing the punishment for their enormous crime, be living witnesses of our redemption. Therefore the church adds these words on behalf of the church: 'Make them totter by your power, and bring them down, O Lord, our shield' (Ps. 59:12). And that is what has happened: Everywhere they have been dispersed they have been brought down. Christian princes have submitted them to harsh slavery. But they will return when the evening begins (Ps. 59:7), and the time will come when they will receive attention. And finally, when the great heathen masses have entered the church, 'all Israel', according to the words of the apostle, 'will be saved' (Rom. ii: 25). But those who die will remain in death . . . What would happen to our hope for their salvation, for their conversion, which has been promised for the end of time, if the Jews were to be totally eradicated?

Source: B. Scott James (trans.) *The Letters of St Bernard of Clairvaux*, 2nd edn (1998) pp. 462–463

One of the frequent accusations against Jews was a supposed role in the spreading of the Black Death which swept across Europe in the middle of the fourteenth century and which signalled the end of the medieval hegemony.

৽ 7.4 Jews and the Black Death ৽

Many wise persons hold the opinion that the Jews are not guilty of poisoning the water, and that they only confessed it in excess of torture, but attribute the poisoning to the great earthquake which took place in January of last year, 1348; this burst open the crust of the earth and allowed the bad, noxious moistures and vapours to enter the wells and springs, as these impurities also fouled the air. This the Jews, of whom a large proportion are physicians and scientists, had learnt from their art and borne in mind, and on that account avoided the wells and springs, and in many places warned the people against them. For it would be impossible for them to have poisoned all wells throughout Christendom. In short, the people were incensed against the Jews, and they could expect no justice.

Source: J. Nohl, *The Black Death, A Chronicle of the Plague* (1926) p. 122

Epidemics and plagues were frightening but occasional visitations, but one group, the lepers, were forced to live a life apart in colonies which had their own restrictions and regimented way of life. Civil authorities might declare lepers legally dead but the church expected the leper's spouse to honour the marriage bond and care for the leper until their death. The religious texts might forbid the use of the rites of Christian burial, but the ritual of Separation was clearly modelled on that for the dead, and, in many places, the leper was required, as part of the ceremony, to stand in an open grave while the words were read to him.

❧ 7.5 Office at the seclusion of a leper ❧

The manner of casting out or separating those who are sick with leprosy from the whole

First of all the sick man or the leper clad in a cloak and in his usual dress, being in his house, ought to have notice of the coming of the priest who is on his way to the house to lead him to the church, and must in that guise wait for him. For the priest vested in surplice and stole, with the cross going before, makes his way to the sick man's house and addresses him with comforting words, pointing out and proving that if he blesses and praises God, and bears his sickness patiently, he may have a sure and certain hope that though he is sick in body he may be whole in soul, and may obtain the gift of everlasting salvation. And then with other words suitable to the occasion let the priest lead the leper to the church, when he has sprinkled him with holy water, the cross going before, the priest following, and last of all the sick man. Within the church let a black cloth, if it can be had, be set upon two trestles at some distance apart before the altar, and let the sick man take his place on bended knees beneath it between the trestles, after the manner of a dead man, although by the grace of God he yet lives in body and spirit, and in this posture let him devoutly hear mass. When this is finished and he has been sprinkled with holy water, he must be led with the cross through the presbytery to a place where a pause must be made. When the spot is reached the priest shall counsel him out of holy scripture, saying: 'Remember thine end and thou shalt never do amiss'. Whence Augustine says: 'He readily esteems all things lightly, who ever bears in mind that he will die.' The priest then with the spade casts earth on each of his feet, saying: 'Be thou dead to the world, but alive again unto God'.

And he comforts him and strengthens him to endure with the words of Isaiah spoken concerning our Lord Jesus Christ: 'Truly He hath borne our griefs and carried our sorrows, yet did we esteem Him as a leper smitten of God and afflicted'. Let him say also: 'If in weakness of body by means of suffering thou art made like unto Christ, thou mayest surely hope that thou wilt rejoice in spirit with God. May the Most High grant this to thee, numbering thee among his faithful ones in the book of life. Amen.'

It is to be noted that the priest must lead him to the church and from the church to his house as a dead man, chanting *Libera me, Domine*, in such wise that the sick man is covered with a black cloth. And the mass celebrated at his seclusion may be chosen either by the priest or by the sick man, but it is customary to say the following . . .

When leaving the church after mass the priest ought to stand at the door to sprinkle him with holy water. And he ought to commend him to the care of the people. Before mass the sick man ought to make his confession in the church, and never again; and in leading him forth the priest again begins the responsorium *Libera me, Domine*, with the other versicles. Then when he has come into the open fields he does as is aforesaid; and he ends by imposing prohibitions upon him in the following manner:

> 'I forbid you ever to enter churches, or to go into a market, or a mill, or a bakehouse, or into any assemblies of people.

I forbid you ever to wash your hands or even any of your belongings in spring or stream of water of any kind; and if you are thirsty you must drink water from your cup or some other vessel.

I forbid you ever henceforth to go out without your leper's dress, that you may be recognised by others; and you must not go outside your house unshod.

I forbid you, wherever you may be, to touch anything which you wish to buy, otherwise than with a rod or staff to show what you want.

I forbid you ever henceforth to enter taverns or other houses if you wish to buy wine; and take care even that what they give you they put into your cup.

I forbid you to have intercourse with any woman except your own wife.

I command you when you are on a journey not to return an answer to any one who questions you, till you have gone off the road to leeward, so that he may take no harm from you; and that you never go through a narrow lane lest you should meet some one.

I charge you if need require you to pass over some toll-way through rough ground, or elsewhere, that you touch no posts or things whereby you cross, till you have first put on your gloves.

I forbid you to touch infants or young folk, whosoever they may be, or to give to them or to others any of your possessions.

I forbid you henceforth to eat or drink in any company except that of lepers. And know that when you die you will be buried in your own house, unless it be, by favour obtained beforehand, in the church.'

And note that before he enters his house, he ought to have a coat and shoes of fur, his own plain shoes, and his signal the clappers, a hood and a cloak, two pairs of sheets, a cup, a funnel, a girdle, a small knife, and a plate. His house ought to be small, with a well, a couch furnished with coverlets, a pillow, a chest, a table, a seat, a candlestick, a shovel, a pot, and other needful articles.

When all is complete the priest must point out to him the ten rules which he has made for him; and let him live on earth in peace with his neighbour. Next must be pointed out to him the ten commandments of God, that he may live in heaven with the saints, and the priest repeats them to him in the presence of the people. And let the priest also point out to him that every day each faithful Christian is bound to say devoutly *Pater Noster, Ave Maria, Credo in Deum,* and *Credo in Spiritum,* and to protect himself with the sign of the cross, saying often *Benedicite.* When the priest leaves him he says: 'Worship God and give thanks to God. Have patience, and the Lord will be with thee. Amen'.

Source: R. M. Clay *The Mediaeval Hospitals of England* (1966) pp. 273–276

Among the most famous of medical hospitals for the sick (but not for lepers) was St Bartholomew's in London founded, during the reign of Henry I by Rahere, or Rayer, an Augustinian canon who had begun his 'professional' life as a jester or jongleur in the court of William Rufus. The work began in 1123 after he had a vision in which St Bartholomew saved him from a winged monster. Clowns and jesters were those whose liminality was formalised.

---

౭ 7.6 Of the vision that he saw in the way, and of the ౩ commandment of St Bartholomew the apostle

---

. . . In a certain night he [Rayer] saw a vision full of dread and of sweetness when, after the labours and sweating that he had by day, his body with rest he would refresh. It seemed to him he was borne up on high by a certain beast having four feet and two wings: and set him in a high place; and when he, from so great a height would inflect and bow down his eye to the lower part he beheld an horrible pit which horrible sight impressed in him, the beholder, great dread and horror. For the deepness of the same pit was deeper than any man might see. Therefore he, the secret knower of his faults, slipped into that cruel pit and he shuddered and for dread trembled and great cries proceeded from his mouth. To whom, dreading and for dread crying, appeared a certain man, possessing in mien the majesty of a king of great beauty and imperial authority and his eye on him fastened, he said good words, words of consolation bringing good tidings, and he should say in this wise, 'O man', he said. 'What and how much service should thou give to him that in so great a peril hath brought help to thee'. Anon he answered to this saying, 'Whatsoever might be of heart and of mighty diligence should I give in recompense to my deliverer.' And then said he, 'I am Bartholomew, the Apostle of Jesus Christ, come to succour thee in thy anguish and to open to thee the secret mysteries of heaven, know me truly by the will and commandment of the high Trinity and the coming favour of the Celestial Court and counsel to have chosen a place in the suburbs of London, at Smithfield; where in mine name thou shalt found a Church and it shall be the house of God, there shall be the tabernacle of the Lamb, the temple of the Holy Ghost. This spiritual house, almighty God, shall inhabit and hallow it and glory it: and his eyes shall be open and his ears attending on this house, night and day that the asker in it shall receive, the seeker shall find and the ringer or knocker shall enter. Truly every soul converted, penitent of his sin, and in this place praying, in heaven shall be heard. The seeker with perfect heart, for whatsoever tribulations, without doubt, he shall find help. To them that with faithful desire knock at the door of the house, assistant Angels shall open the gate of heaven, receiving and offering to God the prayers and vows of faithful people. Wherefore thy hand is, there be comfort in God, having in him trust, do you manly. Neither doubt the cost of this building, only give your diligence and my part shall be proud necessities, direct, build and end this work, and this place to me accept with evident tokens and signs protect and defend it constantly, under the shadows of my wings, and therefore of this work know me the master. And you only the minister. Use diligently your service and I shall show my lordship.' With these words the vision disappeared.

Source: Sir Norman Moore, *The Book of the Foundation of St Bartholomew's Church in London: The Church Belonging to the Priory of the Same in West Smithfield*. Original series, 163. H. Milford (1923) Liber 1: Capitulum 4, pp. 4–6 (adapted)

WELLS CATHEDRAL:
A MEDIEVAL WORLD

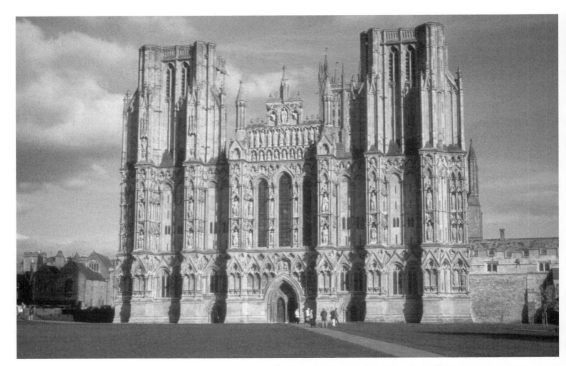

Figure 1 Wells Cathedral in Somerset, England, is in itself a medieval world. The west front, begun about 1230, in its huge array of Gothic carvings reflects a complete worldview

Plate 2 The Three Orders – Those who pray: John Drokensford (bishop 1309–1329) in St Katherine's Chapel retaining much of its original colour

Plate 3 The Three Orders – Those who fight:
West Front, one of the eight knights
depicted

Plate 4 The Three Orders – Those who
work: Cobbler, South Transept

Plate 5 The Hierarchical Church: Three bishops from the West Front

Plate 6 The Hierarchical Church: A canon in the North Porch (thirteenth century). In his hands a scroll with Latin reading 'Enter thou into the joy of the Lord'

Plate 7 The Hierarchical Church: A canon of the cathedral shown in an alabaster panel on a tomb in St Calixtus' Chapel (c. 1450) of an unidentified cleric

Plate 8 The Hierarchical Church: A vicar choral, lower end of the church hierarchy, who sang in place of the not always resident canons (thirteenth century). Chapter House steps

Plate 10
Medieval women:
The Annunciation
portrayed in St
Calixtus' Chapel
(c. 1450)

Plate 9 The Secular Hierarchy: A king from the West Front

Plate 11 (left)
Medieval women:
A queen from the
West Front. The
inverted niche over
the West Door had
a now headless
figure of Christ
crowning His
mother

Plate 12 (right)
Medieval women:
Mary Magdalene
from the West
Front shown with
her alabaster jar of
oil for anointing
Jesus

Plate 13 Outsiders: The jester from the tomb of Thomas Beckynton (bishop, 1443–1465). Bishop Beckynton's tomb was prepared fifteen years before his death

Plate 14 (below) Outsiders: A humiliating scene, 'the world turned upside-down', a man in hood and drawers, riding bareback facing horse's tail. A misericord (*c.* 1335)

Plate 15 Medieval medicine? Man with toothache, one of eleven depictions of this affliction in the cathedral. South Transept (early thirteenth century)

Plate 16 The World of the Bestiary: Spoonbill and frog. Chantry Chapel of Nicholas Bubwith (bishop, 1407–1424)

Plate 17 The World of the Bestiary:
Hawk and rabbit. Misericord (c. 1335)

Plate 18 The World of the Bestiary: Mythical
birds from capital in Western Nave (early
thirteenth century)

Plate 19 The World of the Bestiary: Grotesque from capital in North Nave

Plate 20 Country and Town: a farmer, fox and goose from a capital in the Eastern Nave (early thirteenth century)

Plate 21 Country and Town: Packman,
an itinerant merchant, from Bubwith Chantry

Plate 22 Country and Town:
Artisan. Noah building the ark
shows the clinker-built boat
not just as a block of stone but
properly hollowed out. West
Front

Plate 23 Technology: Master mason, the
cathedral 'architect', probably Adam Lock,
who died in 1229. Head stop at the west end
of North Nave Triforium

Plate 24 Technology: The Cathedral Clock, late fourteenth century, showing the dial which portrays hours, minutes, position of the sun, date of the lunar month and the phases of the moon

Plate 25 Technology: Detail of the clock showing its complexity

Plate 26 (below) Technology: Knights from the clock. The four knights rotate every quarter of an hour in a perpetual tournament

Plate 27 The Heavenly City: The Old Covenant. Moses with the tablets of the ten Commandments, a foundation of the Judeo-Christian tradition. North Transept, thirteenth century

Plate 28 The Heavenly City: The Twelve Apostles in glory, St Andrew, the cathedral's patron, standing centrally, higher than the rest, next to his brother, St Peter

The world of witchcraft, so often associated with the Middle Ages, seems in its identifiable form much more characteristic of the Early Modern period, but some medieval literature on witchcraft survives, often from Church sources.

❧ 7.7 Innocent VIII: Papal Bull, *Summis desiderantes*, ☙
5 December 1484, in which the Pope provided his blessing
and encouragement for witchhunting

Innocent, Bishop, Servant of the servants of God, for an eternal remembrance.

Desiring with the most heartfelt anxiety, even as Our Apostleship requires, that the Catholic Faith should especially in this Our day increase and flourish everywhere, and that all heretical depravity should be driven far from the frontiers and bournes of the Faithful, We very gladly proclaim and even restate those particular means and methods whereby Our pious desire may obtain Its wished effect, since when all errors are uprooted by Our diligent avocation as by the hoe of a provident husbandman, a zeal for, and the regular observance of, Our holy Faith will be all the more strongly impressed upon the hearts of the faithful.

It has indeed lately come to Our ears, not without afflicting Us with bitter sorrow, that in some parts of Northern Germany, as well as in the provinces, townships, territories, districts, and dioceses of Mainz, Cologne, Treves, Salzburg, and Bremen, many persons of both sexes, unmindful of their own salvation and straying from the Catholic Faith, have abandoned themselves to devils, incubi and succubi, and by their incantations, spells, conjurations, and other accursed charms and crafts, enormities and horrid offences, have slain infants yet in the mother's womb, as also the offspring of cattle, have blasted the produce of the earth, the grapes of the vine, the fruits of trees, nay, men and women, beasts of burthen, herd-beasts, as well as animals of other kinds, vineyards, orchards, meadows, pasture-land, corn, wheat, and all other cereals; these wretches furthermore afflict and torment men and women, beasts of burthen, herd-beasts, as well as animals of other kinds, with terrible and piteous pains and sore diseases, both internal and external; they hinder men from performing the sexual act and women from conceiving, whence husbands cannot know their wives nor wives receive their husbands; over and above this, they blasphemously renounce that Faith which is theirs by the Sacrament of Baptism, and at the instigation of the Enemy of Mankind they do not shrink from committing and perpetrating the foulest abominations and filthiest excesses to the deadly peril of their own souls, whereby they outrage the Divine Majesty and are a cause of scandal and danger to very many. And although Our dear sons Henry Kramer and James Sprenger, Professors of Theology, of the Order of Friars Preachers, have been by Letters Apostolic delegated as Inquisitors of these heretical pravities, and still are Inquisitors, the first in the aforesaid parts of Northern Germany, wherein are included those aforesaid townships, districts, dioceses, and other specified localities, and the second in certain territories which lie along the borders of the Rhine, nevertheless not a few clerics and lay folk of those countries, seeking too curiously to know more than concerns them, since in the aforesaid delegatory letters there is no express and specific mention by name of these provinces, townships, dioceses, and districts, and further since the two delegates themselves and the abominations they are to encounter are not designated in detailed and particular fashion, these persons are not ashamed to contend with the most unblushing effrontery that these enormities are not practised in those provinces, and consequently the aforesaid Inquisitors have no legal right to exercise their powers of inquisition in the provinces, townships, dioceses, districts, and territories, which have been rehearsed, and that the Inquisitors may not proceed to punish, imprison, and penalize criminals convicted of the heinous offences and many wickednesses which have been set forth. Accordingly in the aforesaid provinces, townships, dioceses, and districts, the abominations and enormities in question remain unpunished not without open danger to the souls of many and peril of eternal damnation.

Wherefore We, as is Our duty, being wholly desirous of removing all hindrances and obstacles by which the good work of the Inquisitors may be let and tarded, as also of applying potent remedies to prevent the disease of heresy and other turpitudes diffusing their poison to the destruction of many innocent souls, since Our zeal for the Faith especially incites us, lest that the provinces, townships, dioceses, districts, and territories of Germany, which We have specified, be deprived of the benefits of the Holy Office thereto assigned, by the tenor of these presents in virtue of Our Apostolic authority We decree and enjoin that the aforesaid Inquisitors be empowered to proceed to the just correction, imprisonment, and punishment of any persons, without let or hindrance, in every way as if the provinces, townships, dioceses, districts, territories, yea, even the persons and their crimes in this kind were named and particularly designated in Our letters. Moreover, for greater surety We extend these letters deputing this authority to cover all the aforesaid provinces, townships, dioceses, districts, and territories, persons, and crimes newly rehearsed, and We grant permission to the aforesaid Inquisitors, to one separately or to both, as also to Our dear son John Gremper, priest of the diocese of Constance, Master of Arts, their notary, or to any other public notary, who shall be by them, or by one of them, temporarily delegated to those provinces, townships, dioceses, districts, and aforesaid territories, to proceed, according to the regulations of the Inquisition, against any persons of whatsoever rank and high estate, correcting, mulcting, imprisoning, punishing, as their crimes merit, those whom they have found guilty, the penalty being adapted to the offence. Moreover, they shall enjoy a full and perfect faculty of expounding and preaching the word of God to the faithful, so often as opportunity may offer and it may seem good to them, in each and every parish church of the said provinces, and they shall freely and lawfully perform any rites or execute any business which may appear advisable in the aforesaid cases. By Our supreme authority We grant them anew full and complete faculties. At the same time by Letters Apostolic We require Our venerable Brother, the Bishop of Strasburg, that he himself shall announce, or by some other or others cause to be announced, the burthen of Our Bull, which he shall solemnly publish when and so often as he deems it necessary, or when he shall be requested so to do by the Inquisitors or by one of them. Nor shall he suffer them in disobedience to the tenor of these presents to be molested or hindered by any authority whatsoever, but he shall threaten all who endeavour to hinder or harass the Inquisitors, all who oppose them, all rebels, of whatsoever rank, estate, position, pre-eminence, dignity, or any condition they may be, or whatsoever privilege of exemption they may claim, with excommunication, suspension, interdict, and yet more terrible penalties, censures, and punishment, as may seem good to him, and that without any right of appeal, and if he will he may by Our authority aggravate and renew these penalties as often as he list, calling in, if so please him, the help of the secular arm.

Non obstantibus . . . Let no man therefore . . . But if any dare to do so, which God forbid, let him know that upon him will fall the wrath of Almighty God, and of the Blessed Apostles Peter and Paul.

Given at Rome, at S. Peter's, on the 9 December of the Year of the Incarnation of Our Lord one thousand four hundred and eighty-four, in the first Year of Our Pontificate.

> Source: M. Summers, *The Geography of Witchcraft*
> (1978) pp. 533–536

ஓ 7.8 *Malleus Maleficarum* (1486) ஒ

Part 1, Question 15

That Witches Deserve the heaviest Punishment above All the Criminals of the World

The crimes of witches, then, exceed the sins of all others; and we now declare what punishment they deserve, whether as Heretics or as Apostates. Now Heretics, according to S. Raymund, are punished in various ways, as by excommunication, deposition, confiscation of their goods, and death. The reader can be fully informed concerning all these by consulting the law relating to the sentence of excommunication. Indeed even their followers, protectors, patrons and defenders incur the heaviest penalties. For, besides the punishment of excommunication inflicted on them, Heretics, together with their patrons, protectors and defenders and with their children to the second generation on the father's side, and to the first degree on the mother's side, are admitted to no benefit or office of the Church. And if a Heretic have Catholic children for the heinousness of his crime they are deprived of their paternal inheritance. And if a man be convicted, and refuse to be converted and abjure his heresy, he must at once be burned, if he is a layman. For if they who counterfeit money are summarily put to death, how much more must they who counterfeit the Faith? But if he is a cleric, after solemn degradation he is handed over to the secular Court to be put to death. But if they return to the Faith, they are to be imprisoned for life. But in practice they are treated more leniently after recantation than they should be according to the judgement of the Bishops and the Inquisition, as will be shown in the Third Part, where the various methods of sentencing such are treated of; that is to say, those who are arrested and convicted and have recanted their error.

But to punish witches in these ways does not seem sufficient, since they are not simple Heretics, but Apostates. More than this, in their very apostasy they do not deny the Faith for any fear of men or for any delight of the flesh, as has been said before; but, apart from their abnegation, even give homage to the very devils by offering them their bodies and souls. It is clear enough from this that, however much they are penitent and return to the Faith, they must not be punished like other Heretics, with lifelong imprisonment, but must suffer the extreme penalty. And because of the temporal injury which they do to men and beasts in various ways, the laws demand this. It is even equally culpable to learn as it is to teach such iniquities, say the laws concerning Soothsayers. Then how much more emphatically do they speak concerning witches, where they say that the penalty for them is the confiscation of their goods and decapitation. The laws also say much concerning those who by witchcraft provoke a woman to lust, or, conversely, cohabit with beasts. But these matters were touched upon in the First Question.

Source: H. Kramer and J. Sprenger (trans.)
M. Summers, *Malleus Maleficarum* (1996) p. 77

Orthodox Catholicism was confronted by challenges from heretics and schismatics especially from the twelfth century. Some heretical groups, like the Waldensians, who had a radical view of church establishment and evangelical poverty, were not far from the intuitions of contemporary church reformers.

7.9 Reinarius Saccho, *Of the Sects of the Modern Heretics* (1254)

First they say that the Romish Church, is not the Church of Jesus Christ, but a church of malignants and that it apostatised under Sylvester, when the poison of temporalities was infused into the church. And they say, that they are the church of Christ, because they observe both in word, and deed, the doctrine of Christ, of the Gospel, and of the Apostles.

Their second error is that all vices and sins are in the church, and that they alone live righteously.

That scarcely anyone in the church, but themselves, preserves the evangelical doctrine.

That they are the true poor in spirit, and suffer persecution for righteousness and faith.

That they are the Church of Jesus Christ.

That the Church of Rome is the Harlot in the Apocalypse, on account of its superfluous decoration which the Eastern Church does not regard.

That they despise all the statutes of the Church, because they are heavy and numerous.

That the Pope is the head of all errors.

That the Prelates are Scribes; and the Monks, Pharisees.

That the Pope and all Bishops, are homicides on account of wars.

That we are not to obey Prelates; but only God.

That no one is greater than another in the church. Matt. 23. 'All of you are brethren.'

That no one ought to bow the knee before a priest. Rev. ii. where the Angel says to John 'See thou do it not.'

That tithes are not to be given, because first fruits were not given to the church.

That the clergy ought not to have possessions; Deut. xviii. 'The Priests and all the tribe of Levi, shall not have part and inheritance with the people of Israel, because they eat the sacrifices, and they shall receive nothing else.'

That the clergy, and monks, ought not to have Prebends.

That the Bishops and Abbots ought not to have royal rights.

That the land, and the people, are not to be divided into parts.

That it is a bad thing to found and endow churches and monasteries.

That wills are not to be made in favour of Churches – also, that no one ought to be a tenant of the church – also, they condemn all the clergy for idleness, saying that they ought to work with their hands as the Apostles did – also, they reprobate titles of dignity such as Pope, Bishops, etc. – also, that no one is to be forced into belief – also, that they make no account of all ecclesiastical offices – also, that they care nothing for ecclesiastical privileges – also, they despise the immunity of the Church and of ecclesiastical persons and things – also, they condemn Councils, Synods, and Assemblies – also, they say that all parochial rights are invention – also, they say that monastic rules are the traditions of the Pharisees.

Secondly, they condemn all the Sacraments of the Church; in the first place, as to baptism, they say that the Catechism is nothing – also, that the ablution which is given to infants profits nothing . . .

Also, they condemn the sacrament of Marriage, saying that married persons sin mortally if they come together without the hope of offspring – also, they disregard compaternity – also, they despise the degrees of affinity, carnal and spiritual, and the impediments of Orders, and of public decency, and of ecclesiastical prohibitions – also, they say that a woman after child-bearing does not require benediction, or introduction – also, they say that the church has erred in prohibiting the marriage of the Clergy, while even those of the East marry – also, they say that the continent do not sin in kisses and embraces.

The sacrament of Unction, they reprobate, because it is only given to the rich; and because several priests are required for it – also, they say that the sacrament of Orders is nothing – also, they say that every good layman is a priest, as the Apostles were laymen – also, that the prayer of an evil priest does not profit – also, they deride the clerical tonsure – also, that Latin prayer does not profit the vulgar – also, they make it a matter of ridicule that illegitimate persons and wicked sinners are raised to eminence in the church – also, they say that every layman, and even woman ought to preach, 1. Cor. xiv. 'I would that ye spake in tongues, that the church might receive edification' – also, whatever is preached which cannot be proved by the text of Scripture they consider as fabulous . . . also, they say that the doctrine of Christ and the Apostles is sufficient for salvation without the statutes of the church – that the tradition of the church is the tradition of the Pharisees; and that there is more made of the transgression of a human tradition than of a divine law. Matt. xv. 'Why do ye transgress the commands of God by reason of your traditions?' Also, they reject the mystical sense in the holy Scriptures, principally as it regards the sayings and doings delivered in the Church by tradition; as that the cock upon the steeple signifies a doctor.

Source: S. R. Maitland (trans.) *History of the*
Albigenses and Waldenses (1832) pp. 407–413

Others, like the Cathars or Albigensians who were ruthlessly persecuted by a Crusade and by a developing church system of inquisition, made a more fundamental break with the 'official' church.

7.10 Raynaldus: on the Accusations against the Albigensians

First it is to be known that the heretics held that there are two Creators; viz. one of invisible things, whom they called the benevolent God, and another of visible things, whom they named the malevolent God. The New Testament they attributed to the benevolent God; but the Old Testament to the malevolent God, and rejected it altogether, except certain authorities which are inserted in the New Testament from the Old; which, out of reverence to the New Testament, they esteemed worthy of reception. They charged the author of the Old Testament with falsehood, because the Creator said, 'In the day that ye eat of the tree of the knowledge of good and evil ye shall die;' nor (as they say) after eating did they die; when, in fact, after the eating the forbidden fruit they were subjected to the misery of death. They also call him a homicide, as well because he burned up Sodom and Gomorrah, and destroyed the world by the waters of the deluge, as because he overwhelmed Pharaoh, and the Egyptians, in the sea. They affirmed also, that all the fathers of the Old Testament were damned; that John the Baptist was one of the greater demons. They said also, in their secret doctrine, (*in secreto suo*) that that Christ who was born in the visible, and terrestrial Bethlehem, and crucified in Jerusalem, was a bad man, and that Mary Magdalene was his concubine; and that she was the woman taken in adultery, of whom we read in the gospel. For the good Christ, as they said, never ate, nor drank, nor took upon him true flesh, nor ever was in this world, except spiritually in the body of Paul . . .

They said that almost all the Church of Rome was a den of thieves; and that it was the harlot of which we read in the Apocalypse. They so far annulled the sacraments of the Church, as publicly to teach that the water of holy Baptism was just the same as river water, and that the Host of the most holy body of Christ did not differ from common bread; instilling into the ears of the simple this blasphemy, that the body of Christ, even though it had been as great as the Alps, would have been long ago consumed, and annihilated by those who had eaten of it. Confirmation and Confession, they considered as altogether vain and frivolous. They preached that Holy Matrimony was meretricious, and that none could be saved in it, if they should beget children. Denying also the Resurrection of the flesh, they invented some unheard of notions, saying, that our souls are those of angelic spirits who, being cast down from heaven by the apostasy of pride, left their glorified bodies in the air; and that these souls themselves, after successively inhabiting seven terrene bodies, of one sort or another, having at length fulfilled their penance, return to those deserted bodies.

It is also to be known that some among the heretics were called 'perfect' or 'good men'; others 'believers' of the heretics. Those who were called perfect, wore a black dress, falsely pretended to chastity, abhorred the eating of flesh, eggs and cheese, wished to appear not liars, when they were continually telling lies, chiefly respecting God. They said also that they ought not on any account to swear.

Those were called 'believers' of the heretics, who lived after the manner of the world, and who though they did not attain so far as to imitate the life of the perfect, nevertheless hoped to be saved in their faith; and though they differed as to their mode of life, they were one with them in belief and unbelief. Those who were called believers of the heretics were given to usury, rapine, homicide, lust, perjury and every vice; and they, in fact, sinned with more security, and less restraint, because they believed that without restitution, without confession and penance, they should be saved, if only, when on the point of death, they could say a Pater Noster, and received imposition of hands from the teachers. As to the perfect heretics however they had a magistracy whom they called Deacons and Bishops, without the imposition of whose hands, at the time of his death, none of the believers thought that he could be saved; but if they laid their hands upon any dying man, however wicked, if he could only say a Pater Noster, they considered him to be saved, that without any satisfaction, and without any other aid, he immediately took wing to heaven.

Source: S. R. Maitland (trans.) *History of the Albigenses and Waldenses* (1832) pp. 392–394

ཨ 7.11 Inquisitor's Manual of Bernard Gui ঙ

It would take too long to describe in detail the manner in which these same Manichaean heretics preach and teach their followers, but it must be briefly considered here.

In the first place, they usually say of themselves that they are good Christians, who do not swear, or lie, or speak evil of others; that they do not kill any man or animal, nor anything having the breath of life, and that they hold the faith of the Lord Jesus Christ and his gospel as the apostles taught. They assert that they occupy the place of the apostles, and that, on account of the above-mentioned things, they of the Roman Church, namely the prelates, clerks, and monks, and especially the inquisitors of heresy persecute them and call them heretics, although they are good men and good Christians, and that they are persecuted just as Christ and his apostles were by the Pharisees.

Moreover they talk to the laity of the evil lives of the clerks and prelates of the Roman Church, pointing out and setting forth their pride, cupidity, avarice, and uncleanness of life, and such other evils as they know. They invoke with their own interpretation and according to their abilities the authority of the Gospels and the Epistles against the condition of the prelates, churchmen, and monks, whom they call Pharisees and false prophets, who say, but do no.

Then they attack and vituperate, in turn, all the sacraments of the Church, especially the sacrament of the Eucharist, saying that it cannot contain the body of Christ, for had this been as great as the largest mountain Christians would have entirely consumed it before this. They assert that the host comes from straw, that it passes through the tails of horses, to wit, when the flour is cleaned by a sieve (of horse hair); that, moreover, it passes through the body and comes to a vile end, which, they say, could not happen if God were in it.

Of baptism, they assert that the water is material and corruptible and is therefore the creation of the evil power, and cannot sanctify the soul, but that the churchmen sell this water out of avarice, just as they sell earth for the burial of the dead, and oil to the sick when they anoint them, and as they sell the confession of sins as made to the priests.

Hence they claim that confession made to the priests of the Roman Church is useless, and that, since the priests may be sinners, they cannot loose nor bind, and, being unclean in themselves, cannot make others clean. They assert, moreover, that the cross of Christ should not be adored or venerated, because, as they urge, no one would venerate or adore the gallows upon which a father, relative, or friend had been hung. They urge, further, that they who adore the cross ought, for similar reasons, to worship all thorns and lances, because as Christ's body was on the cross during the passion, so was the crown of thorns on his head and the soldier's lance in his side. They proclaim many other scandalous things in regard to the sacraments.

Moreover they read from the Gospels and the Epistles in the vulgar tongue, applying and expounding them in their favour and against the condition of the Roman Church in a manner which it would take too long to describe in detail; but all that relates to this subject may be read more fully in the books they have written and infected, and may be learned from the confessions of such of their followers as have been converted.

> **Source: J. H. Robinson (trans.)** *Readings in European History* (1905) pp. 381–383

Dissent from the Catholic Church could indicate a rising individualism and sometimes incipient calls for reform (and anti-papalism), as was the case with the Oxford theologian John Wyclif and the Bohemian reformer Jan Hus.

≈ 7.12 John Wyclif (c. 1330–1384): *On Indulgences* ≈

I confess that the indulgences of the pope, if they are what they are said to be, are a manifest blasphemy, inasmuch as he claims a power to save men almost without limit, and not only to mitigate the penalties of those who have sinned, by granting them the aid of absolution and indulgences, that they may never come to purgatory, but to give command to the holy angels, that when the soul is separated from the body, they may carry it without delay to its everlasting rest . . . They suppose, in the first place, that there is an infinite number of supererogatory merits, belonging to the saints, laid up in heaven, and above all, the merit of our Lord Jesus Christ, which would be sufficient to save and set the pope. Secondly, that it is his pleasure to distribute it, and, accordingly, infinite number of other worlds, and that, over all this treasure Christ hath, he may distribute therefrom to an infinite extent, since the remainder will still be infinite. Against this rude blasphemy I have elsewhere inveighed . . . This doctrine is a manifold blasphemy against Christ, inasmuch as the pope is extolled above his humanity and deity, and so above all that is called God – pretensions which, according to the declarations of the apostle, agree with the character of the Antichrist; for he possesses Caesarean power above Christ, who had not where to lay his head . . .

> Source: H. E. Fosdick, *Great Voices of the Reformation* (1952) p. 234

☙ 7.13 Jan Hus: *Final Declaration*, 1 July 1415 ❧

I, Jan Hus, in hope a priest of Jesus Christ, fearing to offend God, and fearing to fall into perjury, do hereby profess my unwillingness to abjure all or any of the articles produced against me by false witnesses. For God is my witness that I neither preached, affirmed, nor defended them, though they say that I did.

Moreover, concerning the articles that they have extracted from my books, I say that I detest any false interpretation which any of them bears. But inasmuch as I fear to offend against the truth, or to gainsay the opinion of the doctors of the Church, I cannot abjure any one of them. And if it were possible that my voice could now reach the whole world, as at the Day of Judgement every lie and every sin that I have committed will be made manifest, then would I gladly abjure before all the world every falsehood and error which I either had thought of saying or actually said!

I say I write this of my own free will and choice.

Written with my own hand, on the first day of July.

> M. Spinka (trans.) *The Letters of John Hus* (1972) p. 206

Compared with other marginalised groups in medieval society, the parameters of sexual liminality were more fluid and this fluidity meant that there were often differences between the actual implementation of policies against those involved in homosexuality and same-sex relationships and the rhetoric of marginality. It has been claimed that the *Adelphopoiia Rite*, used in Orthodox and Greek Catholic Churches was, in usage at least, a form of ecclesiastical blessing for same-sex unions.

Marginality is understood as deviance from the norm but this foundation falls short of expressing the many issues which need to be addressed in the context of exploring marginality in the medieval world. The representative, marginalised groups in medieval society explored in this chapter help us to arrive at a working definition of what it meant to be an outsider in the medieval world.

Further reading

M. Aston, *Faith and Fire* (Hambledon, London, 1993).

M. Camille, *Image on the Edge: The Margins of Medieval Art* (Reaktion, London, 1992).

H. Kennedy, *Muslim Spain and Portugal* (Longman, London, 1996).

M. Lambert, *Medieval Heresy* (Blackwell, Oxford, 1992).

H. Le Roy Ladurie, *Montaillou* (Scolar Press, London 1978).

R. I. Moore, *The Origins of European Dissent* (Allen Lane, London, 1977).

S. O'Shea, *The Perfect Heresy, the Revolutionary Life and Death of the Medieval Cathars* (2000).

H. G. Richardson, *The English Jewry under Angevin Kings* (Methuen, London, 1966).

J. J. Saunders, *A History of Medieval Islam* (Routledge & Kegan Paul, London, 1965).

THE WORLD OF
WOMEN

Women in the medieval West were seen in the light of the Bible and Christian tradition. Christianity preached equality but regarded women as morally and physically weaker than men. The ideal life for a women was as a cloistered nun, but throughout the Middle Ages the number of nuns and other women religious remained small compared to men: over 90 percent of Europe's women lived in the countryside and were dependent on the land. Medieval women tended to be classified by their sexual status as virgins, wives or widows. The sources reflect the life of the literate, cloistered elite and indicate the way in which a small minority were able to live a prominent life in what was fundamentally a man's world. The creation of Eve from Adam and the leading role played by the first woman in the Fall was the critical archetype of medieval womanhood.

ड़ 8.1 Medieval women ङ्श

And God said, 'Let the earth bring forth living creatures according to their kinds: cattle and creeping things and beasts of the earth according to their kinds.' And it was so. And God made the beasts of the earth according to their kinds, and everything that creeps upon the ground according to its kind. And God saw that it was good.

Then God said, 'Let us make man in our image, after our likeness, and let them have dominion over the fish of the sea, and over the birds of the air, and over the cattle, and over all the earth, and over every creeping thing that creeps upon the earth.' So God created man in his own image, in the image of God he created him; male and female he created them. And God blessed them, and God said to them, 'Be fruitful and multiply, and fill the earth and subdue it; and have dominion over the fish of the sea and over the birds of the air and over every living thing that moves upon the earth.' And God said, 'Behold, I have given you every plant yielding seed which is upon the face of all the earth, and every tree with seed in its fruit; you shall have them for food. And to every beast of the earth, and to every bird of the air, and to everything that creeps on the earth, everything that has the breath of life, I have given every green plant for food.' And it was so. And God saw everything that he had made, and behold, it was very good. And there was evening and there was morning, a sixth day.

Thus the heavens and the earth were finished, and all the host of them. And on the seventh day God finished his work which he had done, and he rested on the seventh day from all his work which he had done. So God blessed the seventh day and hallowed it, because on it God rested from all his work which he had done in creation.

These are the generations of the heavens and the earth when they were created. In the day that the Lord God made the earth and the heavens, when no plant of the field was yet in the earth and no herb of the field had yet sprung up – for the Lord God had not caused it to rain upon the earth, and there was no man to till the ground; but a mist went up from the earth and watered the whole face of the ground – then the Lord God formed man of dust from the ground, and breathed into his nostrils the breath of life; and man became a living being. And the Lord God planted him a garden in Eden, in the east; and there he put the man whom he had formed. And out of the ground the Lord God made to grow every tree that is pleasant to the sight and good for food, the tree of life also in the midst of the garden, and the tree of the knowledge of good and evil.

The Lord God took the man and put him in the garden of Eden to till it and keep it. And the Lord God commanded the man, saying, 'You may freely eat of every tree of the garden; but of the tree of the knowledge of good and evil you shall not eat, for in the day that you eat of it you shall die.'

Then the Lord God said, 'It is not good that the man should be alone; I will make him a helper fit for him.' So out of the ground the Lord God formed every beast of the field and every bird of the air, and brought them to the man to see what he would call them; and whatever the man called the living creature, that was its name. The man gave names to all cattle, and to the birds of the air, and to every beast of the field; but for the man there was not found a helper fit for him. So the Lord God caused a deep sleep to fall upon the man, and while he slept took one of his ribs and closed up its place with flesh; and the rib which the Lord God had taken from the man he made into a woman and brought her to the man. Then the man said,

This at last is bone of my bones and flesh of my flesh;
she shall be called Woman,
because she was taken out of Man.

Therefore a man leaves his father and his mother and cleaves to his wife, and they become one flesh. And the man and his wife were both naked, and were not ashamed.

Now the serpent was more subtle than any other wild creature that the Lord God had made. He said to the woman, 'Did God say, "You shall not eat of any tree of the garden?"' And the woman said to the serpent, 'We may eat of the fruit of the trees of the garden; but God said, "You shall not eat of the fruit of the tree which is in the midst of the garden, neither shall you touch it, lest you die."' But the serpent said to the woman, 'You will not die. For God knows that when you eat of it your eyes will be opened, and you will be like God, knowing good and evil.' So when the woman saw that the tree was good for food, and that it was a delight to the eyes, and that the tree was to be desired to make one wise, she took of its fruit and ate; and she also gave some to her husband, and he ate. Then the eyes of both were opened, and they knew that they were naked; and they sewed fig leaves together and made themselves aprons.

And they heard the sound of the Lord God walking in the garden in the cool of the day, and the man and his wife hid themselves from the presence of the Lord God among the trees of the garden. But the Lord God called to the man, and said to him, 'Where are you?' And he said, 'I heard the sound of thee in the garden, and I was afraid, because I was naked; and I hid myself.' He said, 'Who told you that you were naked? Have you eaten of the tree of which I commanded you not to eat?' The man said, 'The woman whom thou gavest to be with me, she gave me fruit of the tree, and I ate.' Then the Lord God said to the woman, 'What is this that you have done?' The woman said, 'The serpent beguiled me, and I ate.' The Lord God said to the serpent,

> Because you have done this,
> cursed are you above all cattle, and above all wild animals;
> upon your belly you shall go,
> and dust you shall eat all the days of your life.
> I will put enmity between you and the woman,
> and between your seed and her seed;
> he shall bruise your head, and you shall bruise his heel.
>
> To the woman he said,
> I will greatly multiply your pain in childbearing;
> in pain you shall bring forth children,
> yet your desire shall be for your husband,
> and he shall rule over you.
>
> And to Adam he said,
> Because you have listened to your wife,
> and have eaten of the tree of which I commanded you,
> 'You shall not eat of it,'
> cursed is the ground because of you;
> in toil you shall eat of it all the days of your life;
> thorns and thistles it shall bring forth to you;
> and you shall eat the plants of the field.
> In the sweat of your face you shall eat bread
> till you return to the ground,
> for out of it you were taken;
> you are dust, and to dust you shall return.

The man called his wife's name Eve, because she was the mother of all living.

Source: The Bible: Genesis 1:24–2:9; 2:15–3:20,
New Revised Standard Version **(1993)**

Paul's Epistles (Ephesians 5:22–33; 1 Corinthians 14:34–5; 1 Timothy 2:8–15) highlighted both the equality and the inherent weakness of women. The Fathers of the Church emphasised the special quality of virginity as the ideal way of life for women.

ॐ 8.2 St Jerome (*c.* 320–420) *Marriage and Virginity* ॐ

Letter XXII: To Eustochium

19

Some one may say, 'Do you dare detract from wedlock, which is a state blessed by God?' I do not detract from wedlock when I set virginity before it. No one compares a bad thing with a good. Wedded women may congratulate themselves that they come next to virgins. 'Be fruitful,' God says, 'and multiply, and replenish the earth.' He who desires to replenish the earth may increase and multiply if he will. But the company to which you belong is not on earth, but in heaven. The command to increase and multiply first finds fulfilment after the expulsion from paradise, after the nakedness and the fig-leaves which speak of sexual passion. Let them marry and be given in marriage who eat their bread in the sweat of their brow; whose land brings forth to them thorns and thistles, and whose crops are choked with briars. My seed produces fruit a hundredfold . . . In Paradise Eve was a virgin, and it was only after coats of skins that she began her married life. Now paradise is your home. Keep therefore your birthright, and say: 'Return unto thy rest, O my soul' . . .

20

I praise wedlock, I praise marriage, but it is because they give me virgins. I gather the rose from the thorns, the gold from the earth, the pearl from the shell. 'Doth the ploughman plough all day to sow?' Shall he not also enjoy the fruit of his labour? Wedlock is the more honoured, the more what is born of it is loved. Why, mother, do you grudge your daughter her virginity? She has been reared on your milk, she has come from your womb, she has grown up in your bosom. Your watchful affection has kept her a virgin. Are you angry with her because she chooses to be a king's wife and not a soldier's? She has conferred on you a high privilege; you are now the mother-in-law of God.

21

In those days, as I have said, the virtue of continence was found only in men: Eve still continued to travail with children. But now that a virgin has conceived in the womb and has borne to us a child of which the prophet says that 'Government shall be upon his shoulder, and his name shall be called the mighty God, the everlasting Father,' now the chain of the curse is broken. Death came through Eve, but life has come through Mary. And thus the gift of virginity has been bestowed most richly upon women, seeing that it has had its beginning from a woman, as soon as the Son of God set foot upon the earth, He formed for Himself a new household there; that, as He was adored by angels in heaven, angels might serve Him also on earth.

Source: **W. H. Fremantle (trans.)** *St Jerome:
Letters and Select Works, Select Library of Nicene
and Post-Nicene Fathers*, Ser. 2, Vol. VI (1893)
pp. 375; 383–384

Mary in Christian theology, was both virgin and mother. Her sinlessness made her an unattainable ideal but her humanity made her an attractive advocate for prayer especially during the eleventh and twelfth centuries.

❧ 8.3 From the Sermons of St Anselm ❧

The sky and the stars rejoice; the earth and the waters rejoice; day and night rejoice; all things subject to man, all things appointed for his service rejoice, O Mary, that you have been the means of restoring their lost beauty and filling them with new and ineffable grace . . .

Through the fullness of your grace, O Lady, things of the underworld rejoiced at their liberation, and those on earth and above it, found bliss in their restoration. Indeed, through that same glorious Son of your resplendent virginity, the just who died before his life-giving death exult at their release from captivity, while there is joy among the angels, because the walls of the heavenly Jerusalem, so near to ruin, are seen to rise again.

O Lady, full and more than full of grace, to you I cry praise, since that superabundance rains down to revive all creation. To you I sing hail, Virgin favoured of God and more than favoured, you in whose blessing every nature is blessed, not only creatures by their Creator, but the Creator by his own creatures!

God gave to Mary that very Son who alone is begotten in God's inner life, equal to him, and whom he loves as he loves himself. From Mary God made himself a Son, not another Son, but the very same. Thus was his purpose achieved, that, in the working of nature, one and the same should become the Son both of God and of Mary. All nature is created by God, yet God was born of Mary. God created all things, yet Mary brought forth God. Our God, who made all, made himself from Mary, and thus re-made all that he had made. He who was able to make all things out of nothing did not wish to re-make them, when they were disfigured, without Mary's co-operation.

God is therefore the Father of all created things, and Mary the mother of recreated things. God is the Father who has given universal order, Mary the Mother through whom all was restored to order. For God begot him through whom all things were made, and Mary gave birth to him through whom all things were saved. God begot him without whom nothing has being, and Mary bore him without whom nothing has well-being. The Lord is with you indeed, since he has ordained that Nature should owe to you the abundance of her own restored existence.

Source: H. Ashworth (ed.) *A Word in Season, an Anthology of Readings from the Fathers for General Use* **(1973) pp. 129–130**

The following texts highlight the dangers the cult of Mary could give rise to.

 8.4 Caesarius of Heisterbach

A certain lay-brother of Hemmenrode was rather badly tempted; so as he stood praying he used these words: 'Truly Lord, if thou dost not deliver me from this temptation I will complain of thee to thy mother!' The loving Lord, a lord of humility and lover of simplicity, prevented the brother's complaint and soon relieved his temptation as if he feared to be accused before his mother. Another lay-brother who stood behind the other, smiled at hearing this prayer and repeated it for the edification of the rest.

> **Source: D. Ayerst and A. Fisher, *Records of Christianity*, p. 238**

 8.5 Vincent of Beauvais

I advise you to call upon Mary the mother of Jesus before all others and attend her with perpetual prayers, for she is the only hope of man's reconciliation, she is the first agent of man's salvation.

> **Source: D. Ayerst and A. Fisher, *Records of Christianity*, p. 238**

Humbert of Romans, the thirteenth-century Dominican, declared that after the Virgin Mary, Mary Magdalene 'was shown greater reverence and believed to have greater glory in heaven than any other woman in the world'. She was a repentant sinner and unlike the spotless Virgin Mary could be seen as 'everywoman'.

8.6 Mary Magdalene

Mary's cognomen 'Magdalene' comes from Magdalum, the name of one of her ancestral properties. She was wellborn, descended of royal stock. Her father's name was Syrus, her mother was called Eucharia. With her brother Lazarus and her sister Martha she owned Magdalum, a walled town two miles from Genezareth, along with Bethany, not far from Jerusalem, and a considerable part of Jerusalem itself. They had, however, divided their holdings among themselves . . . Magdalum belonged to

Mary . . . Lazarus kept the property in Jerusalem, and Bethany was Martha's . . . After Christ's ascension, however, they all sold their possessions and laid the proceeds at the feet of the apostles. Magdalene, then, was very rich, and sensuous pleasure keeps company with great wealth. Renowned as she was for her beauty and her riches, she was no less known for the way she gave her body to pleasure – so much so that her proper name was forgotten and she was commonly called 'the sinner'. Meanwhile, Christ was preaching here and there, and she, guided by the divine will, hastened to the house of Simon the leper, where, she had learned, he was at table. Being a sinner she did not dare mingle with the righteous, but stayed back and washed the Lord's feet with her tears, dried them with her hair, and anointed them with precious ointment . . .

Now Simon the Pharisee thought to himself that if this man were a prophet, he would never allow a sinful woman to touch him; but the Lord rebuked him for his proud righteousness and told the woman that all her sins were forgiven. This is the Magdalene upon whom Jesus conferred such great graces and to whom he showed so many marks of love. He cast seven devils out of her, set her totally afire with love of him, counted her among his closest familiars, was her guest, had her do the house-keeping on his travels, and kindly took her side at all times. He defended her when the Pharisee said she was unclean, when her sister implied that she was lazy, when Judas called her wasteful. Seeing her weep he could not contain his tears. For love of her he raised her brother, four days dead, to life, for love of her he freed her sister Martha from the issue of blood she had suffered for seven years . . .

Some fourteen years after the Lord's passion and ascension into heaven, when the Jews had long since killed Stephen and expelled the other disciples from the confines of Judea, the disciples went off into the lands of the various nations and there sowed the word of the Lord. With the apostles at the time was one of Christ's seventy-two disciples, blessed Maximin, to whose care blessed Peter had entrusted Mary Magdalene. In the dispersion Maximin, Mary Magdalene, her brother Lazarus, her sister Martha . . . and many other Christians, were herded by the unbelievers into a ship without pilot or rudder and sent out to sea so that they might all be drowned, but by God's will they eventually landed at Marseilles. There they found no one willing to give them shelter, so they took refuge under the portico of a shrine belonging to the people of that area. When . . . Mary . . . saw the people gathering at the shrine to offer sacrifice to the idols, she came forward, her manner calm and her face serene, and with well-chosen words called them away from the cult of idols and preached Christ fervidly to them. All who heard her were in admiration at her beauty, her eloquence, and the sweetness of her message . . . Then the governor of that province came with his wife to offer sacrifice and pray the gods for offspring. Magdalene preached Christ to him and dissuaded him from sacrificing. Some days later she appeared in a vision to the wife, saying: 'Why, when you are so rich, do you allow the saints of God to die of hunger and cold?' She added the threat that if the lady did not persuade her husband to relieve the saints' needs, she might incur the wrath of God; but the woman was afraid to tell her spouse about the vision. The following night she saw the same vision . . . The third time . . . Mary Magdalene appeared to each of them . . . and said: 'So you sleep, tyrant, limb of your father Satan, with your viper of a wife who refused to tell you what I had said? You take your rest, you enemy of the cross of Christ, your gluttony sated with a bellyful of all sorts of food while you let the saints of God perish from hunger and thirst? You lie here wrapped in silken sheets, after seeing those others homeless and desolate, and passing them by? Wicked man, you will not escape! You will not go unpunished for your long delay in giving them some help!' And, having said her say, she disappeared.

The lady awoke gasping and trembling, and spoke to her husband, who was in like distress: 'My lord, have you had the dream that I just had?' 'I saw it,' he answered, 'and I can't stop wondering and shaking with fear! What are we do?' His wife said: 'It will be better for us to give in to her than to face the wrath of her God whom she preaches.' They therefore provided shelter for the Christians and supplied their needs.

Then one day when Mary Magdalene was preaching, the . . . governor asked her: 'Do you think you can defend the faith you preach?' 'I am ready indeed to defend it,' she replied, 'because my faith is strengthened by the daily miracles and preaching of my teacher Peter, who presides in Rome!' The governor and his wife then said to her: 'See here, we are prepared to do whatever you tell us to if you can obtain a son for us from the God whom you preach.' 'In this he will not fail you,' said Magdalene. Then the blessed Mary prayed the Lord to deign to grant them a son. The Lord heard her prayers and the woman conceived. Now the husband began to want to go to Peter and find out whether what Magdalene preached about Christ was the truth. 'What's this?' snapped his wife. 'Are you thinking of going without me? Not a bit of it! You leave, I leave. You come back, I come back. You stay here, I stay here!' The man replied: 'My dear, it can't be that way! You're pregnant and the perils of the sea are infinite. It's too risky. You will stay home and take care of what we have here!'

But she insisted . . . She threw herself at his feet, weeping . . . and in the end won him over. Mary therefore put the sign of the cross on their shoulders as a protection against the ancient Enemy's interference on their journey. They stocked a ship with all the necessaries, leaving the rest of their possessions in the care of Mary Magdalene, and set sail. A day and a night had not passed, however, when the wind rose and the sea became tumultuous. All aboard, . . . were shaken and fearful as the waves battered the ship. Abruptly she went into labour and, exhausted by her pangs and the buffeting of the storm, she expired as she brought forth her son. The newborn groped about seeking the comfort of his mother's breasts, and cried and whimpered piteously . . . What will the Pilgrim do, seeing his wife dead and the child whining plaintively as he seeks the maternal breast? . . .

The seamen meanwhile were shouting: 'Throw that corpse overboard before we all perish! As long as it is with us, this storm will not let up!' They seized the body and were about to cast it into the sea, but the Pilgrim intervened. 'Hold on a little!' he cried. 'Even if you don't want to spare me or the mother, at least pity the poor weeping little one! Wait just a bit! Maybe the woman has only fainted with pain and may begin to breathe again!'

Now suddenly they saw a hilly coast not far off the bow, and the Pilgrim thought it would be better to put the dead body and the infant ashore there than to throw them as food to the sea monsters. His pleas . . . persuaded the crew to drop anchor there. Then he found the ground so hard that he could not dig a grave, so he spread his cloak in a fold of the hill, laid his wife's body on it, and placed the child with its head between the mother's breasts. Then he wept and said: 'O Mary Magdalene, you brought ruin upon me when you landed at Marseilles! Unhappy me, that on your advice I set out on this journey! Did you not pray to God that my wife might conceive? Conceive she did, and suffered death giving birth, and the child she conceived was born only to die because there is no one to nurse him. Behold, this is what your prayer obtained for me. I commended my all to you and do commend me to your God. If it be in your power, be mindful of the mother's soul, and by your prayer take pity on the child and spare its life.' Then he enfolded the body and the child in his cloak and went back aboard the ship. When the Pilgrim arrived in Rome, Peter came to meet him and, seeing the sign of the cross on his shoulder, asked him who he was and where he came from. He told Peter all that had happened to him, and Peter responded: 'Peace be with you! You have done well to trust the good advice you received. Do not take it amiss that your wife sleeps and the infant rests with her. It is in the Lord's power to give gifts to whom he will, to take away what was given, to restore what was taken away, and to turn your grief into joy.'

Peter then took him to Jerusalem and showed him all the places where Christ had preached and performed miracles, as well as the place where he had suffered and the other from which he had ascended into heaven . . . and after two years . . . he boarded ship, being eager to get back to his homeland . . . in the course of the voyage they came close to the hilly coast where he had left the body of his wife and his son, and . . . he induced the crew to put him ashore. The little boy, whom Mary Magdalene had preserved unharmed, used to come down to the beach and play with the stones and pebbles, as children love to do. As the Pilgrim's skiff drew near to the land, he saw the child playing on the beach. He was dumbstruck at seeing his son alive and leapt ashore from the skiff. The child, who had never seen a man, was terrified at the sight and ran to his mother's bosom, taking cover under the familiar cloak. The Pilgrim, anxious to see what was happening, followed, and found the handsome child feeding at his mother's breast. He lifted the boy and said: 'O Mary Magdalene, how happy I would be, how well everything would have turned out for me, if my wife were alive and able to return home with me! Indeed I know, I know and believe beyond a doubt, that having given us this child and kept him alive for two years on this rock, you could now, by your prayers, restore his mother to life and health.'

As these words were spoken, the woman breathed and, as if waking from sleep, said: 'Great is your merit, O blessed Mary Magdalene, and you are glorious! As I struggled to give birth, you did me a midwife's service and waited upon my every need like a faithful handmaid.' Hearing this, the Pilgrim said: 'My dear wife, are you alive?' 'Indeed I am,' she answered, 'and am just coming from the pilgrimage from which you yourself are returning. And as blessed Peter conducted you to Jerusalem and showed you all the places where Christ suffered, died, and was buried, and many other places, I, with blessed Mary Magdalene as my guide and companion, was with you and committed all you saw to memory.' Whereupon she recited all the places where Christ had suffered, and fully explained the miracles and all she had seen, not missing a single thing.

Now the Pilgrim, having got back his wife and child, joyfully took ship and in a short time made port at Marseilles. Going into the city they found blessed Mary Magdalene with her disciples, preaching. Weeping with joy, they threw themselves at her feet and related all that had happened to them, then received baptism from blessed Maximin . . .

At this time blessed Mary Magdalene, wishing to devote herself to heavenly contemplation, retired to an empty wilderness, and lived unknown for thirty years in a place made ready by the hands of angels. There were no streams of water there, nor the comfort of grass or trees: thus it was made clear that our Redeemer had determined to fill her not with earthly viands but only with the good things of heaven. Every day at the seven canonical hours she was carried aloft by angels and with her bodily ears heard the glorious chants of the celestial hosts. So it was that day by day she was gratified with these supernal delights and, being conveyed back to her own place by the same angels, needed no material nourishment.

There was a priest who wanted to live a solitary life and built himself a cell a few miles from the Magdalene's habitat. One day the Lord opened this priest's eyes, and with his own eyes he saw how the angels descended to the . . . place where blessed Mary Magdalene dwelt, and how they lifted her into the upper air and an hour later brought her back to her place with divine praises. Wanting to learn the truth about this wondrous vision and commending himself prayerfully to his Creator, he hurried with daring and devotion toward the . . . place; but when he was a stone's throw from the spot, his knees began to wobble, and he was so frightened that he could hardly breathe. When he started to go away, his legs and feet responded, but every time he turned around and tried to reach the desired spot . . . he could not move forward.

So the man of God realised that there was a heavenly secret here . . . He therefore invoked his saviour's name and called out: 'I adjure you by the Lord, that if you are a human being or any rational creature living in that cave, you answer me and tell me the truth about yourself!' When he had repeated this three times, blessed Mary Magdalene answered him: 'Come closer, and you can learn the truth about whatever your soul desires.' Trembling, he had gone halfway across the intervening space when she said to him: 'Do you remember what the Gospel says about Mary the notorious sinner, who washed the Saviour's feet with her tears and dried them with her hair, and earned forgiveness for all her misdeeds?' 'I do remember,' the priest replied, 'and more than thirty years have gone by since then. Holy Church also believes and confesses what you have said about her.' 'I am that woman', she said. 'For the space of thirty years I have lived here unknown to everyone; and as you were allowed to see yesterday, every day I am borne aloft seven times by angelic hands, and have been found worthy to hear with the ears of my body the joyful jubilation of the heavenly hosts. Now, because it has been revealed to me by the Lord that I am soon to depart from this world, please go to blessed Maximin and take care to inform him that next year, the day of the Lord's resurrection, at the time when he regularly rises for sins, he is to go alone to his church, and there he will find me present and waited upon by angels.' To the priest the voice sounded like the voice of an angel, but he saw no one.

The good man hurried to blessed Maximin and carried out his errand . . . Maximin, overjoyed, gave fulsome thanks to the Saviour, and . . . at the appointed hour, went alone into the church and saw blessed Mary Magdalene amidst the choir of angels who had brought her there. She was raised up . . . two cubits above the floor, standing among the angels and lifting her hands in prayer to God. When blessed Maximin hesitated about approaching her, she turned to him and said: 'Come closer, father, and do not back away from your daughter.' When he drew near to her . . . the lady's countenance was so radiant, due to her continuous and daily vision of the angels, that one would more easily look straight into the sun than gaze upon her face.

All the clergy . . . were now called together, and blessed Mary Magdalene, shedding tears of joy, received the Lord's Body and Blood from the bishop. Then she lay down full length before the steps of the altar, and her most holy soul migrated to the Lord. After she expired, so powerful an odour of sweetness pervaded the church that for seven days all those who entered there noticed it . . . Maximin embalmed her holy body with aromatic lotions and gave it honourable burial, giving orders that after his death he was to be buried close to her.

Source: W. Granger Ryan (trans.) *Jacobus de Voragine, The Golden Legend* (1993) pp. 375–381

Medieval women were both close to nature and far removed from biological knowledge. In particular, misogynists delighted in regarding menstrual blood with dislike. Writers described the facts of life but monastic sources were generally inclined to concentrate on the lives of virgins and their community enterprises. Not all religious women lived according to men's rules and the place of both female patronage and female insights into religious life emerge clearly from the sources.

8.7 Abelard writing on the Virtue and Delight of Sex

The mere desire to do something immoral is never to be called a sin, but only the consent to it is sinful. We consent to the immorality when we do not draw ourselves back from such a deed, and are prepared to complete it should opportunity offer. He who is discovered in this intention, though he has not completed the deed, is already guilty in the eyes of God, for he is trying hard to sin and, as the blessed Augustine reminds us, he performs as much in his own mind as if he were caught in the act.

Some are highly indignant when we assert that the act of sinning adds no further to the guilt in God's eyes. They argue that in this act a certain delight accrues which increases the sin, as in sexual intercourse or indulgence in food. Their statement is absurd unless they can prove that physical pleasure of this kind is a sin in itself, and that such pleasure cannot be taken without committing a sin. If it is as they say, then no one is permitted to enjoy physical pleasure. Married couples do not avoid sin when they take their physical rights, nor does a man who eats his own fruits with relish . . .

God, the creator of food and of the bodies that receive it, would be guilty for having instilled flavours which must involve the ignorant tasters in sin. Yet why did he supply such things for our consumption or let them be consumed, if it is impossible for us to eat them without sinning? How can there be sin in doing what is allowed? If things which were once unlawful and forbidden are later made lawful and allowed, they can be done entirely without sin. For instance, eating pork and much else which was once forbidden to Jews are now allowed to Christians. When Jews become Christians they gladly eat of these foods their law had prohibited, and we can only defend the rightness of their act by affirming that this freedom has been given to them by God . . . Who then shall say that a man sins in a matter which has been made lawful for him by divine permission? If the marriage-bed or the eating of delicious foods was permitted from the first day of our creation, when we lived in Paradise without sin, who can prove that we sin in these pleasures so long as we do not pass the permitted limits?

Another objection is that sexual intercourse in marriage and the eating of delicious food are only allowed if they are done without pleasure. If this is so, they are allowed to be done in a way in which they never can be done. Such a concession is not reasonable. By what reasoning did the ancient law enforce marriage so that each should leave his seed to Israel? Or how did the apostle order wives to fulfil the mutual debt if these acts could not be done without sinning? . . . I think it is clear that no natural physical delight can be accounted a sin, nor can man be guilty to delight in what, when it is done, must involve the feeling of pleasure.

Source: D. Ayerst and A. Fisher, *Records of Christianity*, pp. 231–232

Augustine of Hippo (354–430), held views which formed the foundation of the medieval theology of marriage. His treatise *On the Good of Marriage* (401) was written in response to the heretical teachings of the theologian, Jovinian, who had claimed that marriage and virginity were states of life of equal merit.

8.8 Augustine of Hippo, *On the Good of Marriage*

3

This is what we now say, that according to the present condition of birth and death, which we know and in which we were created, the marriage of male and female is something good . . .

This does not seem to me to be a good solely because of the procreation of children, but also because of the natural companionship between the two sexes. Otherwise, we would not speak of marriage in the case of old people, especially if they had either lost their children or had begotten none at all. But, in a good marriage, although one of many years, even if the ardour of youth has cooled between man and woman, the order of charity still flourishes between husband and wife. They are better in proportion as they begin the earlier to refrain by mutual consent from sexual intercourse, not that it would afterwards happen of necessity that they would not be able to do what they wished, but that it would be a matter of praise that they had refused beforehand what they were able to do. If, then, there is observed that promise of respect and of services due to each other by either sex, even though both members weaken in health and become almost corpse-like, the chastity of souls rightly joined together continues the purer, the more it has been proved, and the more secure, the more it has been calmed.

Marriage has also this good, that carnal or youthful incontinence, even if it is bad, is turned to the honourable task of begetting children, so that marital intercourse makes something good out of the evil of lust. Finally, the concupiscence of the flesh, which parental affection tempers, is repressed and becomes inflamed more modestly. For a kind of dignity prevails when, as husband and wife they unite in the marriage act, they think of themselves as mother and father.

4

There is the added fact that, in the very debt which married persons owe each other, even if they demand its payment somewhat intemperately and incontinently, they owe fidelity equally to each other . . . 'The wife has not authority over her body, but the husband; the husband likewise has not authority over his body, but the wife.' But the violation of this fidelity is called adultery, when, either by the instigation of one's own lust or by consent of the lust of another, there is intercourse with another contrary to the marriage compact. And so the fidelity is . . .

6

There are also men incontinent to such a degree that they do not spare their wives even when pregnant. Whatever immodest, shameful, and sordid acts the married commit with each other are the sins of the married persons themselves, not the fault of marriage.

Furthermore . . . to have sexual intercourse even without the purpose of procreation, although evil habits impel them to such intercourse, marriage protects them from adultery and fornication. For this is not permitted because of the marriage, but because of the marriage it is pardoned. Therefore, married people owe each other not only the fidelity of sexual intercourse for the purpose of procreating children – and this is the first association of the human race in this mortal life – but also the mutual service, in a certain measure of sustaining each other's weakness, for the avoidance of illicit intercourse, so that, even if perpetual continence is pleasing to one of them, he may not follow this urge except with the consent of the other . . . So, let them not deny either to each other, what the man seeks from matrimony and the woman from her husband, not for the sake of having children but because of weakness and incontinence, lest in this way they fall into damnable seductions through the temptations of Satan because of the incontinence of both or of one of them.

In marriage, intercourse for the purpose of generation has no fault attached to it, but for the purpose of satisfying concupiscence, provided with a spouse, because of the marriage fidelity, it is a venial sin; adultery or fornication, however, is a mortal sin. And so, continence from all intercourse is certainly better than marital intercourse itself which takes place for the sake of begetting children . . .

15

Once, however, marriage is entered upon in the City of our God, where also from the first union of the two human beings marriage bears a kind of sacred bond, it can be dissolved in no way except by the death of one of the parties. The bond of marriage remains, even if offspring, for which the marriage was entered upon, should not follow because of a clear case of sterility, so that it is not lawful for married people who know they will not have any children to separate and to unite with others even for the sake of having children. If they do unite, they commit adultery with the ones with whom they join themselves, for they remain married people . . .

19

Therefore, as many women as there are now, to whom it is said: 'If they do not have self-control, let them marry', are not to be compared even to the holy women who married then. Marriage itself among all races is for the one purpose of procreating children, whatever will be their station and character afterwards; marriage was instituted for this purpose, so that children might be born properly and decently.

> Source: C. T. Wilcox (trans.) *Treatises on Marriage and Other Subjects* (1955) pp. 12–14, 16–17, 19–20, 24–26, 31, 33

Biography and individual correspondence is dominated by male clerics, but a number of individual women rise the above the hagiographical and can be seen as clear individuals. The role of individual women is apparent from the beginning of the period and at times women could adapt to what was seen as predominantly male roles as religious or secular leaders.

Female religious life adopted its own rules which operated in parallel to male religious orders.

---

৪ 8.9 The Ancren Riwle for Nuns ৯

Of Evil Speaking

Hope is a sweet spice within the heart, which spits out all the bitter that the body drinketh. And whoever cheweth spices should shut her mouth, that the sweet breath and the strength thereof may stay within. But she that openeth her mouth, with much talking, and breaketh silence, spits out hope entirely, and the sweetness thereof, with worldly-words, and loseth spiritual strength against the fiend. For what maketh us strong to ensure hardships in God's service, and in temptations to wrestle stoutly against the assaults of the devil? What, but hope of high reward? Hope keeps the heart sound, whatever the flesh may suffer, or endure; as it is said, 'Were there no hope the heart would break.' Ah, Jesus, thy mercy! How stands it with those who are in that place where dwells all woe and misery, without hope of deliverance, and yet the heart may not break?

Wherefore, as ye would keep hope within you, and the sweet breath of her that giveth strength to the soul – with mouth shut chew her within your heart. Blow her not out with babbling mouth nor with gaping lips. 'See,' saith St Jerome, 'that ye have neither itching tongue nor ears'; that is to say, that ye neither desire to speak nor to hear worldly talk. Thus far we have spoken of your silence, and how your speech shall be infrequent. 'Of silence and of speech there is but one precept'; and, therefore, in the writing they run both together. We shall now speak somewhat of your hearing, against evil speech; that ye may shut your ears against it, and, if need be, shut your eyes.

Of Hearing

Against all evil speech, my dear sisters, stop your ears, and have a loathing of the mouth that vomiteth out poison. Evil speech is threefold – poisonous, foul, idle: idle speech is evil; foul speech is worse; poisonous speech is the worst . . . How, then, shall men give account of the three evils, and especially of the worst? . . . Foul speech is of lechery and of other uncleanness, which unwashen mouths speak at times. Men should stop the mouth of him who spitteth out such filth in the ears of any recluse, not with sharp words, but with hard fists. Poisonous speech is heresy, and direct false-hood, backbiting, and flattery. These are the worst . . . St Austin saith 'That thou shouldest not tell a lie to shield thy father from death.' God himself saith that he is truth; and what is more against truth than is lying and falsehood? 'The devil,' we are told, 'is a liar, and the father of lies.' She then, who moveth her tongue in lying, maketh of her tongue a cradle to the devil's child, and rocketh it diligently as nurse. Backbiting and flattery . . . are not fit for man to speak; but they are the devil's blast and his own voice. If these ought to be far from all secular men, what! how ought recluses to hate and shun them, that they may not hear them? Hear them, I say, for she who speaketh with them is no recluse at all. 'The serpent,' saith Solomon, 'stingeth quite silently; and she who speaketh behind another what she would not before is not a whit better.' Hearest thou how Solomon eveneth a backbiter to a stinging serpent? Such she certainly is. She is of serpents' kindred, and she who speaketh evil behind another beareth poison in her tongue. The flatterer blinds a man, and puts a prickle in the eyes of him whom he flattereth . . .

There are three kinds of flatterers. The first are bad enough; yet the second are worse; but the third are worst of all. The first, if a man is good, praiseth him in his presence, and, without scruple, maketh him still better than he is; and, if he saith or doth well, he extolleth it too highly with excessive praise and commendation. The second, if a man is depraved and sins so much in word and deed, that his sin is so open that he may nowise wholly deny it, yet he, the flatterer, in the man's own presence extenuates his guilt. 'It is not, now,' saith he, 'so exceeding bad as it is repre-sented. Thou art not, in this matter, the first, nor wilt thou be the last. Thou hast many fellows. Let it be, my good man. Thou goest not alone. Many do much worse.' The third flatterer cometh after, and is the worse, as I said before, for he praiseth the wicked and his evil deeds; as he who said to the knight who robbed his poor vassals, 'Ah, sir! truly thou doest well. For men ought always to pluck and pillage the churl; for he is like the willow, which sprouteth out the better that it is often cropped.' Thus doth the false flatterer blind those who listen to him, as I said before, and covereth their filth so that it may not stink: and that is a great calamity. For, if it stunk, he would be disgusted with it, and so run to confession, and there vomit it out, and shun it thereafter.

Source: J. Morton, *The Nun's Rule* (1905) pp. 61–68

Once a year Scholastica, (d. 543) the sister of Saint Benedict, who had been dedicated to God from her youth, used to visit her brother. The man of God would go down to meet her in a house belonging to the monastery not far from the gate.

ૐ 8.10 Saint Scholastica ૐ

And she coming thither on a time according to her custom, her venerable brother with his monks went to meet her, where they spent the whole day in the praises of God and spiritual talk: and when it was almost night they supped together, and as they were yet sitting at the table, talking of devout matters, and darkness came on, the holy nun his sister entreated him to stay there all night, that they might spend it in discoursing of the joys of heaven. But by no persuasion would he agree to that, saying that he might not by any means tarry all night out of his Abbey. At that time, the sky was so clear that no cloud was to be seen. The nun, receiving this denial of her brother, joining her hands together, laid them upon the table; and so, bowing down her head upon them, she made her prayers to Almighty God, and lifting her head from the table, there fell suddenly such a tempest of lightning and thundering, and such abundance of rain, that neither venerable Benedict nor his monks that were with him, could put their head out of door: for the holy nun, resting her head upon her hands, poured forth such a flood of tears upon the table that she drew the clear air to a watery sky, so that after the end of her devotions, that storm of rain followed; and her prayer and the rain did so meet together, that as she lifted up her head from the table, the thunder, so that in one and the very same instant she lifted up her head and brought down the rain. The man of God, seeing that he could not by reason of such thunder and lightning and great abundance of rain return back to his Abbey, began to be heavy and to complain of his sister, saying: 'God forgive you, what have you done?' to whom she answered: 'I desired you to stay, and you would not hear me, I have desired our good Lord, and he hath vouchsafed to grant my petition: wherefore if you can now depart, in God's name return to your monastery, and leave me here alone.' But the good father, being not able to go forth, tarried there against his will, where willingly he would not stay. And so by that means they watched all night, and with spiritual and heavenly talk did mutually comfort one another: and therefore by this we see, as I said before that he would have had that thing, which yet he could not: for if we respect the venerable man's mind, no question but he would have had the same fair weather to have continued as it was, when he set forth, but he found that a miracle did prevent his desire, which, by the power of almighty God, a woman's prayers had wrought. It is not a thing to be marvelled at, that a woman which of long time had not seen her brother, might do more at that time than he could, seeing, according to the saying of St John, 'God is charity' and therefore of right she did more which loved more . . .

The next day the venerable woman returned to her nunnery, and the man of God to his Abbey: who three days after, standing in his cell, raising up his eyes to heaven, beheld the soul of his sister, which was departed from her body, in the likeness of a dove to ascend into heaven: who rejoicing much to see her great glory, with hymns and lauds gave the almighty God, and did impart the news of this her death to his monks, whom also he sent presently to bring her corpse to his Abbey, and had it buried in that grave which he had provided for himself; by means whereof it fell out that, as their souls were always one in God whiles they lived, so their bodies continued together after their death.

Source: H. J. Coleridge (ed.) *The Dialogues of
St Gregory the Great,* 2 vols (1874) Vol. II,
Chaps. 33, 34, pp. 108–111

Even in the dark days of Merovingian Gaul, Queen Radegund (518–587) founded a religious house for women which allowed her to be a patron of the arts and the liturgy.

ह 8.11 Radegund's Letter of Foundation ≼

To the holy fathers in Christ and most worthy occupants of their apostolic seats, the bishops, Radegund of Poitiers.

The first steps of a meet project can only move strongly to fulfilment when the matter is brought to the ears of our common fathers, the physicians and the shepherds of the fold, and commended likewise to their hearts. For the active sympathy proceeding from their love, the sage counsel proceeding from their power, the support proceeding from their prayers all unite to give it furtherance. Since in time past, delivered from the chains of secular life by the providence and inspiration of the divine mercy, I turned of my own will to the Rule of religion under Christ's guidance, and with ardent mind also considered how I might help forward others, that with the approval of the Lord my desires might become profitable to the rest, I established at Poitiers a monastery for nuns, founded and enriched by the most excellent lord King Lothar; this monastery after its foundation I myself endowed by the gift of all the property which the royal munificence had bestowed upon me. Moreover, I appointed for this community gathered together under Christ's protection the Rule according to which the holy Caesaria lived, and which the care of the blessed Caesarius, bishop of Arles, had compiled to suit her needs from the institutions of the holy Fathers. With the approval of the most blessed bishops of Poitiers and the other sees, and by the choice of our own community, I appointed as abbess the lady Agnes, my sister, whom I have loved and brought up from her earliest youth; and I submitted myself in regular obedience to her authority next to that of God. And following the apostolic example, I myself and my sisters, when we entered the monastery, made over by deed all our substance in earthly possessions, reserving nothing for ourselves . . .

And since I cannot in person throw myself at your feet, I make prostration vicariously through this letter, and by the Father, Son and Holy Spirit, and by the tremendous Day of Judgement, I adjure you, as if ye stood before me, to protect us from any tyrant, and secure to us the favour of our rightful king. And if haply after my death anyone, whether the bishop of the city, or a royal officer, or any other person shall, as I trust shall never befall, either by suggestion of wicked men or by action of law, seek to trouble the sisterhood, or to break the Rule, or appoint any other abbess than my sister Agnes, whom the most blessed Germanus in the presence of his brethren consecrated with his benediction; or if the community itself, which I may not think possible, shall murmur and seek change; or if any person, were it even the bishop of the City, shall seek to claim, by new privileges over and above those enjoyed by his predecessors or any other persons in my lifetime, either power in the monastery or over its property; or if any shall essay against the Rule to go forth thence; or if any prince or bishop or other powerful person, or any of the sisters, shall with sacrilegious intent diminish or appropriate the property which the most excellent lord Lothar or the most excellent kings his sons bestowed upon me, and I, by his injunction and permission, transferred to the monastery to have and hold, of which transmission I obtained confirmation by letters of the most excellent lords the kings Charibert, Guntram, Chilperic, and Sigibert under their oath and signature, or the gifts which others have given for the good of their souls or the sisters have bestowed out of their own possessions; may they through my prayer and the will of Christ in such wise be confronted with God's wrath, and that of yourselves and your successors, that as robbers and despoilers of the poor they may be shut out from your grace. Resist in such wise that none may ever avail to diminish or to change in anything either our Rule or the possessions of the monastery. This also I pray, that when it shall be the will of God that the . . . lady Agnes, my sister, shall pass away, an abbess shall be appointed out of our congregation, who shall find favour in God's sight, who shall safely guard the Rule, and in nothing diminish the intent of holy living; let neither her own will nor that of another person be suffered to ruin them. If any, which God forbid, contrary to the command of the Lord and the authority of our kings, shall do aught against the conditions heretofore cited and commended to your protection by prayer before the Lord and His saints, or against the welfare of the monastery, either as regards its occupants or its possessions, or shall in any way vex my . . . sister Agnes, the abbess, may he incur the judgement of God and of the Holy Cross and of the blessed Mary, and may he have as his enemies and pursuers the blessed confessors Hilary and Martin, to whom, after God, I have entrusted the protection of my sisters.

Thou also, holy bishop, and thy successors . . . if there should be found any . . . to make attempts against these my dispositions, shrink not from appeal to the king who then shall rule over this place, or to the city of Poitiers, on behalf of that which hath been commended to your guardianship before the Lord, or from toil in shielding and defending justice against the unjust attack of others, that the enemy of God may be confounded and driven back. So shall no Catholic king in his own times brook such infamy, or suffer to be destroyed that which hath been founded firm by God's will and mine intent, and the will of the kings themselves. Likewise also I conjure the princes that live after me . . . in the name of the King whose reign shall have no end and by whose nod kingdoms consist, who hath given them their very life and their dominion: them I conjure to take under their ward the abbess Agnes and this monastery which . . . I have built and duly ordered and endowed. Let them not suffer it, that this our abbess . . . be by any man harassed or molested, or aught pertaining to our monastery be hereafter diminished, or in any wise changed; but rather see that all these be defended and secured, which cause I commend to them . . . and in accordance with my prayer to the Redeemer of all peoples; that they may be for ever united in the eternal kingdom with the defender of the poor and the spouse of virgins, in whose honour they protect the handmaids of God. And I conjure you, holy bishops, and our most excellent lords and kings, and the whole Christian people, by the Catholic faith in which ye are baptised, when . . . I pass from the light of this world, let my poor body be buried in that basilica, be it at the time completed or unfinished, which I have begun to build in honour of the holy Mary, the mother of the Lord, and wherein many of our sisters are already laid to rest. May it be that if any shall desire or attempt aught contrary, by virtue of the Cross of Christ and of the blessed Mary, he may incur divine vengeance, and that I, by your mediation, be held worthy to obtain a resting-place in that church among the congregation of my sisters. And I beseech with many tears that this my petition, signed by my own hand, be preserved among the archives of the cathedral church; and that if the action of the wicked shall compel my sister the abbess Agnes, or her community, to entreat your succour and protection . . . they shall not proclaim themselves forsaken of me, when God hath prepared for them the protection of your grace.

This request I lay before your eyes, omitting nothing! through the grace of Him who from His glorious Cross did commend His virgin mother to the blessed apostle John; that as by him the Lord's commendation was fulfilled, so by you may be fulfilled that which I in my unworthiness and humility commend to you my lords, the fathers of the Church, who now bear the apostolic name. And when ye shall have kept this trust which I leave you as beseemeth your high estate, ye shall be partakers in His merits whose apostolic charge ye fulfil, and worthily renew His example.

> **Source: O. M. Dalton (trans.)** *Gregory of Tours,*
> *The History of the Franks,* 2 vols (1927) Vol. II, 42,
> pp. 418–422

ॐ

Clare (1194–1253) the disciple of St Francis of Assisi, made her own Spiritual Testament, although this source like many other 'female' documents of the period often owes more to male spiritual directors or confessors.

ॐ 8.12 *The Testament of St Clare* ॐ

In the Name of Our Lord, Amen.

Among the many graces which we have already received and which we receive still every day from the liberality of the Father of Mercies, and for which we glorify him by giving our deepest thanks, the principal grace is our vocation. And we are all the more grateful for it, because it is the greatest and the most perfect of them.

Hence the apostle says: 'Know your vocation.'

The Son of God became for us the Way, which our blessed father Francis has shown and taught to us by word and example . . .

The saint himself did not yet have either friars or companions. It was almost immediately after his conversion when he was repairing the church of St Damian, where after a visitation by the Lord and being filled with his consolations, he was led to abandon the world wholly. It was then, in the transports of a holy joy and in the splendour of the Holy Spirit, that he uttered that prophecy concerning us which the Lord later fulfilled. For after having mounted the wall of this church, and addressed himself to some poor folk of the neighbourhood, he said to them in a loud voice in French, 'Come, help me to build the monastery of St Damian, for it will be the dwelling of Ladies whose fame and holy life will glorify the Heavenly Father throughout his holy Church.' . . .

The Lord, in fact has placed us as an example, as models and mirrors, not only for other faithful but also for our sisters whom he has called to the same vocation, so that in turn they may be mirrors and models for those living in the world. The Lord, therefore, has called us to such great things so that our sanctity should serve as a model and as a mirror in which even those who are models and mirrors for others may behold themselves. Consequently we are truly bound to bless and praise the Lord and to be strengthened more and more in him so that we may do good.

Wherefore, by living in accordance with the present Rule, we shall leave a noble example to others, and through a labour of short duration we shall gain the prize of eternal bliss.

After the Most High Heavenly Father, through his mercy and grace, had deigned to illumine my heart and inspire me to do penance, according to the example and following the teaching of our blessed father Francis, shortly after his conversion, in concert with some sisters whom God had given to me soon after my conversion, I voluntarily put my vow of obedience into his hands, according to the light and the grace which the Lord had granted us by the holy life and the teaching of his servant. The blessed Francis perceived that we were weak and fragile of body, but that nevertheless neither hardship, poverty, work, tribulation and ignominy, nor the contempt of the world, in short that nothing of all this made us retreat. Rather he saw that all these things seemed to be unutterable delights, after the example of his friars and saints. Indeed, he and his friars often remarked this and rejoiced greatly in the Lord . . .

Thus by the will of God and our blessed father Francis, we came to dwell at the church of St Damian. There in a short time the Lord, by his grace and mercy, increased our number so that what had been foretold through His holy servant might come to pass. Before that we had sojourned at another place, but briefly.

Afterwards St Francis prescribed a form of life for us, above all so that we might persevere always in holy poverty. During his life he was not content to exhort us often, by words and example, to the love and observance of most holy poverty, for he also bequeathed us many writings so that after his death we would never turn aside from it in any way.

And I, Clare, who though unworthy, am the handmaid of Christ and of the poor sisters of the monastery of St Damian and the little plant of the holy patriarch, have with my sisters given consideration to our most high calling and the command of so great and good a father, and also the frailty of others, fearing for ourselves after the death of our father St Francis, who was our pillar, and after God our only consolation and our support . . .

And since I myself have always taken diligent care and solicitude to observe and have others observe holy poverty, which we have promised to the Lord and to our father Francis, so the other abbesses who shall succeed me in my office are bound always to observe and have it observed by their sisters unto the end.

In addition, for greater surety, I had recourse first of all to Pope Innocent, whose pontificate witnessed the beginning of our Institute and then to his successors, and I had our profession of most holy poverty confirmed and strengthened by their pontifical privilege.

Wherefore, on bended knee and prostrated in body and soul at the feet of our Holy Mother, the Roman Church, and of the Sovereign Pontiff, and especially of the Lord Cardinal, who is assigned to the Order of the Friars Minor and to us, I commend all my sisters present and to come. And for the love of Jesus, who was so poor in his crib, who was so poor during his life, and who hung naked on the Cross, for love of him, I pray the Cardinal to protect this little flock which the Most High Heavenly Father has begotten in the holy Church through the word and example of the blessed father Francis, imitator of the poverty and of the humility of the Son of God and of the glorious Virgin, his Mother; I pray the Cardinal to preserve this flock and to encourage it always in the observance of the holy poverty that we have promised to God and to our blessed father Francis.

And since the Lord has given us our blessed father Francis as founder, father and support in the service of Christ and in our promises to God and to this blessed father who placed so much diligence in his words and works to foster the growth of us his plants; now, in my turn, I commend my sisters, present and to come, to the successor of our blessed father Francis, and to the friar of all his Order, so that they will aid us in ever progressing in the good and in the better service of God and above all in the better observance of most holy poverty.

And if it should ever come to pass that my sisters should leave this place and be transferred elsewhere, let them nevertheless be bound, wherever they may be after my death, to the observance of the same form of poverty as we have promised God and our blessed father Francis. But let her who will be in my office and the other sisters ever show the care and prudence not to acquire or accept land around their dwelling except for the strict necessity of a vegetable garden . . .

I also beseech the sister who shall be entrusted with the guidance of the sisters to govern them more by her virtues and the holiness of her life, than by the dignity of her office, so that the sisters, inspired by her example, will obey her not only out of duty, but rather out of love.

In addition, let her show the discretion and solicitude of a good mother for her daughters, and above all provide all of them with the alms given by the Lord, giving to each according to her need. Let her also be so kind and so approachable to all, that they may disclose their needs to her with surety and have recourse to her with confidence, as they may deem necessary for themselves or for their sisters. For their part the sisters subject to her should remember that they have renounced their wills for God's sake.

Therefore, I will that they obey their mother, with a spontaneous will, as they have promised the Lord, so that this mother, seeing the charity, humility and the unity that reigns among them, may bear the burden of her duties more lightly, and their holy life may change what is painful and bitter into sweetness for her . . .

Now, it is written, 'Cursed are they who turn aside from thy commandments.' For this reason I bend my knees before the Father of Our Lord Jesus Christ, so that, through the prayers and merits of the glorious and holy Virgin, his Mother, and those of our blessed father Francis and of all the saints the Lord himself who has given us a good beginning will also give us increase and perseverance to the end. Amen.

**Source: H. Daniel-Rops, *The Call of St Clare*
(1963) pp. 133–140**

Joan of Arc (*c.* 1412–1431) is so familiar to us that it is difficult to fully comprehend just how remarkable her life was. Many influential plays and films have helped to immortalise Joan and the image we have of her today is of a young woman, secure in the knowledge of her immortal destiny, about to suffer a cruel death. However, the following text, from the French chronicler, Jean de Waurin, is less adulatory than most other accounts.

8.13 Jean de Waurin

While Orléans was besieged, there came to King Charles of France, at Chinon where he was then staying, a young girl who described herself as a maid of twenty years of age or thereabout, named Joan, who was clothed and habited in the guise of a man. This Joan had remained a long time at an inn and she was very bold in riding horses and leading them to drink and also in performing other feats and exercises which young girls are not accustomed to do; and she was sent to the king of France by a knight named Sir Robert de Baudricourt, captain of the palace of Vaucouleurs appointed on behalf of King Charles. This Sir Robert gave her horses and five or six companions, and likewise instructed her, and taught her what she ought to say and do, and the way in which she could conduct herself, since she asserted that she was a maid inspired by divine providence, and sent to King Charles to restore him and bring him back into the possession of all his kingdom generally, from which he was, as she said, wrongfully driven away and put out. And the maid was, at her coming, in very poor estate; and she was about two months in the house of the king, whom she many times admonished by her speeches, as she had been instructed, to give her troops and aid, and she would repel and drive away his enemies, and exalt his name, enlarging his lordships, certifying that she had had a sufficient revelation concerning this. And she was then considered at court only as one deranged and deluded, because she boasted herself as able to achieve so great an enterprise, which seemed to the great princes a thing impossible, considering that all they together could not effect it. Nevertheless, after the maid had remained a good space at the king's court, she was brought forward and aided, and she raised a standard whereon she had painted the figure and representation of Our Lord Jesus Christ; indeed, all her words were full of the name of God. And she was many times examined by famous clerks and men of great authority in order to inquire and know more fully her intention, but she always held to her purpose, saying that if the king would believe her she would restore him to his dominion. Maintaining this purpose she accomplished some operations successfully, whereby she acquired great renown, fame, and exaltation.

This maid went with the Duke of Alençon from Chinon to Poitiers, where he ordered that the marshal should take provisions and artillery and other necessary things to Orléans in force, whither the maid Joan wished to go; and she made request that they would give her a suit of armour to arm herself, which was delivered to her. Then, with her standard raised, she went to Blois where the muster was being made, and then to Orléans with the others; and she was always armed, in complete armour, and on this same journey many men-at-arms placed themselves under her.

When the maid had come into the city of Orléans, they gave her a good reception, and some were greatly rejoiced at seeing her in their company. And when the French troops who had brought the provisions into Orléans returned to the king, the maid remained there. And she was urged to go out to skirmish with the others by La Hire and some captains, but she made answer that she would not go unless the men-at-arms who had brought her were also with her: these were recalled from Blois and from the other places whither they had now withdrawn. And they returned to Orléans, where they were joyfully received by the maid. So she went out to them to welcome them, saying that she had well seen and considered the governance of the English, and that if they would believe in her she would make them all rich.

So she began that day to sally out of the town, and went with great alacrity to attack one of the English towers, which she took by force; and going on from that time she did some very marvellous things.

Source: A. R. Meyers (ed.) *English Historical Documents, 1327–1485* (1969) Vol. IV, pp. 242–243

Towards the latter part of the period Christine de Pisan (1364–c. 1429) took upon herself the task of defending women from their male detractors. She was a prolific writer, producing many works which included a biography of Charles V, and several polemical treatises against the men who slandered women. The most famous of these texts is *The City of Ladies* (1405), in which she questioned Reason, Rectitude and Justice about the lies of men concerning the inferiority, virtues and achievements of women.

࿐ 8.14 Christine de Pisan ࿐

'My lady [Reason], according to what I understand from you, woman is a most noble creature. But even so, Cicero says that a man should never serve any woman and that he who does so debases himself, for no man should ever serve anyone lower than him.'

She replied, 'The man or the woman in whom resides greater virtue is the higher; neither the loftiness nor the lowliness of a person lies in the body according to the sex, but in the perfection of conduct and virtues. And surely he is happy who serves the Virgin, who is above all the angels.'

'My lady, one of the Catos – who was such a great orator – said, 'nevertheless, that if this world were without women, we would converse with the gods.'

She replied, 'You can now see the foolishness of the man who is considered wise, because, thanks to a woman, man reigns with God. And if anyone would say that man was banished because of Lady Eve, I tell you that he gained more through [the Virgin] Mary than he lost through Eve when humanity was conjoined to the Godhead, which would never have taken place if Eve's misdeed [eating the forbidden fruit] had not occurred. Thus man and woman should be glad for this sin, through which such an honour has come about. For as low as human nature fell through this creature woman, was human nature lifted higher by this same creature. And as for conversing with the gods, as this Cato has said, if there had been no woman, he spoke truer than he knew, for he was a pagan, and among those of this belief, gods were thought to reside in Hell as well as in Heaven, that is, the devils whom they called the gods of Hell – so that it is no lie that these gods would have conversed with men, if Mary had not lived.'

'. . . But please enlighten me again, whether it has ever pleased this God, who has bestowed so many favours on women, to honour the feminine sex with the privilege of the virtue of high understanding and great learning, and whether women ever have a clever enough mind for this. I wish very much to know this because men maintain that the mind of women can learn only a little.'

She [Lady Reason] answered, 'My daughter, since I told you before, you know quite well that the opposite of their opinion is true, and to show you this even more clearly, I will give you proof through examples. I tell you again – and don't doubt the contrary – if it were customary to send daughters to school like sons, and if they were then taught the natural sciences, they would learn as thoroughly and understand the subtleties of all the arts and sciences as well as sons. And by chance there happen to be such women, for, as I touched on before, just as women have more delicate bodies than men, weaker and less able to perform many tasks, so do they have minds that are freer and sharper whenever they apply themselves.'

'My lady, what are you saying? With all due respect, could you dwell longer on this point, please. Certainly men would never admit this answer is true, unless it is explained more plainly, for they believe that one normally sees that men know more than women do.'

She answered, 'Do you know why women know less?'

'Not unless you tell me, my lady.'

'Without the slightest doubt, it is because they are not involved in many different things, but stay at home, where it is enough for them to run the household, and there is nothing which so instructs a reasonable creature as the exercise and experience of many different things.'

'My lady, since they have minds skilled in conceptualising and learning, just like men, why don't women learn more?'

She replied, 'Because, my daughter, the public does not require them to get involved in the affairs which men are commissioned to execute, just as I told you before. It is enough for women to perform the usual duties to which they are ordained. As for judging from experience, since one sees that women usually know less than men, that therefore their capacity for understanding is less, look at men who farm the flatlands or who live in the mountains. You will find that in many countries they seem completely savage because they are so simpleminded. All the same, there is no doubt that Nature provided them with the qualities of body and mind found in the wisest and most learned men . . .'

Following these remarks, I, Christine, spoke, 'My lady, I realize that women have accomplished many good things and that even if evil women have done evil, it seems to me, nevertheless, that the benefits accrued and still accruing because of good women – particularly the wise and literary ones and those educated in the natural sciences whom I mentioned above – outweigh the evil. Therefore, I am amazed by the opinion of some men who claim that they do not want their daughters, wives, or kinswomen to be educated because their mores would be ruined as a result.'

She responded, 'Here you can clearly see that not all opinions of men are based on reason and that these men are wrong. For it must not be presumed that mores necessarily grow worse from knowing the moral sciences, which teach the virtues, indeed, there is not the slightest doubt that moral education amends and ennobles them. How could anyone think or believe that whoever follows good teaching or doctrine is the worse for it? Such an opinion cannot be expressed or maintained. I do not mean that it would be good for a man or a woman to study the art of divination or those fields of learning which are forbidden – for the holy Church did not remove them from common use without good reason – but it should not be believed that women are the worse for knowing what is good . . . To speak of more recent times, without searching for examples in ancient history, Giovanni Andrea, a solemn law professor in Bologna not quite sixty years ago, was not of the opinion that it was bad for women to be educated. He had a fair and good daughter, named Novella, who was educated in the law to such an advanced degree that when he was occupied by some task and not at leisure to present his lectures to his students, he would send Novella, his daughter, in his place to lecture to the students from his chair. And to prevent her beauty from distracting the concentration of her audience, she had a little curtain drawn in front of her. In this manner she could on occasion supplement and lighten her father's occupation . . .'

Source: E. J. Richards (trans.) *Christine de Pisan, The Book of the City of Ladies* (1983) pp. 24, 63–64, 153–154

The Middle Ages may be seen as repressive but women suffered from fewer restrictions and enjoyed greater opportunities than in subsequent centuries. The dominance of men in all spheres of life has tended to obscure the contribution of women, but recent research makes it clear that women formed an active and vital role in society, not only in the traditional household roles but in other fields as well. What we see from these texts is that, although in the medieval world nobody questioned the universal subordination of women, their work was both essential and respected.

Further reading

E. Amt, *Women's Lives in Medieval Europe* (Routledge, London, 1998).

B. Anderson and J. Zinser, *A History of Their Own*, Vol. 1 (Penguin, Harmondsworth, 1988).

D. Baker (ed.) *Medieval Women* (Blackwell, Oxford, 1978).

C. W. Bynum, *Holy Feast and Holy Fast: The Religious Significance of Food to Medieval Women* (University of California Press, Berkley, 1986).

S. Haskins, *Mary Magdalen, Myth and Metaphor* (HarperCollins, London, 1993).

H. Jewell, *Women in Medieval England* (Manchester University Press, Manchester, 1996).

H. Leyser, *Medieval Women* (Weidenfeld and Nicolson, London, 1995).

J. Murray (ed.) *Love, Marriage and Family in the Middle Ages* (Broadview Press, Ontario, 2001).

E. Power, *Medieval Women* (Cambridge University Press, Cambridge, 1975).

B. Radice (trans.), *The Letters of Abelard and Heloise* (Penguin, Harmondsworth, 1975).

S. M. Stuard (ed.), *Women in Medieval Society* (University of Pennsylvania Press, Philadelphia, 1976).

THE WORLD
OF THE MIND

Science and technology are not generally associated with medieval Christendom, but this way of thinking is to misunderstand the period. If science is about the detailed understanding of the material world expressed in the form of mathematical equations that enable the course of phenomena to be predicted with great accuracy, then its origins can be found in the western Europe of the medieval epoch. Such an approach to 'natural philosophy' was based on the beliefs that stem from the doctrines of creation and incarnation: that the material world is good, rational and open to the human mind. Indeed, the Christian belief in the creation of the world in time broke the strength of the Aristotelian views that had curtailed the rise of science for many centuries. Medieval natural philosophers were in awe of nature and sought a unified world picture, a theme summarised in the 1272 inscription on the pavement of Westminster Abbey: 'Here is the perfectly rounded sphere which reveals the eternal pattern of the universe.'

Questions of sight, space and time were particular preoccupations. Roger Bacon (c. 1214–c. 1292), the Oxford Franciscan, suggested that 'the whole truth of things in the world lies in the literal sense . . . because nothing is fully intelligible unless it is presented before our eyes'. Theories of how the eye grasped an object fell into two main beliefs: extramission (with the eye as a lamp sending out visual rays) and intromission (the image, not the eye, sends forth rays). Intromission was favoured in the thirteenth century, especially by those who believed that in the developing science of optics the closer vision was related to geometry the more reliable it was thought to be. Such reasoning is far away from the speculative alchemy which is often presented as the medieval scientific ideal. In their search for a complete vision, medieval scientists could at times appear rather more mystical than experimental.

ঌ 9.1 Robert Grosseteste, *On the Six Days of Creation* ঌ

Chapter IX

1

In a spiritual sense: light is made both in the church and in any holy soul when its rational knowledge rises up to the contemplation of the Trinity through a contemplation which is stripped of images, or to the theoretical consideration of intellectual and incorporeal creatures through the intellect; or, again, to the knowledge of those things that are laid down and cared for in time by faith, for the salvation of the human race. The darkness means when there is an obscuring of the understanding of divine things, or of the understanding of spiritual things, or of faith in the sacraments that exist in time, through ignorance or error. And this light is divided from this darkness, and it gets the names of day and light in a way similar to the way dealt with above, when we commented on the division of light from darkness as being the distinction between the thing as formed and the same thing as formless.

2

In the same way as 'light' is understood to mean the knowledge of the truth, with regard to the glance of the mind, in just that way it is understood as the love of the known truth in the desire of the mind. And darkness means the vicious lack of ordering of love. Also, in an allegorical sense, the light is the wise and spiritual prelates of the church, who shine with the knowledge of the truth, with love, and with the outward shining of good works. The darkness is their subjects who are wrapped in the darkness of ignorance, and are animal and carnal. Also light comes to be when the fleshly sense of Scripture breaks through into the spiritual sense: it is as if light then shines out in the darkness, when the historical and fleshly sense of Scripture becomes bright by moving into a spiritual understanding.

3

Also, the establishment of light can be understood as the forming of our first parent in a state of grace in paradise: darkness and night and evening, as his fall from the grace he had received and the damaging by this fall of the natural goods with which he had been established. Morning can be understood as his return to grace through penance. Likewise, in the baptised the establishment of light is when by that sacrament they put on the Lord Jesus Christ and become light in the Lord, though before they were, in their own right, darkness. And those who fall away from the grace of baptism by sin, fall, as it were, through evening into the darkness of night. Those among them who return through penance, receive the renewed light of morning.

4

Also the establishment of light is the vision of the truth through contemplation, the evening is descent to action, and the morning is return to contemplation.

5

In all these ways of understanding the text it is easy, from what has been said above, to understand what is the division of light and darkness, and what is the calling of them 'day' and 'night'.

Source: C. F. J. Martin (trans.) *On the Six Days of Creation: A Translation of the Hexaëmeron* (1999) pp. 96–97

Astronomy attempted to map the heavens, and the medieval zodiac, again based on classical models, provided a codified picture of the constellations, twelve in number, which provided the basis for astrology that identified the planets with human life and activity. John Gower (*c.* 1325–1408) the English vernacular poet, celebrated the astrological tradition and the zodiac's deep levels of meaning.

9.2 *Confessio Amantis*, Bk. VII, lines 974–1234

. . . Hou that the Signes sitte arowe,
Ech after other be degree
In substance and in proprete
The zodiaque comprehendeth
Withinne his cercle, as it appendeth.

The ferste of whiche natheles
Be name is cleped Aries,
Which lich a wether of stature
Resembled is in his figure.
And as it seith in Almageste,
Of Sterres tuelve upon this beste
Ben set, wherof in his degre
The wombe hath tuo, the heved hath thre,
The Tail hath sevene, and in this wise,
As thou myht hiere me divise,
Stant Aries, which hot and drye
Is of himself, and in partie
He is the receipte and the hous
Of myhty Mars the bataillous.
And overmore ek, as I finde,
The creatour of alle kinde
Upon this Signe ferst began
The world, whan that he made man.
And of this constellacioun
The verray operacioun
Availeth, if a man therinne
The pourpos of his werk beginne;
For thanne he hath of proprete
Good sped and gret felicite.

The tuelve Monthes of the yeer
Attitled under the pouer
Of these tuelve Signes stonde;
Wherof that thou schalt understonde
This Aries on of the tuelve
Hath March attitled for himselve,
Whan every bridd schal chese his make,
And every neddre and every Snake

And every Reptil which mai moeve,
His myht assaieth forto proeve,
To crepen out ayein the Sonne,
Whan Ver his Seson hath begonne.

Taurus the seconde after this
Of Signes, which figured is
Unto a Bole, is dreie and cold;
And as it is in bokes told,
He is the hous appourtienant
To Venus, somdiel descordant.
This Bole is ek with sterres set,
Thurgh whiche he hath hise hornes knet
Unto the tail of Aries,
So is he noght ther sterreles.
Upon his brest ek eyhtetiene
He hath, and ek, as it is sene,
Upon his tail stonde othre tuo.
His Monthe assigned ek also
Is Averil, which of his schoures
Ministreth weie unto the floures.

The thridde signe is Gemini,
Which is figured redely
Lich to tuo twinnes of mankinde,
That naked stonde; and as I finde,
Thei be with Sterres wel bego:
The heved hath part of thilke tuo
That schyne upon the boles tail,
So be thei bothe of o parail;
But on the wombe of Gemini
Ben fyve sterres noght forthi,
And ek upon the feet be tweie,
So as these olde bokes seie,
That wise Tholomeus wrot.
His propre Monthe wel I wot
Assigned is the lusti Maii,
Whanne every brid upon his lay
Among the griene leves singeth,
And love of his pointure stingeth
After the lawes of nature
The youthe of every creature.

Cancer after the reule and space
Of Signes halt the ferthe place.
Like to the crabbe he hath semblance,
And hath unto his retienance
Sextiene sterres, wherof ten,
So as these olde wise men

Descrive, he berth on him tofore,
And in the middel tuo be bore,
And foure he hath upon his ende.
Thus goth he sterred in his kende,
And of himself is moiste and cold,
And is the propre hous and hold
Which appartieneth to the Mone,
And doth what longeth him to done.
The Monthe of Juin unto this Signe
Thou schalt after the reule assigne.

The fifte Signe is Leo hote,
Whos kinde is schape dreie and hote,
In whom the Sonne hath herbergage.
And the semblance of his ymage
Is a leoun, which in baillie
Of sterres hath his pourpartie:
The foure, which as Cancer hath
Upon his ende, Leo tath
Upon his heved, and thanne nest
He hath ek foure upon his brest,
And on upon his tail behinde,
In olde bokes as we finde.
His propre Monthe is Juyl be name,
In which men pleien many a game.

After Leo Virgo the nexte
Of Signes cleped is the sexte,
Wherof the figure is a Maide;
And as the Philosophre saide,
Sche is the welthe and the risinge,
The lust, the joie and the likinge
Unto Mercurie: and soth to seie
Sche is with sterres wel beseie,
Wherof Leo hath lent hire on,
Which sit on hih hir heved upon,
Hire wombe hath fyve, hir feet also
Have other fyve: and overmo
Touchende as of complexion,
Be kindly disposicion
Of dreie and cold this Maiden is.
And forto tellen over this
Hir Monthe, thou schalt understonde,
Whan every feld hath corn in honde
And many a man his bak hath plied,
Unto this Signe is Augst applied.

After Virgo to reknen evene
Libra sit in the nombre of sevene,

Which hath figure and resemblance
Unto a man which a balance
Berth in his hond as forto weie:
In boke and as it mai be seie,
Diverse sterres to him longeth,
Wherof on hevede he underfongeth
Ferst thre, and ek his wombe hath tuo,
And doun benethe eighte othre mo.
This Signe is hot and moiste bothe,
The whiche thinges be noght lothe
Unto Venus, so that alofte
Sche resteth in his hous fulofte,
And ek Saturnus often hyed
Is in this Signe and magnefied.
His propre Monthe is seid Septembre,
Which yifth men cause to remembre,
If eny Sor be left behinde
Of thing which grieve mai to kinde.

Among the Signes upon heighte
The Signe which is nombred eighte
Is Scorpio, which as feloun
Figured is a Scorpioun.
Bot for al that yit natheles
Is Scorpio noght sterreles;
For Libra granteth him his ende
Of eighte sterres, wher he wende,
The whiche upon his heved assised
He berth, and ek ther ben divised
Upon his wombe sterres thre,
And eighte upon his tail hath he.
Which of his kinde is moiste and cold
And unbehovely manyfold;
He harmeth Venus and empeireth,
Bot Mars unto his hous repeireth,
Bot war whan thei togedre duellen.
His propre Monthe is, as men tellen,
Octobre, which bringth the kalende
Of wynter, that comth next suiende.

The nynthe Signe in nombre also,
Which folweth after Scorpio,
Is cleped Sagittarius,
The whos figure is marked thus,
A Monstre with a bowe on honde:
On whom that sondri sterres stonde,
Thilke eighte of whiche I spak tofore,
The whiche upon the tail ben bore
Of Scorpio, the heved al faire

Bespreden of the Sagittaire;
And eighte of othre stonden evene
Upon his wombe, and othre sevene
Ther stonde upon his tail behinde.
And he is hot and dreie of kinde:
To Jupiter his hous is fre,
Bot to Mercurie in his degre,
For thei ben noght of on assent,
He worcheth gret empeirement.
This Signe hath of his proprete
A Monthe, which of duete
After the sesoun that befalleth
The Plowed Oxe in wynter stalleth;
And fyr into the halle he bringeth,
And thilke drinke of which men singeth,
He torneth must into the wyn;
Thanne is the larder of the swyn;
That is Novembre which I meene,
Whan that the lef hath lost his greene.

The tenthe Signe dreie and cold,
The which is Capricornus told,
Unto a Got hath resemblance:
For whos love and whos aqueintance
Withinne hise houses to sojorne
It liketh wel unto Satorne,
Bot to the Mone it liketh noght,
For no profit is there wroght.
This Signe as of his proprete
Upon his heved hath sterres thre,
And ek upon his wombe tuo,
And tweie upon his tail also.
Decembre after the yeeres forme,
So as the bokes ous enforme,
With daies schorte and nyhtes longe
This ilke Signe hath underfonge.

Of tho that sitte upon the hevene
Of Signes in the nombre ellevene
Aquarius hath take his place,
And stant wel in Satornes grace,
Which duelleth in his herbergage,
Bot to the Sonne he doth oultrage.
This Signe is verraily resembled
Lich to a man which halt assembled
In eyther hand a water spoute,
Wherof the stremes rennen oute.
He is of kinde moiste and hot,
And he that of the sterres wot

Seith that he hath of sterres tuo
Upon his heved, and ben of tho
That Capricorn hath on his ende;
And as the bokes maken mende,
That Tholomeus made himselve,
He hath ek on his wombe tuelve,
And tweie upon his ende stonde.

Thou schalt also this understonde,
The frosti colde Janever,
Whan comen is the newe yeer,
That Janus with his double face
In his chaiere hath take his place
And loketh upon bothe sides,
Somdiel toward the wynter tydes,
Somdiel toward the yeer suiende,
That is the Monthe belongende
Unto this Signe, and of his dole
He yifth the ferste Primerole.

The tuelfthe, which is last of alle
Of Signes, Piscis men it calle,
The which, as telleth the scripture,
Berth of tuo fisshes the figure.
So is he cold and moiste of kinde,
And ek with sterres, as I finde,
Beset in sondri wise, as thus:
Tuo of his ende Aquarius
Hath lent unto his heved, and tuo
This Signe hath of his oghne also
Upon his wombe, and over this
Upon his ende also ther is
A nombre of twenty sterres bryghte,
Which is to sen a wonder sighte.
Toward this Signe into his hous
Comth Jupiter the glorious,
And Venus ek with him acordeth
To duellen, as the bok recordeth.
The Monthe unto this Signe ordeined
Is Februer, which is bereined . . .

Source: G. C. Macaulay (ed.) *The English Works of John Gower*, EETS e.x. 81–82 (1900–1901) pp. 259–266

Table 9.1 The humours and elements

Elements	Humours	Temperament	Organs
water	phlegm	phlegmatic	brain
air	blood	sanguine	heart
fire	yellow bile	choleric	liver
earth	black bile	melancholic	spleen

The signs of the zodiac became incorporated into a pseudo-medical theory in which each sign governed a part of the body; to the medievals the human body (microcosm) reflected the universe (macrocosm). The foundation of medieval medicine was Greek medicine, and the idea of the four humours and four elements, and their proper balance, attributed to Hippocrates of Cos (5 BC), provided a paradigm of diagnosis and treatment (see Table 9.1).

Galen (132–201 AD) provided a firm astronomical knowledge for the Medievals who were handicapped by a growing church suspicion of medical practice. Indeed, monks and canons were prohibited from studying medicine in the twelfth century and it was through Muslim medics like Avicenna (c. 980–1037) and Averröes (1126–1198) that the science developed.

‌9.3 The doctrine of medieval medicine ‌

Medicine considers the human body as to the means by which it is cured and by which it is driven away from health. The knowledge of anything, since all things have causes, is not acquired or complete unless it is known by its causes. Therefore in medicine we ought to know the causes of sickness and health. And because health and sickness and their causes are sometimes manifest, and sometimes hidden and not to be comprehended except by the study of symptoms, we must also study the symptoms of health and disease. Now it is established in the sciences that no knowledge is acquired save through the study of its causes and beginnings, if it has had causes and beginnings; nor completed except by knowledge of its accidents and accompanying essentials. Of these causes there are four kinds: material, efficient, formal, and final.

Material causes, on which health and sickness depend, are . . . the affected member, which is the immediate subject, and the humours; and in these are the elements. And these two are subjects that, according to their mixing together, alter. In the composition and alteration of the substance which is thus composed, a certain unity is attained.

Efficient causes are the causes changing and preserving the conditions of the human body; as airs, and what are united with them; and evacuation and retention; and districts and cities, and habitable places, and what are united with them; and changes in age and diversities in it, and in races and arts and manners, and bodily and animate movings and restings, and sleepings and wakings on account of them; and in things which befall the human body when they touch it, and are either in accordance or at variance with nature. Formal causes are physical constitutions, and combinations and virtues which result from them. Final causes are operations. And in the science of operations lies the science of virtues, as we have set forth. These are the subjects of the doctrine of medicine; whence one inquires concerning the disease and curing of the human body. One ought to attain perfection in this research; namely, how health may be preserved and sickness cured. And the causes of this kind are rules in eating and drinking, and the choice of air, and the measure of exercise and rest; and doctoring with medicines and doctoring with the hands. All this with physicians is according to three species: the well, the sick, and the medium of whom we have spoken.

> Source: C. F. Horne (ed.) *The Sacred Books and Early Literature of the East* (1917), Vol. VI: *Medieval Arabia*, pp. 90–91

At Salerno, open to Muslim influence, a great medieval medical tradition developed. In 1316 Mordino de'Luzzi wrote his *Anothomica*, the first work entirely devoted to anatomy. Dissections were conducted at about the same time in Bologna and Padua, places noted both for their medical and legal traditions, but surgery remained a primitive art. Only perhaps in the field of herbalism did medieval medicine show any real quality.

'Judicial' astronomy concerned the influence of the planets on human behaviour rather than bodily functions; a subject of considerable debate. In his *De gestis regum Anglorum,* William of Malmesbury, the best informed and most reliable historian in twelfth-century England, tells us how, shortly before the Norman invasion of England in 1066, Eilmer, a monk of Malmesbury, saw for the second time, what was later to be recognised as Halley's Comet. The appearance of the comet in April 1066 caused such a stir that it is pictured in the Bayeux Tapestry.

₹ 9.4 Eilmer's account of the comet ₹

The same year, Henry, King of France, a good and active warrior, died by poison. Soon after, a comet, a star, denoting as they say change in kingdoms appeared trailing its extended and fiery train along the sky. Wherefore a certain Monk of our Monastery, by name Eilmer, bowing down with terror at the sight of the brilliant star, wisely exclaimed 'Thou art come, a matter of lamentation to many, more terrible, threatening to hurl destruction on this country'. He was a man of good learning for those times, of mature age and in his early youth had hazarded an attempt of singular temerity. He had by some contrivance fastened wings to his hands and feet in order that looking upon the fable as true he might fly like Daedalus, and collecting the air on the summit of a tower had flown for more than the distance of a furlong, but agitated by the violence of the wind and the current of air, as well as by the consciousness of his rash attempt, he fell and broke his legs and was lame ever after. He used to relate as the cause of his failure his forgetting to provide himself a tail.

> Source: M. Woosnam, *Eilmer: 11th Century Monk of Malmesbury. The Flight and the Comet* (1986) pp. 3–4

Scientific speculation could, however, be practically applied and this is no more clearly shown than in the mechanical clock, one of medieval Europe's great innovations. The mechanical clock was perfected in the last quarter of the thirteenth century. It reflected the fact that Western medieval men were so mechanically minded that they could believe that angels were in charge of the mechanism of the universe rather as mechanics regulated the clocks. The mathematical division of time into hours, minutes and seconds, reflected in the mechanical clock, challenged the East's concept of the eternity of time, but underlined the medieval world picture. The surviving fourteenth-century clock at Wells Cathedral provides a medieval universe in miniature. Richard of Wallingford undertook, on a grand scale, the building of the clock at St Albans. Although he cannot be credited with the invention of the astronomical clock it was the application of his exceptional mechanical flair and mathematical genius which perhaps proved a turning point in clock design.

ঌ 9.5 Thomas Walsingham, *Gesta Abbatum,* ঌ

[Richard] constructed a horologe in the church, and that he did nobly, with great expenditure of money and industry. He did not abandon the work as the result of its disparagement by the brethren, although they, wise in their own eyes, regarded it as the height of folly. He had the excuse, however, that his original intention was to construct the horologe at less expense, on account of the poor state of repair of the church, of which he often spoke; but that in his absence, as the result of the management of certain of the brethren, and the greed of the workmen, it was begun on such a costly scale that it would have been unseemly and caused him shame, not to have completed what had been begun.

Indeed, when on some occasion the illustrious King Edward, the Third from the Conquest, had come to the monastery to pray, and saw that so sumptuous a work had been put in hand, while the church was still not rebuilt after the ruin which had come about in Abbot Hugh's time, he modestly upbraided Abbot Richard, on the score that he had neglected the fabric of the church, and spent so much on a less important work, namely the aforementioned horologe. To this rebuke it was replied with due reverence, that abbots enough would succeed him who would find workmen for the fabric of the monastery, but no successor, once he was dead, would be able to finish the work he had begun. Indeed, he was quite right; for in that art he left none like him, nor in his lifetime did he find an equal.

Source: J. D. North (ed. and trans.) *Richard of Wallingford,* 3 vols (1976) Vol. 2, p. 361

The Middle Ages introduced machinery into Europe on a scale which no previous civilisation had known, allowing work to be done by machines which had previously only been possible, if at all, by hard labour. At the centre of this technological revolution was the mill and all its connotations, and at its summit lay the construction of some of the greatest places of worship ever erected. The status of the architect-engineer of the Gothic cathedrals which represented the culmination of this tradition was a high one, reflected in the thirteenth and fourteenth-century miniatures, which show God himself as the architect-engineer, measuring the universe with a large compass. It is, as Jean Gimpel has reminded us, as if today, in a film, God was to be represented as a computer programmer. The Gothic cathedral was a signpost to the world beyond, but its mastery and manipulation of space reflected a confidence in the control of this world. Michael Camille in his *Gothic Art* (1996), pp. 27–28, has described Gothic cathedrals as 'a new vision of space' and part of a great growth in French cultural influence. He writes, 'It has been estimated that eighty cathedrals were built in France between 1180 and 1270, part of the massive geographical and political expression of the royal domain under King Philip Augustus (r. 1180–1223), which made it the wealthiest country in the West. If people of the time referred to what we call Gothic architecture as anything, it was with the term *opus francigenum* (French work), or sometimes as the "new style" . . . Gothic architecture represented a break with tradition . . . the "new light" helped to create more complex interiors . . . and exerted its influence on the structuring of new forms of public and private space.'

The Gothic cathedral spread across Europe, but its chief publicist remained the French Abbot Suger of Saint Denis (1081–1151) who worked to put into stone a vision of the Heavenly Jerusalem.

---

৯ 9.6 Abbot Suger of St Denis ৯

Chp. XXVII

Of the Cast and Gilded Doors
Bronze casters having been summoned and sculptors chosen, we set up the main doors on which are represented the Passion of the Saviour and His Resurrection, or rather Ascension, with great cost and much expenditure for their gilding as was fitting for the noble porch. Also [we set up] others, new ones on the right side and the old ones on the left beneath the mosaic, which, though contrary to modern custom, we ordered to be executed there and to be affixed to the tympanum of the portal. We also committed ourselves richly to elaborate the tower[s] and the upper crenelations of the front, both for the beauty of the church and, should circumstances require it, for practical purposes. Further we ordered the year of the consecration, lest it be forgotten, to be inscribed in copper-gilt letters in the following manner:

> 'For the splendour of the church that has fostered and exalted him,
> Suger has laboured for the splendour of the church.
> Giving thee a share of what is thine, O Martyr Denis,
> He prays to thee to pray that he may obtain a share of Paradise.
> The year was the One Thousand, One Hundred, and Fortieth
> Year of the Word when [this structure] was consecrated.'

The verses on the door, further, are these:

'Whoever thou art, if thou seekest to extol the glory of these doors,
Marvel not at the gold and the expense but at the craftsmanship of the work.
Bright is the noble work; but, being nobly bright, the work
Should brighten the minds, so that they may travel, through the true lights,
To the True Light where Christ is the true door.
In what manner it be inherent in this world the golden door defines:
The dull mind rises to truth through that which is material
And, in seeing this light is resurrected from its former submersion.'

And on the lintel:

'Receive, O stern Judge, the prayers of Thy Suger;
Grant that I be mercifully numbered among Thy own sheep.'

> Source: E. Panofsky (ed. and trans.) *Abbot Suger on
> the Abbey Church of St.-Denis and its Art Treasures*
> (1946) pp. 47, 49

The physical space of the church buildings took on an organic unity. The greatest of England's Gothic cathedrals, Lincoln, was in part built during the episcopate of St Hugh, bishop from 1186 to 1200, and its building (like the clocks alluded to already) could to be viewed allegorically.

৯৵ 9.7 Lincoln Cathedral ৶৭

Of the allegory of the separate parts
These parts, though they have been described with a child's simplicity, import an allegory. On the outside of the church is like a hard shell, but inside is formed a kernel; outside is like wax, but inside it is a honeycomb; and the fire shines more enjoyably being in the shadow. For the foundation, wall, roof, hewn white stone, the marble that is so smooth, eye-catching, and black, the two rows of the windows, and the pair of windows which as it were look down northward and southward, great as they are in themselves, image forth still greater things.

That of the parts of the whole cathedral
The foundation is the body, the wall is the man, the roof is the spirit: the division of the church is thus threefold. The body has as its portion earth, the man has the clouds, the spirit has the stars.

That of the white stones
The white hewn stone signifies the pure and wise: the whiteness is modesty and the hewing is doctrine.

That of the marble shafts
In the guise of marble, which is smooth, shining and dark, is signified the bride, simple, meticulous, and toiling. The smoothness indeed correctly represents her simplicity, the sheen her meticulousness, and the dark colour her toil.

That of the glass windows
Illuminating the world with heavenly light is the distinguished band of the clergy, and this is expressed by the bright windows. There is a ranking order on either side, which can be remarked: in the clerestory range the rank of canon, and in the aisle range that of vicar. And since, while a canon is handling the world's affairs, his vicar is perpetually and diligently carrying out the divine offices, the top range of windows shine illustrious with flower-petals, signifying the varied beauty of the world, while the lower range presents the names of the holy fathers.

That of the two circular windows
The twin windows that offer a circular light are the two Eyes of the cathedral; and rightly the greater of these is seen to be the bishop and the lesser the dean. For north represents the devil, and south the Holy Spirit and it is in these directions that the two Eyes look. The bishop faces the south in order to invite in, and the dean the north in order to avoid; the one takes care to be saved, the other takes care not to perish. With these Eyes the cathedral's face is on the watch for the candelabra of heaven and the darkness of Lethe.

The summing up of the whole allegory
Thus unconscious stones enclose the mysteries of animate ones, the fabric made with hands represents that of the spirit, and the face of the cathedral has a double refulgence, adorned as it is with the twofold appointment.

> **Source: B. Garton (trans.) *The Metrical Life of
> Saint Hugh* (1986) pp. 57, 59, 61**

The movement in the direction of superabundant decoration and richly layered meaning offended religious purists like Bernard of Clairvaux who issued a celebrated diatribe against those, especially those in the Cluniac monasteries, who built overripe churches.

࿇ 9.8 Bernard of Clairvaux ࿇

But these are small matters. I pass on to greater ones ... I will not speak of the immense height of the churches, of their immoderate length, of their superfluous breadth, costly polishing, and strange designs, which, while they attract the eyes of the worshipper, hinder the soul's devotion, and somehow remind me of the old Jewish ritual. However, let all this pass; we will suppose it is done, as we are told, for the glory of God. But, a monk myself, I do ask other monks . . . 'Tell me, O ye professors of poverty, what does gold do in a holy place?' The case of bishops and monks is not the same. We know that they, as debtors to the wise and foolish, when they cannot rouse the sense of religion in the carnal multitude by spiritual means, must do so by ornaments that appeal to the senses. But among us, who have gone out from among the people; among us, who have forsaken whatever things are fair and costly for Christ's sake; who have regarded all things beautiful to the eye, soft to the ear, agreeable to the smell, sweet to the taste, pleasant to the touch – all things, in a word, which can gratify the body – as dross and dung, that we might gain Christ, of whom among us, I ask, can devotion be excited by such means? Or, to speak plainly, is it not avarice – that is, the worship of idols – which does all this? from which we do not expect spiritual fruit, but worldly benefit . . . So carefully is the money laid out, that it returns multiplied many times. It is spent that it may be increased, and plenty is born of profusion. By the sight of wonderful and costly vanities men are prompted to give rather than to pray. Some beautiful picture of a saint is exhibited – and the brighter the colours the greater the holiness attributed to it; men run, eager to kiss; they are invited to give, and the beautiful is more admired than the sacred is revered. In the churches are suspended, not *coronae,* but wheels studded with gems, and surrounded by lights, which are scarcely brighter than the precious stones which are near them. Instead of candlesticks, we behold great trees of brass, fashioned with wonderful skill, and glittering as much through their jewels as their lights. What do you suppose is the object of all this? The repentance of the contrite, or the admiration of the gazers? Oh, vanity of vanities! but not more vain than foolish. The church's walls are resplendent, but the poor are not there . . . The curious find wherewith to amuse themselves; the wretched find no stay for them in their misery. Why, at least, do we not reverence the images of the saints, with which the very pavement we walk on is covered? Often an angel's mouth is spilt into, and the face of some saint trodden on by the passers by . . . But if we cannot do without images, why can we not spare the brilliant colours? What has all this to do with monks, with professors of poverty, with men of spiritual minds?

Again, in the cloisters, what is the meaning of those ridiculous monsters, of that deformed beauty, that beautiful deformity, before the very eyes of the brethren when reading? What are disgusting monkeys there for, or ferocious lions, or monstrous centaurs, or spotted tigers, or fighting soldiers, or huntsmen sounding the bugle? You may see there one head with many bodies, or one body with numerous heads. Here is a quadruped with a serpent's tail; there is a fish with a beast's head; there a creature, in front a horse, behind a goat; another has horns at one end, and a horse's tail at the other. In fact, such an endless variety of forms appears everywhere, that it is more pleasant to read in the stonework than in books, and to spend the day in admiring these oddities than in meditating on the law of God. Good God! If we are not ashamed of these absurdities, why do we not grieve at the cost of them?

Source: J. Cotter Morison, *The Life and Times of Saint Bernard* (1901) pp. 130–132

It is to be noted that however heavy the polemic, Bernard's own Cistercians built churches of splendid mathematical integrity and to the highest workmanship. The technical skill of architects, builders and artisans is clear, not only from the buildings themselves, but from surviving records. Costing, patronage and expertise reveal the more practical side of medieval craftsmanship, sometimes concealed in the ecclesiastical verbiage.

֍ 9.9 Reconstructing cathedrals ֎

Reconstruction of Cambrai Cathedral (Gestum pontificum Cameracensium, 1023–1030)

The Lord Bishop Gérard first entered the town. When he saw that the buildings of the monastery of St Mary were as small as they were decrepit and he suspected their ancient walls were cracking, he swiftly conceived the project of putting them into a more satisfactory state, if only he were given the necessary time, with the help of God. But he could not undertake the project before the year of the Incarnation 1023 . . . because he was prevented . . . by internal as well as external conflict. But then, trusting in divine mercy and reassured by the prayers of many of the faithful whom he had taken into his confidence, he gave orders to demolish the old walls. Once the necessary funds were pledged, he devoted all his energy to reconstructing a building that presented such great difficulties, for he had a fear of leaving the work unfinished, either because death might overtake him, or because some other reason might hinder him from completing it. In this respect, he realised that among the obstacles that might delay the project he had at heart, none was more difficult to overcome than the slowness of the transport of columns, cut a long way from the town, almost at the thirtieth milestone. And so he prayed Divine Mercy grant him assistance nearer at hand. One day while riding his horse, he explored the hidden depths of the earth in many surrounding places. At last, with the help of God who never fails those who put their trust in Him, he had a trench dug in the village that has always been known as Lesdain, four miles from the town, and found stone suitable for the columns. And this was not the only place: on digging nearer, to be precise on the estate of Nigella, he had the joy of finding good quality stones of another kind. Giving thanks to God for this find, he devoted all his zeal to this pious work. And to cut short the story, in the space of seven years, with the help of Divine Mercy, he brought this huge work to its conclusion, that is in the year of the Incarnation of Our Lord 1030.

The Rebuilding of Canterbury Cathedral (Chronicle of Gervase of Canterbury)

Meantime the brotherhood sought counsel as to how and in what manner the burnt church might be repaired, but without success; for the columns of the church, commonly termed the pillars, were exceedingly weakened by the heat of the fire, and were scaling in pieces and hardly able to stand, so that they frightened even the wisest out of their wits.

French and English artificers were therefore summoned, but even these differed in opinion. On the one hand, some undertook to repair the aforesaid columns without mischief to the walls above. On the other hand, there were some who asserted that the whole church must be pulled down if the monks wished to exist in safety. This opinion, true as it was, excruciated the monks with grief, and no wonder, for how could they hope that so great a work should be completed in their days by any human ingenuity?

However, amongst the other workmen there had come a certain William of Sens, a man active and ready, and as a workman most skilful both in wood and stone. Him, therefore, they retained, on account of his lively genius and good reputation, and dismissed the others. And to him, and to the providence of God was the execution of the work committed.

And he, residing many days with the monks and carefully surveying the burnt walls in their upper and lower parts, within and without, did yet for some time conceal what he found necessary to be done, lest the truth should kill them in their present state of pusillanimity.

But he went on preparing all things that were needful for the work, either of himself or by the agency of others. And when he found that the monks began to be somewhat comforted, he ventured to confess that the pillars rent with the fire and all that they supported must be destroyed if the monks wished to have a safe and excellent building. At length they agreed, being convinced by reason and wishing to have the work as good as he promised, and above all things to live in security; thus they consented patiently, if not willingly, to the destruction of the choir.

And now he addressed himself to the procuring of stone from beyond the sea. He constructed ingenious machines for loading and unloading ships, and for drawing cement and stone. He delivered moulds for shaping the stones to the sculptors who were assembled, and diligently prepared other things of the same kind. The choir thus condemned to destruction was pulled down, and nothing else was done in this year.

As the new work is of a different fashion from the old, it may be well to describe the old work first and then the new. Edmer, the venerable singer, in his Opuscula, describes the ancient church built in the Roman manner, which Archbishop Lanfranc, when he came to the See, utterly destroyed, finding it in ashes. For Christ Church is recorded to have suffered thrice from fire; first, when the blessed martyr Elfege was captured by the Danes and received the crown of martyrdom; secondly, when Lanfranc, abbot of Caen, took the rule of the church of Canterbury; thirdly, in the days of Archbishop Richard and Prior Odo . . . Leaving out, therefore, all that is not absolutely necessary, let us boldly prepare for the destruction of this old work and the marvellous building of the new, and let us see what our master William has been doing in the meanwhile. The master began, as I stated long ago, to prepare all things necessary for the new work, and to destroy the old. In this way the first year was taken up. In the following year, that is after the feast of St Bertin before the winter, he erected four pillars, that is, two on each side, and after the winter two more were placed, so that on each side were three in order, upon which and upon the exterior wall of the aisles he framed seemly arches and a vault, that is three [bays] on each side . . . In the third year he placed two pillars on each side, the two extreme ones of which he decorated with marble columns placed around them, and because at that place the choir and [transepts] were to meet, he constituted these principal pillars. To which, having added the keystones and the vault, he intermingled the lower triforium from the great tower to the aforesaid pillars, that is, as far as the [transept], with many marble columns. Over which he adjusted another triforium of the other materials, and also the upper windows. And in the next place, three [bays] of the great vault, from the tower, namely, as far as the [transept]. All which things appeared to us and to all who saw them, incomparable and most worthy of praise. And at so glorious a beginning we rejoiced and conceived good hopes to the end, and provided for the acceleration of the work with diligence and spirit. Thus was the third year occupied and the beginning of the fourth.

In the summer, commencing from the cross, he erected ten pillars, that is, on each side five. Of which the first two were ornamented with marble columns to correspond with the other two principal ones. Upon these ten he placed the arches and vaults. And having, in the next place, completed on both sides the triforia and upper windows, he was, at the beginning of the fifth year, in the act of preparing with machines for the turning of the great vault, when suddenly the beams broke under his feet, and he fell to the ground, stones and timbers accompanying his fall, from the height of the capitals of the upper vault, that is to say, of fifty feet. Thus sorely bruised by the blows from the beams and stones, he was rendered helpless alike to himself and for the work, but no other than himself was in the least injured. Against the master only was this vengeance of God or spite of the devil directed.

The master, thus hurt, remained in his bed for some time under medical care in expectation of recovering, but was deceived in this hope, for his health amended not. Nevertheless, as the winter approached, and it was necessary to finish the upper vault, he gave the charge of the work to a certain ingenious and industrious monk, who was the overseer of the masons; an appointment whence much envy and malice arose, because it made this young man appear more skilful than richer and more powerful ones. But the master reclining in bed commanded all things that should be done in order. And thus was completed the [bay] between the four principal pillars. In the keystone of this [bay] the choir and [transepts] seem as it were to meet. Two [bays] on each side were formed before the winter; when the heavy rains beginning stopped the work. In these operations the fourth year was occupied and the beginning of the fifth. But on the eighth day from the said fourth year, on the ides of September, there happened an eclipse of the sun at about the sixth hour, and before the master's accident.

And the master, perceiving that he derived no benefit from the physicians, gave up the work, and crossing the sea returned to his home in France. And another succeeded him in charge of the works; William by name, English by nation, small in body, but in workmanship of many kinds acute and honest. In the summer of the fifth year he finished the [transepts] on each side, that is, the south and the north, and [built the vault] which is above the great Altar, which the rains of the previous year had hindered, although all was prepared. Moreover he laid the foundation for the enlargement of the church at the eastern part, because a chapel of St Thomas was to be built there . . . Moreover, in the same summer, that is of the sixth year, the outer wall round the chapel of St Thomas, begun before the winter, was elevated as far as the turning of the vault. But the master had begun a tower at the eastern part outside the circuit of the wall as it were, the lower vault of which was completed before the winter.

The chapel of the Holy Trinity above mentioned was then levelled to the ground; this had hitherto remained untouched out of reverence to St Thomas, who was buried in the crypt. But the saints who reposed in the upper part of the chapel were translated elsewhere, and lest the memory of what was then done should be lost, I will record somewhat thereof. On the eighth idus of July the altar of the Holy Trinity was broken up, and from its materials the altar of St John the Apostle was made; I mention this lest the history of the holy stone should be lost.

It has been above stated, that after the fire nearly all the old portions of the choir were destroyed and changed into somewhat new and of a more noble fashion. The differences between the two works may now be enumerated. The pillars of the old and new work are alike in form and thickness but different in length. For the new pillars were elongated by almost twelve feet. In the old capitals the work was plain, in the new ones exquisite in sculpture. There the circuit of the choir had twenty-two pillars, here are twenty-eight. There the arches and everything else was plain, or sculptured with an axe and not with a chisel. But here almost throughout is appropriate sculpture. No marble columns were there, but here are innumerable ones. There, in the circuit around the choir, the vaults were plain, but here they are arch-ribbed and have keystones. There a wall set upon the pillars divided the crosses from the choir, but here the crosses are separated from the choir by no such partition, and converge together in one keystone, which is placed in the middle of the great vault which rests on the four principal pillars. There, there was a ceiling of wood decorated with excellent painting, but here is a vault beautifully constructed of stone and light tufa. There, was a single triforium, but here are two in the choir and a third in the aisle of the church. All which will be better understood from inspection than by any description.

This must be known, however, that the new work is higher than the old by so much as the upper windows of the body of the choir, as well as of its aisles, are raised above the marble tabling.

And as in future ages it may be doubtful why the breadth which was given to the choir next the tower should be so much contracted at the head of the church, it may not be useless to explain the causes thereof. One reason is, that the two towers of St Anselm and St Andrew, placed in the circuit on each side of the old church, would not allow the breadth of the choir to proceed in the direct line. Another reason is, that it was agreed upon and necessary that the chapel of St Thomas should be erected at the head of the church, where the chapel of the Holy Trinity stood, and this was much narrower than the choir. The master, therefore, not choosing to pull down the said towers, and being unable to move them entire, set out the breadth of the choir in a straight line, as far as the beginning of the towers. Then, receding slightly on either side from the towers, and preserving as much as he could the breadth of the passage outside the choir on account of the processions which were there frequently passing, he gradually and obliquely drew in his work, so that from the opposite the altar, it might begin to contract, and from thence, at the third pillar, might be so narrowed as to coincide with the breadth of the chapel, which was named of the Holy Trinity. Beyond these, four pillars were set on the sides at the same distance as the last, but of a different form; and beyond these other four were arranged in a circle, and upon these the superposed work was brought together and terminated. This is the arrangement of the pillars. The outer wall, which extends from the aforesaid towers, first proceeds in a straight line, is then bent into a curve, and thus in the round tower the wall on each side comes together in one, and is there ended. All which may be more clearly and pleasantly seen by the eyes than taught in writing. But this much was said that the differences between the old and new work might be made manifest.

Now let us carefully examine what were the works of our mason in this seventh year from the fire, which, in short, included the completion of the new and handsome crypt, and above the crypt the exterior walls of the aisles up to their marble capitals. The windows, however, the master was neither willing nor able to turn, on account of the approaching rains. Neither did he erect the interior pillars. Thus was the seventh year finished, and the eighth begun. In this eighth year the master erected eight interior pillars and turned the arches and the vault with the windows in the circuit. He also raised the tower up to the bases of the highest windows under the vault. In the ninth year no work was done for want of funds. In the tenth year the upper windows of the tower, together with the vault, were finished.

> **Source: A. Erlande-Brandenburg, *The Cathedral Builders of the Middle Ages* (1995) pp. 146–152**

Medieval technology and science was often at the service of the state through the growing sophistication of castle-building and fortifications and it benefited from the insights of the ancient world and on the discoveries of Arab science. Its highest expression, however, was in the architecture of space and light exemplified in the Gothic cathedral.

The Classical tradition, inherited from Greece and Rome, sometimes only dimly present owing to the paucity of texts, dominated medieval learning. Medieval education, which remained principally the preserve of ecclesiastics, appropriated the ancient liberal tradition for the service of Christianity. The basic framework of study, as in the ancient world, remained the sevenfold division, and seven was seen as the number of perfection, of the *trivium* (grammar, logic and rhetoric) and the *quadrivium* (arithmetic, music, geometry and astronomy). On the west front of the cathedral of Chartres, the portal portrays the Mother of God, the seat of wisdom, surrounded in the archivolts by statues personifying the liberal arts, each supported by a great classical master of the discipline.

In the first part of the Middle Ages, there was a strong emphasis on the word and text with the Bible as the principal authority. The chief educators were the monks and the principal arenas of learning were the monastic schools. Grammar was seen as the foundation of study.

ঽ 9.10 Masters and teachers to inculcate the liberal arts ৡ

Complaints have been made that in some places no masters nor endowment for a Grammar School is found. Therefore all bishops shall bestow all care and diligence, both for their subjects and for other places in which it shall be found necessary, to establish masters and teachers who shall assiduously teach grammar schools and the principles of the liberal arts, because in these chiefly the commandments of God are manifested and declared.

> **Source: A. F. Leach (trans.) *Educational Charters and Documents* (1911) p. 21**

In the twelfth century the deepening and flowering of learning was so profound that some scholars have talked about a twelfth-century renaissance. Some monastic schools, like that at Bec in Normandy, with its two famous northern Italian monks, Lanfranc (*c.* 1005–1089) and Anselm (1033–1107), who both went on to be archbishop of Canterbury continued to be full of intellectual vitality. Anselm saw reason as defending rather than opposing faith and suggesting the existence of God.

ৡ 9.11 St Anselm, *Monologion* ঙ

That of all the things that exist, there is one nature that is the best, greatest and supreme.

Of all the things that exist, there is one nature that is supreme. It alone is self-sufficient in its eternal happiness, yet through its all-powerful goodness it creates and gives to all other things their very existence and their goodness. Now, take someone who either has never heard of, or does not believe in, and so does not know this, or indeed any of the numerous other things which we necessarily believe about God and his creation. I think that they can, even if of average ability, convince themselves, to a large extent, of the truth of these beliefs, simply by reason alone. Now, since this could be done in several ways, I will set down here the one that I consider to be the most readily available. For, given that all desire only what they think is good, anyone can easily avail himself of the following opportunity: he can at any time turn the mind's eye to look for the source of the things that are good – things that one would not want unless one judged them to be good. In this way, then, guided by reason, he may make rational progress towards what he, unreasoningly, does not know.

But if I say something along the way that greater authority does not teach, then I wish it to be taken in the following way: it is, indeed, reached as a necessary conclusion from reasoning which seems right to me. Nevertheless, it is not thereby asserted as necessary without qualification. Rather I assert it as possible – for the present at least.

Anyone, then, can quite easily ask himself the following question: 'Given that there is such an uncountable number of good things, the sheer multiplicity of which is simply a datum of bodily sense as well as something we perceive by means of the rational mind – given this, are we to believe that there is some one thing through which all good things whatsoever are good? Or do different goods have their existence through different things?' Quite certain, indeed, and clear to all who are willing to see, is the following: take some things that are said to be (say) X, and relative to each other are said to be less, more, or equally X. It is through this X that they are said to be so, and this X is understood as the very same thing in the various cases and not something different in each case (whether X is considered to be in them equally or not equally). Take, for example, some things that are said, relative to each other, to be, either equally, or more, or less just. They cannot be understood to be just except through justice, and justice is not something different in each of the various cases. Therefore, since it is certain that all good things when compared with each other are either equally or not equally good, necessarily all good things are good through something, and this something is understood to be the same thing in each of various good things.

Different good things may none the less appear to be called good through different things. Thus a horse may appear to be called good through one thing, because it is strong, and through something else, because it is swift. For it seems to be called good through strength and good through speed, and yet strength and speed do not seem to be the same thing. And if the horse is good because it is strong and swift, how come the thief that is swift and strong is bad? Rather, it is the case that the swift and strong thief is bad because he does harm, and the strong and swift horse is good because it is beneficial. (And indeed ordinarily nothing is thought to be good except on the grounds either of what is beneficial, e.g. health and what makes for it – or of what is excellent, e.g. beauty and what contributes to it.) Now, the reasoning above is irrefutable. Necessarily, therefore, everything beneficial or excellent is, if it is truly good, good through that same one thing, through which all good things necessarily are good, whatever that thing may be. And who would doubt that that through which all things are good is a great good?

Because, then, it is that through which every good thing is good, it is good through itself. It therefore follows that all the other good things are good through something other than what they themselves are, while this thing alone is good through itself. But nothing that is good through something other than itself is equal to or greater than that good which is good through itself. The one thing, therefore, that is good through itself is the one thing that is supremely good. For the supreme is that which so over-tops the others that it has no equal and no superior. But what is supremely good is also supremely great. There is therefore one thing that is supremely good and supremely great, and this is of all the things that exist, the supreme.

Source: B. Davies and G. R. Evans (eds) *Anselm of Canterbury, The Major Works* (1998) pp. 11–12. © Simon Harrison 1998. Reprinted from *Anselm of Canterbury: The Major Works*, edited with an introduction by Brian Davies and G. R. Evans (Oxford World Classics, 1998) by permission of Oxford University Press

The monastic reform movements, the reformation rather than the renaissance of the twelfth century, tended towards anti-intellectualism.

---

৯৯ 9.12 The fifty-eighth Treatise of St Peter Damian: ৯৯ Concerning true happiness and wisdom

---

Chapter Three

Indeed, just as heavenly wisdom makes spiritually-minded and lawful sons of the Church, so earthly prudence makes them carnal-minded and bastards. Of these,

Baruch says: 'And the sons of Agar, who sought out diligently that wisdom which is of this world, the merchants of Merrha and Theman, the spinners of tales and seekers of knowledge, knew not the way of wisdom, nor did they remember her paths.' Those who desire to pursue worldly knowledge and who despise the wisdom of the spirit are sons of Agar, not of Sarah; and, being bastards, are to be judged by the law of Ishmael, not that of Israel. And, since the name Agar means 'stranger', they are not the children of wisdom, but strangers and pilgrims, but not of the number of those to whom the Apostle says: 'Now therefore ye are no more strangers and pilgrims, but fellow-citizens with the saints, and of the household of God.' Do you too, dearly beloved (if I may once more use the words of Baruch), learn where wisdom dwells. For she is to be found in her essence only in God, and of him you must certainly seek her. But because the place you hold in the world is not a lowly one, and because you cannot abandon it, you will find it useful, in avoiding the cadences of pagan rhetoric in conversation, and in shunning at all times the sophistication of literary elegance, to observe a certain discretion. Be almost slothful in worldly matters; but stretch all the sinews of your mind in the discipline of the spirit. Be heedless of the former, but eager in the latter. Because you cannot of yourself hope entirely to avoid the cunning of the serpent in the transaction of worldly affairs, let this be enough for you: that the wisdom of the spirit may devour your earthly prudence, and transform it into the secret substance of her body. The Scriptures tell us, concerning Pharaoh's magicians: 'They cast down every man his rod, and they became serpents, but Aaron's rod swallowed up their rods.' Now, the rod of Aaron swallowed up the rods of the sorcerers because the wisdom of Christ, which it signified, has made void all the wisdom of the world, and has united in the bowels of His body, the Church, the wise men of this world.

Besides, it is absurd and disgraceful that we should show the same care and precision in human affairs that we devote to the things of God and of the spirit. That is why the Lord said to Moses: 'Take unto thee sweet spices, stacte and onycha and sweet-smelling galbanum and pure frankincense, and thou shalt make it a perfume, a confection after the art of the apothecary, tempered together, pure and holy.'

We make a perfume of sweet spices when we diffuse the odour of a multiplicity of virtues around the altar of good works. And it is tempered together and pure, because the more we add to virtue, the more purely does the incense of good works rise up. And to these words of the Lord were added others: 'And thou shalt beat it very small, and put of it before the testimony in the tabernacle of the congregation.' We beat all these spices very small when we pound our good works in the pestle of our hearts by secret examination of our consciences and carefully consider whether they are truly good. To reduce the spices to dust is to grind our virtues by means of reflection and to subject them to the refinement of inner inquiry.

Source: P. McNulty (trans.) *St Peter Damian:*
Selected Writings on the Spiritual Life (1959)
pp. 140–141

The cathedral schools, especially those in northern France, came to be centres of exciting and new ideas in the twelfth century. Students flocked from across the whole of Europe to such masters of the mind as Peter Abelard (1079–1142) whose early work *Sic et Non* (*Yes and No*) challenged his students with 168 topics of great complexity. He did not attempt to tell his students what to think, but rather he explained to them how to think and how to set about studying texts.

ৡৈ 9.13 Peter Abelard, On how to study ৡৈ

We must be careful not to be led astray by attributing views to the Fathers which they did not hold. This may happen if a wrong author's name is given to a book or if a text is corrupt. For many works are falsely attributed to one of the Fathers to give them authority, and some passages, even in the Bible, are corrupt through the errors of copyists . . . We must be equally careful to make sure that an opinion quoted from a Father was not withdrawn or corrected by him in the light of later and better knowledge (as, for instance, blessed Augustine often did). Again the passage in question may not give the Father's own opinion, but that of some other writer whom he is quoting . . .

We must also make a thorough inquiry when different decisions are given on the same matter under canon law. We must discover the underlying purpose of the opinion, whether it is meant to grant an indulgence or exhort to some perfection. In this way we may clear up the apparent contradiction . . . If the opinion is a definitive judgement, we must determine whether it is of general application or directed to a particular case . . . The when and why of the order must also be considered because what is allowed at one time is often forbidden at another, and what is often laid down as the strict letter of the law may be sometimes moderated by a dispensation . . .

Furthermore we customarily talk of things as they appear to our bodily senses and not as they are in actual fact. So judging by what we see we say it is a starry sky or it is not, and that the sun is hot or has no heat at all, when these things though variable in appearance are ever constant. Can we be surprised, then, that some matters have been stated by the Fathers as opinions rather than the truth? Then again many controversies would be quickly settled if we could be on our guard against a particular word used in different senses by different authors . . .

A careful reader will employ all these ways of reconciling contradictions in the writings of the Fathers. But if the contradictions are so glaring that they cannot be reconciled, then the rival authorities must be compared and the view that has the heaviest backing be adopted . . .

By collecting contrasting divergent opinions I hope to provoke young readers to push themselves to the limit in the search for truth, so that their wits may be sharpened by their investigation. It is by doubting that we come to investigate, and by investigating that we recognise the truth.

Source: D. Ayerst and A. Fisher, *Records of Christianity, Vol. II: Christianity* (1977) pp. 196–197

Abelard's intellectualism and his personal arrogance both attracted adulation and created opposition.

ࣝ 9.14 Bernard of Clairvaux on Peter Abelard ࣝ

We have in France an old teacher turned into a new theologian, who in his early days amused himself with dialectics, and now pours out wild baseless speculations about the Bible. He is trying to revive false ideas long since condemned and buried – his own and other people's; and he is adding fresh errors. I can think of nothing in heaven above or on earth beneath which he will admit that he does not understand. He looks up to heaven and explores the deep things of God. Coming back to us he reports things which cannot be expressed, words which it is not lawful for a man to speak. He has the temerity to give a reason for everything, even for those things which are above reason; he makes unwarranted assertions against reason and against faith – for what is more unreasonable than to try by reason to transcend reason? And what is more against faith than to be unwilling to believe what reason cannot reach? . . . But our theologian says: 'What is the use of speaking of doctrine unless what we wish to teach can be explained in an intelligible way?' And so he promises that his hearers will understand even those most sublime and sacred truths which lie hidden in the bosom itself of our faith . . . On the very threshold of his theology, or rather of his 'foolology', he defines faith as private judgement . . .

Is not our hope baseless if our faith is subject to change? Surely our martyrs were fools if they accepted such cruel tortures for an uncertainty, and entered without hesitation on an eternal exile by bitter death, if there was a doubt about the reward that awaited them. But far be it from us to think – with him – that anything in our faith or hope depends on an individual's judgement, when the whole of it rests upon sure, solid truth, certified by miracles and revelations from heaven, founded and consecrated by the Son of the Virgin, by the Blood of the Redeemer, by the glory of the risen Christ . . . 'I know in whom I have believed, and I am confident' (2 Tim. 1, 12) the Apostle proclaims; you mutter in my ear that faith is only an opinion . . .

But now notice other points. I pass over his saying . . . that the Holy Spirit is the world-soul; . . . Here, while he exhausts himself to make Plato a Christian, he proves himself a heathen. All these things and his numerous other silly stories I leave on one side and come to graver matters . . .

Source: D. Ayerst and A. Fisher, *Records of
Christianity, Vol. II: Christianity* (1977) pp. 200–201

ࣝ❦ࣝ

By the beginning of the thirteenth century, the major schools were developing into universities, corporations of masters and students who formed a unit independent of the cathedral establishments and the monasteries. Theology was the highest aspiration of the student's curriculum, the queen of the sciences, and Paris became the pre-eminent theological faculty. Others had different specialisations: Bologna for law, Salerno and

Montepellier for medicine. The two English medieval universities of Oxford and Cambridge were provincial reflections of Paris, although Oxford had some masters of great distinction. There is no clear date of foundation for Oxford, the oldest English university, but teaching existed in some form as early as 1096 and developed rapidly from 1167, when Henry II banned English students from attending the University of Paris. By 1201, Oxford was headed by a *magister scolarum Oxonie*, on whom the title of Chancellor was conferred in 1214, and in 1231, the masters were recognised as a *universitas* or corporation. In 1209, scholars taking refuge from hostile townsmen in Oxford migrated to Cambridge and settled there. They were numerous enough by 1226 to have set up an organisation and arranged regular courses of study, taught by their own members. The documentation for the Paris schools reflects the life of all the European universities.

৶ 9.15 The Statutes of Robert Curzon for the ৶⁹ University of Paris (1215)

R., servant of the cross of Christ, by the divine mercy cardinal priest with the title of St Stephen in Monte Celio and legate of the apostolic seat, to all the masters and scholars at Paris – eternal safety in the Lord.

Let all know, that having been especially commanded by the lord pope to devote our energy effectively to the betterment of the condition of the students at Paris, and wishing by the advice of good men to provide for the tranquillity of the students in the future, we have ordered and prescribed the following rules:

No one is to lecture at Paris in arts before he is twenty years old. He is to listen in arts at least six years, before he begins to lecture. He is to promise that he will lecture for at least two years, unless he is prevented by some good reason, which he ought to prove either in public or before the examiners. He must not be smirched by any infamy. When he is ready to lecture, each one is to be examined according to the form contained in the letter of lord P. bishop of Paris (in which is contained the peace established between the chancellor and the students by the judges appointed by the lord pope, approved and confirmed namely by the bishop and deacon of Troyes and by P. the bishop, and J. the chancellor of Paris).

The treatises of Aristotle on logic, both the old and the new, are to be read in the schools in the regular and not in the extraordinary courses. The two Priscians, or at least the second, are also to be read in the schools in the regular courses. On the feast-days nothing is to be read except philosophy, rhetoric, *quadrivialia,* the Barbarisms, the Ethics, if one so chooses, and the fourth book of the Topics. The books of Aristotle on Metaphysics or Natural Philosophy, or the abridgements of these works, are not to be read, nor 'the doctrine' of master David de Dinant, of the heretic Amalric, or of Maurice of Spain.

In the inceptions and meetings of the masters and in the confutations or arguments of the boys or youths there are to be no festivities. But they may call in some friends or associates, but only a few. We also advise that donations of garments and other things be made, as is customary or even to a greater extent, and especially to the poor. No master lecturing in arts is to wear anything except a cope, round and black and reaching to the heels – at least, when it is new. But he may well wear a pallium. He is not to wear under the round cope embroidered shoes and never any with long bands.

If anyone of the students in arts or theology dies, half of the masters of arts are to go to the funeral, and the other half to the next funeral. They are not to withdraw until the burial is completed, unless they have some good reason. If any master of arts or theology dies, all the masters are to be present at the vigils, each one is to read the psalter or have it read. Each one is to remain in the church, where the vigils are celebrated, until midnight or later, unless prevented by some good reason. On the day when the master is buried, no one is to lecture or dispute.

We fully confirm to them the meadow of St Germain in the condition in which it was adjudged to them.

Each master is to have jurisdiction over his scholars. No one is to receive either schools or a house without the consent of the occupant, if he is able to obtain it. No one is to receive a licence from the chancellor or anyone else through a gift of money or furnishing a pledge or making an agreement. Also, the masters and students make among themselves or with others agreements and regulations, confirmed by a pledge, penalty or oath, about the following matters: namely, if a student is killed, mutilated or receives some outrageous injury and if justice is not done; for taxing the rent of *Hospitia*; concerning the dress, burial, lectures and disputations; in such a manner, however, that the university is not scattered nor destroyed on this account.

We decide concerning the theologians that no one shall lecture at Paris before he is thirty-five years old, and not unless he has studied at least eight years, and has heard the books faithfully and in the schools. He is to listen in theology for five years, before he reads his own lectures in public. No one of them is to lecture before the third hour on the days when the masters lecture. No one is to be received at Paris for the important lectures or sermons unless he is of approved character and learning. There is to be no student at Paris who does not have a regular master.

In order moreover that these may be inviolably observed, all who presume contumaciously to violate these our statutes, unless they take care, within fifteen days from the date of the transgression, to correct their presumption in the presence of the university of masters and scholars, or in the presence of some appointed by the university, by the authority of the legation with which we are entrusted, we bind with the bonds to read the excommunication.

Done in the year of grace 1215, in the month of August.

Source: *Translations and Reprints from Original Sources of European History* (1894–1900) II, Vol. 3, pp. 12–15

❧ 9.16 Of the reformation of the University of Paris ❧

1255

At this time, also, the university of the clerks of Paris was re-established and reformed, which had been exposed to danger, owing to the suspension of its lectures and disputations, and the dispersion of many of its scholars, through the disturbances caused by the Preacher brethren, who wished to alter the old-established custom of the university. But the condition of these brethren, as they were supported by charity and alms, was much altered for the worse; whilst, owing to the insults and reproaches of the Preachers and Minors, much improvement and increase was daily felt by the house of monks of the Cistercian order, who was studying at Paris; which house had been founded by the abbat of Clairvaux, who was an Englishman by birth, named Lexinton; and their honourable and orderly behaviour gave pleasure to God, the prelates, and the people. They did not wander, like vagabonds, through cities and towns; nor was the ocean their barrier and limit; but they remained quietly shut up within the walls of their domicile, obeying their superior, according to the rule of St Benedict, which will obtain the praise of everyone who chooses to study the rule of that saint. For at the commencement of it, in distinguishing the different kinds of monks he rebukes the Sarabaites and Gyrivagos. However, these same brethren, zealously pursuing their office of preaching, and weakening the authority of the ordinary preachers, gained the commendation of many, whilst to many others they rendered themselves objects of reproach; for many of them assumed horns of audacity in their delinquencies, because they were not obliged to confess their sins to their priest. And here was the harm: some refused to confess to their proper priest, because he was perhaps a drunkard, or for some other secret reasons, but flew with confidence to make their confessions under the shelter of the wings of consolation and counsel, spread out to them by passing Preachers and Minors. And what was the remedy and utility which resulted from it?

> Source: J. A. Giles (trans.) *Matthew of Paris, English History, from the year 1235–1273*, 3 vols (1852) Vol. 3, p. 149

❧❧

The universities provided the context for the scholastic theology and philosophy which tried to accommodate a universal learning. It owed much to the rediscovery of the philosophical works of Aristotle and to the great thirteenth-century theologians, notably Thomas Aquinas, who applied the philosopher's thinking to Christianity.

❧ 9.17 Thomas Aquinas, *Summa Theologica*, ❧
'The Natural Law' (Qu. 94)

Precepts of the Natural Law

(Art. 2, concl.)
The order of the precepts of the natural law corresponds to the order of our natural inclinations. For there is in man a natural and initial inclination to good which he has in common with all substances; in so far as every substance seeks its own preservation according to its own nature. Corresponding to this inclination, the natural law contains all that makes for the preservation of human life, and all that is opposed to its dissolution. Secondly, there is to be found in man a further inclination to certain more specific ends, according to the nature which man shares with other animals. In virtue of this inclination there pertains to the natural law all those instincts 'which nature has taught all animals', such as sexual relationship, the rearing of offspring, and the like. Thirdly, there is in man a certain inclination to good, corresponding to his rational nature: and this inclination is proper to man alone. So man has a natural inclination to know the truth about God and to live in society. In this respect there come under the natural law, all actions connected with such inclinations: namely, that a man should avoid ignorance, that he must not give offence to others with whom he must associate and all actions of like nature.

The Universality of the Natural Law

(Art.4, concl.)
As we have just said, all those actions pertain to the natural law to which man has a natural inclination: and among such it is proper to man to seek to act according to reason. Reason, however, proceeds from general principles to matters of detail, as is proved in the Physics. The practical and the speculative reason, however, go about this process in different ways. For the speculative reason is principally employed about necessary truths, which cannot be otherwise than they are; so that truth is to be found as surely in its particular conclusions as in general principles themselves. But practical reason is employed about contingent matters, into which human actions enter: thus, though there is a certain necessity in its general principles, the further one departs from generality the more is the conclusion open to exception. So it is clear that as far as the general principles of reason are concerned, whether speculative or practical, there is one standard of truth or rightness for everybody, and that this is equally known by every one. With regard to the particular conclusions of speculative reason, again there is one standard of truth for all; but in this case it is not equally known to all: it is universally true, for instance, that the three interior angles of a triangle equal two right angles; but this conclusion is not known by everybody. When we come to the particular conclusions of the practical reason, however, there is neither the same standard of truth or rightness for every one, nor are these conclusions equally known to all. All people, indeed, realise that it is right and true to act according to reason. And from this principle we may deduce as an immediate conclusion that debts must be repaid. This conclusion holds in the majority of cases. But it could happen in some particular case that it would be injurious, and therefore

irrational, to repay a debt; if for instance, the money repaid were used to make war against one's own country. Such exceptions are all the more likely to occur the more we get down to particular cases: take, for instance, the question of repaying a debt together with a certain security, or in some specific way. The more specialised the conditions applied, the greater is the possibility of an exception arising which will make it right to make restitution or not. So we must conclude that the law of nature, as far as general first principles are concerned, is the same for all as a norm of right conduct and is equally well known to all. But as to more particular cases which are conclusions from such general principles it remains the same for all only in the majority of cases, both as a norm and as to the extent to which it is known. Thus in particular instances it can admit of exceptions: both with regard to rightness, because of certain impediments, (just as in nature the generation and change of bodies is subject to accidents caused by some impediment), and with regard to its knowability. This can happen because reason is, in some persons, depraved by passion or by some evil habit of nature; as Caesar relates in *De Bello Gallico* (VI, 23), of the Germans, that at one time they did not consider robbery to be wrong; though it is obviously against natural law.

The Immutability of Natural Law

(Art. 5)
There are two ways in which natural law may be understood to change. One, in that certain additions are made to it. And in this sense there is no reason why it should not change. Both the divine law and human laws do, in fact, add much to the natural law which is useful to human activity.

Or again the natural law would be understood to change by having something subtracted from it. If, for instance, something ceased to pertain to the natural law which was formerly part of it. In this respect, and as far as first principles are concerned, it is wholly unchangeable. As to secondary precepts, which, as we have said, follow as immediate conclusions from first principles, the natural law again does not change; in the sense that it remains a general rule for the majority of cases that what the natural law prescribes is correct. It may, however, be said to change in some particular case, or in a limited number of examples; because of some special causes which make its observation impossible; as we have already pointed out.

Things may be said to pertain to the natural law for two reasons. First, if there is a natural inclination to them: as, for example, that it is wrong to do injury to one's neighbour. Secondly, if nature does not lead us to do what is contrary. So we might say that man has a natural right to go naked because, nature not having provided him with clothing he has had to fashion it for himself. In this sense the 'common possession of all things and the equal liberty of all' can be said to pertain to the natural law. For neither private possession nor servitude were imposed by nature: they are the adoptions of human reason in the interests of human life. And in these cases the natural law is not altered but is added to.

Source: A. P. D'Entreves (ed.), J. G. Dawson
(trans.) *Aquinas: Selected Political Writings* (1965)
pp. 123–127

Medieval learning was never narrow. The medieval mind was, within the limits of technology and cosmology, always searching for the truth.

Further reading

J. H. Burns (ed.), *The Cambridge History of Medieval Thought* (Cambridge University Press, Cambridge, 1988).

M. Camille, *Gothic Art: Visions and Revelations of the Medieval World* (Weidenfeld and Nicolson, London, 1996).

M. Clanchy, *Abelard: A Medieval Life* (Blackwell, Oxford, 1997).

A. B. Cobban, *English University Life in the Middle Ages* (UCL Press, London, 1999).

A. Erlande-Brandenburg, *The Cathedral Builders of the Middle Ages* (Thames & Hudson, London, 1995).

J. Gimpel, *The Medieval Machine* (Holt, Rinehart & Winston, New York, 1976).

J. Gimpel, *The Cathedral Builders* (Grove Press, New York, 1983).

J. Harvey, *The Master Builders* (Thames & Hudson, London, 1971).

C. H. Haskins, *The Renaissance of the Twelfth Century* (Thames & Hudson, London, 1927).

D. Hassig, *Medieval Bestiaries: Text, Image Ideology* (Cambridge University Press, Cambridge, 1995).

D. Hill, *A History of Engineering in Classical and Medieval Towns* (Croom Helm, London, 1984).

A. Murray, *Reason and Society in the Middle Ages* (Clarendon Press, Oxford, 1978).

L. F. Salzmann, *Building in England Down to 1540* (Clarendon Press, Oxford, 1982).

R. W. Southern, *Medieval Humanism and Other Studies* (Blackwell, Oxford, 1970).

L. White, Jr, *Medieval Technology and Social Change* (Clarendon Press, Oxford, 1962).

C. Wilson, *The Gothic Cathedral: The Architecture of the Great Church, 1130–1530* (Thames & Hudson, London, 1980).

❧ 10 ❧

THE WORLD OF
THE COUNTRYSIDE

In pre-industrial western Europe, country people made up the vast majority of the population and most of these were peasants, varying in status from slavery to independence. The third *ordo* is difficult to document despite the compelling evidence of non-literary sources. Visual sources proliferate for country life even if they betray the bias of a condescending non-peasant source; the early fourteenth-century English Luttrell Psalter, which is in the Bodleian Library, Oxford, prepared for a Lincolnshire knight, shows many country activities but, as has been wryly remarked before, it shows peasants in their proper role: at work. Archaeological evidence in the form of field patterns, houses and villages (which retain their medieval pattern with church and alehouse at their centre) provide valuable evidence of everyday life. The study of place names has provided much information concerning the development of the medieval countryside that witnessed the gradual increase of cultivated land and the clearance of the primeval forest. In England, where place names from the sixth to the eleventh century predominate, they show how many places owe their origin to a lord (whose name is attracted to a place) and how many were new settlements. By the middle of the eleventh century, in England at least, a framework had been established which was to remain largely intact until the Industrial Revolution. By the end of the twelfth century many scattered households began to congregate in small villages with adjoining open fields.

Legal evidence provides some useful background material on the dynamics of rural society. The piece that follows comes from the Carolingian period and is a Frankish administrative directive or *capitulary* about estate management (*De Villis*).

❧ 10.1 The Carolingian Capitulary ❧

---

1. We wish that our estates, which we have established to serve our needs, shall serve entirely for our benefit and not of other men.
2. That the people on our estates be well taken care of, and that they be reduced to poverty by no one.
3. That the stewards do not dare to enlist our people in their own service. They should not force them to perform agricultural labours, to cut wood or to do other work for them. Nor should the stewards accept any gifts from them, neither a horse nor an ox nor cow nor pig nor sheep nor piglet nor lamb nor anything else, excepting bottles of wine, garden produce, fruits, chickens and eggs.
4. If any of our people commit against our interests the crime of robbery or other offence, let him make good the damage, and further, let him be punished by

whipping in satisfaction of the law, except in cases of murder and arson, for which fines may be collected. The stewards should strive to render to other men the justice which they may deserve, according to the law. Our people, as we have said, instead of paying fines, are to be whipped. Freemen, however, who reside on our properties and estates, should strive to make good whatever injuries they may commit according to their law. Whatever they give in fines, whether in cattle or other payments, should be collected for our use.

5. Whenever our stewards are to see that our work is performed – sowing, ploughing, harvesting, cutting of hay or gathering of grapes – let each of them at the proper time and place supervise and give directions how the work is to be done, so that it may be done well. If the steward is not within his district and cannot come to a particular place, let him send a good messenger from among our people or another reliable man, in order to supervise our affairs and conduct them to a good end. The steward should diligently see to it that he sends a faithful man to take care of this matter.

6. We wish that our stewards pay a full tenth of all produce to the churches which are on our property, and do not let our tenth be given to the church of another, unless in places where this is an ancient custom. Other clerics should not hold these churches, but only our own or those from our people or from our chapel.

7. That every steward should perform his full service as he has been directed. And if necessity requires that he should serve additional time, he should determine whether he should increase the service or the night service.

8. That our stewards take care of our vineyards which are in their territory, and make sure that they are worked well. Let them place the wine in good containers and let them diligently see to it that nothing is lost in shipping it. Let them acquire through purchase special kinds of wine, in order to send it to the royal estates. And when more of this wine has been purchased than is needed for the provisioning of our estates, they should inform us of this, so that we may command whatever may be our will. They should have vine slips from our vineyards sent for our use. The rents from our estates which are paid in wine are to be stored in our cellars.

9. We wish that every steward keep in his territory measures of *modia, sextaria,* containers of eight *sextaria,* and baskets, of the same type as we have in our palace.

10. That our mayors, foresters, stablemen, cellarers, deans, toll collectors and other servants do regular services and pay pigs for their farms. In place of manual labour let them perform their offices well. And whatever mayor may have a benefice, let him send a substitute, who may perform for him the manual labour and other service.

11. That no steward take lodging for himself or for his dogs from our men or from those living outside our estates.

12. That no steward should commend any hostage on our estates.

13. That the stewards should take good care of our stallions and not allow them to remain too long in one place, lest the pasturage be damaged. And if a stallion should be unhealthy or old so as to be likely to die soon, they should inform us of this at the proper time, before the season comes when they are to be placed with the mares.

14. That they should watch our mares well, and segregate the colts at the proper time. And if the fillies should increase in number, they should be separated so as to form a new herd by themselves.

15. Let them have our foals sent to our winter palace at the feast of St Martin.

16. We wish that whatever we or the queen should command to any steward, or whatever our servants, the seneschal or the butler, should order, the stewards in our name or that of the queen, they should perform as was told them. Whoever should

fail to do so through negligence, let him abstain from drink from the time he has been told until he appears in our presence or that of the queen and requests pardon from us. And if the steward was in the army or on guard duty or on a mission or elsewhere, and ordered his subordinates to perform something and they did not do so, they should come on foot to the palace. They should abstain from drink and meat while they give the reasons why they were negligent. Then they should accept their punishment, either in whipping or however else it may please us or the queen.

17. The steward should appoint as many men as there are estates in his territory, to keep bees for our needs.

18. At our mills the stewards should keep chickens and geese according to the quality of the mill and as many more as can be maintained.

19. The stewards should keep in the barns of our principal estates no fewer than 100 chickens and 30 geese; on smaller farms let them have no fewer than 50 chickens and 12 geese.

20. Every steward should always send the produce [of the fowls] to our court abundantly throughout the year, except when they make visits three or four or more times.

21. Every steward should keep fish ponds on our estates where they were in the past. He should enlarge them if possible. And if they were not there in times past but can now be made, let them be made.

22. Those who hold our vineyards should keep for our use no fewer than three or four crowns of grapes.

23. The stewards should maintain in each of our estates cow barns, pig pens, folds for sheep and goats, as many as possible. No estate should be without them. Moreover, let them have cows delivered, by our serfs in fulfilment of their service, so that our cow barn or plough teams are not diminished by service on our demesne. Let them also obtain, in order to supply meat, lame but healthy oxen and cows, horses which are not mangy, or other healthy beasts. As we have said, our cow barns or plough teams should not be diminished for this.

24. Every steward should see to it that whatever is provided for our table be good and of highest quality, and that whatever they deliver has been prepared carefully and cleanly. And whenever someone serves at our table, he should receive for his service two meals of wheat every day. The other provisions, whether in flour or in meat, should similarly be of good quality.

25. The stewards should report on the first of September whether or not there is pasturage for the hogs.

26. Mayors should not administer a territory which is too large for them to ride through and inspect in a single day.

27. Our manor houses should have continuous watch fires and guards so that they may be secure. When our *missi* or a legation come to or from the palace, they should not take lodging in the royal manor houses, unless by our special permission or that of the queen. The count in his district or those men who have been traditionally accustomed to care for the *missi* or legations should continue to provide pack horses in the usual fashion and all things needed by them. Thus they may journey to and from our palace with ease and dignity.

28. We wish that every year, on Palm Sunday in Lent, which is called *Hosanna Sunday*, the stewards should deliver to us at our command the monetary part of our revenue, after we find out for the present year how great our revenue is.

29. Every steward should see to it that those of our men who wish to plead cases are not required to come into our presence to plead. He should not through negligence allow those days to be lost which the man should serve. If our serf should have to seek justice outside our estates, his master should expend every effort to gain justice for him. If the serf is unable to obtain justice in a particular locale, the master should not allow our serf to suffer for this, but through himself or his messenger he should inform us of this.

30. We wish that our stewards separate from the entire revenue that which is needed in our service. Similarly, let them take out supplies needed to fill the carts sent into the army, both those of householders and those of shepherds. And let them know how much they send for this purpose.

31. That they should similarly deduct each year what is to be given to the household servants or to the women working in the women's quarters. Let them give it fully at the proper time and let them inform us how they have done so and from where it was taken.

32. That every steward should see to it that he always has good seed of highest quality, by purchase or otherwise.

33. After all these parts of our revenue have been allocated or sown or consumed, whatever is left from the produce should be kept in expectation of our order, so that it may be sold or stored according to our command.

34. Whatever is made by hand should be closely supervised with all diligence, so that they are made or prepared with the maximum cleanliness: that is, lard, smoked meat, sausage, newly salted meat, wine, vinegar, mulberry wine, boiled wine, garn, mustard, cheese, butter, malt, beer, mead, honey, wax, and flour.

35. We wish that tallow be made from fat sheep and also from pigs. Furthermore, let them keep in each estate no less than two fattened oxen, whether to be fattened there or to be delivered to us.

36. That our woods and forests be well protected. And where there is room for clearing, let the stewards clear it, and they should not allow fields to become overgrown with woods. And where woods should be, they should not allow them to be excessively stripped and damaged. Let them guard well our wild beasts within the forests. Similarly, let them take care of our falcons and hawks for our use, and collect our rents diligently. If our stewards or mayors or their men let their hogs forage in our forest for fattening, let them be the first to pay a tenth, in order to set a good example, so that in the future other men will pay their tenth fully.

37. That our stewards maintain our fields and cultivated lands well, and let them guard our meadows in season.

38. That they should always keep fat geese and chickens for our needs, when they ought to provide them for us or deliver them to us.

39. Let them receive the chickens and eggs which serfs or residents of farms return every year; when they are not needed, they should sell them.

40. Let every steward always keep for the sake of ornament on every estate swans, peacocks, pheasants, ducks, pigeons, partridges and turtledoves.

41. Let the buildings within our manors and the fences about them be well cared for, and let stables, kitchens, bakeries or wine presses be carefully constructed, so that our servants can perform their tasks properly and cleanly.

42. Let every estate have within its hall beds, mattresses, pillows, bed linens, table cloths, seat covers, vessels of bronze, lead, iron and wood, andirons, chains, pot hangers, planes, axes, hatchets, knives and all sorts of tools, so that it will not be

necessary to seek them elsewhere or to borrow them. Let the stewards also have the responsibility of seeing to it that the iron tools which they provide for the army are good and that when they are returned they are sent to the manor hall.

43. To the workshop of the women they should provide material to work at suitable times, as has been commanded: that is, linen, wool, woad, red dye, madder, carding implements, combs, soap, oil, containers, and other small things which are needed there.

44. Concerning Lenten food, let two-thirds be sent every year for our use, in vegetables, fish or cheese, butter, honey, mustard, vinegar, millet, panic, dry or green herbs, roots, turnips and wax or soap or other small items. Let them inform us by letter what is left over. They should by no means fail to do this, as they have in the past, because through those two parts we wish to learn about the third part which remains.

45. That every steward should have in his territory good artisans: that is, smiths, blacksmiths, gold- and silversmiths, tailors, turners, carpenters, shield makers, fishermen, falconers . . . soap makers, brewers . . . bakers who can make bread for our need, net makers who know how to make nets for hunting, fishing or fowling, and other servants. It would be too long to name them all.

46. That the stewards should take good care of our woods, which the people call *brogilos*, and let them always repair them in good time, and not delay until it should be necessary to rebuild them entirely. Let them take similar care of every building.

47. That our hunters and falconers and other servants, who serve us zealously in the palace, should receive help in our villages, as we or the queen may command through our letters, when we send them forth for any errand, or when the seneschal and butler should command them to do anything on our behalf.

48. The wine presses on our estates should be kept ready for use, and let the stewards take care that no one dare crush our grape harvest with his feet, but everything should be clean and orderly.

49. That our women's workshops be well arranged, that is, their houses, heated rooms, and living rooms. Let them have good fences throughout and strong doors, in order that they may perform our work well.

50. That every steward should determine how many horses should remain in one stable and how many grooms should stay with the horses. And those grooms who are freemen and have benefices for their service should support themselves by their benefices; freemen too, who have farms on our public property which feed them. Whoever does not have this, should be given support from the demesne.

51. Every steward should take care lest wicked men conceal our seed under the ground or elsewhere. This makes our harvest grow sparser. Similarly, they should beware of other wicked deeds, to make sure that they never happen.

52. We wish that serfs on the public lands or our own serfs or freemen who are settled on our properties or estates give full and complete justice, whatever is fitting, to men.

53. That every steward should see to it that the men of their territory in no wise become thiefs or criminals.

54. That every steward should see to it that our people work well at their tasks and do not go about wasting time at markets.

55. We wish that the stewards write in one document whatever income they have been given or provided or received in our service, and in another whatever they have spent. They should inform us by letter what is left over.

56. That every steward in his territory hold frequent hearings, dispense justice and see to it that our people live law-abiding lives.

57. If any of our serfs should wish to inform us of anything which is to our interest concerning his master, he should not be prevented from coming to us. And if the steward knows that those under his charge wish to come to the palace to complain against him, then the steward should deliver to us at the palace arguments against them, why their complaint should not cause resentment in our ears. And thus we wish to know, whether the subordinates are coming from necessity or under pretence.

58. When our puppies are given to stewards to be raised, the steward should feed them at his own expense or commend them to his subordinates, that is, the mayors, deans or cellarers, in order that they should feed them from their own property, unless by our own order or that of the queen they are to be raised on our estate. Then the steward should send a man to feed them, and should set aside that from which they are to be fed. It will not be necessary for the man to go daily to the kennels.

59. Every steward, during the time that he is on service, should give each day three pounds of wax, and eight *sextaria* of soap. Furthermore, at the feast of St Andrew, he should give six pounds of wax, wherever we may be with our people. He should give the same in mid-Lent.

60. Mayors should never be chosen from powerful men, but from those of moderate station who are faithful.

61. During the time the steward performs his service, he should have his malt delivered to the palace. Similarly, let masters come who know how to make good beer there.

62. That every steward should make known to us yearly on Christmas, with everything arranged in the proper order, what we have received by way of income, so that we may learn what and how much we possess of all things; what land our ploughmen work with their cattle; what holdings they ought to plough; what taxes, rents, judgement costs, fees, fines for taking animals in our forests without our permission, and payments for other reasons; what income from mills, forests, fields, bridges or ships; what payments from freemen and from hundreds who serve our fisc; what revenues from markets, vineyards and those who pay in wine; what revenue from hay, wood, torches, planks or other lumber; what from wastelands, vegetables, millet and panic; wool, linen or hemp, fruits of trees, large or small nuts and graftings of various trees, gardens, turnips, fish ponds, skins, furs, horns, honey and wax; what from mulberry wine, cooked wine, mead and vinegar; what from beer, new and old wine, new and old grain, chickens, eggs and geese; what from fishermen, smiths, shield makers or tailors; what from kneading troughs, boxes or cases; what from turners or saddlers; what from forges and mines, that is, iron diggings or other lead diggings; what from persons liable to tribute payments; what from colts and fillies.

63. Concerning the above mentioned things, it should not disturb our stewards if we make inquiry, for we wish that they in like fashion require all these things from their subordinates without causing resentment. And all things whatsoever that a man ought to have in his house or estates, our stewards should have on our estates.

64. That our carts which go to the army, that is, the war carts, be well constructed, and that their coverings be well made of skins. They should be so sewn together that, if it is necessary to cross water, they can go across the rivers with their provisions inside and no water can enter. It should be possible to cross, as we have said, with our provisions protected. We wish that flour be placed in each cart at our expense,

that is, twelve *modia* of farina. In those carts which carry wine let them put twelve *modia* according to our measurement. And let them supply for each cart a shield, lance, quiver and bow.

65. That the fish from our ponds be sold and others put in their place, so that there will always be a supply of fish. However, when we do not visit the estates, then they should be sold and the stewards should make profit from them to our advantage.

66. Let the stewards give us an accounting of the male and female goats and of their horns and skins; and let them bring to us yearly newly salted meat of fat goats.

67. Concerning deserted farms and newly acquired slaves, the stewards should inform us if they have any surplus and cannot find a place for them.

68. We wish that all stewards have always ready good barrels bound with iron, which they can send to the army and to the palace. They should not make containers of skins.

69. They should at all times keep us informed concerning wolves, how many each one has caught, and they should send us the skins. In May, they should hunt wolf cubs and catch them, both with poison and with hooks, as well as with traps and dogs.

70. We wish that they should have in the garden all kinds of plants: that is, lily, roses, fenugreek, costmary, sage, rue, southernwood, cucumbers, pumpkins, gourd, pea, cumin, rosemary, caraway, chick-pea, squill, gladiola, estragon, anise, colosynth, heliotrope, spicknel, seseli, lettuce, spider's foot, rocket salad, garden cress, burdock, penny royal, hemlock, parsley, celery, lovage, juniper, dill, sweet-fennel, endive, dittany, white mustard, summer savory, water mint, garden mint, wild mint, tansy, catnip, centaury, garden poppy, beets, hazelwort, marshmallows, hollyhock, mallows, carrots, parsnip, garden-orach, amaranth, kohlrabi, cabbages, onions, chives, leeks, radishes, shallots, cibols, garlic, madder, teasel, broad beans, large peas, Moorish peas, chervil, capers, clary. And the gardener should have love's beard [house-leek] growing on his house.

Concerning trees we wish that they have apple, pear, plum, sorb, medlar, chestnut and peach trees of different kinds; quince, hazel, almond, mulberry, laurel, pine, fig nut, and cherry trees of different kinds.

The names of apple trees are *gozmaringa, geroldinga, crevedella, spirauca,* sweet, bitter, those which keep well and those to be eaten at once, and early apples. They shall have three or four kinds of pears, those which keep well, sweet, cooking and late pears.

Source: D. Herlihy (ed. and trans.) *Medieval Culture and Society* (1968) pp. 43–52

The typical manor, even within a specific country, area or region, exists only in theory, and manorial documents reveal a great breadth of customs and variation.

---

੪ 10.2 Deed illustrating the distribution of strips, 1397 ੬

To all Christ's faithful to whom the present writing shall come, Morgan Gogh, greeting in the Lord. Know ye that I have demised, granted and by this my present writing indented confirmed to John Druwere a cottage with a curtilage situate in Modbury between the cottage of John Janekyns on the east side and the tenement of Thomas Cobbe on the west side and three acres, one rood of arable land lying in the fields of Modbury, whereof one acre lies in Brokeryg between the lord's land on either side, one acre in Totecombe between the lord's land and the land of Thomas Cobbe, three roods in Brokeryg between the lord's land and the land of William Cockes, a half acre there between the land of Thomas Cobbe and the land of Ralph Smale, and a half acre of meadow lies in Sturtilmede between the meadow of Gilbert Scolemaystre on either side, with pasture for one plough-beast and two draught beasts in common; which land, meadow and pasture John Pipere lately held for term of his life; to have and to hold all the aforesaid cottage with the curtilage, land, meadow, and pasture, to the aforesaid John for term of his life, of me and my heirs or my assigns freely, quietly, well and in peace rendering therefor yearly to the aforesaid Morgan and his heirs or his assigns 3s. 4d. sterling at the four principal terms of the year by equal portions for all services, saving the royal service, and doing suit to my court yearly upon reasonable summons . . . Nor shall it be lawful for the aforesaid John to demise to any man the said cottage, with the curtilage, land, meadow and pasture, as well in parcels as in whole, during his life, under penalty of loss of the aforesaid cottage with all it appurtenances . . . In witness whereof the parties aforesaid, have interchangeably set their seals to these indentures. These witnesses: Richard Pokeswell, Thomas Wodham, Robert Grey, John Hunte, John Iryssh and many others. Given at Modbury on Thursday next after Michaelmas, 21 Richard 11.

> Source: A. E. Bland, P. A. Brown and R. H. Tawney (comp. and ed.) *English Economic History* (1930) p. 76

---

੪ 10.3 Regulation of the common fields ੬ of Wimeswould, *c.* 1425

For neat pasture we ordain Orrow and Breeches, Woldsyke and Wylougbybroke, for to be broken on Crowchmesseday; and whoso break this, every man shall pay for each beast that may be taken in any other several pasture a penny to the church;

therefor to go a seven nightday. Also, for the neat pasture, after that be eaten, all the wheat-field, to wit, Hardacre field namely, save Strete headlands, where they may not go for destroying of corn; this for to endure another sevennightday under the pain before said.

Also, on Holy Thursday eve we ordain the commons of the Peasfield for horses to be broken, and no other beasts to come therein. For if there be any man that have any horse that is feeble and may not do his work for fault of meat, and this may reasonably be known, let him relieve of his own, so that he save his neighbour from harm, for if any man may . . . which beasts 'lose' in corn or in grass, he shall for each beast pay a penny to the church, and make amends to his neighbour.

Also, on Whitsun eve every man break his several pasture as he likes, and no man tie his horse on other . . . his own for to be several till Lammas, each man to eat his own, under the pain beforesaid. Furthermore, if any man . . . plough-oxen for to be relieved on his several grass, let him tie them in his best manner or hold them in, as other men do their horses . . . on no other man's grass going to or fro abroad, as they will pay for each beast a penny to the church and make [amends] . . . to him that has the harm.

Also, if any man tie his horse or reach on any headlands or by brookside into any man's corn, he shall make amends to him that has the harm, and for each foot that is within the corn pay a penny to the church.

Also if any man shall be taken at night time destroying other corn or grass, he shall be punished as the law will, and pay 4d. to the church.

Also, all manner of men that have any pease in the field when codding time comes, let them cod in their own lands and in no other man's lands. And other men or women that have no peas of their own growing, let them gather them twice in the week on Wednesday and on Friday, reasonably going in the land-furrows and gathering with their hands and with no sickles, once before noon and no more, for if any man or woman other that has any peas of his own and goes into any other, for each time pay a penny to the church and lose his cods, and they that have none and go oftener than it before said, with sickle or without, shall lose the vessel they gather them in and the cods, and a penny to the church.

Also, no man with common herd nor with shed herd come on the wold after grass be mown till it be made and led away, but on his own, and then let them go all together God's name; and if they do, each man pay for his quantity of his beasts a certain to the church, that is for to say, a penny for each beast.

Also, if there be any man that throws in any sheaves on any land for to tie on his horses, he shall make a large amends to them that have the harm, and for each foot pay a penny to the church, but on his own. Furthermore, if any man tie his horse in any stubble and it be mown in reasonable time he shall pay the aforesaid pain.

Also, if any man may be taken at nighttime in the field with cart or with bearing of any other carriage in unreasonable time between bell and bell pay 40d. to the church, save as thus, if any man in peas harvest, he and his servants, in furthering of his work and saving of his corn, bind at morning or till it be moonshine, all other works at nighttime except save this.

Also, all manner of labourers that dwell in the town and have commons among us shall work harvest work and other works for their hire reasonable as custom is, and not to go to other towns but if they have no work or else no man speak to them so that they may be excused, for if they do, they shall be chastised as the law will.

Also, no man or woman that works harvest work bear home no sheaves of no man's, but if they be given them well and truly, for if it may be wist, for each sheaf that they bear home without leave shall pay a penny to the church.

Also, no man or woman glean no manner of corn that is able to work for his meat and twopence a day at the least to help to save his neighbour's corn; nor no other gleaners, that may not work, glean in no manner of wise among no sheaves, for if they do, they shall lose the corn and a penny to the church for each burden.

Also, neither common herd nor shed herd come in the wheat cornfield till the corn be led away, nor in the peas cornfield in the same wise till the peas be led away, and the common herd and shed herd may go together as they should do, on pain of each beast a penny to the church.

Also, that no man take away his beasts from the common herd from Michaelmas tide to Yule to go in the wheatfield to 'lose' the wheat, for if any man may take any beast therein, they shall pay for each beast a penny to the church as often as they may be taken destroying the corn, and the herd his hire.

Also, if our hayward pen a flock of neat of the country, he shall take six pence, for a flock of sheep four pence, and for each horse a penny. And that our wold be laid in several at Candlemas, for if any herd let his beasts come thereon after, pay for each time four pence to the church.

Also, whosoever has any meadows within the corns, my lord or any man else, let make them to *dele* them out and take a profit of them on God's behalf, and whoso trespass, let make amends.

> Source: A. E. Bland, P. A. Brown and R. H. Tawney
> (comp. and ed.) *English Economic History* (1930)
> pp. 77–79

Landlords were a privileged minority throughout the period. At the time of Domesday in 1086 there were in England almost eleven hundred tenants-in-chief, holding land directly from the king, with about six thousand sub-tenants. By 1300, there were some one hundred earls and barons, eleven hundred knights and perhaps ten thousand lesser gentry. In addition there were ecclesiastical landlords, both episcopal, and increasingly, monastic. Yet, peasants were not entirely subservient. In many regions a tradition of ancestral freedom persisted and peasants, despite their lack of literacy, took out lawsuits.

ॐ 10.4 An Assize allowed to a villein, 1225 ॐ

The justices in eyre in the county of Essex were ordered to take a grand assize between Thomas of Woodford, claimant, and John de la Rille, tenant, of a virgate and a half of land with the appurtenances in Woodford. And the said John and Thomas came before the justices at Chelmsford and offered themselves, and the bailiff of the Abbot of Waltham came and said both claimant and tenant were villeins, and the tenement was the Abbot's villeinage and therefore the assize thereof ought not to proceed. He was questioned by the tenant whether the latter was a villein or not, and he said Yes, asserting that the said tenement was the Abbot's villeinage.

And Thomas comes [and says] that this ought not to hurt him, because when he impleaded the aforesaid John in the court of the lord Abbot by writ of the lord the King, no mention was made by the Abbot nor by John that the tenement was villeinage nor that John was a villein, but because the Abbot failed to do him right in his court, Thomas went to the county court and complained in the county court that the lord Abbot had failed to do him right in his court, and the Abbot, summoned hereon, came not, and the suit proceeded so far in the county court that the tenant asked and obtained view of the land. Afterwards he put himself on a grand assize as to which of the two had greater right in the aforesaid land without any challenge of villeinage being made on the part of the Abbot or of John. And this he sought to be allowed him.

And the Abbot's bailiff comes and denies the whole, as the court of the lord the King should award. And he said that unknown to the Abbot and without his court failing to do Thomas right, the suit was taken away to the county court, and this he asked to be allowed him. And owing to the doubt a day was given to the parties at Westminster, etc. And because the Abbot permitted John to be impleaded in his court first and in the county court afterwards until he put himself on a grand assize, the Abbot not having lodged the claim which he should have made, it is awarded that the assize proceed.

Source: A. E. Bland, P. A. Brown and R. H. Tawney
(comp. and ed.) *English Economic History* (1930)
p. 95

The crisis of the fourteenth century, with its climate changes, famine and disease and culminating in the great pestilence of the Black Death was to hit the peasants and the peasants' way of life hard. The classical description of Giovanni Boccaccio, whose father was carried off by the plague in 1348, evokes the impact of the disease on the city of Florence.

৯৬ 10.5 The Black Death reaches Florence ৩৬

I say, then, that the years of the beatific incarnation of the Son of God had reached the tale of one thousand three hundred and forty-eight, when in the illustrious city of Florence, the fairest of all the cities of Italy, there made its appearance that deadly pestilence, which, whether disseminated by the influence of the celestial bodies, or sent upon us mortals by God in His just wrath by way of retribution for our iniquities, had had its origin some years before in the East, whence, after destroying an innumerable multitude of living beings, it had propagated itself without respite from place to place, and so, calamitously, had spread into the West.

In Florence, despite all that human wisdom and forethought could devise to avert it, as the cleansing of the city from many impurities by officials appointed for the purpose, the refusal of entrance to all sick folk, and the adoption of many precautions for the preservation of health; despite also humble supplications addressed to God, and often repeated both in public procession and otherwise, by the devout; towards the beginning of the spring of the said year the doleful effects of the pestilence began to be horribly apparent by symptoms that shewed as if miraculous.

Not such were they as in the East, where an issue of blood from the nose was a manifest sign of inevitable death; but in men and women alike it first betrayed itself by the emergence of certain tumours in the groin or the armpits, some of which grew as large as a common apple, others as an egg, some more, some less, which the common folk called gavoccioli. From the two said parts of the body this deadly gavocciolo soon began to propagate and spread itself in all directions indifferently; after which the form of the malady began to change, black spots or livid making their appearance in many cases on the arm or the thigh or elsewhere, now few and large, now minute and numerous. And as the gavocciolo had been and still was an infallible token of approaching death, such also were these spots on whomsoever they shewed themselves. Which maladies seemed to set entirely at naught both the art of the physician and the virtues of physic; indeed, whether it was that the disorder was of a nature to defy such treatment, or that the physicians were at fault – besides the qualified there was now a multitude both of men and of women who practised without having received the slightest tincture of medical science – and, if being in ignorance of its source, failed to apply the proper remedies; in either case, not merely were those that recovered few, but almost all within three days from the appearance of the said symptoms, sooner or later, died, and in most cases without any fever or other attendant malady.

Moreover, the virulence of the pest was the greater by reason that intercourse was apt to convey it from the sick to the whole, just as fire devours things dry or greasy when they are brought close to it. Nay, the evil went yet further, for not merely by speech or association with the sick was the malady communicated to the healthy with consequent peril of common death; but any that touched the clothes of the sick or aught else that had been touched or used by them, seemed thereby to contract the disease.

So marvellous sounds that which I have now to relate, that, had not many, and I among them, observed it with their own eyes, I had hardly dared to credit it, much less to set it down in writing, though I had had it from the lips of a credible witness.

I say, then, that such was the energy of the contagion of the said pestilence, that it was not merely propagated from man to man but, what is much more startling, it was frequently observed, that things which had belonged to one sick or dead of the disease, if touched by some other living creature, not of the human species, were the occasion, not merely of sickening, but of an almost instantaneous death. Whereof my own eyes (as I said a little before) had cognisance, one day among others, by the following experience. The rags of a poor man who had died of the disease being strewn about the open street, two hogs came thither, and after, as is their wont, no little trifling with their snouts, took the rags between their teeth and tossed them to and fro about their chaps; whereupon, almost immediately, they gave a few turns, and fell down dead, as if by poison, upon the rags which in an evil hour they had disturbed.

In which circumstances, not to speak of many others of a similar or even graver complexion, divers apprehensions and imaginations were engendered in the minds of such as were left alive, inclining almost all of them to the same harsh resolution, to wit, to shun and abhor all contact with the sick and all that belonged to them, thinking thereby to make each his own health secure. Among whom there were those who thought that to live temperately and avoid all excess would count for much as a preservative against seizures of this kind. Wherefore they banded together and, dissociating themselves from all others, formed communities in houses where there were no sick, and lived a separate and secluded life, which they regulated with the utmost care, avoiding every kind of luxury, but eating and drinking very moderately of the most delicate viands and the finest wines, holding converse with none but one another, lest tidings of sickness or death should reach them, and diverting their minds with music and such other delights as they could devise. Others, the bias of whose minds was in the opposite direction, maintained, that to drink freely, frequent places of public resort, and take their pleasure with song and revel, sparing to satisfy no appetite, and to laugh and mock at no event, was the sovereign remedy for so great an evil: and that which they affirmed they also put in practice, so far as they were able, resorting day and night, now to this tavern, now to that, drinking with an entire disregard of rule or measure, and by preference making the houses of others, as it were, their inns, if they but saw in them aught that was particularly to their taste or liking; which they were readily able to do, because the owners, seeing death imminent, had become as reckless of their property as of their lives; so that most of the houses were open to all comers, and no distinction was observed between the stranger who presented himself and the rightful lord. Thus, adhering ever to their inhuman determination to shun the sick, as far as possible, they ordered their life. In this extremity of our city's suffering and tribulation the venerable authority of laws, human and divine, was abased and all but totally dissolved, for lack of those who should have administered and enforced them, most of whom, like the rest of the citizens, were either dead or sick, or so hard bested for servants that they were unable to execute any office; whereby every man was free to do what was right in his own eyes.

Source: G. Boccaccio, *Decameron*, 2 vols (1930)
Vol. 1, pp. 4–11

ह Etched into a wall of the tower of St Mary's Church, ह
Ashwell, Hertfordshire

MCX.   *penta miseranda ferox violenta*
       superest plebs pessima testis in fineque ventus validus
       oc anno maurus in orbe tonat

1350   The people who remain are driven wild and miserable. They are
       wretched witnesses to the end. A strong wind is thundering over the
       whole earth. Written on St Maurus' Day.

ह∿ह

The Peasants' Revolt of 1381 was less a reaction to the desperation of the post-plague
years than the reaction of better-off peasants and town workers to the social oppression
and corrupt authorities which they saw as holding them back from prosperity.

ह 10.6 The final meeting of Richard II ह
and Wat Tyler

Then the King caused a proclamation to be made that all the commons of the country
who were still in London should come to Smithfield, to meet him there; and so they
did.

And when the King and his train had arrived there they turned into the Eastern
meadow in front of St Bartholomew's, which is a house of canons: and the commons
arrayed themselves on the west side in great battles. At this moment the Mayor of
London, William Walworth, came up, and the King bade him go to the commons,
and make their chieftain come to him. And when he was summoned by the Mayor,
by the name of Wat Tiyler of Maidstone, he came to the King with great confidence,
mounted on a little horse, that the commons might see him.

And he dismounted, holding in his hand a dagger which he had taken from
another man, and when he had dismounted he half bent his knee, and then took the
King by the hand, and shook his arm forcibly and roughly, saying to him, 'Brother,
be of good comfort and joyful, for you shall have, in the fortnight that is to come,
praise from the commons even more than you have yet had, and we shall be good
companions.' And the King said to Walter, 'Why will you not go back to your own
country?' But the other answered, with a great oath, that neither he nor his fellows
would depart until they had got their charter such as they wished to have it, and had
certain points rehearsed and added to their charter which they wished to demand.
And he said in a threatening fashion that the lords of the realm would rue it bitterly
if these points were not settled to their pleasure. Then the King asked him what were
the points which he wished to have revised, and he should have them freely, without
contradiction, written out and sealed. Thereupon the said Walter rehearsed the points

which were to be demanded; and he asked that there should be no law within the realm save the law of Winchester, and that from henceforth there should be no outlawry in any process of law, and that no lord should have lordship save civilly, and that there should be equality among all people save only the King, and that the goods of Holy Church should not remain in the hands of the religious, nor of parsons and vicars, and other churchmen; but that clergy already in possession should have a sufficient sustenance from the endowments, and the rest of the goods should be divided among the people of the parish. And he demanded that there should be only one bishop in England and only one prelate, and all the lands and tenements now held by them should be confiscated, and divided among the commons, only reserving for them a reasonable sustenance. And he demanded that there should be no more villeins in England, and no serfdom or villeinage, but that all men should be free and of one condition. To this the King gave an easy answer, and said that he should have all that he could fairly grant, reserving only for himself the regality of his crown. And then he bade him go back to his home, without making further delay.

During all this time that the King was speaking, no lord or counsellor dared or wished to give answer to the commons in any place save the King himself. Presently Wat Tyler, in the presence of the King, sent for a flagon of water to rinse his mouth, because of the great heat that he was in, and when it was brought he rinsed his mouth in a very rude and disgusting fashion before the King's face. And then he made them bring him a jug of beer, and drank a great draught, and then, in the presence of the King, climbed on his horse again. At this time a certain valet from Kent, who was among the King's retinue, asked that the said Walter, the chief of the commons, might be pointed out to him. And when he saw him, he said aloud that he knew him for the greatest thief and robber in all Kent . . . And for these words Wat tried to strike him with his dagger, and would have slain him in the King's presence; but because he strove so to do, the Mayor of London, William Walworth, reasoned with the said Wat for his violent behaviour and despite, done in the King's presence, and arrested him. And because he arrested him, the said Wat stabbed the Mayor with his dagger in the stomach in great wrath. But, as it pleased God, the Mayor was wearing armour and took no harm, but like a hardy and vigorous man drew his cutlass, and struck back at the said Wat, and gave him a deep cut on the neck, and then a great cut on the head. And during this scuffle one of the King's household drew his sword, and ran Wat two or three times through the body, mortally wounding him. And he spurred his horse, crying to the commons to avenge him, and the horse carried him some four score paces, and then he fell to the ground half dead. And when the commons saw him fall, and knew not how for certain it was, they began to bend their bows and to shoot, wherefore the King himself spurred his horse, and rode out to them, commanding them that they should all come to him to Clerkenwell Fields.

Meanwhile the Mayor of London rode as hastily as he could back to the City, and commanded those who were in charge of the twenty four wards to make proclamation round their wards, that every man should arm himself as quickly as he could, and come to the King in St John's Fields, where were the commons, to aid the King, for he was in great trouble and necessity . . . And presently the aldermen came to him in a body, bringing with them their wardens, and the wards arrayed in bands, a fine company of well-armed folks in great strength. And they enveloped the commons like sheep within a pen, and after that the Mayor had set the wardens of the city on their way to the King, he returned with a company of lances to Smithfield, to make an end of the captain of the commons. And when he came to Smithfield he found not there the said captain Wat Tiyler, at which he marvelled much, and asked what was become of the traitor. And it was told him that he had been carried by some of the commons to the hospital for poor folks by St Bartholomew's, and was put to bed in the chamber of the master of the hospital. And the Mayor went thither and found him, and had him carried out to the middle of Smithfield, in presence of his fellows, and there beheaded. And thus ended his wretched life. But the Mayor had his head set on a pole and borne before him to the King, who still abode in the Fields. And when the King saw the head he had it brought near him to abash the commons, and thanked the Mayor greatly for what he had done. And when the commons saw that their chieftain, Wat Tyler, was dead in such a manner, they fell to the ground there among the wheat, like beaten men, imploring the King for mercy for their misdeeds. And the King benevolently granted them mercy, and most of them took to flight. But the King ordained two knights to conduct the rest of them, namely the Kentishmen, through London, and over London Bridge, without doing them harm, so that each of them could go to his own home . . .

Afterwards the King sent out his messengers into divers parts, to capture the malefactors and put them to death. And many were taken and hanged at London, and they set up many gallows around the City of London, and in other cities and boroughs of the south country. At last, as it pleased God, the King seeing that too many of his liege subjects would be undone, and too much blood spilt, took pity in his heart, and granted them all pardon, on condition that they should never rise again, under pain of losing life or members, and that each of them should get his charter of pardon, and pay the King as fee for his seal twenty shillings, to make him rich. And so finished this wicked war.

Source: C. Oman, *The Great Revolt of 1381* (1906) pp. 200–203, 205

It would be a mistake, however, to see the fourteenth and fifteenth centuries as an era of total stagnation and disorder. Villages remained centres of administrative and legal energy regulating every local activity from football to animal husbandry. Parish churches were rebuilt with great magnificence and provided the core of local social life. Recovery from the plague in many parts of Europe was ushering in a new period of communalism. The historians of the *Annales* school in their search for 'total' history have tried to reconstruct peasant life and mentality from every available source, and the work of Le Roy Ladurie on the settlement of Montaillou in southern France, based on Inquisition records, has famously captured something of the variety and surprising individuality of the poor as well as the prosperous. Superstition and folklore wait in the wings and rather like the marginalia on medieval manuscripts threaten to take centre stage. A document from the early Middle Ages, the later sixth century, from the pen of a Spanish bishop captures something of the raw energy of the peasant mind.

❧ 10.7 Martin of Braga, *On the Correction of Peasants* ❧

Here begins the letter of the saint and bishop Martin to Bishop Polemius, on the correction of peasants.

Bishop Martin to the most blessed lord and brother in Christ Bishop Polemius, whom I miss sorely.

1. I have received the letter of your holy charity, in which you write to me that I should send to you some things written on the origin of idols and on their crimes, a few words on a large subject, for the chastisement of peasants who, still restrained by the former superstition of the pagans, pay more honour to demons than to God. But since it is necessary to provide, as a kind of appetiser, some little information on the reason for their existence from the beginning of the world, I have had to treat the gigantic forest of past times and deeds in abbreviated speech of slight weight, and to prepare food for the rustics in rustic language. And therefore, with God aiding you, this shall be the beginning of your sermon . . .

9. However, God Almighty, when he made heaven and earth, himself then created light, which was turned seven times according to the division of his works. On the first revolution, God made light, which was called the day; on the second, the firmament of heaven was made; on the third, the land was divided from the sea; on the fourth, the sun and moon and stars were made; on the fifth, the quadrupeds and flying things and swimming things; on the sixth, man was formed; however, on the seventh day, as the whole world and its ornament were completed, God called for a rest. One light, therefore, which was first made among the works of God, which was revolved seven times according to the different works of God, was called a week. What folly is it, therefore, that a man baptised in the faith of Christ should not observe the Lord's day, in which Christ rose, and should say that he honours the day of Jupiter and Mercury and Venus and Saturn, who have no day, but were adulterers and magicians and evil men and died badly in their provinces. But, as we have stated, under the form of these names, stupid men give worship and honour to demons.

10. Likewise this error holds ignorant and rustic men, that they think that January 1st is the beginning of the year. This is altogether most false. For, as Sacred Scripture says, the beginning of the year was established on 25th March at the time of the equinox. For thus is it written: and God divided the light front the darkness (Genesis 1: 4). For all right division has equality, as on 25th March the day has the same length of hours as the night. And therefore it is false that the beginning of the year is on 1st January.

11. What should be said in sorrow concerning this most stupid error: they observe days of moths and mice and, if it is allowed to say it, a Christian man venerates mice and moths in place of God? If the protection of a cupboard or casket did not keep bread or cloth away from these pests, they would by no means spare whatever they might find, in spite of the feasts in their honour. However, the miserable man makes these prognostications without cause; as if, should he be sated and happy with all things in the beginning of the year, thus it will be with him throughout the year. All these auguries of the pagans are interpreted according to the inventions of the demons. But woe to that man who may not have had a merciful God and who may not have received from him satiety of bread and security of life! Behold, you perform

these vain superstitions either secretly or openly, and never refrain from these sacrifices of the demons. And why do they not grant to you that you are always full and
secure and happy? Why, when God is angry, do not the empty sacrifices defend you
from the locust, the mouse and from the many other tribulations, which an angry
God sends upon you?

12. Do you not fully understand that the demons are deceiving you in these your
views which you hold vainly, and that they deceive you in the auguries which you
attend so frequently. For as the most wise Solomon said: divinations and omens are
vanities (Eccl. 34: 5); and the more a man has fear of these things, so much the more
is his heart deceived. Set not thy heart upon them, for dreams have deceived many
(Eccl. 34:6–7). Behold, Sacred Scripture says this, and it is most certain. As long as
demons persuade unhappy men through the voices of birds, until they lose even the
faith of Christ through silly and empty things, they themselves will encounter the
destruction of their own death without warning. God has not ordered man to know
future things. He has ordered him to live always in his fear, and to seek from him
guidance and aid in his life. It is God's alone to know something before it happens.
Demons, however, deceive men with diverse arguments, until they lead them to
offend God and they drag their souls with them into hell. From the beginning
they have done this out of envy, lest man should enter the kingdom of heaven, from
which they were thrown out.

13. For this reason, when God saw that miserable men were so deceived by the devil
and his bad angels that, forgetting their creator, they adored demons for God, he sent
his Son, that is wisdom and his word, to lead them back from the error of the devil
to the worship of the true God. Because the divinity of the Son of God could not be
seen by men, he took on human flesh from the womb of the Virgin Mary, conceived
not by marriage with a man, but by the Holy Spirit. The Son of God was born, therefore, into human flesh, invisible God concealed within but on the outside a visible
man. He preached to men and taught them to escape from the power of the devil,
leaving behind idols and evil works, and to return to the worship of their creator.
After he taught, he wished to die for the human race. He suffered death voluntarily,
under no compulsion. He was crucified by the Jews under the judge Pontius
Pilate, who, a native of the province of Pontus, at that time ruled the province of
Syria. Taken down from the cross, he was placed in a sepulchre; the third day he rose
again alive from the dead, and for forty days lived with his twelve disciples. In order
to show them that his true flesh had been resurrected, he ate after the resurrection
before his disciples. After forty days had passed, he ordered his disciples to proclaim
to all nations the resurrection of the Son of God. They should baptise them in the
name of the Father and of the Son and of the Holy Spirit in remission of their sins,
and they should teach those who were baptised to abandon evil works, that is, idols,
murders, thefts, perjury, and fornication. They should not do to others what they did
not want done to themselves. After he commanded these things, he ascended into
heaven in the sight of these disciples. There he sits at the right hand of the Father,
from whence at the end of this world he shall come with that flesh which he took
with himself into heaven.

14. When the end of this world shall come, all nations and every man who took their
origin from these first men, that is, from Adam and Eve – all shall rise, both the good
and the evil. All shall come before the judgement seat of Christ. Those who were in
their lives faithful and good are then separated from the evil. They enter into the
kingdom of God with the holy angels. Their souls shall be with their flesh in eternal

rest, never again to die. There shall be for them neither labour nor pain nor sorrow nor hunger nor thirst nor heat nor cold nor darkness nor night. Forever happy, satisfied, they shall be like to the angels of God in splendour and glory, for they merited to enter into the place whence the devil with his like-minded angels fell. There all who have been faithful to God shall remain for eternity. But those who have not believed or were not baptised or, if they might have been baptised, returned after their baptism to idols and murders or adulteries or perjuries and other evils and died without penance – all who may be found such are damned with the devil and with all the demons whom they worshipped and whose work they did. They are sent into eternal fire with their flesh in hell. There unquenchable fire burns forever, and the flesh already received from the resurrection is tortured forever, groaning. The flesh wishes again to die, so that it may not feel the pains, but it is not allowed to die, so that it may bear eternal tortures. Behold, this says the law, this say the prophets, these things the gospel of Christ, these things the Apostle, these things the entire Holy Scripture attests. We say these things simply to you now, a few things out of many. Yours it is from now on, dearly beloved sons, to remember the things which we have said. By doing good, hope for future rest in the kingdom of God, or (God forbid!) by doing evil, expect perpetual fire to come in hell. For both eternal life and eternal death are placed in the decision of man. Whatever each one chooses for himself, this he shall have.

15. You therefore, faithful people, who have come to Christ's baptism in the name of the Father and of the Son and of the Holy Spirit, consider what sort of agreement you made with God in that baptism. For when you individually gave your name at the baptismal font, as, for example, Peter or John or any name, you were asked this by the priest: 'How are you called?' You answered, if you were already able to answer or, at any rate, he answered who made faith for you, 'He is called John.' The priest then asked: 'John, do you renounce the devil and his angels, his worship and his idols, his thefts and frauds, fornications and his drunkenness, and all his evil works?' You answered: 'I do renounce.' After this renunciation of the devil you were asked again by the priest: 'Do you believe in God the Father Almighty?' You answered: 'I do believe.' 'And in Jesus Christ His only Son, God and our lord, who was born of the Holy Spirit from the Virgin Mary, suffered under Pontius Pilate, was crucified and was buried; he descended into hell, the third day he rose again from the dead; he ascended into heaven; he sits at the right hand of the Father, from whence he shall come to judge the living and the dead. Do you believe?' And you answered: 'I do believe.' And again you were asked: 'Do you believe in the Holy Spirit, the holy Catholic Church, the remission of all sins, the resurrection of the flesh, and life everlasting?' And you answered: 'I do believe.' Behold, therefore, and consider what agreement you made with God in baptism. You promised to renounce the devil and his angels and all his evil works, and you confessed that you believed in the Father and the Son and the Holy Spirit and that you hoped for the resurrection of the flesh in the end of the world and life everlasting.

16. Behold by what sort of promise and confession you are bound before God! And how is it that some of you, who renounced the devil and his angels and his worship and his evil works, now again return to the worship of the devil? For to light candles before rocks and trees and streams and at crossroads – is this anything else but the worship of the devil? To observe divinations and auguries and days of the idols – is this anything else but the worship of the devil? To observe *vulcanalia* and the kalends [feasts at the first day of the months], to decorate table and place wreaths and watch

your step, to place fruit and pour wine into a fire on the trunk of a tree, to place bread upon the stream – is this anything else but the worship of the devil? For women at their looms to call on Minerva; to observe for marriages the day of Venus; to pay attention as to what day to begin a journey – is this anything else but the worship of the devil? To cast spells over herbs for the purpose of evil, to call upon the names of demons in casting spells – is this anything else but the worship of the devil? Many other things are done which are too numerous to mention! Behold, you do all these things after renouncing the devil, after baptism. You return to the worship of demons and to the wicked works of idols. You break your faith and violate the agreement which you made with God. You put aside the sign of the cross, which you received in baptism, and you pay attention to other signs of the devil in little birds and sneezings and through many other things. How does a divination not injure me or any right Christian? Because, where the sign of the cross precedes, the sign of the devil is nothing. Why does it injure you? Because you scorn the sign of the cross, and you fear that which you yourselves imagine is in the sign. Likewise you put aside holy incantations. These are the creed which you accepted at baptism, which is 'I believe in God the Father Almighty,' and the Lord's prayer, which is 'Our Father who art in heaven.' You keep diabolical incantations and songs. Therefore, whosoever scorns the sign of the cross of Christ and takes other signs, loses the sign of the cross which he received in baptism. Similarly he who holds other incantations invented by magicians and criminals, loses the incantation of the holy creed and of the Lord's prayer, which he received in the faith of Christ. He treads upon the faith of Christ, because both God and the devil cannot be at once adored.

17. If therefore you recognise, dearly beloved sons, all these things which we have said, if anyone knows that he himself has done these things after having received baptism and that he has broken the faith of Christ, let him not despair of himself nor should he say in his heart: 'Because I have done so many evil things after baptism, perhaps God will not forgive me my sins.' Do not doubt the mercy of God. Only make in your heart an agreement with God, that you will no more honour the worship of demons, nor adore anything else but the God of heaven, nor commit murder, nor adultery nor fornication, nor rob nor perjure. And when you promise this to God with your whole heart and commit these sins no more, faithfully hope for pardon from God, because God says through prophetic scripture: In whatever day the wicked should forget his iniquities and do justice, I will not remember all his iniquities (Ezech. 18: 21–22). For God awaits the penance of the sinner. This however is true penitence, that a man should do no more the evils that he has done, but that he should seek indulgence for past sins, and should not care for the future lest he return again to them, but on the other hand, he should in particular do good works. He should show mercy to the starving pauper, refresh the tired stranger, and should do to another whatever he wishes done to him by another. And what he does not wish done to him, let him not do this to another, because in this word the commandments of God are fulfilled.

18. We therefore ask you, dearly beloved brothers and sons, that you hold in mind these commands, which God has deigned to give to you through us, though we are humble and lowly. Think how you can save your souls. You should consider not only this present life and the passing utility of this world, but you should especially remember that which you promised to believe in the creed, that is, the resurrection of the flesh and life eternal. If therefore you have believed and now believe that there will be a resurrection of the flesh and life eternal in the kingdom of heaven among

the angels of God, as we have said to you above, think about this as much as possible, and not just about the misery of this world. Prepare your way in good works. Frequently visit the church to pray to God or the places of the saints. Do not scorn the Lord's day, which is called the Lord's for this reason, that the Son of God, our Lord Jesus Christ, on that day rose from the dead, but keep it with reverence. Do not do servile work, that is, in the field, meadow, vineyard or whatever is heavy, except only as much as pertains to the needs of restoring the body through cooking food and the necessity of a long journey. It is licit to travel to nearby places on the Lord's day, not however for evil purposes but rather for good reasons, that is, to visit holy places or to visit a brother or a friend; to console the sick; to give counsel to the troubled; or to bring help for a good cause. It is fitting for a Christian man to venerate the Lord's day in such a manner. For it is sufficiently evil and base that those who are pagans and ignore the Christian faith, worshipping the idols of demons, honour the day of Jupiter or some other demon and refrain from work, although it is certain that the demons neither created a day nor have one. And we, who adore the true God and believe that the Son of God rose from the dead, do not venerate at all the day of his resurrection, that is, the Lord's day. Do not therefore do injury to the Lord's resurrection, but honour it and keep it with reverence for our hope which we have in it. For as our Lord Jesus Christ, Son of God, who is our head, on the third day rose again from the dead, so also we, who are his members, hope ourselves to rise in our flesh at the end of the world, so that everyone shall receive either eternal rest or eternal punishment, as he chose in his body in this world.

19. Behold, in this sermon, with the testimony of God and the holy angels who heard us, we have paid to your charity our debt and we have lent you the coin of the Lord, as we were commanded. Yours it is now to think and to see to it that everyone shall return as much: as he received with interest, when the Lord comes in the day of judgement. We invoke the mercy of the Lord, that he may guard you from all evil and make you worthy companions of the holy angels in his kingdom, with the help of him who lives and reigns forever and ever. Amen.

Source: D. Herlihy (ed. and trans.) *Medieval Culture and Society* (1968) pp. 33–42

It will never be clear to what extent 'paganism' was tamed by the Christian Church and to what level of Christian observance the peasantry were educated, but it is clear that by the fifteenth century in the countryside, as well as in the towns, fierce communal loyalties were the very stuff of life.

Further reading

J. Aberth, *From the Brink of the Apocalypse: Confronting Famine, War, Plague, and Death in the later Middle Ages* (Routledge, London, 2001).

J. L. Bolton, *The Medieval English Economy* (J. M. Dent, London, 1980).

G. Duby, *Rural Economy and Country Life in the Medieval West* (Edward Arnold, London, 1968).

C. Dyer, *Standards of Living in the Later Middle Ages: Social Change in Europe, c. 1200–1520* (Cambridge University Press, Cambridge, 1989).

B. Hanawalt, *The Ties that Bound* (Oxford University Press, Oxford, 1986).

D. Herlihy, *Medieval Households* (Harvard University Press, MA, 1985).

D. Herlihy, *The Black Death and the Transformation of the West* (Harvard University Press, MA, 1997).

M. M. Postan, *The Medieval Economy and Society* (Weidenfeld & Nicolson, 1972).

W. Rösener, *The Peasantry of Europe* (Blackwell, Oxford, 1994).

W. Rösener, *Peasants in the Middle Ages* (Polity Press, Oxford, 1996).

P. Ziegler, *The Black Death* (Collins, London, 1969).

THE WORLD
OF THE TOWN

The Middle Ages began in a world where town life seemed to be in terminal decline and ended in a renaissance where urban centres again celebrated their communal life in art and learning. The re-birth of towns stemmed, like the manor and the village, from defensive considerations which soon gave way to, or were complemented by, trade and industry. Small towns are difficult to distinguish from villages or even from manors but the growth of self-government, the emergence of a community of a distinctly urban kind often associated with markets and fairs (although these were not necessarily urban phenomena) was characteristic of medieval Christendom. An example, typical as in all towns chiefly of itself, might be Wells in Somerset where a prosperous town developed alongside an independent ecclesiastical corporation of a cathedral. This could be a contentious juxtaposition, because although a royal borough in England (like Wells) could manage its own affairs through a mayor and council, the proximity of a great lord (like the Bishop of Bath and Wells) could sometimes lead townspeople to think that their political privileges did not match their economic status.

ॐ 11.1 Charter of King John to Wells, Somerset, ॐ
7 September 1201

John, by the grace of God king of England, lord of Ireland, duke of Normandy and Aquitaine, count of Anjou, to his archbishops, bishops, abbots, earls, barons, justiciars, sheriffs, stewards, servants, and all his bailiffs and liegemen, greetings. Know that we have granted and by our present charter have confirmed that Wells in Somerset shall be a free borough, and that the men of the same town and their heirs shall be free burgesses; and that there shall be a free market there every Sunday just as there is and always has been, and free fairs just as there are yearly, on the feast of blessed Andrew, blessed Callistus, Invention of Holy Cross, on the morrow of blessed John the Baptist; and that there shall be moreover a fair every year in our gift, on the Translation of blessed Andrew, to continue for eight days within the streets of the same borough in the places where the fair of blessed Andrew has always been held, provided it be not a nuisance to neighbouring fairs. Wherefore we will and firmly enjoin that the town of Wells shall be a free borough, and that all its men and their heirs shall be free burgesses for ever; and that they shall have a free market and fairs just as there have always been, together with the eight day fair in our gift; and that they and their heirs shall have all the liberties and free customs of a free borough and of free burgesses, and those that pertain to a market and to fairs of this kind, well and peacefully, freely and quietly, completely and honourably for ever. We also will that they, their goods and possessions shall be in our hand, charge and protection, forbidding anyone to trouble or disturb them or their heirs against this our charter on pain of our penalty.

Witnesses: William the Marshal earl of Pembroke, William earl of Salisbury, William des Roches seneschal of Anjou, Stephen de Perche, Gerard de Furnival, Warin Fitzgerold, Peter de Stoke, Fulk de Cantilupe, Robert de Plessey.

Given under the hand of Simon archdeacon of Wells at Chinon on the seventh day of September in the third year of our reign.

Source: W. Smith (trans.) *Wells, 1201–2001: Eight
Hundred Years of Royal Charter* (2001) p. 12

The urban elites, institutionalised in the town councils, also exercised patronage and authority through the guilds, corporations of town self-improvement. Some of the guilds were principally philanthropic, devoted to pious exercises and good works. This can be shown in the Holy Trinity Guild at Hull, a town which grew rich on shipping.

11.2 Constitutions Ordained in 1369

In the Name of God, Amen. On the fourth day of the month of June, in the year of our Lord, 1369, was begun a certain Fraternity, called the Guild of Holy Trinity of Kingston-upon-Hull, in these words:
Know all men present and to come, that we, Robt. Marshall, Alderman, Wm. Scott, John de Wormsley and my wife, Hugo de Hughtoft and my wife, Rich. Ward and my wife, Thos. de Chestre and my wife, Simon Sergeant and my wife, William Say and my wife, John de Blacktoft and my wife, Henry de Hullbank and my wife, John de Wolfreton and my wife, Thos. de Hodelston and my wife, Adam Forbesco and my wife, Thomas de Swanland and my wife, Emma, formerly the wife of Thomas Taverner, Robert Taverner and my wife, John de Wrawby Cachman and my wife, John Lebster Cachman and my wife, Elena Car, Johanna Baxter, Robert Scope, Robert de Flynston and my wife, John Rudd, Catherine Racy, Christina Kyng, William Dunegeton and my wife, William de Driffield and my wife, Simon Cutt, Robert de Cunescliffe and my wife, Richard Seagle and my wife, Hugo Sergestan and my wife, Margaret, formerly the wife of Martin Coke, Thomas de Sitheray and my wife, Robert Wing and my wife, with one assent and consent, have ordained, founded, and appointed, the aforesaid Guild to the honour of the Holy Trinity, to be held yearly at Kingston-upon-Hull, on the day of the Holy Trinity, and to the maintaining and perpetually supporting of the aforesaid Guild well and faithfully, We, the afore-named, for ourselves and our successors of our own free and good will have given and

granted, and by this present writing have confirmed, and each of us severally hath given and granted to the aforesaid Guild, a certain revenue of Two Shillings of Silver, to be paid out of our goods and chattels, and of our successors, at four times of the year, that is to say, at the Feast of the Nativity of the Blessed John the Baptist, Saint Michael, the Nativity of our Lord and Easter, by equal portions to have and to hold the aforesaid yearly revenue of 2s. to the aforesaid Guild, well and peaceably according to law and custom, without the contradiction of us, or our successors for ever. And if it shall happen that the said revenue of two shillings shall at any of the times in part, or in the whole, be in arrear by any of us, or of our successors (which God forbid), we will and grant, for us and our successors, and each of us willeth and granteth, that from that time it may be lawful for the aforesaid Aldermen for the time being, with the assistance of the Fraternity, to take and levy in double the afore-said sum without any contradiction, unless it be by the special favour of the said Fraternity. Moreover, it is ordained, that when any of the Fraternity of the aforesaid Guild shall become surety for anyone of the said Society, for the goods and chattels of the said Guild, until a certain day, at which day, the principal debtor fails in payment of the said debt, or hath not wherewithal to pay the aforesaid debt, it shall, without plea or delay, be forthwith levied of such surety. And if the aforesaid Aldermen in demanding any debt of the aforesaid Guild shall find such debtors, or their sureties, rebellious or refractory without cause, in word or deed, then by virtue of this our writing, double the aforesaid debt for the contempt done to us, shall be taken and levied of such rebellious or refractory person without abatement, for supporting the said Guild. And we will and grant, for us and our successors, that when any of the said Fraternity into the office of Alderman shall be chosen the same Alderman with the assistance of the aforesaid Fraternity, shall choose two Constables and four other sufficient and discreet men, who shall be sworn in the presence of the whole Fraternity, to hold authentic and agreeable, whatsoever shall be done or ordained for the benefit of the said Guild, in our and our successors names. And if any person defraud the said Fraternity, or be rebellious towards the aforesaid Alderman, Constables, and Elect, in demand of the revenues or profits touching our said Guild which may be well proved. We will that two pounds of wax be taken and levied of him, in aid of the aforesaid Guild, by the aforesaid Constables and Elect.

And that no one be received into this our Fraternity without the will and assent of the Alderman, Constables, and four Elect aforesaid. And if anyone shall enter this Fraternity, upon his entrance, upon the Holy Evangelists of God, and by his faith, shall be obliged faithfully to pay his yearly sum, and to his utmost power to main-tain and support the aforesaid Guild.

Moreover, We order and strictly enjoin that all of us be present in the Church of the Holy Trinity, in Hull, on the day of the Holy Trinity as well at the Offertory, as to carry the Candle of our Guild (as the custom is), not absenting or excusing ourselves, under the penalty of one pound of wax, to be paid to the said Guild the next day, in aid of the same Guild by each so absent without a reasonable cause. And whensoever any of the Brothers or Sisters of the said Guild shall die, the funeral shall be cele-brated in the town of Kingston, and all the Brothers and Sisters shall be present at the Placebo dirge, and at Mass, making offerings there for the soul of the deceased, everyone under the penalty of one pound of wax for the aid aforesaid, unless they have a reasonable excuse; and four tapers of the goods of the said Guild shall be burning, and thirty masses for the soul of the same deceased shall be celebrated immediately after the burial, or at least within the first week. And if a child of the said Brothers and Sisters shall die, two tapers shall be burning, and the Brothers and Sisters shall offer at mass. Also, if any Brother or Sister of the said Guild be rebellious whensoever it shall happen that the said Fraternity are met together, which can be proved by the major part of the said Fraternity, immediately one pound of wax shall be levied of such rebellious person for the support of the said Guild.

And if any discord shall arise among the Brothers or Sisters aforesaid, it is our will, that by the Alderman and Brothers aforesaid concord be restored. And if any shall be rebellious or behave contrary to reason and concord, two pounds of wax shall be immediately levied of him for the use of the said Guild. And if he be a second or third time rebellious and contumelious, he shall immediately be ejected out of the said Fraternity without recovery, unless by the favour of the Alderman and others of the said Guild.

And if any of the Brothers or Sisters of the said Guild languish in a perpetual infirmity, so that they have not of their own to support themselves with, We ordain that such infirm man or woman shall take every week of the goods of the said Guild eightpence; and at the Feast of Saint Martin, in winter, one tunic and a little cap; and in case the goods of the said Guild shall not be sufficient for this (which God forbid), then there shall be a collection among the Brothers and Sisters of the said Guild to support the said infirm man or woman. It is also our will and we ordain, that when it shall happen, that one shall come into this our Guild, at his entrance and reception, the articles of this our writing, shall be read openly and distinctly before him; lest our constitutions and ordinances aforesaid should hereafter be contradicted or changed by any of the Brothers or Sisters of the said Guild. And faithfully to hold, and firmly to support all and singular these things, we, the aforenamed Brothers, for us and the example of our successors have taken our corporal oaths upon the Holy Evangelists of God.

In witness whereof we have alternately put our seals to this our present writing. These being witnesses: Robert de Selby, then Mayor of Kingston-upon-Hull; William de Cane and William de Bubwith, Bailiffs of the said town; Thomas de Sancton, Peter de Grimsby, Henry de Selby, William de Snaynton, John Lambert, and others.

Given at Kingston-upon-Hull, the 12th day of the month of December, in the year of our Lord above said.

Andrew Davy and Johanna his wife.

William Best and Alicia his wife.

Thomas Bellerwell and Johanna his wife.

William Power and his wife.

Afterwards received into the Fraternity aforesaid, that is to say: William Wymonk and Julian, his wife, Robert Brise and Alicia his wife, Richard de Walton and his wife, Richard Dundale and his wife, Robert de Weighton and his wife, Robert Bowes and Anna his wife, William de Lepton and Constance his wife, Richard Wilberry and Johanna his wife, Thomas de Hornsea and his wife, Roger Bassett, Alicia Bower, John de Swanland and his wife, John Page and Katherine his wife, Robert Stolfyn and his wife, Thomas de Walton and his wife, John Campion and his wife, John Lilie and his wife, John Baker and his wife, John Ravon and Agnes my wife, William de Meton Bocher and Anna my wife, John de Clee and Alice my wife, Peter Barker and Margaret his wife, Robert Guerdson and Johanna his wife.

Source: J. Malet Lambert, *Two Thousand Years of Gild Life* (1891) pp. 128–131

Craft guilds and guild merchants, dedicated to the pursuit of wealth and self-interest, emerged in large numbers in the twelfth and thirteenth centuries, and their payments for independence provided a rich source of income for the crown. In the fourteenth and fifteenth centuries the craft guilds closed ranks, laying down elaborate rules for membership and restricting competition.

৯ 11.3 Incorporation of the Fraternity of the Haberdashers ৩৫ of London (1448)

The king to all to whom, etc., greeting. Know ye that of our especial grace and the inspiration of charity, and for the especial devotion which we bear and have towards the Blessed Virgin Catherine, we have granted and given licence for us and our heirs, as much as in us lies, to our beloved lieges, the men of the mistery of Haberdashers within our city of London, that they may begin, unite, found, create, erect and establish a gild or fraternity in honour of the same Virgin of men of the mistery aforesaid and others, and have and hold that gild or fraternity so begun, united, founded, created, erected and established, and enjoy and exercise the same to them and their successors for all future times to endure; and that they and their successors may increase and augment the same gild or fraternity and hold the gild or fraternity aforesaid of the said mistery of Haberdashers and any persons whom they will receive within the fraternity aforesaid, and may elect and make four wardens from themselves as often as they shall please or need shall be for the governance, custody and rule of the said fraternity for ever, as shall best please them; and that the said wardens and their successors each year may make a livery of vesture of one suit among the brethren and sisters of the same fraternity, and their meetings and gatherings in places of our city aforesaid, and there in honest manner hold and keep their feast of food and drink at the feast of St Catherine the Virgin, and make ordinances among themselves as often as they shall please and as they shall deem most necessary and opportune, and ordain and rule their mistery and correct and amend defects of their servants by view of the Mayor of the city aforesaid for the time being or of any person whom he shall depute hereto in his place, as they shall deem fit to be done for the greater utility of the commonalty of our people; and that none within the liberty of the city aforesaid keep a shop or house of that mistery, unless he be of the liberty of that city, nor any be admitted to the liberty of the said city in the same mistery, unless he be presented by the aforesaid wardens or their successors and by four other good and lawful men of the same mistery, and it be testified to the Mayor of our said city for the time being that he is good, faithful and fit for the same. And further of our more abundant grace and at the supplication of our said lieges, the men of the mistery aforesaid, we will and grant for us and our heirs, as much as in us lies, that the same wardens and their successors be perpetual and capable and the said fraternity be by itself a solid and perpetual and corporate fraternity, and that that fraternity be hereafter named the fraternity of St Catherine the Virgin of Haberdashers in the city of London, and the said wardens and their successors [the wardens] of the fraternity of St Catherine the Virgin of Haberdashers in the city of London, and we incorporate the said wardens and their successors and the fraternity aforesaid to endure for ever, and we make them as it were one body and declare, accept and approve them for one body and hold them for one body. We have granted also for us and our heirs, as far as in us lies, to the aforesaid wardens, that they and their successors, by the name of the wardens of the fraternity of St Catherine the Virgin of Haberdashers in the city of London, may acquire to them and their successors in fee and perpetuity lands, tenements, rents, annuities and other possessions as well of those which are held of us in free burgage as others, provided, that by inquisitions to be taken thereon in due form and returned into the Chancery of us and our heirs it be found that it can be done without damage or prejudice to us or our heirs or others whomsoever, and that they may have a common seal and be impleaded and implead others by the name of the wardens of the fraternity of St Catherine the Virgin of Haberdashers in the city of London for ever before any judges in any courts, and that they may have and hold to them and their successors all lands and tenements, rents, annuities and other possessions whatsoever acquired by the aforesaid wardens and their successors, and enjoy the same for ever without obstacle, impeachment or hindrance of us or our heirs, our justices, escheators, sheriffs or other bailiffs or ministers of us or our heirs whomsoever, the Statute published touching lands and tenements not to be put in Mortmain, or any other Statute or ordinance made to the contrary, notwithstanding. And further of our more abundant grace we have granted for us and our heirs to our aforesaid lieges and wardens and their successors aforesaid for ever that the same wardens and their successors, wardens of the fraternity aforesaid for the time being, have and make full search as well in and of the mistery of Haberdashers and of every thing touching it, as of all goods and things in any wise belonging to or incumbent on the craft of Haberdashers aforesaid brought or hereafter to be brought by any alien or any aliens from parts remote into our realm of England, when they or any of them shall bring the same to the same our city or the suburbs thereof or within three miles distant round about the said city, and also of each such alien and of such misteries and things which they, our privileged lieges, use or have used before these times, and may present all defects in that behalf found by them as well upon our said lieges as upon aliens, according to their discretions, to the Mayor of our city aforesaid for the time being or his deputy in this behalf, if need be, and correct and reform the same by his survey. And further we will and by these our letters we grant to our aforesaid lieges, the men of the mistery aforesaid, that no officer, minister, artificer, merchant or any other whosoever hereafter search or presume to search in any wise any our privileged liege employing the craft aforesaid nor his goods of haberdashery, save only the four wardens of the craft aforesaid for the time being; so that it be not to the prejudice of the Mayor of our city of London. In witness, etc. Witness the King at Westminster the 3rd day of June. By the King himself and of the said date, etc.

Source: A. E. Bland, P. A. Brown and R. H. Tawney (comp. and ed.) *English Economic History* (1930) pp. 144–147

࿇ 11.4 Indenture of Apprenticeship (1459) ࿇

This indenture made between John Gibbs of Penzance in the county of Cornwall of the one part and John Goffe, Spaniard, of the other part, witnesses that the aforesaid John Goffe has put himself to the aforesaid John Gibbs to learn the craft of fishing, and to stay with him as apprentice and to serve from the feast of Philip and James next to come after the date of these presents until the end of eight years then next ensuing and fully complete; throughout which term the aforesaid John Goffe shall well and faithfully serve the aforesaid John Gibbs and Agnes his wife as his masters and lords, shall keep their secrets, shall everywhere willingly do their lawful and honourable commands, shall do his masters no injury nor see injury done to them by others, but prevent the same as far as he can, shall not waste his master's goods; nor lend them to any man without his special command. And the aforesaid John Gibbs and Agnes his wife shall teach, train and inform or cause the aforesaid John Goffe, their apprentice, to be informed in the craft of fishing in the best way they know, chastising him duly and finding for the same John, their apprentice, food, clothing linen and woollen, and shoes, sufficiently, as befits such an apprentice to be found, during the term aforesaid. And at the end of the term aforesaid the aforesaid John Goffe shall have of the aforesaid John Gibbs and Agnes his wife 20s. sterling without any fraud. In witness whereof the parties aforesaid have interchangeably set their seals to the parts of this indenture. These witnesses: Richard Bascawen, Robert Martyn and Robert Cosyn and many others.

Given at Penzance, 1st April in the 37th year of the reign of King Henry the Sixth after the Conquest of England.

> Source: A. E. Bland, P. A. Brown and R. H. Tawney
> (comp. and ed.) *English Economic History* (1930)
> pp. 147–148

࿇ 11.5 A runaway apprentice (*c.* 1425) ࿇

To the most reverend father in God and his most gracious lord, the bishop of Winchester, chancellor of England.

Beseecheth meekly William Beverley of London that whereas William Batyngham has been arrested and detained in prison in Salisbury at the suit of the said beseecher, for that he was his apprentice and departed from his service here in London, and has been the whole time since . . . wandering in divers towns, as in Winchester, Bristol and elsewhere, so that the said beseecher could not find him until now of late suddenly, and so it is that upon the matter abovesaid his said suit cannot be determined in Salisbury, for that the retaining and departing did not take place within the said town: Please it your most gracious discretion to grant to the said beseecher a writ directed to the mayor, bailiffs and keeper of the gaol there and to each of them to have the body of the said William Batyngham with such a clause 'by whatsoever name he be known', before you at a certain day to be limited by you, considering that he has no other remedy, and that for God and in work of charity.

Source: A. E. Bland, R. A. Brown and R. H. Tawney (comp. and ed.) *English Economic History* (1930) p. 148

ॐ✿ॐ

The development of commerce was aided by fairs and markets which were often 'international' in their clientele.

ॐ 11.6 Inquisition touching a proposed market ॐ and fair (1252)

Henry by the grace of God King of England, Lord of Ireland, Duke of Normandy and Aquitaine and Count of Anjou, to his mayor and bailiffs of Bristol, greeting. We command you that by the oath of good and lawful men of your town, by whom the truth of the matter may the better be known, you make diligent enquiry if it would be to the nuisance of the town aforesaid if we should grant to our beloved abbot of Pershore that he have a market at his manor of Hawksbury on Monday and a fair there at the feast of St Matthew in Autumn; and if it be to your nuisance, to what extent; and that without delay you send to us the inquisition made thereon under your seal and the seals of those by whom it shall be made, and this writ. Witness myself at Westminster, 26 February in the 36th year of our reign.

Inquisition made by command of the lord the King by the mayor and bailiffs of Bristol, if it would be to the nuisance of the town of Bristol if there were a market on Monday at the manor of Hawksbury which E. abbot of Pershore holds, and if there were a fair there at the feast of St Matthew in Autumn, by William de Feria, clerk . . . Who say by their oath that it would not be to the nuisance of the town of Bristol in any wise if there were a market on the aforesaid Monday at the said manor of Hawksbury, and a fair there on the aforesaid feast of St Matthew in Autumn.

Source: A. E. Bland, P. A. Brown and R. H. Tawney (comp. and ed.) *English Economic History* (1930) pp. 157–158

ॐ✿ॐ

ॐ 11.7 Grant of a fair at St Ives to the Abbey of Ramsey (1202) ॐ

John by the grace of God King of England, etc., greeting. Know ye that we, for our salvation and for the souls of our ancestors and successors, have granted and by our present charter have confirmed to God and the church of St Mary and St Benedict of Ramsey, and to the abbot and monks there serving God, a fair at St Ives, to begin on the fourth day before the feast of St Laurence and to endure for eight days; to have and to hold for ever, so nevertheless that it be not to the nuisance of neighbouring fairs.

Wherefore we will and straitly command that the aforesaid abbot and monks have and hold the aforesaid fair well and in peace, freely and quietly, entirely, fully and honourably, with all liberties and free customs to such fair pertaining.

Witnesses: Robert earl of Leicester, William earl of Arundel, and others.

Given by the hand of Simon, archdeacon of Wells, at Harcourt on the seventh day of June in the fourth year of our reign.

Source: A. E. Bland, P. A. Brown and R. H. Tawney (comp. and ed.) *English Economic History*, p. 158

11.8 Grant of a market at St Ives to the Abbey of Ramsey (1293)

Edward by the grace of God King of England, lord of Ireland and Duke of Aquitaine, to archbishops, bishops, abbots, priors, earls, barons, justices, sheriffs, reeves, ministers and all his bailiffs and faithful, greeting. Know ye that we have granted and by this our charter confirmed to our beloved in Christ, the abbot and convent of Ramsey, that they and their successors for ever have a market every week on Monday at their manor of St Ives in the county of Huntingdon, unless that market be to the nuisance of neighbouring markets. Wherefore we will and straitly command, for us and our heirs, that the aforesaid abbot and convent and their successors for ever have the aforesaid market at their manor aforesaid with all the liberties and free customs to such market pertaining, unless that market be to the nuisance of neighbouring markets, as is aforesaid. These witnesses: the venerable fathers John, of Winchester, Anthony, of Durham, William, of Ely, bishops, William de Valencia, our uncle, Roger le Bygod, earl of Norfolk and marshal of England, John de Warenna, earl of Surrey, Henry de Lascy, earl of Lincoln, William de Bello Campo, earl of Warwick, Robert de Tybetot, Gilbert de Thornton, John de Metingham, Robert de Hertford, Robert Malet, and others. Given by our hand at Westminster on the fourteenth day of May in the twenty-first year of our reign.

Source: A. E. Bland, P. A. Brown and R. H. Tawney (comp. and ed.) *English Economic History*, pp. 158–159

Control by the crown and the maintenance of order was always an urban problem.

---

৪৯ 11.9 The recovery of debt on a ৫৯
recognisance (1293)

To the reverend and discreet and their dearest lord, J. de Langton, chancellor of the illustrious King of England, Robert le Venur, guardian of the city of Lincoln, and Adam son of Martin of the same city, clerk, deputed to receive recognisances of debts, greeting. With all reverence and honour we make known to your reverend discretion by these presents that Simon le Sage of Scarborough and William Kempe of the same town, of the county of York, and each of them for the whole sum, acknowledged before us that they owe to William le Noyr of Lincoln 28s. sterling to be paid to him or his attorney at the feast of St Michael in the twenty-first year of the reign of King Edward, according to the form of the statute of the said lord the King published at Westminster. And because the aforesaid Simon and William have not kept the term of their payment at all, we beseech your reverend discretion humbly and devoutly, that you will order a writ to be sent to the sheriff of York to compel the same Simon and William to pay the said money according to the form of the statute aforesaid. May your reverend discretion prosper long and well. Given at Lincoln on Friday next after the feast of St Martin in the year aforesaid.

> Source: A. E. Bland, R. A. Brown and R. H. Tawney
> (comp. and ed.) *English Economic History*,
> pp. 161–162

---

৪৯ 11.10 J. A. Giles (trans.) *Matthew of Paris* ৫৯

1242

About the same time, as the laborious season of autumn drew on, the French king, in a very unbecoming manner, gave orders to seize the bodies of English merchants who were trafficking with their wares throughout his kingdom; thus inflicting an enormous injury on the ancient dignity of Gaul, which formerly afforded a safe asylum and protection to all exiles and proscribed men, especially the peaceable ones; from which circumstance it originally obtained the name of France in its own language. This dishonourable and cruel proceeding soon reached the ears as well as the feelings of the king of England, on which he also gave orders that the French traders found in any part of England should undergo a just retaliation . . .

1244

In this same year the king of England prohibited the wool of the Cistercian monks from being conveyed to the continent to be sold for their benefit, endeavouring by these means to oppress and injure them, because they would not, indeed they were not able to, give him pecuniary assistance when he was in Gascony.

> Source: J. A. Giles (trans.) *English History, from the year 1235–1273*, 3 vols (1852) Vol. I, pp. 410, 511

Urban workers, too, increasingly came under royal legislation in England.

11.11 The Ordinance of Labourers (1349)

The King to the sheriff of Kent, greeting. Because a great part of the people and specially of the workmen and servants has now died in this plague, some, seeing the necessity of lords and the scarcity of servants, will not serve unless they receive excessive wages, and others preferring to beg in idleness rather than to seek their livelihood by labour: we, weighing the grave disadvantages which might arise from the dearth specially of tillers and workmen, have had deliberation and treaty hereon with the prelates and nobles and other learned men in session with us, by whose unanimous counsel we have thought fit to ordain that every man and woman of our realm of England, of whatsoever condition, free or servile, able-bodied and under the age of sixty years, not living by trade nor exercising a certain craft, nor having of his own whereof he shall be able to live, or land of his own, in the tilling whereof he shall be able to occupy himself, and not serving another man, shall be bound to serve him who shall require him, if he be required to serve in a suitable service, regard being had to his rank, and shall receive only the wages, liveries, hire or salaries which used to be offered in the places where he should serve in the twentieth year of our reign of England, or in the five or six common years last preceding; provided that lords be preferred to others in the bondmen or tenants of their lands so to be retained in their service; so however that such lords so retain as many as shall be necessary and not more; and if such a man or woman, so required to serve, refuse so to do, the same being proved by two trusty men before the sheriff, bailiff, lord, or constable of the town where this shall come to pass, he shall be taken forthwith by them or any of them and sent to the nearest gaol, there to stay in strait keeping until he find security to serve in the form aforesaid.

And if a reaper, mower or other workman or servant, of whatsoever rank or condition he be, retained in the service of any man, withdraw from the said service without reasonable cause or licence before the end of the term agreed upon, he shall undergo the penalty of imprisonment, and none, under the same penalty, shall presume to receive or retain such an one in his service. Furthermore no man shall pay or promise to pay to any man more wages, liveries, hire or salaries than is accustomed, as is aforesaid, nor shall any man in any wise demand or receive the same, under penalty of the double of that which shall be so paid, promised, demanded or received, to go to him who shall feel himself aggrieved hereby; and if none such will prosecute, it shall go to anyone of the people who shall prosecute; and such prosecution shall be made in the court of the lord of the place where such a case shall befal; and if the lords of towns or manors shall presume in any wise to contravene our present ordinance, by themselves or their ministers, then prosecution shall be made against them in the form aforesaid in counties, wapentakes and ridings, or other such courts of ours, at a penalty of threefold of that so paid or promised by them, or their ministers; and if by chance anyone shall have covenanted with any man so to serve for a greater salary before the present ordinance, the latter shall in no wise be bound by reason of the said covenant to pay to such a man more than has been customary at other times; nay, rather, he shall not presume to pay more under the penalty aforesaid.

Moreover saddlers, skinners, sawyers, shoemakers, tailors, smiths, carpenters, masons, tilers, boatmen, carters and other artificers and workmen whosoever shall not take for their labour and craft more than used to be paid to such in the twentieth year and other common years preceding in the places in which they chance to be employed, as is aforesaid; and if any shall receive more, he shall be committed to the nearest gaol in the manner aforesaid.

Moreover butchers, fishermen, hostlers, brewers, bakers, poulterers and all other sellers of victuals whatsoever shall be bound to sell such victuals for a reasonable price, regard being had to the price at which such victuals are sold in the neighbouring places; so that such sellers have a moderate profit and not excessive, as shall be reasonably required by the distance of the places wherefrom such victuals are carried; and if any man sell such victuals otherwise and be convicted thereof in the form aforesaid, he shall pay the double of that which he shall receive to him that suffered loss, or, for lack of such, to him who will prosecute in this behalf; and the mayor and bailiffs of cities and boroughs, market and other towns, and ports and places by the sea, shall have power to enquire of all and singular who in any wise transgress against this ordinance, at the penalty aforesaid to be levied to the use of those at whose suit such transgressors shall be convicted: and in case the same mayor and bailiffs shall neglect to execute the premises and shall be convicted hereof before the justices appointed by us, then the same mayor and bailiffs shall be compelled by the same justices to pay to such as suffered loss, or, for lack of him, to any other prosecuting, threefold the value of the thing so sold, and none the less shall incur grievous punishment at our hands.

And because many sturdy beggars, so long as they can live by begging for alms, refuse to labour, living in idleness and sin and sometimes by thefts and other crimes, no man, under the aforesaid penalty of imprisonment, shall presume under colour of pity or alms to give anything to such as shall be able profitably to labour, or to cherish them in their sloth, that so they may be compelled to labour for the necessaries of life.

We order you, straitly enjoining upon you, that you cause all and singular the premises to be publicly proclaimed and kept in the cities, boroughs and market towns, seaports and other places in your bailiwick where you deem expedient, as well within liberties as without, and due execution to be made thereof, as is aforesaid; and that in no wise you omit this, as you love us and the common utility of our realm and will save yourself harmless. Witness the King at Westminster, the eighteenth day of June. By the King himself and the whole council.

The like writs are directed to the several sheriffs throughout England. The King to the venerable father in Christ, W. by the same grace bishop of Winchester, greeting. Because a great part of the people, etc., as above, as far as 'to labour for the necessaries of life', and then thus: and therefore we request you that you cause the premises to be proclaimed in the several churches and other places of your diocese where you shall deem expedient; commanding rectors, vicars of such churches, ministers and other your subjects that by salutary warnings they beseech and persuade their parishioner to labour and to keep the ordinances aforesaid, as instant necessity demands; and that you constrain the wage-earning chaplains of your said diocese, who, as is said, refuse in like manner to serve without excessive salary, and compel them, under penalty of suspension and interdict, to serve for the accustomed salary, as is expedient; and that you in no wise omit this as you love us and the common utility of our said realm. Witness as above.

By the King himself and the whole council. The like letters of request are directed to the several bishops of England and to the guardian of the archbishopric of Canterbury, the see being vacant, under the same date.

> **Source: A. E. Bland, R. A. Brown and R. H. Tawney (comp. and ed.)** *English Economic History,* pp. 164–167

ह•~•३

English examples have been used for the sake of accessibility, but throughout the Middle Ages England was dependent on the continent for its most successful businessmen, especially in the cloth trade; throughout the period high quality English wool was exported to the European mainland, and especially to Flanders, where cloth was made and exported back to England.

Economic history can sometimes distort the high aspirations of medieval civic institutions. In Flanders, and even more dramatically in Northern Italy, high notions of benign self-government were developing. In the Palazzo Pubblico in Siena, for example, the great fresco series of Ambrogio Lorenzetti, executed between 1337 and 1339, reflects, especially in the Sala della Pace, a philosophy of the common good. In his portrayal of the effects of good government, safety, prosperity and unity are expressed by the portrayal of a walled city (Siena itself) surrounded by a verdant countryside in which peasants work on the fields and merchants roam unmolested by criminals, a reflection of divine order.

ह• 11.12 Thomas Aquinas, *Summa Contra Gentiles* •३

Of the Ordering of Men among Themselves and with respect to Other Creatures

Compared with other intellectual substances the human soul takes the lowest place, because, as has already been stated, it is, when first created, only a general apprehension of the order of divine providence: consequently, it must perfect its knowledge of what pertains to that order in the particular, by reference to things themselves, in which the order of divine providence is already established in detail. So it is that the human soul must rely on bodily organs to acquire knowledge from the sensible world. But, such is the weakness of its intellectual light, that it could never acquire a perfect knowledge of all that concerns man unless it were assisted and enlightened by higher spirits; for it is the disposition of divine providence, as we have seen, that lower spirits shall reach their perfection aided by the higher. Furthermore, because man possesses a certain measure of the light of intelligence, it is disposed by divine providence that brute animals, being altogether without intelligence, shall be subject to him. So it is said, 'Let us make man to our own image and likeness' – that is as far as his intellectual powers are concerned – 'and let him have dominion over the fishes of the sea, and the fowls of the air, and the beasts and the whole earth' (Genesis I, 26).

Brute animals, though without intelligence, do arrive at a certain knowledge, and, in consequence, are placed by the order of divine providence over plants and all else that is without knowledge. So it is said: 'Behold I have given you every herb bearing seed upon the earth, and all trees that have in themselves seed of their own kind, to be your meat: and to all beasts of the earth' (Genesis I, 29–30). As for those things which are altogether without knowledge one is superior to the other in so far as it has greater power to produce effects; for such things are not determined as to their values by divine providence but only as to their effects. Now since man has both intelligence and sense and also bodily strength, these, by the disposition of divine providence, are subordinated to one another on the pattern of that order which is found throughout the universe. Bodily strength being subordinate to the sensitive and intellectual powers and ready to obey their commands, while the senses are subject to the intelligence and follow its dictates.

For the same reason there is an order to be found among men themselves; for men of outstanding intelligence naturally take command, while those who are less intelligent but of more robust physique, seem intended by nature to act as servants; as Aristotle points out in the Politics. Solomon also was of like opinion, for he said: 'Let the foolish serve the wise' (Proverbs, XI, 29); and again: 'Seek out from the people wise and God-fearing men who shall be judges over the people at all times' (Exodus, XVIII, 21–22). So, just as in the case of a man there is a lack of balance if his reason follows the dictates of his senses, or his sensible powers are affected by some bodily infirmity, as happens for instance in lameness, so also in human government. Lack of order arises from the fact that somebody is in control, not because of his superior intelligence, but because he has seized power by physical violence or has been set up to rule through ties of sensible affection. Nor does Solomon fail to remark upon such injustice, but says: 'There is an evil I have seen under the sun, as it were by an error proceeding from the face of the prince: a tool set in high dignity' (Ecclesiastes, X, 5, 6). Such lack of order is, however, not incompatible with divine providence. It comes about by divine permission, and because of defects in subordinate agents, as we have already pointed out in the case of other sorts of evil. Nor is the natural order wholly perverted in such cases: for the rule of the foolish must needs be weak if it be not aided by counsel from the wise. So it is said: 'Designs are strengthened by counsels; and wars are to be managed by governments' (Proverbs, XX, 18). And again: 'A wise man is strong: and a knowing man stout and valiant. Because war is managed by due ordering: and there shall be safety where there are many counsels' (Proverbs, XXIV, 5–6). And, because a counsellor rules whoever accepts his counsel, and, in a sense, commands him, it is said: 'The wise servant shall rule over foolish children' (Proverbs, XVII, 2).

So it is clear that divine providence imposes an order on all things and manifests the truth of the Apostle's saying: 'All things that are, are set in order by God' (Romans, XIII, 1).

Source: A. P. D'Entreves (ed.) J. G. Dawson (trans.)
Aquinas: Selected Political Writings (1965)
pp. 99, 101

In such cities as Florence prosperity and civic pride exuded confidence, as is demonstrated in the following description of the city in the years 1336–1338, written by a contemporary chronicler, Giovanni Villani.

11.13 Cronica di Giovanni Villani

Now that we have spoken of the revenues and expenses of the commune of Florence in these times, I think it appropriate, to mention this and the other great things about our city. Thus, our successors, who in times to come shall follow us, may become aware of the rise and decline of the wealth and power which our city achieved. Thus they may also, through the wise and courageous citizens who at various times shall govern her, see to it that she advances in wealth and great power, through the memory and example of this our chronicle.

We have diligently discovered that in these times there were in Florence about 25,000 men able to bear arms, from 15 years up to 70, all citizens. Among them there were 1500 noble and powerful citizens who as magnates posted bond with the commune. There were then in Florence upwards of 75 liveried knights. We have diligently discovered that before the popular regime, which rules at present, was established, there were more than 250 knights. Since the popular government was created, the magnates have not had the possessions or the power as before, and therefore few become knights.

It has been estimated that there are in Florence upwards of 90,000 mouths, including men, women and children, from the evidence of the bread which is continuously needed in the city, as one can well understand. It has been guessed that there were continuously in the city more than 1500 foreigners, transients and soldiers, not counting in the total religious, friars and cloistered nuns, of whom we shall make mention soon. It has been estimated that there were in these times in the countryside and district of Florence upwards of 80,000 men. We have discovered from the priest who baptised the babies that they numbered every year in these times from 5500 to 6000, with the masculine sex larger than the feminine by up to 500 per year. (The priest sets aside a black bean for every male baptised in San Giovanni and a white bean for every female, in order to know their number). We have discovered, that the boys and girls who are learning to read number from 8000 to 10,000. The boys who are learning the abacus and calculation in six schools number from 1000 to 1200. And those who are learning Latin and logic in four large schools number from 550 to 600.

The churches which were then in Florence and in her suburbs, including the abbeys and the churches of the religious friars, have been found to be 110. Among them are 57 parishes with congregations, five abbeys with two priors and upwards of 80 monks, 24 convents of nuns with upwards of 500 women, 10 houses of friars, 30 hospitals with more than 1000 beds to serve the poor and infirm, and from 250 to 300 ordained chaplains.

The shops of the wool craft were 200 or more, and produced from 70,000 to 80,000 cloths, which were worth upwards of 1,200,000 gold florins. A third of this value remained in the country to pay for labour, without regarding the profit which the wool merchants made from that labour. More than 30,000 persons were supported by it. We have accurately discovered, that thirty years ago there were 300 shops or thereabouts, and that they made every year more than 100,000 cloths. But these cloths were cruder and worth half the present value, since wool from England was not then imported, nor was it known how to work it, as has subsequently been done. The shops of the guild of Calimala, which deals with cloth brought from France and beyond the mountains, number upwards of twenty, and import every year more than 10,000 cloths worth 300,000 gold florins. These they sell entirely in Florence, and we do not include those cloths which are shipped outside of Florence. The tables of money-changers were upwards of eighty. The gold money which was coined was upwards of 350,000 gold florins and sometimes 400,000; and of pennies worth four *piccioli* each, there were coined every year about 20,000 pounds. The college of judges was upwards of 80. The notaries were more than 600. The pharmacists, physicians and surgeons numbered upwards of 60. The pharmacies were more than 100. Merchants and dealers in dry goods were of great number. One cannot estimate the shops of the makers of shoes, slippers and boots. Those who went outside of Florence to trade numbered 300 or more, and many other masters of many crafts, and masters of stone and wood, did likewise. There were then in Florence 146 furnaces, We have discovered by the tax of milling and for the furnaces, that every day the city needed for internal consumption 140 moggia of grain. From this one can estimate what was needed every year. And we do not consider that the greater part of the rich, noble and affluent citizens spent with their families four months every year in the countryside, and some even more. We have discovered that in the year 1280, when the city was in happy and good circumstances, that it needed every week upward of 800 moggia. We have discovered by the tax at the gates that every year Florence imported upwards of 55,000 cogna of wine, and when it was plentiful about 10,000 cogna more. The city required every year about 400 cows and calves; 60,000 muttons and sheep; 20,000 she-goats and he-goats; and 30,000 pigs. In the month of July through the gate of San Frediano there entered 4000 loads of melons, which were all distributed in the city. In these times there were in Florence the following magistracies held by foreign officials. Each held court and had the authority to torture. They were the podesta, the captain, the defender of the people and the guilds; the executor of the Ordinances of Justice; the captain of the guard, or defender of the people, who had more authority than the others. All these four [*sic*] magistrates had the option of inflicting personal punishment: the judge of auditing and appeals; the judge of taxes; the official supervising women's ornaments; the official over commerce; the official over the wool guild; the ecclesiastical officials; the court of the bishop of Florence; the court of the bishop of Fiesole; the inquisitor concerning heretical depravity. And other high and magnificent offices of our city of Florence ought not to be omitted, but remembered, in order to provide information to those who shall follow us.

The city was well laid out within, and constructed with many beautiful houses. Construction was going on continually in these times. Buildings were improved, to make them comfortable and elegant, and fine examples of all sorts of improvements were sought from outside the city. There were cathedral churches, and churches of brothers of every discipline, and magnificent monasteries. Besides that, there was not a citizen, of popular or magnate status, who had not built or would not build in the countryside great and rich estates, and very rich habitations, with beautiful buildings, much better than in the city. And in this they all sinned, and were considered insane for their extravagant expenditures.

And it was such a magnificent thing to behold, that foreigners coming from afar, not familiar with Florence, believed (or most of them) that the rich buildings and beautiful palaces which were outside the city about three miles were part of the city, as they are at Rome. We do not speak of the rich palaces, towers, courts and walled gardens even farther from the city, which in other regions would be called castles. In conclusion, it has been estimated, that around the city for a distance of six miles there are so many rich and noble habitations that two Florences would not contain as many. We have said enough of the facts of Florence.

> **Source: D. Herlihy (ed. and trans.)** *Medieval Culture and Society* (1968) pp. 185–189

Dante, in his role as political writer and publicist of the Empire, a citizen of Florence, warned against the dangers of centrifugalism.

---

৪ 11.14 Letter from Dante ৬

Letter VI

Dante Alighieri, a Florentine in undeserved exile, to the arrant scoundrels within the city.

1. The merciful providence of the everlasting King, who does not abandon in contempt our world below while maintaining the heavens above by his goodness, has entrusted to the Holy Roman Empire the governance of human affairs so that mankind might have peace under the cloudless sky that such a protection affords and that everywhere, in accord with the dictates of nature, the organised life of society may be upheld. Although this is proved by Holy Scripture and is warranted by the ancient world on the basis of reason alone, it is nevertheless no slight confirmation of the truth that, when the throne of Augustus is vacant, the whole world loses its way, the pilot and oarsmen in the ship of St Peter fall asleep, and Italy, unhappy and forsaken, abandoned to private caprice and deprived of all public direction, drifts in such a battering from wind and wave as words could not express, and even the Italians themselves in their misery can scarcely measure it by their tears. Let everyone,

therefore, who by blind presumption is puffed up to resist this unmistakable evidence of God's will, now betray himself by turning pale before the imminent approach of the stern Judge's assize, even if the sword of Him who says 'vengeance is mine' has not yet flashed from heaven to strike.

2. But you have been lured, all too apt pupils in crime, by the monstrous maw of your greed into every trespass against the laws of God and man: are you not haunted by dread of the second death, since you, first and alone in your abhorrence of the discipline of liberty, have raged against the majesty of the Roman Emperor, the King of the world and the lieutenant of God, and, on the plea of prescriptive right, have denied your duty of proper obedience and preferred to work yourselves into a frenzy of rebellion? Are you unaware, crazy and contrary as you are, that Public Right is not to be criticised on the ground of prescription but expires only with the end of time itself? Surely the venerable precepts of our Roman Law aver, and human reason, after prolonged reflection, concurs, that sovereignty, however long neglected, admits neither obsolescence, diminution, nor question.

For whatever tends to the advantage of all cannot perish or be even impaired without damage to all. This is contrary to the intention of God and of nature, and mankind would agree in utterly rejecting it.

Why are you stirred by this will o' the wisp to abandon the Holy Empire and, like builders of a second tower of Babel, to embark on new forms of state so that the Florentine sovereignty should be co-ordinate with the Roman? Why do you not choose to feel the same envy of the ecclesiastical hierarchy, and to duplicate the sun, the celestial symbol of the Papacy, at the same time as the moon of the Empire? But if reflection on your monstrous designs does not give you pause, let this at least strike terror into your hardened hearts, that the penalty of your crime is your deprivation, not merely of wisdom, but even of the beginning of wisdom. For there is no more alarming symptom in a sinner than his doing as he likes without shame and without the fear of God. This is of course the punishment which so often strikes down the wicked man, that on his deathbed he takes no account of what he is, as in life he took no account of God.

3. But if your insolent arrogance has indeed so far cut you off from the dew of heaven's grace, like the mountains of Gilboa, that resistance to the decree of the Eternal Senate has given you no qualms and you are not even afraid of your own lack of fear, will you really be able to silence that other fear, the merely human and secular fear of ruin, when you are hurried to the inevitable shipwreck of your proud race and of what will cost you many tears, your snatching at the prize of absolute sovereignty? You trust, doubtless, that you can defend yourselves somehow, because you have a contemptible ring of ramparts? What a union of hearts is yours – for evildoing only, how you are blinded by your incredible ambition! What help will it be to have built your ring of ramparts and fortified yourselves with bulwarks and battlements, when there swoops upon you the eagle in the field of gold, which, soaring now over Pyrenees, now over Caucasus, now over Atlas, once looked down upon vast expanses of sea in its flight, aided and supported by the hosts of heaven? What indeed, when you stand dumbfounded, you most miserable of men, before the Emperor at your doors to check the delirium of Italy? The inordinate hope that you vainly cherish will certainly not be furthered by this rebellion of yours, but this barring of the just king's way will be fuel to the flame of his coming, and the mercy that always accompanies his army will take wing in indignation. Your self-styled defence of the threshold of false liberty will throw you down into the penitentiary of real slavery. For we cannot

help believing that sometimes by the irony of God's judgement the means whereby the sinner plans to evade his deserts are made only to hurry him the more fatally to meet them; and the man who consciously and deliberately has defied the will of God is, without his knowledge and against his will, subserving it.

4. To your sorrow you will see your palaces, which you have not raised with prudence to meet your needs but have thoughtlessly enlarged for your pleasures, fallen, since no walls of a revived Troy encircle them, fallen under the battering-ram or consumed by fire. You will see your populace, now a raging mob, disorganised and divided against itself, part for, part against you, soon united against you in howls of fury, since a starving mob can know no fear. You will see with remorse your churches, now thronged every day by crowds of your ladies, pillaged, and your children doomed to pay for their fathers' sins in bewilderment and ignorance. And if my prophetic soul is not deceived in delivering a message brought home to me by unmistakable omens as well as by incontrovertible arguments, your small remnant, when the greater part has perished by slaughter or been taken prisoner, will witness with tears, before it passes into exile, the final delivery of your city, worn out with prolonged grief, into the hands of strangers. In short, the disasters which that glorious city of Saguntum endured in its loyalty for liberty's sake will be shamefully visited on your treachery to enslave you.

5. Nor may you take courage from the unexpected success of Parma: under pressure of famine, 'that evil counsellor', her citizens whispered to each other, 'let us rather rush into the midst of battle and be killed', and broke into Caesar's camp, when Caesar was away. For although they won a victory over Victoria, they too none the less earned thereby woe upon woe unforgettably. But reflect on the lightning strokes of Frederick I; be warned by the example of Milan as well as of Spoleto, since the thought of their perverse oversight linked so closely with their overthrow will give you no stomach for the fight, but strike a chill into your too expansive hopes and contract with fear your too sanguine hearts.

You, the most empty-headed of all the Tuscans, crazy by nature and crazy by corruption, in your ignorance you neither care nor conceive that in the eyes of the fully fledged the feet of your warped minds go astray in the darkness of night. For the fully fledged, the 'undefiled in the way' (as the Psalmist has it), see you as though you stood at the gates of a prison driving off anyone who takes pity on you, for fear that he might perhaps free you from your imprisonment, bound hand and foot as you are. Nor do you notice in your blindness that greed is your master, luring you on with venomous whispers and curbing you with insubstantial threats, bringing you into 'captivity to the law of sin' and forbidding obedience to the most sacred laws, which are made in the image of natural law. Now the observance of these laws, if whole-hearted and spontaneous, can not only be shown to be no slavery, but much rather reveals itself to a penetrating mind as the essence of perfect liberty. For what is liberty but the unhampered translation of will into act? and the law paves the way to act for her votaries. If therefore only those who give willing obedience to law are free, what will you call yourselves who, behind the screen of devotion to liberty, break every law to conspire against the lawgiver?

6. You pitiable offshoot of Fiesole, barbarians now due for a second chastisement, does this foretaste not strike panic enough into your hearts? I am sure that you tremble in your waking hours, for all that you put a show of hope on your faces and in your lying claims, and that you often wake out of dreams in alarm at the future foreshadowed in them, or perhaps at the review of what you were plotting the day

before. But if in your well-founded alarm you regret your madness yet without remorse, these further points remain to be brought home to you, so that the streams of fear and remorse may join to form the bitter river of repentance, that this our Elect, our triumphant Henry, who carries the burden of the Roman Commonwealth, thirsting not for his own personal interests, but for the general good of the world, has undertaken for our sakes his high task, sharing our pains by his own free will, as though to him, after Christ, the prophet Isaiah had pointed the finger of, prophecy, when he foretold what the Spirit of God revealed: 'Surely he hath himself borne our griefs and himself carried our sorrows'. So you see, if you will consent not to deny it, that the time is at hand for your bitterest repentance of your rash presumption. But belated repentance of this kind will not be productive of pardon, much rather will it be the opening scene of your well-timed punishment. This is so, because 'the sinner is smitten so that he shall surely die' without appeal.

Source: Dante, *Monarchy and Three Political Letters* (1954) pp. 103–108

Further reading

C. Dyer, *Standards of Living in the Later Middle Ages: Social Change in England, c. 1200–1520* (Cambridge University Press, Cambridge, 1989).

R. MacKenney, *Tradesmen and Traders: the World of the Gilds in Venice and Europe c. 1250 – c. 1650* (Barnes & Noble, NJ, 1987).

M. M. Postan, *Cambridge Economic History of Europe 2. Trade and Industry in the Middle Ages* (Cambridge University Press, Cambridge, 1987).

S. Reynolds, *An Introduction to the History of English Medieval Towns* (Clarendon Press, Oxford, 1970).

THE MEDIEVAL WORLD
SELF-OBSERVED

The medieval universe was generously proportioned. The world itself was at the physical centre of creation but was only a pale reflection of the ultimate reality of God. Its shape and structure were understood not only in the language of Christianity but also in the classical tradition of Greek and Roman science. God's creation of the visible universe *ex nihilo*, poetically described in the *Book of Genesis*, the opening chapter of the Old Testament, was generally accepted, but an understanding of the universe's structure and form owed more to observation than revelation. Certain key classical texts, passed on either completely or in part, gave substance to the observations of the intelligent observer. The most influential of these was the so-called *Almagest* (Arabic for *Great Work*) of Claudius Ptolemy (fl. 150 AD) which presented the earth as a static sphere at the centre of the universe around which the heavenly bodies rotated.

It cannot be assumed, as modern detractors of the Middle Ages so often do, that people in the medieval West regarded the earth as flat and, indeed, some scholars were aware of the fact that the circumference of the earth had been accurately computed by Eratosthenes (d. 196 BC) as 24,662 miles. Knowledge of the earth's surface was largely confined to the northern hemisphere, which made the Christian tradition that the inhabited world consisted of three interlinked continents whose populations were descendants of Noah's three sons, more compelling. The Antipodes was seen through a glass darkly.

The *Mappa Mundi*, world maps of the medieval period, of which the finest surviving big-scale example is at Hereford cathedral, in England, charted time as well as space. Places were not so much geographically located as shown for their pedagogical significance; Jerusalem was shown at the world's centre, Santiago de Compostella at the far west of the inhabited world to demonstrate how wide Christian evangelisation had reached and how close was the end of the world. World maps were much more visual encyclopaedias, contained in a disc, a common view of communicating knowledge, than route-finders. By the thirteenth century, however, itineraries were being produced and maps charted which were far more secular and less universalist, even if their function was to guide pilgrims from shrine to shrine.

The pilgrimage was the ideal journey of medieval Christendom and there were numerous cosmopolitan and regional shrines. Rome (and for a time the Holy Land) remained firm favourites, but Compostella in Galician Spain, the burial place of St James, attracted numerous visitors.

৯১ 12.1 Pilgrims of St James ৯১

Chapter XI

Of the Reception to be given to Pilgrims of St James
Pilgrims, whether poor or rich, returning from St James or going there must be received with charity and compassion; for whosoever receives them and gives them hospitality has for his guest not only St James but our Lord Himself. As the Lord says in His gospel, 'He that receiveth you receiveth me'. Many are those who have incurred the wrath of God because they would not take in the pilgrims of St James and the needy.

A weaver in Nantua, a town between Geneva and Lyons, refused bread to a pilgrim of St James who asked for it; and at once he saw his cloth fall to the ground, rent asunder. At Villeneuve a poor pilgrim of St James asked for alms, for the love of God and the blessed James, from a woman who was keeping bread under hot ashes. She told him that she had no bread: whereupon the pilgrim said, 'May the bread that you have turn into stone!' The pilgrim had left the house and gone some distance on his way when the wicked woman went to take her bread out of the ashes and found a round stone in the place where the bread had been. Struck with remorse, she set out to look for the pilgrim, but could not find him.

At Poitiers two valiant French pilgrims, returning from St James in great need, asked for hospitality, for the love of God and St James, in the street running from the house of Jean Gautier to the church of Saint-Porchaire, but found none. Finally, at the last house in the street, by the church, they were taken in by a poor man; and that night, by the operation of divine vengeance, a fierce fire broke out and quickly destroyed the whole street, beginning with the house where they had first asked for hospitality and going right up to the house where they were taken in. Some thousand houses were destroyed, but the one where the servants of God were taken in was, by His grace, spared.

Thus we learn that the pilgrims of St James, whether rich or poor, should be given hospitality and a considerate reception.

> **Source: J. Hogarth (trans.) *The Pilgrim's Guide:
> A 12th Century Guide for the Pilgrim to St James
> of Compostella* (1992) pp. 87–88**

৯১ 12.2 William Wey's pilgrimage to St James ৯১

An Account of the Pilgrimage Made by Master William Wey, Bachelor of Sacred Theology, sometime Fellow of the Royal College of the Most Blessed Mary at Eton, to St James in Spain.

In the name of my God, I, William Wey, Fellow of the Royal College at Eton, in the Year of Our Lord 1456, inspired by divine grace and with the leave of my King and Founder, Henry the Sixth, set out on a pilgrim journey on my own account to St James in Compostella in Spain. Leaving the Royal College on 27 March and arriving at the port of Plymouth on the last day of April, I waited there until 17 May. On that day six pilgrim ships set sail in company: one ship was from Portsmouth, another from Bristol, another from Weymouth, another from Lymington, another called the *Cargreen* and a Plymouth ship called the *Mary White*. We were at sea until 21 May, when we came to the port of La Coruña about noon. The first place which we saw in that area of Spain is called *Ortyngez,* the second place we saw is called *Cappryez* (on the opposite quarter is the island called *Sesarke*); the third place we saw is called the *Delavale Tower*. When these had been sighted the sailors lowered one sail and we entered the port of La Coruña. From there we went to St James in Compostella on the Eve of the Feast of the Holy Trinity.

There I heard from the clergy of that Church of St James of Compostella that there is an archbishop who has under him in that church, seven cardinals, a dean, a precentor, five archdeacons, a chancellor and two judges, all of whom have mitres and croziers. In addition there are 80 canons of that church. There are also 12 *parceners;* three of them hold one prebend jointly. Moreover there are 12 *parceners* of the Holy Spirit and four *duplarii,* who receive a double stipend. These cardinals and bishops receive 50 ducats each year; and, if they are all in residence, a canon will receive 20 ducats each year. These cardinals do not wear amices or furred hoods in the choir, but merely surplices.

At Vespers for the Holy Trinity there were six rectors choral in scarlet capes holding in their hands long croziers covered with silver. They sang the versicle and the *Benedicamus.* Two cardinals in pontificals and wearing mitres, with pastoral staffs and a thurible in the right hand, censed the high altar with one hand and then, in similar fashion, the clergy in the choir. In the procession before Mass on the day of Holy Trinity there were nine bishops and cardinals in pontificals. The clergy of that church enquired if there were any gentlemen from England present. When the reply was given that there were, they were chosen before all other nationalities to carry the canopy over the Body of Christ. There were six there who carried the canopy and the names of four of them are: Austile, Gale, Ule and Fulford. The Archbishop of St James at Compostella has 12 bishops under him, apart from those who are in his church. In the whole kingdom there are three archbishops: first the Archbishop of Compostella; second the Archbishop of Seville, which is a great Spanish city; the third is the Archbishop of Toledo. The last two have canons, not cardinals, under them. The offerings to St James in Compostella are divided into three. The archbishop has one, the canons, cardinals and bishops have the second and the third is reserved for the church fabric.

Next I came to the port of La Coruña where we stayed three days. We used these days in three activities. First in conversation throughout those days with a Jew, then on the Wednesday we had a procession and a *Saint Mary* Mass with music, while on Corpus Christi we had a procession in the Franciscan church, followed by a sermon in the same church by an Englishman, a Bachelor of Sacred Theology, whose text was, Here am I, for thou calledst me. He concluded from his text that all the Englishmen present could say these words to St James, Here am I, since by God's grace thou calledst me to come here and visit thy place. There was no other nation which had a conversation with a Jew, processions, a Mass and a sermon except the English.

In the port of La Coruña there were 80 ships with topcastles and four without. They included English, Welsh, Irish, Norman, French, Bretons and others. The total of English vessels was 32. We left the port of La Coruña on 28 May, and had vessels sailing ahead of us and astern in the Spanish sea. On 3 June we returned to the port of La Coruña and on 5 June we set out to sea again from La Coruña arriving in Plymouth on 9 June. The first part of England to be recognised and sighted by our crew is called the Browsam Rock; the second is called Long Ships, and there are three rocks; the third is called Popyl Hopyl, the fourth Mount's Bay and the fifth the Lizard, of which it is commonly said:

'Be the churl ne'er so hard,
He'll quake by the beard
Ere he pass the Lizard'.

The highest mountain in Spain is called Sturies and it always has snow on top. The University of Spain is called Salamanca. There are five regions in Spain: the region of Spain, the region of Castile and Leon, and the region of Portugal, which are Christian; the region of Granada and the region of Balmaria are both Saracen regions. Of these regions the Saracen King of Granada was captured by Lord Henry, King of Castile and Leon, in the year of Our Lord 1456. In this year he captured the largest city of Granada, which is called Malaga. (It is from here that the figs known as *Figs of Malike* come.) He held that Saracen king in custody in his kingdom and he wrote under his own seal to that king's cities and towns and to those living in them. As a token of his victory the King of Castile and Leon sent that King of Granada's crown, which was made of gold or gilded, to St James in Compostella. This crown was placed on the head of the seated image of St James in the middle of the high altar on the day of the Holy Trinity in the year of Our Lord mentioned above, being a year of Indulgence at St James.

In the same year a great tower built by the French at Bordeaux using St Peter's bell-tower as a fortress was swept away from the land.

In the same year a man from the County of Somerset, who had vowed to make the pilgrimage to St James because of a great infirmity which he had, on arriving at the port of Plymouth, came to me for advice. Because he was afraid he would die from that infirmity he wanted to know if he could return home after making the vow. He believed that he could not escape this infirmity and therefore he preferred to die at home rather than on the way to St James. I advised him to go to St James telling him that it would be better to die on that journey rather than at his home on account of the indulgences granted to those on pilgrimage to St James. Despite this advice he began his journey back to his own country. After travelling 20 miles in one day with great pain and distress, when he reached the inn where he intended to spend the night, he was healed from the infirmity which he had suffered for a long time. Realising that he was completely cured he started his journey back to Plymouth covering in the half day following as great a distance as he had completed in the whole of the previous day. He re-embarked and came to St James. I met him in the house of the Franciscans at La Coruña where he told me this story on Corpus Christi Day. I asked him if he had confessed about his journey homewards and he told me that he had. Another miracle! One of those sailing on our ship had his purse cut from his belt. He lost his valuables and all the money he had. He immediately made a vow to St James that if he recovered his property he would go to him stripped. After he had made this vow, a Breton, who had cut his purse, was caught in the act of cutting another man's purse. The pilgrim's purse was discovered in the thief's pocket, and so, with St James's help, he got it back. Immediately he set off for St James, stripped, as he had vowed. At that time the ship in which he had previously sailed was carried towards England with a favourable wind, but for four days she was so tossed about at sea that the sailors brought her back to La Coruña. Three days later the sailors set sail again now carrying with them in their ship that pilgrim who had been robbed earlier and whom they had previously sent off on his pilgrimage.

The song of the Spanish children who danced before pilgrims for shillings and pennies:

> St James of Compostella, grant you to return to your land.
> St James, good Lord, grant you true forgiveness,
> Fine weather, a good road, and a fair wind. Fare ye well.
> Of your generosity give those who are here a shilling.

These are the relics which are kept in the aforementioned places:

First and foremost the holy stone which is called *The Patron*, on which the body of the Blessed James, son of Zebedee, lay. This stone is now beneath the altar of St James in the church at Padrón.

Also *The Most Holy Boat*. This is in the river. Pilgrims approach it and touch it physically in summer when the water level is low and the river dry.

On the hill in Padrón is the spring where St James set his staff together with the great stone on which he stood when he first preached in Spain.

Also these are the relics which are kept in the church of St Mary of Iria at Padrón. First on the altar in the chapel of St Martin are the relics of the tunic of Our Lord, Jesus Christ, together with the relics of St Paul and St Andrew, Apostles, St Stephen, St Saturninus, St Romanus, St Isidore, St Emilianus, St Leocadia and St Eugenia. This altar was built in honour of St Mary and All Saints.

The following are the relics which are kept in the church at Compostella where rests the body of St James, son of Zebedee. First and foremost the body of St James, son of Zebedee, nephew of the Virgin Mary, brother of St John, Apostle and Evangelist, whole and uncorrupted. Next the body of St Fructuosus, Bishop, the body of St Athanasius, the body of St Cucufatus, the body of St Theodore, a disciple of the Apostle himself, and the body of St Silvester, martyr and companion of the Apostle. Moreover the head of St James, son of Alphaeus, Apostle, is displayed to all in the treasury of the aforementioned church most clearly.

These are the indulgences granted by the Holy Fathers to the aforesaid church at Compostella:

Whoever has come on pilgrimage to the church of St James, son of Zebedee, at any time, has one third of all his sins remitted. If he should die on his way there, while there or during his return, provided he repents of his sins, they are all remitted to him.

Moreover, all who go on any Sunday in the procession of the church of St James have, for each procession and ministration of the sacrament, 40 days of indulgence, and similarly throughout the whole week. If it is a feast day they have 300 days in addition to the aforesaid indulgence of a third of all their sins.

Moreover, on the eve of St James's Day and on the day itself and the feast of the dedication of his church, all who have gone there on pilgrimage have 600 days, both on the eve and on the day itself, in addition to the aforementioned indulgence of a third part of all their sins.

Likewise, all who hear Mass said by an Archbishop, Bishop or Cardinal at the altar of St James have 200 days indulgence for each Mass, in addition to the aforesaid indulgences. All these privileges, listed above, have been granted and confirmed, in the manner described, to St James's pilgrims, who have confessed and are truly penitent, by Bulls issued by the Holy Fathers of the Apostolic See. Likewise Pope Callixtus granted that, for the whole of the year when the Feast of St James falls on a Sunday, those who come there on pilgrimage and are truly penitent and have confessed should be absolved from punishment and guilt. Again, by a Bull of the Pope, St Callixtus, who was strongly devoted to St James, when the Feast of St James falls on a Sunday, all pilgrims who come to the mother church at Compostella in Galicia on pilgrimage, both on the Eve and on the Day itself, are granted full indulgence from all their sins. This privilege applies throughout the whole year starting on the first day of January right up to the last day of the month of December next following, inclusively. Again by a Bull of the aforesaid Pope Callixtus, which has been confirmed by his successors, it is granted and enjoined that anyone who doubts and does not firmly believe these remissions, privileges and indulgences of the aforesaid church at Compostella shall incur the grave sentence of excommunication by apostolic authority.

The aforesaid indulgences have been confirmed and granted by the lord Pope, Innocent II and by Leo of blessed memory and by other Supreme Pontiffs. The Supreme Pontiffs have graciously granted, moreover, to this same church at Compostella that on the Feast of the Apostle and on his Translation and at any time, anyone who intends to go to the aforesaid church on pilgrimage may have the right, from the day that he leaves home on his journey, to choose a confessor, who shall have the power, by apostolic authority, to absolve, even in 'papal cases', the pilgrims themselves, while they are on their way thither, or there or returning thence. Moreover it is contained in the said Bull that any pilgrim coming to the church at Compostella who, having made his confession and being repentant, dies on the way there or there or returning thence shall be completely absolved from all his sins. Amen.

Source: F. Davey, *William Wey: An English Pilgrim to Compostella in 1456* (2000) pp. 20–40

Margery Kempe, in her book of 1436, reflected on many journeys, including one to Rome and another to Jerusalem.

ࣾ 12.3 Margery Kempe's reflections ࣾ

Chapter 29

When this creature with her fellowship came to the grave where Our Lord was buried, anon, as she entered that holy place, she fell down with her candle in her hand, as if she would have died for sorrow. And later she rose up again with great weeping and sobbing, as though she had seen Our Lord buried even before her.

Then she thought she saw Our Lady in her soul, how she mourned and how she wept for her Son's death, and then was Our Lady's sorrow her sorrow. And so, wherever the friars led them in that holy place, she always wept and sobbed wonderfully, and especially when she came where Our Lord was nailed on the Cross. There cried she, and wept without measure, so that she could not restrain herself.

Also they came to a stone of marble that Our Lord was laid on when He was taken down from the Cross, and there she wept with great compassion, having mind of Our Lord's Passion.

Afterwards she was houselled on the Mount of Calvary, and then she wept, she sobbed, she cried so loud that it was a wonder to hear it. She was so full of holy thoughts and meditations and holy contemplations on the Passion of Our Lord Jesus Christ, and holy dalliance that Our Lord Jesus Christ spoke to her soul, that she could never express them after, so high and so holy were they. Much was the grace that Our Lord shewed to this creature whilst she was three weeks in Jerusalem.

Another day, early in the morning, they went again amongst great hills, and their guides told her where Our Lord bore the Cross on His back, and where His Mother met with Him, and how she swooned and fell down and He fell down also. And so they went forth all the fore-noon till they came to Mount Sion. And ever this creature wept abundantly, all the way that she went, for compassion of Our Lord's Passion. On Mount Sion is a place where Our Lord washed His disciples' feet and, a little therefrom, He made His Maundy with His disciples.

And therefore this creature had great desire to be houselled in that holy place where Our Merciful Lord Christ Jesus first consecrated His precious Body in the form of bread, and gave it to His disciples. And so she was, with great devotion and plenteous tears and boisterous sobbings, for in this place is plenary remission, and so there is in four other places in the Temple. One is on the Mount of Calvary; another at the grave where Our Lord was buried; the third is at the marble stone that His precious Body was laid on, when It was taken from the Cross; the fourth is where the Holy Cross was buried; and in many other places in Jerusalem.

And when this creature came to the place where the apostles received the Holy Ghost, Our Lord gave her great devotion. Afterwards she went to the place where Our Lady was buried, and as she knelt on her knees the time of two masses, Our Lord Jesus Christ said to her:

> Thou comest not hither, daughter, for any need except merit and reward, for
> thy sins were forgiven thee ere thou came here and therefore thou comest

here for the increasing of thy reward and thy merit. And I am well pleased with thee, daughter, for thou standest under obedience to Holy Church, and because thou wilt obey thy confessor and follow his counsel who, through authority of Holy Church, hath absolved thee of thy sins and dispensed thee so that thou shouldst not go to Rome and Saint James unless thou wilt thine own self. Notwithstanding all this, I command thee in the Name of Jesus, daughter, that thou go visit these holy places and do as I bid thee, for I am above Holy Church, and I shall go with thee and keep thee right well.

Then Our Lady spoke to her soul in this manner, saying:

Daughter, well art thou blessed, for my Son Jesus shall flow so much grace into thee that all the world shall wonder at thee. Be not ashamed, my dear-worthy daughter, to receive the gifts that my Son shall give thee, for I tell thee in truth, they shall be great gifts that He shall give thee. And therefore, my dearworthy daughter, be not ashamed of Him that is thy God, thy Lord and thy love, any more than I was, when I saw Him hanging on the Cross – my sweet Son, Jesus – to cry and to weep for the pain of my sweet Son Jesus Christ. Mary Magdalene was not ashamed to cry and weep for my Son's love. Therefore, daughter, if thou will be partaker in our love, thou must be partaker in our sorrow.

This sweet speech and dalliance had this creature at Our Lady's grave, and much more than she could ever repeat.

Afterwards she rode on an ass to Bethlehem, and when she came to the temple and the crib where Our Lord was born, she had great devotion, much speech and dalliance in her soul, and high ghostly comfort with much weeping and sobbing, so that her fellows would not let her eat in their company, and therefore she ate her meat by herself alone.

And then the Grey Friars, who had led her from place to place, received her to them and set her with them at the meat so that she should not eat alone. And one of the friars asked one of her fellowship if she were the woman of England whom, they had heard said, spoke with God. And when this came to her knowledge, she knew well that it was the truth that Our Lord said to her, ere she went out of England:

Daughter, I will make all the world to wonder at thee, and many a man and many a woman shall speak of Me for love of thee, and worship Me in thee.

> **Source: W. Butler-Bowdon (ed.)** *The Book of Margery*
> *Kempe, 1436* (1936) pp. 111–114

Margery Kempe's reflections, as rambling as they are, indicate the medieval tendency to blur disciplines and specialities. Topographical writers, like the compilers of bestiaries, combined sound geographical knowledge with a fantastic erudition which some would call credulous.

৪৬ 12.4 Writings of the Middle Ages ৪৩

There is an animal called the elephant, which has no desire to mate. The Greeks believe that the name of the elephant comes from the size of his body, because he looks like a mountain: *elephio* is the Greek for mountain. The Indians call him *barro* (bhri) from the sound of his voice: *barritus* means the roar of an elephant, and 'ivory' the teeth of the elephant. His nose is called a trunk because he uses it to put food in his mouth; the trunk is like a snake and is protected by a rampart of ivory. There is no beast greater than this. The Persians and Indians put wooden towers on his back and fight with arrows as if they were on top of a wall. Elephants have a lively intelligence and memory. They move about in herds, flee from mice, and mate with their backs to each other. Pregnancy lasts for two years: nor do they give birth more than once, and never to several young, but to only one. They live for three hundred years. If, however, they want to have off-spring, they go to the east, near the earthly paradise, where a tree called mandragora grows. The elephant and his mate go there, and she picks a fruit from the tree and gives it to him. And she seduces him into eating it; after they have both eaten it, they mate and the female at once conceives. When the time comes for her to give birth, she goes to a pond, and the water comes up to her udder. The male elephant guards her while she gives birth, because the dragon is the enemy of the elephant. If the elephant finds a snake he will kill it by trampling on it until it is dead. The elephant strikes terror into bulls, and yet is terrified by a mouse. His nature is such that, if he falls down, he cannot stand up again. Yet he will fall if he leans against a tree in order to sleep. For he has no joints in his knees, and the hunter cuts a little way into the tree, so that as soon as the elephant leans against it, he falls with the tree. When he falls, he trumpets loudly, and at once a huge elephant comes, but is unable to lift him. Then they both trumpet together, and twelve elephants come, and are unable to lift him. They all trumpet, and at once a little elephant appears and puts his trunk under the large elephant, and lifts him up. The little elephant has the following characteristic: wherever some of his hair and bones are burnt, nothing evil can do harm, not even a dragon.

The elephant and his wife represent Adam and his wife, who pleased God in the flesh before their sin, and knew nothing of mating or of sin. When the woman ate of the tree, that is, gave the herb mandragora which brought understanding to her husband, she became pregnant and for that reason left paradise. For as long as they were in paradise, Adam did not know her in the flesh. For it is written: 'And Adam knew Eve his wife; and she conceived' (Genesis 4:1) and bore a son amid the waters of shame of which the prophet says: 'Save me a God, for the waters are come in unto my soul' (Psalm 69:1). And at once they were seduced by the dragon and banished from their haven, that is, they were no longer pleasing to God. Then the great elephant came, namely the Law, and could not help him to rise, any more than the priest could help the man who fell among thieves (Luke 10:30). And even the twelve elephants (that is, all the prophets) could not help him, like the Levite and the wounded man of whom we spoke. But the cunning elephant, that is our Lord Jesus Christ, although He was greatest of all, became very small, in that He humbled Himself before death, in order to raise mankind up, a true compassionate Samaritan who set the man who had fallen among thieves on his beast of burden. For He Himself was wounded, and took upon Himself our weaknesses and bore our sins: the Samaritan means a guardian. But where God is present, the devil cannot come near.

Whatever an elephant picks up in its trunk it breaks, and what it tramples underfoot it crushes to death beneath the debris of a giant ruin. They never fight over their females, because adultery is unknown among them. The goodness of mercy is within them. For when they see men wandering in the desert, they lead them back into familiar ways, and when they meet a flock of sheep huddling together they protect them on their journey, so that no missile kills any of them. If they fight in a battle, they always take great care of the weary and the wounded.

> Source: R. Barber (trans.) *Bestiary* (1999)
> pp. 39–43

Gerald of Wales (*c.* 1146–1223), who made several visits to Ireland, the first in 1185, presents in his *History and Topography of Ireland* a wild land full of wild people.

ಶ 12.5 Gerald of Wales, *The History and* ಶ
Topography of Ireland

The Third Part

The nature, customs and characteristics of the people
I have thought it not superfluous to say a few things about the nature of this people both in mind and body, that is to say, of their mental and physical characteristics.

To begin with: when they are born, they are not carefully nursed as is usual. For apart from the nourishment with which they are sustained by their hard parents from dying altogether, they are for the most part abandoned to nature. They are not put in cradles, or swathed; nor are their tender limbs helped by frequent baths or formed by any useful art. The midwives do not use hot water to raise the nose, or press down the face, or lengthen the legs. Unaided nature according to her own judgement arranges and disposes without the help of any art the limbs that she has produced.

As if to prove what she can do by herself she continually shapes and moulds, until she finally forms and finishes them in their full strength with beautiful upright bodies and handsome and well-complexioned faces.

But although they are fully endowed with natural gifts, their external characteristics of beard and dress, and internal cultivation of the mind are so barbarous that they cannot be said to have any culture.

They use very little wool in their dress and that itself nearly always black – because the sheep of that country are black – and made up in a barbarous fashion. For they wear little hoods, close-fitting and stretched across the shoulders and down to a length of about eighteen to twenty-two inches, and generally sewn together from cloths of various kinds. Under these they wear mantles instead of cloaks. They also use woollen trousers that are at the same time boots, or boots that are at the same time trousers, and these are for the most part dyed. When they are riding, they do not use saddles or leggings or spurs. They drive on, and guide their horses by means of a stick with a crook at its upper end, which they hold in their hand. They use reins to serve the purpose both of a bridle and a bit. These do not keep the horses, accustomed to feeding on the grass, from their food.

Moreover, they go naked and unarmed into battle. They regard weapons as a burden, and they think it brave and honourable to fight unarmed. They use, however, three types of weapons – short weapons, spears, two darts (in this they imitate the Basclenses), and big axes well and carefully forged, which they have taken over from the Norwegians and the Ostmen, about which we shall speak later.

They are quicker and more expert than any other people in throwing, when everything else fails, stones as missiles, and such stones do great damage to the enemy in an engagement.

They are a wild and inhospitable people. They live on beasts only, and live like beasts. They have not progressed at all from the primitive habits of pastoral living.

While man usually progresses from the woods to the fields, and from the fields to settlements and communities of citizens, this people despises work on the land, has little use for the money-making of towns, condemns the rights and privileges of citizenship, and desires neither to abandon, nor lose respect for, the life which it has been accustomed to lead in the woods and countryside. They use the fields generally as pasture, but pasture in poor condition. Little is cultivated, and even less sown. The fields cultivated are so few because of the neglect of those who should cultivate them. But many of them are naturally very fertile and productive. The wealth of the soil is lost, not through the fault of the soil, but because there are no farmers to cultivate fruit-bearing trees even on the best land: 'the fields demand, but there are no hands'. How few kinds of fruit-bearing trees are grown here! The nature of the soil is not to be blamed, but rather the want of industry on the part of the cultivator. He is too lazy to plant the foreign types of trees that would grow very well here.

The different types of minerals too, with which the hidden veins of the earth are full, are not mined or put to any use, precisely because of the same laziness. Even gold, of which they are very desirous – just like the Spaniards – and which they would like to have in abundance, is brought here by traders that search the ocean for gain.

They do not devote their lives to the processing of flax or wool, or to any kind of merchandise or mechanical art. For given only to leisure, and devoted only to laziness, they think that the greatest pleasure is not to work, and the greatest wealth is to enjoy liberty.

This people is, then, a barbarous people, literally barbarous. Judged according to modern ideas, they are uncultivated, not only in the external appearance of their dress, but also in their flowing hair and beards. All their habits are the habits of barbarians. Since conventions are formed from living together in society, and since they are so removed in these distant parts from the ordinary world of men, as if they were in another world altogether and consequently cut off from well-behaved and law-abiding people, they know only of the barbarous habits in which they were born and brought up, and embrace them as another nature. Their natural qualities are excellent. But almost everything acquired is deplorable.

Source: J. J. O'Meara (trans.) *Gerald of Wales, The
History and Topography of Ireland* (1982) pp. 100–104

The missionary activities of the Irish people led to great journeys which, when recollected, presented not the travel writing of actual journeys, but tales and yarns to pass away the dark nights of the winter.

⇒ 12.6 Tales of Irish missionaries ⇐

The Promised Land of the Saints

Saint Brendan and those who were with him sailed to the island of the steward, who was with them, and there they took on board provision for forty days. Their voyage was for forty days towards the east. The steward went to the front of the boat and showed them the way. When the forty days were up, as the evening drew on, a great fog enveloped them, so that one of them could hardly see another. The steward, however, said to Saint Brendan:

'Do you know what fog that is?'

Saint Brendan replied:

'What?'

Then the other said:

'That fog encircles the island for which you have been searching for seven years.'

After the space of an hour a mighty light shone all around them again and the boat rested on the shore.

On disembarking from the boat they saw a wide land full of trees bearing fruit as in autumn time. When they had gone in a circle around that land, night had still not come on them. They took what fruit they wanted and drank from the wells and so for the space of forty days they reconnoitred the whole land and could not find the end of it. But one day they came upon a great river flowing through the middle of the island. Then Saint Brendan said to his brothers:

'We cannot cross this river and we do not know the size of this land.'

They had been considering these thoughts within themselves when a youth met them and embraced them with great joy and, calling each by his name, said: 'Happy are they that live in your house. They shall praise you from generation to generation.'

When he said this, he spoke to Saint Brendan:

'There before you lies the land which you have sought for a long time. You could not find it immediately because God wanted to show you his varied secrets in the great ocean. Return, then, to the land of your birth, bringing with you some of the fruit of this land and as many of the precious stones as your boat can carry. The final day of your pilgrimage draws near so that you may sleep with your fathers. After the passage of many times this land will become known to your successors, when persecution of the Christians shall have come. The river that you see divides the island. Just as this land appears to you ripe with fruit, so shall it remain always without any shadow of night. For its light is Christ.'

Saint Brendan with his brothers, having taken samples of the fruits of the land and of all its varieties of precious stones, took his leave of the blessed steward and the youth. He then embarked in his boat and began to sail through the middle of the fog. When they had passed through it, they came to the island called the Island of Delights. They availed themselves of three days' hospitality there and then, receiving a blessing, Saint Brendan returned home directly.

> Source: J. J. O'Meara (trans.) *The Voyage of St Brendan: Journey to the Promised Land* (1978) pp. 67–70

⁂

The movement of population, from the Barbarian invasions onwards, was characteristic of the Middle Ages. One of the best documented of such movements is the 'Viking' life of the Northern World. The word 'Viking' has been applied to all early medieval Scandinavians, but as used by contemporaries the word *víkingr* applied only to someone who went *í víkingr*, that is plundering. Monastic chroniclers, not surprisingly, had a low opinion of 'the heathen' who came to devastate their monasteries. In 793, the *Anglo Saxon Chronicle* reported that 'the harrying of the heathen miserably destroyed God's church in Lindisfarne by rapine and slaughter'. The life of the Northern travellers, however, also had its heroic side and in the Icelandic Sagas, compiled in the period from the twelfth to the fourteenth century we have an epic source. In the *Saga of the Greenlanders* there is an indication of a settlement in the Northern American continent, Vinland as the voyagers call it.

❧ 12.7 K. Kunz, *The Saga of the Greenlanders* ☙

2

Following this, Bjarni Herjolfsson sailed from Greenland to Earl Eirik, who received him well. Bjarni told of his voyage, during which he had sighted various lands, and many people thought him short on curiosity, since he had nothing to tell of these lands, and he was criticised somewhat for this. Bjarni became one of the earl's followers and sailed to Greenland the following summer. There was now much talk of looking for new lands.

Leif, the son of Eirik the Red of Brattahlid, sought out Bjarni and purchased his ship. He hired himself a crew numbering thirty-five men altogether. Leif asked his father Eirik to head the expedition.

Eirik was reluctant to agree, saying he was getting on in years and not as good at bearing the cold and wet as before. Leif said he still commanded the greatest good fortune of all his kinsmen. Eirik gave in to Leif's urgings and, when they were almost ready, set out from his farm on horseback. When he had but a short distance left to the ship, the horse he was riding stumbled and threw Eirik, injuring his foot. Eirik then spoke: 'I am not intended to find any other land than this one where we now live. This will be the end of our travelling together.' Eirik returned home to Brattahlid, and Leif boarded his ship, along with his companions, thirty-five men altogether. One of the crew was a man named Tyrkir, from a more southerly country.

Once they had made the ship ready, they put to sea and found first the land which Bjarni and his companions had seen last. They sailed up to the shore and cast anchor, put out a boat and rowed ashore. There they found no grass, but large glaciers covered the highlands, and the land was like a single flat slab of rock from the glaciers to the sea. This land seemed to them of little use. Leif then spoke: 'As far as this land is concerned it can't be said of us as of Bjarni, that we did not set foot on shore. I am now going to name this land and call it Helluland (Stone-slab land).'

They then returned to their ship, put out to sea and found a second land. Once more they sailed close to the shore and cast anchor, put out a boat and went ashore. This land was flat and forested, sloping gently seaward, and they came across many beaches of white sand.

Leif then spoke: 'This land will be named for what it has to offer and called Markland (Forest Land).' They then returned to the ship without delay.

After this they sailed out to sea and spent two days at sea with a north-easterly wind before they saw land. They sailed towards it and came to an island, which lay to the north of the land, where they went ashore. In the fine weather they found dew on the grass, that they collected in their hands and drank, and thought they had never tasted anything as sweet.

Afterwards they returned to their ship and sailed into the sound which lay between the island and the headland that stretched out northwards from the land. They rounded the headland and steered westward. Here there were extensive shallows at low tide and their ship was soon stranded, and the sea looked far away to those aboard ship.

Their curiosity to see the land was so great that they could not be bothered to wait for the tide to come in and float their stranded ship, and they ran aground where a river flowed into the sea from a lake. When the incoming tide floated the ship again, they took the boat and rowed to the ship and moved it up into the river and from there into the lake, where they cast anchor. They carried their sleeping-sacks ashore and built booths. Later they decided to spend the winter there and built large houses.

There was no lack of salmon both in the lake and in the river, and this salmon was larger than they had ever seen before. It seemed to them the land was so good that livestock would need no fodder during the winter. The temperature never dropped below freezing, and the grass only withered very slightly. The days and nights were much more equal in length than in Greenland or Iceland. In the depth of winter the sun was aloft by mid-morning and still visible at mid-afternoon.

When they had finished building their houses, Leif spoke to his companions: 'I want to divide our company into two groups, as I wish to explore the land. One half is to remain at home by the longhouses while the other half explores the land. They are never to go any farther than will enable them to return that same evening and no one is to separate from the group.'

This they did for some time. Leif accompanied them sometimes, and at other times remained at home by the houses. Leif was a large, strong man, of very striking appearance and wise, as well as being a man of moderation in all things.

3

One evening it happened that one man, the southerner Tyrkir, was missing from their company. Leif was very upset by this, as Tyrkir had spent many years with him and his father and had treated Leif as a child very affectionately. Leif criticised his companions harshly and prepared to search for Tyrkir, taking twelve men with him. When they had gone only a short way from the houses, however, Tyrkir came towards him and they welcomed him gladly. Leif soon realised that the companion of his childhood was pleased about something. Tyrkir had a protruding forehead and darting eyes, with dark wrinkles in his face; he was short in stature and frail-looking, but a master of all types of crafts. Leif then asked him, 'Why were you so late returning, foster-father, and how did you become separated from the rest?'

For a long time Tyrkir only spoke in German, with his eyes darting in all directions and his face contorted. The others understood nothing of what he was saying.

After awhile he spoke in Norse: 'I had gone only a bit farther than the rest of you. But I have news to tell you: I found grapevines and grapes.'

'Are you really sure of this, foster-father?' Leif said. 'I'm absolutely sure,' he replied, 'because where I was born there was no lack of grapevines and grapes.'

They went to sleep after that, and the following morning Leif spoke to his crew: 'We'll divide our time between two tasks, taking one day for one task and one day for the other, picking grapes or cutting vines and felling the trees to make a load for my ship.' They agreed on this course.

It is said that the boat which was drawn behind the ship was filled with grapes. Then they cut a load for the ship.

When spring came they made the ship ready and set sail. Leif named the land for its natural features and called it Vinland (Wineland). They headed out to sea and had favourable winds, until they came in sight of Greenland and the mountains under its glaciers. Then one of the crew spoke up, asking, 'Why do you steer a course so close to the wind?'

Leif answered, 'I'm watching my course, but there's more to it than that: do you see anything of note?'

The crew said they saw nothing worthy of note.

'I'm not sure,' Leif said, 'whether it's a ship or a skerry that I see.'

They then saw it and said it was a skerry. Leif saw so much better than they did, that he could make out men on the skerry.

'I want to steer us close into the wind,' Leif said, 'so that we can reach them; if these men should be in need of our help, we have to try to give it to them. If they should prove to be hostile, we have all the advantages on our side and they have none.'

They managed to sail close to the skerry and lowered their sail, cast anchor and put out one of the two extra boats they had taken with them.

Leif then asked who was in charge of the company.

The man who replied said his name was Thorir and that he was of Norwegian origin. 'And what is your name?'

Leif told him his name.

'Are you the son of Eirik the Red of Brattahlid?' he asked.

Leif said he was. 'Now I want to invite all of you,' Leif said, 'to come on board my ship, bringing as much of your valuables as the ship can carry.'

After they had accepted his offer, the ship sailed to Eiriksfjord with all this cargo until they reached Brattahlid, where they unloaded the ship. Leif then invited Thorir to spend the winter with him there, along with Thorir's wife Gudrid and three other men, and found places for the other members of both his own and Thorir's crew. Leif rescued fifteen men from the skerry. After this he was called Leif the Lucky. Leif had now become very wealthy and was held in much respect.

That winter Thorir's crew were stricken by illness and he himself died, along with most of his company. Eirik the Red also died that winter.

There was great discussion of Leif's Vinland voyage and his brother Thorvald felt they had not explored enough of the land. Leif then said to Thorvald, 'You go to Vinland, brother, and take my ship if you wish, but before you do so I want the ship to make a trip to the skerry to fetch the wood that Thorir had there.'

And so this was done.

> Source: From K. Kunz (trans.) 'The Saga of the
> Greenlanders' in Ö. Thorssen, *The Sagas of
> Icelanders* (1997) pp. 638–642. © Leifur Eiricksson
> Publishing, 2000

The *Sagas*, as befits the literature of a maritime people, contained sound navigational hints and good descriptive passages as well as magical and mythical excurses.

The *Travels* of the Venetian, Marco Polo (*c.* 1254–1324), provided an imaginative reconstruction of his journeys, stronger on anecdote than on topographical accuracy, not too far in their story-telling in spirit from the Icelandic sagas, as these extracts, one about Iran, and the other about China, attest.

---

৪৯ 12.8 Extracts from *Travels of Marco Polo* ৬৫

Chapter XXI

Of the journey from Kobiam to the province of Timochain on the northern confines of Persia – and of a particular species of tree

Leaving Kobiam you proceed over a desert of eight days' journey exposed to great drought; neither fruits nor any kind of trees are met with, and what water is found has a bitter taste. Travellers are therefore obliged to carry with them so much as may be necessary for their sustenance. Their cattle are constrained by thirst to drink such as the desert affords, which their owners endeavour to render palatable to them by mixing it with flour. At the end of eight days you reach the province of Timochain, situated towards the north, on the borders of Persia, in which are many towns and strong places. There is here an extensive plain remarkable for the production of a species of tree called the tree of the sun, and by Christians *arbor secco,* the dry or fruitless tree. Its nature and qualities are these: It is lofty, with a large stem, having its leaves green on the upper surface, but white or glaucous on the under. It produces husks or capsules like those in which the chestnut is enclosed, but these contain no fruit. The wood is solid and strong, and of a yellow colour resembling the box. There is no other species of tree near it for the space of a hundred miles, excepting in one quarter, where trees are found within the distance of about ten miles.

It is reported by the inhabitants of this district that a battle was fought there between Alexander, King of Macedonia, and Darius. The towns are well supplied with every necessary and convenience of life, the climate being temperate and not subject to extremes either of heat or cold. The people are of the Mahometan religion. They are in general a handsome race, especially the women, who, in my opinion, are the most beautiful in the world.

Chapter XVI

Of the Grand Khan's proceeding to the chase, with his gerfalcons and hawks – of his falconers – and of his tents

When his majesty has resided the usual time in the metropolis, and leaves it in the month of March, he proceeds in a north-easterly direction, to within two days' journey of the ocean; attended by full ten thousand falconers, who carry with them a vast number of gerfalcons, peregrine falcons, and sakers, as well as many vultures, in order to pursue the game along the banks of the river. It must be understood that he does not keep all this body of men together in one place, but divides them into several parties of one or two hundred or more, who follow the sport in various directions, and the greater part of what they take is brought to his majesty. He has likewise with him ten thousand men of those who are termed *taskaol,* implying that their business is to be upon the watch, and, who, for this purpose, are detached in small parties of two or three to stations not far distant from each other, in such a manner as to encompass a considerable tract of country. Each of them is provided with a call and a hood, by which they are enabled, when necessary, to call in and to secure the birds. Upon the command being given for flying the hawks, those who let them loose are not under the necessity of following them because the others, whose duty it is, look out so attentively that the birds cannot direct their flight to any quarter where they are not secured, or promptly assisted if there should be occasion. Every bird belonging to his majesty, or to any of his nobles, has a small silver label fastened to its leg, on which is engraved the name of the owner and also the name of the keeper. In consequence of this precaution, as soon as the hawk is secured, it is immediately known to whom it belongs and restored accordingly. If it happens that, although the name appears, the owner, not being personally known to the finder, cannot be ascertained in the first instance, the bird is, in that case, carried to an officer termed *bulangazi,* whose title imports that he is the 'guardian of unclaimed property'. If a horse, therefore, a sword, a bird, or any other article is found, and it does not appear to whom it belongs, the finder carries it directly to this officer, by whom it is received in charge and carefully preserved. If, on the other hand, a person finds any article that has been lost, and fails to carry it to the proper depositary, he is accounted a thief. Those by whom any parties' property has been lost make their application to this officer, by whom it is restored to them. His situation is always in the most elevated part of the camp, and distinguished by a particular flag, in order that he may be the more readily found by such as have occasion to apply to him. The effect of this regulation is, that no articles are ultimately lost.

When his majesty makes his progress in this manner, towards the shores of the ocean, many interesting occurrences attend the sport, and it may truly be said that it is unrivalled by any other amusement in the world. On account of the narrowness of the passes in some parts of the country where the grand khan follows the chase, he is borne upon two elephants only, or sometimes a single one, being more convenient than a greater number; but under other circumstances he makes use of four, upon the backs of which is placed a pavilion of wood, handsomely carved, the inside being lined with cloth of gold, and the outside covered with the skins of lions, a mode of conveyance which is rendered necessary to him during his hunting excursions, in consequence of the gout, with which he is troubled. In the pavilion he always carries with him twelve of his best gerfalcons, with twelve officers, from amongst his favourites, to bear him company and amuse him. Those who are on horseback by his side give him notice of the approach of cranes or other birds, upon which he raises the curtaill of the pavilion, and when he espies the game, gives direction for letting fly the gerfalcons, which seize the cranes and over power them after a long struggle. The view of this sport as he lies upon his couch, affords extreme satisfaction to his majesty, as well as to the officers who attend him, and to the horsemen by whom he is surrounded. After having thus enjoyed the amusement for some hours, he repairs to a place named Kakzarmodin, where are pitched the pavilions and tents of his sons, and also of the nobles, the life-guards, and the falconers; exceeding ten thousand in number, and making a handsome appearance. The tent of his majesty, in which he gives his audiences, is so long and wide that under it ten thousand soldiers might be drawn up, leaving room for the superior officers and other persons of rank. Its entrance fronts the south, and on the eastern side it has another tent connected with it, forming a capacious saloon, which the emperor usually occupies, with a few of his nobility, and when he thinks proper to speak to any other persons, they are introduced to him in that apartment. In the rear of this there is a large and handsome chamber, where he sleeps; and there are many other tents and apartments (for the different branches of the household), but which are not immediately connected with the great tent. These halls and chambers are all constructed and fitted up in the following manner. Each of them is supported by three pillars of wood, richly carved and gilt. The tents are covered on the outside with the skins of lions, streaked white, black, and red, and so well joined together that neither wind nor rain can penetrate. Withinside they are lined with the skins of ermines and sables, which are the most costly of all furs; for the latter, if of a size to trim a dress, is valued at two thousand besants of gold, provided it be perfect; but if otherwise, only one thousand. It is esteemed by Tartars the queen of furs. The animal, which in their language in which is named *rondes,* is about the size of a polecat. With these two kinds of skin, the halls as well as the sleeping-rooms are handsomely fitted up in compartments, arranged with much taste and skill. The tent-ropes, or cords by which they stretch the tents, are all of silk. Near to the grand tent of his majesty are situated those of his ladies, also very handsome and splendid. They have in like manner their gerfalcons, their hawks, and other birds and beasts, with which they partake in the amusement. The number of persons collected in these encampments is quite incredible, and a spectator might conceive himself to be in the midst of a populous city, so great is the assemblage from every part of the empire. The grand khan is attended on the occasion by the whole of his family and household; that is to say, his physicians, astronomers, falconers, and every other description of officer.

In these parts of the country he remains until the first vigil of our Easter, during which period he never ceases to frequent the lakes and rivers, where he takes storks, swans, herons, and a variety of other birds. His people also being detached to several different places, procure for him a large quantity of game. In this manner, during the season of his diversion, he enjoys himself to a degree that no person who is not an eye-witness can conceive; the excellence and the extent of the sport being greater than it is possible to express. It is strictly forbidden to every tradesman, mechanic, or husbandman throughout his majesty's dominions, to keep a vulture, hawk, or any other bird used for the pursuit of game, or any sporting dog; nor is a nobleman or cavalier to presume to chase beast or bird in the neighbourhood of the place where his majesty takes up his residence (the distance being limited to five miles, for example, on one side, ten on another, and perhaps fifteen in a third direction), unless his name be inscribed in a list kept by the grand falconer, or he has a special privilege to that effect. Beyond those limits it is permitted. There is an order, however, which prohibits every person throughout all the countries subject to the grand khan, whether prince, nobleman, or peasant, from daring to kill hares, roebucks, fallow deer, stags, or other animals of that kind, or any large birds, between the months of March and October; to the intent that they may increase and multiply; and as the breach of this order is attended with punishment, game of every description increases prodigiously. When the usual time is elapsed, his majesty returns to the capital by the road he went; continuing his sport during the whole of the journey.

Source: *Travels of Marco Polo* (1936) pp. 72–73, 195–200

The travels of Sir John Mandeville, originally written in French, a series of tales of travels culled, in the fourteenth century, from a variety of sources, were a delight for readers but could not have been used as a travel guide.

ॐ 12.9 Tales of travels of Sir John Mandeville ॐ

Chapter XVII (1322)

Of the Evil Customs in the Isle of Lamary; and how the Earth and the Sea are of Round Form, as is proved by the Star called Antarctic, which is fixed in the south.

From that country men go by the Sea of Ocean, and by many divers isles and countries which it would be too long to describe. Fifty-two days from the land I have spoken of there is another extensive land, which they call Lamary, in which the heat is very great; and it is the custom there for men and women to go all naked. And they scorn when they see foreigners going clothed, because they say that God made Adam and Eve all naked, and that no man should be ashamed of what is according to nature. And they say that they that are clothed are people of another world, or people who believe not in God. And they marry there no wives, for all the women are common; and they say they sin if they refuse any man; for God commanded Adam and Eve, and all that come of him, that they should increase and multiply and fill the land, therefore may no man in that country say, 'This is my wife;' and no woman may say, 'This is my husband.' And when they have children, they may give them to what man they will, who has companied with them. And all land and property also is common, nothing being shut up, or kept under lock, one man being as rich as another. But in that country there is a cursed custom, for they eat more gladly man's flesh than any other flesh, although their country abounds in flesh, fish, corn, gold, and silver, and all other goods. Thither merchants go, who bring with them children to sell to them of the country, and they buy them; and if they are fat they eat them anon: and if they are lean they feed them till they are fat, and then eat them; and they say that it is the best and sweetest flesh in the world.

Neither in that land, nor in many others beyond it, may any man see the polar star, which is called the Star of the Sea, which is immoveable, and is towards the north, and which we call the lode-star. But they see another star opposite to it, towards the south, which is called antarctic. And right as shipmen here govern themselves by the lode-star, so shipmen beyond these parts are guided by the star of the south, which appears not to us. This star, which is towards the north, that we call the lode-star, appears not to them. For which cause, we may clearly perceive that the land and sea are of round shape and form, because the part of the firmament appears in one country which is not seen in another country. And men may prove by experience and their understanding, that if a man found passages by ships, he might go by ship all round the world, above and beneath; which I prove thus, after what I have seen. For I have been towards the parts of Brabant, and found by the astrolabe that the polar star is fifty-three degrees high; and further, in Germany and Bohemia, it has fifty-eight degrees; and still further towards the north it is sixty-two degrees and some minutes; for I myself have measured it by the astrolabe. Now you shall know that opposite the polar star is the other star, called antarctic, as I have said before. These two stars are fixed; and about them all the firmament turns as a wheel that turns on its axle-tree; so that those stars bear the firmament in two equal parts; so that it has as much above as it has beneath. After this I have gone towards the south, and have found, that in Lybia we first see the antarctic star; and I have gone so far in those countries that I have found that star higher, so that, towards Upper Lybia, it is eighteen degrees and certain minutes. After going by sea and land towards the country of which I spoke last, and to other isles and lands beyond that country, I have found the antarctic star thirty-three degrees in altitude, and some minutes. And if I had had company and shipping to go further, I believe certainly that we should have seen all the roundness of the firmament all about. For, as I have told you before, the half of the firmament is between the two stars, which half I have seen. And the other half I have seen towards the north, under the polar star, sixty-two degrees and ten minutes; and, towards the south, I have seen under the antarctic thirty-three degrees and sixteen minutes; and the half of the firmament in all contains but one hundred and eighty degrees, of which I have seen sixty-two on the one part, and thirty-three on the other, which makes ninety-five degrees, and nearly the half of a degree; so that I have seen all the firmament except eighty-four degrees and the half of a degree; and that is not the fourth part of the firmament. By which I tell you, certainly, that men may go all round the world, as well under as above, and return to their country, if they had company, and shipping, and guides; and always they would find men, lands, and isles, as well as in our part of the world. For they who are towards the antarctic are directly feet opposite feet of them who dwell under the polar star; as well as we and they that dwell under us are feet opposite feet. For all parts of sea and land have their opposites, habitable or passable.

And know well that, after what I may perceive and understand, the lands of Prester John, emperor of India, are under us; for in going from Scotland or from England, towards Jerusalem, men go always upwards; for our land is in the low part of the earth, towards the west; and the land of Prester John is in the low part of the earth, towards the east; and they have there the day when we have night; and, on the country, they have the night when we have the day; for the earth and the sea are of a round form, as I have said before; and as men go upward to one part, they go downward to another. Also you have heard me say that Jerusalem is in the middle of the world; and that may be proved and shown there by a spear which is fixed in the earth at the hour of midday, when it is equinoxial, which gives no shadow on any side. They, therefore, that start from the west to go towards Jerusalem, as many days as they go upward to go thither, in so many days may they go from Jerusalem to other confines of the superficialities of the earth beyond. And when men go beyond that distance, towards India and to the foreign isles, they are proceeding on the roundness of the earth and the sea, under our country. And therefore hath it befallen many times of a thing that I have heard told when I was young, how a worthy man departed once from our country to go and discover the world; and so he passed India, and the isles beyond India, where are more than five thousand isles; and so long he went by sea and land, and so environed the world by many seasons that he found an isle where he heard people speak his own language, calling on oxen in the plough such words as men speak to beasts in his own country, whereof he had great wonder, for he knew not how it might be. But I say that he had gone so long, by land and sea, that he had gone all round the earth, that he was come again to his own borders, if he would have passed forth till he had found his native country. But he turned again from thence, from whence he was come; and so he lost much painful labour, as himself said, a great while after, when he was coming home; for it befell after, that he went into Norway, and the tempest of the sea carried him to an isle; and when he was in that isle, he knew well that it was the isle where he had heard his own language spoken before, and the calling of the oxen at the plough. But it seems to simple and unlearned men that men may not go under the earth, but that they would fall from under towards the heaven. But that may not be any more than we fall towards heaven from the earth where we are; for from what part of the earth that men dwell, either above or beneath, it seems always to them that they go more right than any other people. And right as it seems to us that they be under us, so it seems to them that we are under them; for if a man might fall from the earth unto the firmament, by greater reason the earth and the sea, that are so great and so heavy, should fall to the firmament; but that may not be, and therefore saith our Lord God, 'He hangeth the earth upon no thing.' And although it be possible so to go all round the world, yet of a thousand persons not one might happen to return to his country: for, from the greatness of the earth and sea, men may go by a thousand different ways, that no one could be sure of returning exactly to the parts he came from, unless by chance or by the grace of God; for the earth is very large, and contains in roundness and circuit, above and beneath, 20,425 miles, after the opinion of the old wise astronomers; and, after my little wit, it seems to me, saving their reverence, that it is more; for I say thus: let there be imagined a figure that has a great compass; and, about the point of the great compass, which is called the centre, let there be made another little compass; then, afterwards, let the great compass be divided by lines in many parts, and all the lines meet at the centre; so that in as many parts as the great compass shall be divided, in so many shall the little one that is about the centre be divided, although the spaces be less. Let the great compass be represented for the firmament, and the little compass for the earth; now the firmament is divided by astronomers into twelve signs, and every sign is divided into thirty degrees. Also let the earth be divided into as many parts as the firmament, and let every part answer to a degree of the firmament; and I know well that, after the authorities in astronomy, seven hundred furlongs of earth answer to a degree of the firmament, that is eighty-seven miles and four furlongs. Now, multiplied by three hundred and sixty times, it makes 31,500 miles, each of eight furlongs, according to miles of our country. So much hath the earth in circuit after my opinion and understanding.

Source: T. Wright, *Early Travels in Palestine* (1848)
pp. 218–222

Travel to new found lands was accompanied, in the later medieval period, by an increasing introspection, a mystical interior journey which expressed itself in contemplative prayer. Meister Eckhart (*c.* 1260–1328), a German Dominican, taught, for example, that true union with God could only be achieved by ridding the mind of all images and the heart of all attachments providing an access to God which required no spiritual mentoring or ecclesiastical structures, 'a wayless way'.

12.10 Meister Eckhart's teaching

But now I ask: 'What is the prayer of a heart that has detachment?' And to answer it I say that purity in detachment does not know how to pray, because if someone prays he asks God to get something for him, or he asks God to take something away from him. But a heart in detachment asks for nothing, nor has it anything of which it would gladly be free. So it is free of all prayer, and its prayer is nothing else than for uniformity with God. That is all its prayer consists in. To illustrate this meaning we may consider what Saint Dionysius said about Saint Paul's words, when he said: 'There are many of you racing for the crown, but it will be given only to one' (1 Co. 9:24). All the powers of the soul are racing for the crown, but it will be given only to the soul's being – and Dionysius says: 'The race is nothing but a turning away from all created things and a uniting oneself with that which is uncreated.' And as the soul attains this, it loses its name and it draws God into itself, so that in itself it becomes nothing, as the sun draws up the red dawn into itself so that it becomes nothing. Nothing else will bring man to this except pure detachment. And we can also apply to this what Augustine says: 'The soul has a secret entry into the divine nature when all things become nothing to it.' This entry here on this earth is nothing else than pure detachment. And when this detachment ascends to the highest place, it knows nothing of knowing, it loves nothing of loving, and from light it becomes dark. To this we can also apply what one teacher says: 'The poor in spirit are those who have abandoned all things for God, just as they were his when we did not exist.' No one can do this but a heart with pure detachment. We can see that God would rather be in a heart with such detachment than in all hearts. For if you ask me: 'What is it God seeks in all things?' then I answer you out of the Book of Wisdom, where he says: 'In all things I seek rest' (Si. 14: 11). Nowhere is there complete rest, except only in the heart that has found detachment. Hence God would rather be there than in other virtues or in any other things. And you should also know that the more a man applies himself to becoming susceptible to the divine inflowing, the more blessed will he be; and whoever can establish himself in the highest readiness, he will also be in the highest blessedness. Now no one can make himself susceptible to the divine inflowing except through uniformity with God, for as each man becomes uniform with God, to that measure he becomes susceptible to the divine inflowing. And uniformity comes from man's subjecting himself to God; and the more a man subjects himself to created things, the less is he uniform with God. Now a heart that has pure detachment is free of all created things, and so it is wholly submitted to God, and so it achieves the highest uniformity with God, and is most susceptible to the divine inflowing. This is what Saint Paul means when he said: 'Put on Jesus Christ' (Rm. 13:14). He means through uniformity with Christ, and this putting-on cannot happen except through uniformity with Christ. And you must know that when Christ became man, it was not just a human being he put on himself; he put on human nature. Therefore, do you too go out of all things, and then there will be only what Christ accepted and put on, and so you will have put on Christ.

Whoever now wishes to see properly what is the excellence and the profit of perfect detachment, let him take good heed of Christ's words, when he spoke about his human nature and said to his disciples: 'It is expedient for you that I go from you, for if I do not go, the Holy Spirit cannot come to you' (Jn. 16:7). This is just as if he were to say: 'You have taken too much delight in my present image, so that the perfect delight of the Holy Spirit cannot be yours. So detach yourselves from the image, and unite yourselves to the formless being, for God's spiritual consolation is delicate; therefore he will not offer it to anyone except to him who disdains bodily consolations.'

Now, all you reasonable people, take heed! No one is happier than a man who has attained the greatest detachment. No one can accept fleshly and bodily consolations without spiritual damage, 'because the flesh longs in opposition to the spirit and the spirit to the flesh' (Ga. 5:17). Therefore whoever sows in the flesh inordinate love will reap everlasting death, and whoever in the spirit sows a well-ordered love will from the spirit reap everlasting life (Ga. 6:8). So it is that the sooner a man shuns what is created, the sooner will the creator come to him. So take heed, all you reasonable people! Since the delight we might have in Christ's bodily image deprives us of receptivity for the Holy Spirit, how much more shall we be deprived of God by the ill-ordered delight that we take in transient consolations! So detachment is the best of all, for it purifies the soul and cleanses the conscience and enkindles the heart and awakens the spirit and stimulates our longings and shows us where God is and separates us from created things and unites itself with God.

Now, all you reasonable people, take heed! The fastest beast that will carry you to your perfection is suffering, for no one will enjoy more eternal sweetness than those who endure with Christ in the greatest bitterness. There is nothing more gall-bitter than suffering, and nothing more honey-sweet than to have suffered; nothing disfigures the body more than suffering, and nothing more adorns the soul in the sight of God than to have suffered. The firmest foundation on which this perfection can stand is humility, for whichever mortal crawls here in the deepest abasement, his spirit will fly up into the highest realms of the divinity, for love brings sorrow, and sorrow brings love. And therefore, whoever longs to attain to perfect detachment, let him struggle for perfect humility, and so he will come close to the divinity.

That we may all be brought to this, may that supreme detachment help us which is God himself. Amen.

Source: E. Colledge, B. McGinn (trans.) *Meister Eckhart, the Essential Sermons, Commentaries, Treatises and Defence* (1981) pp. 292–294

෧෨ඁ෧

Such a mystical way to God was particularly prevalent in Northern Europe. An example of this is the classically entitled *The Cloud of Unknowing* by an English writer of the fourteenth century.

---

෧ 12.11 *The Cloud of Unknowing* ෨

The Sixteenth Chapter

That by virtue of this work a sinner truly turned and called to contemplation cometh sooner to perfection than by any other work; and by it soonest may get of God forgiveness of sins.

Look that no man think it presumption that he that is the wretchedest sinner of this life dare take upon him – after the time that he hath lawfully amended him, and after he hath felt himself stirred to that life that is called contemplative, by the assent of his counsel and of his conscience – for to proffer a meek stirring of love to his God, secretly setting upon the cloud of unknowing betwixt him and his God. For our Lord said to Mary, in person of all sinners that be called to contemplative life: Thy sins be forgiven thee. Not for her great sorrow, nor for her thought of her sins, nor yet for her meekness that she had in the beholding of her wretchedness only. But why then? Surely because she loved much. Lo! here may be seen what a secret setting of love may purchase of our Lord, before all other works that man may think. And yet I grant well that she had full much sorrow and wept full sore for her sins, and full much was she meeked in the thought of wretchedness. And so should we too – that have been wretches and customary sinners – all our lifetime make hideous and wonderful sorrow for our sins, and full much be meeked in the thought of our wretchedness. But how? Surely as Mary did. She, although she might not unfeel the deep hearty sorrow for her sins – for why, all her lifetime she had them with her whereso she went, as it were in a burthen bounden together and laid up full privily in the hole of her heart, in manner never to be forgotten – nevertheless it may be said and confirmed by Scripture that she had a more hearty sorrow, a more doleful desire, a more deep sighing: and more she languished – yea! almost to the death – for lacking of love, although she had full much love – and have no wonder thereat, for it is the condition of a true lover that the more he loveth, the more he longeth to love – than she had for any thought of her sins.

And yet she knew well and felt well in herself with a sober certainty that she was a wretch most foul of all other, and that her sins had made a division betwixt her and her God that she loved so much: and also that they were in great part the cause of her languishing sickness for lacking of love. But what of that? Came she therefore down from the height of desire into the depth of her sinful life, and searched in the foul stinking fen and dunghill of her sins, searching them up one by one, with all the circumstances of them, and sorrowed and wept so upon them each one by himself? Nay, surely she did not so. And why? Because God let her know by his grace within her soul that she should never so bring it about. For so she might sooner have raised in herself an ableness to have often sinned, than have purchased by that work any plain forgiveness of all her sins.

And therefore she hung up her love and her longing desire in this cloud of unknowing, and learned to love a thing the which she might not see clearly in this life by light of understanding in her reason, nor yet verily feel in sweetness of love in her affection. Insomuch, that she had ofttimes little special thought whether she ever had been a sinner or none. Yea! and full ofttimes I think that she was so deeply disposed to the love of his Godhead that she had but right little special beholding unto the beauty of his precious and blessed body, in the which he sat full lovely, speaking and preaching before her; nor yet to anything else, bodily or ghostly. That this be truth it seemeth by the Gospel.

> Source: J. McCann (ed.) *The Cloud of Unknowing*
> (1924) pp. 49–52

The journey within, the spiritual path to perfection, was to lead ultimately to a reality more vivid and vital than could be imagined, 'the Beatific Vision', the everlasting life promised by Christ and given by God. Dante Alighieri (1265–1321) evoked the future life in his *La Divina Commedia* which takes the reader on a grand tour of the cosmology of time and through the terrors of Hell (*Inferno*) and Purgatory (*Purgatorio*) to Heaven (*Paradiso*) and to the medieval world to which all Christendom aspired. *La Divina Commedia* describes a vision in which Dante travels for a week at Easter, 1300, from a dark forest on this side of the world , down through hell to Satan at the centre of the Earth and up the seven terraces to the mount of Purgatory, to its summit, the Earthly Paradise where Adam and Eve were created. Virgil, the classical poet, then Beatrice, who conducts him through the nine planetary and stellar spheres to the *Empyrean*, where St Bernard of Clairvaux takes her place. St Bernard presents Dante to the Blessed Virgin Mary, at whose intercession the poet is granted a glimpse of the Beatific Vision, the vision of the Divine Being in Heaven.

ঌ 12.12 Dante Alighieri, *La Divina Commedia* ঌ

Paradiso

'Virgin mother, daughter of thy son, lowly and uplifted more than any creature, fixed goal of the eternal counsel, art she who didst human nature so ennoble that its own Maker scorned not to become its making.

In thy womb was lit again the love under whose warmth in the eternal peace this flower hath thus unfolded.

Here art thou unto us the meridian torch of love and there below with
  mortals art a living spring of hope.
Lady, thou art so great and hast such worth, that if there be who would
  have grace yet betaketh not himself to thee, his longing seeketh to fly
  without wings.
Thy kindliness not only succoureth whoso requesteth, but doth oftentimes
  freely forerun request.
In thee is tenderness, in thee is pity, in thee munificence, in thee united
  whatever in created being is of excellence.
Now he who from the deepest pool of the universe even to here hath seen
  the spirit-lives one after one
imploreth thee, of grace, for so much power as to be able to uplift his eyes
  more high towards final bliss;
and I, who never burned for my own vision more than I do for his, proffer
  thee all my prayers, and pray they be not scant,
that thou do scatter for him every cloud of his mortality with prayers of
  thine, so that the joy supreme may be unfolded to him.
And further do I pray thee, Queen who canst all that thou wilt, that thou
  keep sound for him, after so great a vision, his affections.
Let thy protection vanquish human ferments; see Beatrice, with how many
  Saints, for my prayers folding hands.'
Those eyes, of God beloved and venerated, fixed upon him who prayed,
  showed us how greatly devout prayers please her.
Then to the eternal light they bent themselves, wherein we may not ween
  that any creature's eye findeth its way so clear.
And I, who to the goal of all my longings was drawing nigh, even as was
  meet the ardour of the yearning quenched within me.
Bernard gave me the sign and smiled to me that I should look on high,
  but I already of myself was such as he would have me;
because my sight, becoming purged, now more and more was entering
  through the ray of the deep light which in itself is true.
Thenceforward was my vision mightier than our discourse, which faileth at
  such sight, and faileth memory at so great outrage.
As is he who dreaming seeth, and when the dream is gone the impression
  stamped remaineth, and naught else cometh to the mind again;
even such am I; for almost wholly faileth me my vision, yet doth the
  sweetness that was born of it still drop within my heart.
So doth the snow unstamp it to the sun, so to the wind on the light leaves
  was lost the Sibyl's wisdom.
O light supreme who so far dost uplift thee o'er mortal thoughts, re-lend
  unto my mind a little of what then thou didst seem,
and give my tongue such power that it may leave only a single sparkle of
  thy glory unto the folk to come;
for by returning to my memory somewhat, and by a little sounding in
  these verses, more of thy victory will be conceived.
I hold that by the keenness of the living ray which I endured I had been
  lost, had mine eyes turned aside from it.
And so I was the bolder, as I mind me, so long to sustain it as to unite my
  glance with the Worth infinite.

Oh grace abounding, wherein I presumed to fix my look on the eternal
    light so long that I consumed my sight thereon!

Within its depths I saw ingathered, bound by love in one volume, the
    scattered leaves of all the universe;

substance and accidents and their relations, as though together fused, after
    such fashion that what I tell of is one simple flame.

The universal form of this complex I think that I beheld, because more
    largely, as I say this, I feel that I rejoice.

A single moment maketh a deeper lethargy for me than twenty and five
    centuries have wrought on the emprise that erst threw Neptune in
    amaze at Argo's shadow.

Thus all suspended did my mind gaze fixed, immovable, intent, ever
    enkindled by its gazing.

Such at that light doth man become that to turn thence to any other sight
    could not by possibility be ever yielded.

For the good, which is the object of the will, is therein wholly gathered,
    and outside it that same thing is defective which therein is perfect.
    Now shall my speech fall farther short even of what I can remember
    than an infant's who still bathes his tongue at breast.

Not that more than a single semblance was in the living light whereon I
    looked, which ever is such as it was before;

but by the sight that gathered strength in me one sole appearance even as I
    changed worked on my gaze.

In the profound and shining being of the deep The Three light appeared to
    me three circles, of three in One colours and one magnitude;

one by the second as Iris by Iris seemed reflected, and the third seemed a
    fire breathed equally from one and from the other.

Oh but how scant the utterance, and how faint, to my conceit! and it, to
    what I saw, is such that it sufficeth not to call it little.

O Light eternal who only in thyself abidest, only thyself dost understand,
    and to thyself, self-understood self-understanding, turnest love and
    smiling!

That circling which appeared in thee to be conceived as a reflected light,
    by mine eyes scanned some little,

in itself, of its own colour, seemed to be painted with our effigy, and
    thereat my sight was all committed to it.

As the geometer who all sets himself to measure the circle and who findeth
    not, think as he may, the principle he lacketh;

such was I at this new seen spectacle; I would perceive how the image
    consorteth with the circle, and how it settleth there;

but not for this were my proper wings, save that my mind was smitten by
    a flash wherein its will came to it.

To the high fantasy here power failed; but already my desire and will were
    rolled – even as a wheel that moveth equally – by the Love that moves
    the sun and the other stars.

Source: J. A. Carlyle, T. Okey and P. H. Wicksteed
(eds) *Dante Alighieri, La Divina Commedia* (1933)
Canto XXXIII

Further reading

M. Clanchy, *From Memory to Written Word: England 1066–1307*, 2nd edn (Blackwell, Oxford, 1993).

W. R. Cook, *The Medieval World View: an introduction* (Oxford University Press, Oxford, 1983).

N. R. Kline, *Maps of Medieval Thought* (Boydell, Woodbridge, 2001).

E. Peters, *Limits of Thought and Power in Medieval Europe* (Ashgate, Aldershot, 2001).

J. R. S. Phillips, *The Medieval Expansion of Europe*, 2nd edn (Clarendon Press, Oxford, 1998).

B. Smalley, *The Study of the Bible in the Middle Ages*, 3rd edn (Blackwell, Oxford, 1953).

J. Sumption, *Pilgrimage: An Image of Medieval Religion* (Faber, London, 1975).

R. W. Southern, *Scholastic Humanism and the Unification of Europe*, Vol. 1 (Blackwell, Oxford, 1995).

A. Vauchez, *Sainthood in the Late Middle Ages* (Cambridge University Press, Cambridge, 1997).

BIBLIOGRAPHY

Aelfric: *Those Who Pray, Work, and Fight, Aelfric's Grammar* (W. W. Norton & Co. [Norton On-line]) (http://www.wwnorton.com/nael/nto/middle/estates/aelfricfrm.htm).

A. J. Andrea, *The Medieval Record* (Houghton Mifflin, Boston, 1997).

H. Ashworth (ed.), *A Word in Season, an Anthology of Readings from the Fathers for General Use* (Talbot Press, Dublin, 1973).

D. Ayerst and A. Fisher, *Records of Christianity. Vol. II; Christendom* (Blackwell, Oxford, 1977).

R. Barber (trans.), *Bestiary* (Boydell, Woodbridge, 1999).

F. Barlow (ed. and trans.), *The Life of King Edward Who Rests at Westminster*, 2nd edn (Clarendon Press, Oxford, 1992).

H. Bettenson (trans.), *Documents of the Christian Church*, 3rd edn, C. Maunder (ed.) (Oxford University Press, Oxford, 1993).

A. E. Bland, P. A. Brown and R. H. Tawney (comp. and ed.), *English Economic History* (G. Bell, London, 1930).

G. Boccaccio, *Decameron*, 2 vols (Dent, Letchworth, 1930).

H. E. Butler (ed.), *The Chronicle of Jocelin of Brakelond* (Thomas Nelson, Edinburgh, 1951).

W. Butler-Bowdon (ed.), *The Book of Margery Kempe*, 1436 (Cape, London, 1936).

R. Canning (trans.), *The Rule of Saint Augustine* (Darton, Longman & Todd, London, 1984).

J. A. Carlyle, T. Okey and P. H. Wicksteed (eds), *Dante Alighieri, La Divina Commedia* (A. Dent, London, 1933).

G. Chaucer, *The Canterbury Tales* (trans.), D. Wright (Oxford University Press, Oxford, 1986).

C. R. Cheney and W. H. Semple, *Selected Letters of Pope Innocent III Concerning England* (Thomas Nelson, Edinburgh, 1953).

R. M. Clay, *The Mediaeval Hospitals of England* (Cass, London, 1966).

H. J. Coleridge (ed.), *The Dialogues of St Gregory the Great*, 2 vols (Burns & Oates, London, 1874).

B. Colgrave and R. A. B. Mynors (eds), *Venerable Bede, Ecclesiastical History of the English People* (Clarendon Press, Oxford, 1979).

E. Colledge and B. McGinn (trans.), *Meister Eckhart, the Essential Sermons, Commentaries, Treatises and Defence* (SPCK, London, 1981).

E. Conybeare, *Alfred in the Chronicles* (Elliott Stock, London, 1900).

J. Cotter Morison, *The Life and Times of Saint Bernard, Abbot of Clairvaux, AD 1091–1153*, 2nd edn (London, 1901).

O. M. Dalton (trans.), *Gregory of Tours, The History of the Franks*, 2 vols (Clarendon Press, Oxford, 1927).

H. Daniel-Rops, *The Call of St Clare* (Hawthorn Books, New York, 1963).

Dante, *Monarchy and Three Political Letters* (Weidenfeld, London, 1954).

F. Davey, *William Wey: An English Pilgrim to Compostella in 1456* (CSJ, London, 2000).

B. Davies and G. R. Evans (eds), *Anselm of Canterbury, The Major Works* (Oxford University Press, Oxford, 1998).

A. P. D'Entreves (ed.), J. G. Dawson (trans.), *Aquinas: Selected Political Writings* (Blackwell, Oxford, 1965).

D. Devas, *A Franciscan View of the Spiritual and Religious Life, Being Three Treatises from the Writing of Saint Bonaventure* (Thomas Baker, London, 1922).

N. de Wailly and J. Evans (trans.), *Joinville, The History of St Louis* (Oxford University Press, Oxford, 1938).

D. C. Douglas and G. W. Greenaway, *English Historical Documents, 1042–1189*, vol. II (Eyre & Spottiswoode, London, 1953).

L. Eberle (trans.), *The Rule of the Master* (Cistercian Publications, Michigan, 1977).

A. Erlande-Brandenburg, *The Cathedral Builders of the Middle Ages* (Thames & Hudson, London, 1995).

J. Evans (trans.), *The Unconquered Knight* (Routledge, London, 1926).

J. Evans, *Monastic Life at Cluny, 910–1157* (Oxford University Press, Oxford, 1931).

R. A. Fletcher, *The Conversion of Europe: From Paganism to Christianity, 371–1386 AD* (Harper-Collins, London, 1997).

H. E. Fosdick, *Great Voices of the Reformation* (Random House, New York, 1952).

W. H. Fremantle (trans.), *St Jerome: Letters and Select Works, Select Library of Nicene and Post-Nicene Fathers*, Ser. 2, Vol. vi (Parker, Oxford, 1892).

B. Garton (trans.), *The Metrical Life of Saint Hugh* (Lincoln Cathedral Publications, Lincoln, 1986).

A. Gewirth (trans.), *Marsilius of Padua: the Defender of Peace* (Columbia University Press, New York, 1967).

J. A. Giles (trans.), *Matthew of Paris, English History, from the year 1235–1273* (Bohn, London, 1852).

J. A. Giles (trans.), *William of Malmesbury, Chronicle of the Kings of England from the Earliest Period to the Reign of King Stephen* (Bohn, London, 1847).

J. A. Giles (trans.), *Roger of Wendover, Flowers of History: Compromising the History of England from the Descent of the Saxons to A.D. 1235*, 2 vols (Bohn, London, 1849).

W. Granger Ryan (trans.), *Jacobus de Voragine, The Golden Legend* (Princeton University Press, New Jersey, 1993).

M. A. Habig (ed.), *St Francis of Assisi: Writings and Early Biography* (Franciscan Herald Press, Chicago, 1983).

G. D. G. Hall (trans.), *The Treatise on the Laws and Customs of the Realm of England Commonly called Glanvill* (Thomas Nelson, Edinburgh, 1965).

J. Healey (trans.), *St Augustine: The City of God* (Dent, London, 1931).

E. F. Henderson (ed. and trans.), *Select Historical Documents of the Middle Ages* (G. Bell, London, 1925).

D. Herlihy (ed. and trans.), *Medieval Culture and Society* (Macmillan, London, 1968).

P. K. Hitti (trans.), *The Memoirs of An Arab-Syrian Gentleman* (Khayat, Beirut, 1964).

J. Hogarth (trans.), *The Pilgrim's Guide: 12th Century Guide for the Pilgrim to St James of Compostella* (CSJ, London, 1992).

J. C. Holt, *Robin Hood* (Thames & Hudson, London, 1983).

C. F. Horne (ed.), *The Sacred Books and Early Literature of the East*, Vol. VI: *Medieval Arabia* (Park, Austin Lipscomb, New York, 1917).

P. L. Hughes and J. P. Larkin (eds), *Tudor Royal Proclamations: Vol. I, The Early Tudors, 1485–1553* (Yale University Press, New Haven, 1964).

H. Krämer and J. Sprenger, *Malleus Maleficarum* (1484) (Random House, Bracken Books, London, 1996).

A. F. Leach (trans.), *Eduational Charters and Documents* (Cambridge University Press, Cambridge, 1911).

G. A. Loud and T. Wiedemann (trans.), *The History of the Tyrants of Sicily by 'Hugo Falcandus' 1154–69* (Manchester University Press, Manchester, 1998).

G. C. Macaulay (ed.), *The English Works of John Gower*, EETS e.x. 81–82 (EETS, London, 1900–1901).

G. C. Macaulay (ed.), Lord Berners (trans.), *The Chronicles of Froissart* (Macmillan, London, 1904).

S. R. Maitland (trans.), *Facts and Documents Illustrating the History, Doctrines and Rites of the Ancient Albigenses and Waldenses* (Rivington, London, 1832).

J. Malet Lambert, *Two Thousand Years of Gild Life* (A. Brown, Hull, 1891).

T. Malory, *Le Morte D'Arthur*, 2 vols (Macmillan, London, 1903).

C. F. J. Martin (trans.), *On the Six Days of Creation: A Translation of the Hexaëmeron* (Oxford University Press, Oxford, 1999).

D. D. Martin, *Carthusian Spirituality, the Writings of Hugh of Balma & Guigo de Ponte* (Paulist Press, New York, 1997).

F. Marzials (trans.), *Joinville and Villehardouin, Chronicles of the Crusades* (Dent, London, 1908).

P. Matarasso (trans., ed.), *The Cistercian World: Monastic Writings of the Twelfth Century* (Penguin, Harmondsworth, 1993).

J. McCann (ed.), *The Cloud of Unknowing* (Burns, Oates & Washburn, London, 1924).

J. McCann, *The Rule of St Benedict* (Burns & Oates, London, 1952).

P. McNulty (trans.), *St Peter Damien: Selected Writings on the Spiritual Life* (Faber & Faber, London, 1959).

A. R. Meyers (ed.), *English Historical Documents, 1327–1485*, Vol. IV (Eyre & Spottiswoode, Oxford, 1969).

C. C. Mierow (ed.), *Otto of Freising, The Deeds of Frederick Barbarossa* (Columbia University Press, Toronto, 1994).

H. Milford (ed.), Sir Norman Moore, *The Book of the Foundation of St Bartholomew's Church in London: The Church Belonging to the Priory of the Same in West Smithfield*, EETS, Original series, 163 (EETS, Oxford, 1923).

J. Morton, *The Nun's Rule* (Burns & Oates, London, 1905).

J. Nohl, *The Black Death, A Chronicle of the Plague* (Allen & Unwin, London, 1926).

J. D. North (ed. and trans.), *Richard of Wallingford*, 3 vols (Clarendon Press, Oxford, 1976).

J. O'Hagan (trans.), *The Song of Roland* (Kegan, Paul, Trench, London, 1883).

U. Ó Maidín (trans.), *The Celtic Monk* (Cistercian Publications, Michigan, 1996).

J. J. O'Meara (trans.), *The Voyage of St Brendan: Journey to the Promised Land* (Dolman Press, Dublin, 1978).

J. J. O'Meara (trans.), *Gerald of Wales, The History and Topography of Ireland* (Penguin, Harmondsworth, 1982).

C. Oman, *The Great Revolt of 1381* (Clarendon Press, Oxford, 1906).

W. Page (ed.), *A History of Somerset*, 5 vols (Victoria County History, London, 1911).

E. Panofsky (ed. and trans.), *Abbot Suger on the Abbey Church of St.-Denis and its Art Treasures* (Princeton University Press, New Jersey, 1946).

A. Paravicini-Bagliani, *The Pope's Body*, D. S. Peterson (trans.) (University of Chicago Press, Chicago, 2000).

M. Polo, *Travels of Marco Polo* (Dent, London, 1936).

J. F. Powers (trans.), *The Code of Cuenca: Municipal Law on the Twelfth-century Castilian Frontier* (University of Pennsylvania Press, Philadelphia, 2000).

E. J. Richards (trans.), *Christine de Pisan, The Book of the City of Ladies* (Macmillan, London, 1983).

C. C. Richardson *et al.* (trans.), *Early Christian Fathers*, Vol. I (SCM Press, London, 1953).

M. R. Ridley, *Sir Gawain and the Green Knight* (Kaye & Ward, London, 1968).

J. H. Robinson (trans.), *Readings in European History* (Ginn, Boston, 1905).

H. J. Schroder (trans.), *Disciplinary Decrees of the General Councils* (B. Herder, St Louis, 1937).

B. Scott James (trans.), *The Letters of St Bernard of Clairvaux*, 2nd edn (Sutton, Stroud, 1998).

V. D. Scudder, *Saint Catherine of Siena as Seen in her Letters* (Dent, London, 1905).

G. Sitwell (ed. and trans.), *St Odo of Cluny: Being the Life of St Odo of Cluny by John of Salerno* (Sheed & Ward, London, 1958).

W. Smith (trans.), *Wells, 1201–2001: Eight Hundred Years of Royal Charter* (City of Wells Council, Somerset, 2001).

M. Spinka (trans.), *The Letters of John Hus* (Manchester University Press, Manchester, 1972).

J. Stevenson (ed. and trans.), *The Church Historians of England*, 5 vols (Seeley, London, 1858).

J. Stevenson (ed.), *A New Eusebius: Documents Illustrative of the History of the Church to AD 337* (SPCK, London, 1968).

M. Summers, *The Geography of Witchcraft* (Routledge & Kegan Paul, London, 1978).

R. V. G. Tasker (ed.), J. Healey (trans.), *The City of God*, 2 vols (Dent, London, 1945).

O. J. Thatcher, E. H. McNeal (trans.), *A Source Book for Mediaeval History* (Charles Scribner, New York, 1905).

The High History of Saint Benedict and his Monks, Collated by a Monk of Douai Abbey (Sands, London, 1945).

New Revised Standard Version Bible (Geoffrey Chapman, London, 1993).

C. and F. Thorne (eds), *Domesday Book: Somerset* (Phillimore, Chichester, 1980).

L. Thorpe (trans.), *The Life of Charlemagne* (Penguin, Harmondsworth, 1970).

Ö. Thorssen, *The Sagas of Icelanders* (Alan Lane, Harmondsworth, 1997).

B. Tierney, *The Crisis of Church and State, 1050–1300*, 2nd edn (Prentice-Hall, New Jersey, 1964).

Translations and Reprints from Original Sources of European History (University of Pennsylvania, Philadelphia, 1894–1900).

S. Tugwell (ed.), *Early Dominicans: Selected Writings* (SPCK, London, 1982).

J. M. Upton-Ward, *The Rule of the Teplars* (Boydell, Woodbridge, 1992).

H. W. Wells (trans.), *William Langland, The Vision of Piers Plowman* (Sheed & Ward, London, 1935).

C. T. Wilcox (trans.), *Augustine, Treatises on Marriage and Other Subjects*. Fathers of the Church Series 27 (Catholic University of America Press, Washington, 1955).

M. Woosnam, *Eilmer: 11th Century Monk of Malmesbury The Flight and the Comet* (Malmesbury Abbey, Malmesbury, 1986).

T. Wright, *Early Travels in Palestine* (Bohn, London, 1848).

INDEX